TRIPLE CROSS

TRIPLE CROSS

Carlos Fuentes: HOLY PLACE

José Donoso: HELL HAS NO LIMITS

Severo Sarduy: FROM CUBA WITH A SONG

E. P. DUTTON & CO., INC. | New York | 1972

Contents

Carlos Fuentes: Holy Place   5

José Donoso: Hell Has No Limits   145

Severo Sarduy: From Cuba with a Song   231

Carlos Fuentes: HOLY PLACE

translated by Suzanne Jill Levine

To Marie-José and Octavio Paz

Contents

1

Happily Ever After

2

Portrait of My Mother
The Kidnappers
In and Out of the Enchanted Grottos
The White Telephone
Domestic Life
Another Visit
Formica Sanguinae
Some Smoothie That Jesús
The Absent Lady
The Dauphins
Autographs
Name of the Game
Wherein It Is Declared and Related
Erinyes
This Is the Truth
The Swallows
Silver Screen

3

Card Tricks
Holy Place

1

Happily Ever After

O vous que lirez cette historie . . .
—Marquis de Sade,
Les infortunes de la vertu

It is Sunday and the whole town is gathered on the beach, watching the boys play soccer. But your look is elsewhere. The islands are close by; you know their legend. You point to them with your hand and tell me what I do not know.

They are the islands of the sirens who watch over the route to Capri. You say that if you listen to their song you must accept the risk. And Ulysses was prudent. What were those rumors? I can't tell if I'm really listening to you. The young men of Positanio, bums and students, porters and waiters (summertime gigolos?), play with that nervous energy, that muscular agility. At dawn, they planted the stakes in the sand to mark the playing field: the holy place. All morning, while you and I drink in the outdoor café, they shoot the ball toward the sea; gentle waves push it back to the beach. Yes, the Tyrean Sea is a lake. The boys were thrown on the sand by a tide full of caresses: you don't feel the effort. During the week, the sailors' labor too is invisible. A silent coming and going of blue, green, and orange fishing boats; an imperceptible unfolding of nets; a quiet exchange of octopuses and squid.

And the fishing boats come out of the sea in silence, move in silence over the carved poles which the fishermen, in an agile play of reliefs, pass from prow to keel to stern to prow. The fishing boats are another horse, mounted on wooden tracks, bound for a conquered Troy: Positano, port of Poseidon, climbs the cliffs; ramps of smooth tile and alleys of damp lime connect the pale hamlets. I look toward the grapevines and the orange trees and you toward the islands: two rocks cleaved by a strait, the silhouette of a sleeping whale.

Today I could say that I saw it all from a distance. The suntanned youths, with their white T-shirts and blue shorts, short curls and golden chests, kick, pitch their heads, run: a goal. The barges go out to sea, slide over the beach. The narrow village streets go up the sides of the bare mountain, toward the high mist of the morning. And you do not travel all those distances. You belong to one image alone, the islands of the sirens.

You take risks. But Ulysses was prudent. You pass judgment on him. You say that he didn't let the sirens' song seduce him; he plugged his crews' ears with wax and tied himself to the mast of his ship. Then he did listen to the song, but he avoided its effect. He thought he had listened without risk: he heard and didn't hear. The sirens sing to make men give in. They put to the test their power of transfiguration. And also their vocation of permanence, which is only their mortal leap toward license. The sirens say: don't go on, surrender. Ulysses answers: they are waiting for me somewhere else. Somewhere else. You say all this. I only repeat what you have said.

We order two Campari bitters.

The mist opens and cars go up and down the cliff, meet, cautiously, at the narrow curves. They blow their horns. Danger: *massi cadenti*.

The town idiot walks by us, he's probably insulting us with his hoarse dialect and with the rage of his bare feet and eyes. He turns his back on us and sticks his hands in his torn, loose, blue canvas pants. He smokes the butt of a raisin-colored cigar.

An ageless woman,, wrapped in shawls, kicks off her golden slippers and walks toward the rocks followed by a frankfurter dog with a wolf's head. The steel claws of the dog and his mistress plow the sand.

Only to fulfill all the acts of the myth. The myth—you drink—must have an ending, happy or unhappy, but predicted. You ask me: how does the myth of Ulysses end? I answer: Ulysses always returns, always kills the suitors, Penelope puts down the loom forever; Telemachus, always, comes home again. The classic male, the faithful wife, the prodigal son. And they lived happily ever after.

You keep laughing. You ask me to ignore all the distractions and listen to the song of those who wish to break the natural order, which is also the resolvable, predictable order of the myth.

"Turned into a ritual."

If Ulysses had yielded to the song, he wouldn't have been prudent; there wouldn't be a story; there would be another story. I cannot listen the way you do; I am distracted by beauty, the game, life.

Nostalgia: we are in ancient Posidonia. I don't know how we got here; how we managed to overcome the dangers. It's like being on the throne of Neptune: it will be a kingdom of written dust and bottomless glass. I can't listen the way you do. Are you listening to a song which, you say, is also part of nature, the hidden, forbidden part, absent from the accepted inventory of things? Above or below the normal sound, but separated from it because of this? The bat's pavilions. The cry under the water. The words the guillotined head is still able to pronounce. The statues' laugh. What does the fetus babble inside the maternal womb: what stories does he tell himself to relieve the long wait of months? Only the stories he learned from the dead, perhaps: he sings to kill time, you say; he listens to all that has remained in the air: Adam's words upon realizing and God's upon realizing that his creature is no longer innocent (which are God's first words: the warning: thou shalt not eat of that fruit) continue to live, dead, on the wavelengths of the universe and some day there will be machines capable (and even worthy) of receiving them. Industrious, prudent, wily Odysseus, tied to the mast, listening without danger. The truth is, he didn't hear anything.

The sirens didn't sing to him. The lost ship passes in silence before the enchanted islands; the deaf crew imagined that temptation. The bound leader said he had listened and resisted. He lied. A matter of prestige, legend-conscious. Ulysses his own public relations man. The sirens, that time, only that time—the time history registered their song—did not sing. Nobody knows, because those matrons of scales and seaweed did not have chroniclers; they had a different audience, fetuses and corpses. Ulysses could pass without danger, Ulysses only wanted to protagonize antagonizing: always, the pulse of agony; never, the song of the sirens which is only heard by those who no longer travel, no longer exert themselves, who are exhausted, and want to remain transfigured in a single place which contains all places.

You tell me the truth, what the official chronicle of the myth keeps silent. But I cannot hear you. You are lost in the single image of the islands; I, distracted by all that's happening on the beach. One of the players, a stout, dark boy who's swinging his arms like windmill wings, knocks the referee down on the sand. I don't quite understand; it seems that everybody has placed bets on either one team or the other, the white or the blue. Another young man, who during the week waits obsequiously on tables in the hotel dining room, and who is now in his Sunday best, jumps on the player; they try to separate them; the waiter shouts that he bet his wages and tips on the team which is losing because of the angry player; they try to separate them, but everyone, player and spectator, immediately turns against the nearest person. They forget they wanted to interrupt the fight, they all begin to beat each other up and the sand sprays the air and on the shore the kicks sound like frogs croaking.

A blond sweaty boy falls back on our table; I catch his curly nape; you hold him near us, grab him tightly by the shoulders. He grunts, breaks loose, spits at our feet and runs away along the beach, toward the rocky caves of the coast and the road to Amalfi: an ochre horse comes galloping out of a cavern, a blond girl astride, the horse's mane and the girl's hair are the same color, his back and her skin the same color, the girl rides and raises clouds of sand the same color: the sea, like them, is ochre, the players shout, the spectators make way, a beautiful and fleeting ghost rides her horse far away from us, along the shore: she looks toward the islands of the sirens, her tousled hair hides her face: the tight pants, the wet blouse. The beach and cliffs are long. The girl comes from Amalfi, from the caverns of Neptune. She will ride every morning, from now on, on Positano beach.

2

Portrait of My Mother

> *Me chi non ha bisogna della Mamma?*
> —Fellini,
> *Giulietta degli spiriti*

I'm walking in, as usual, at the wrong time. After turning off the motor I will sit for a moment, with the keys in my hand, and before leaning back against the red leather seat of this black, convertible Lancia—which she gave me—I will press the lighter, take the Pall Mall out of the pocket of my blue cashmere jacket—which she bought me—and I will wait with the cigarette in my mouth till the lighter jumps out with a slight click and I lift it to the tip of the cigarette and finally lean back to smoke while I observe, in the twilight, that house of sharp angles, hidden, like all Mexican houses, behind a wall topped with broken glass.

I know that as I walk in, there will be an English lawn and hedges as trimmed and geometric as the house itself. All the glass doors on the ground floor are open to extend the drawing room, the library, and the dining room onto the volcanic stone terraces and, at the same time, to bring the walled garden into the house. The shadow of the *pirul* trees—and also their light, which filters through the large windows and the china figures and cut glass—will play, with those almost cathedral blues, yellows and grays, upon the portraits of my mother, the oil paintings framed in burnished gold and patinaed silver.

When I least want to, I remember her in those paintings, silent and disdainful, haughty and beautiful. I don't know which of them I identify her with. If in one she appears clearly outlined, all her contours visible, like a reality of sensuous flesh and aggressive bones, with her arched eyebrows and straight black hair, barefoot and surrounded by pelicans, in another she vanishes, like the lace covering her, and her flesh seems to dissolve in the ivory tones of the air and materials invented by the painter. I would say, nevertheless, that Claudia, my mother, is really the figure in the triptych by Leonora Carrington who knows how to preserve her famous face and turn her body into a perpetual metamorphosis of bird and ash, flame and dragon. Here, the pelicans give way to spikenards and weeping willows: the background is an open cemetery.

But when I walk into this house I also know that Claudia's presence will dominate these paintings which so obviously try to immortalize her. I stop in the marble hall and the familiar and repeated spectacle that the drawing room offers, with its clean Scandinavian furniture, matters less to me than my own presence, my knowing that I'm there, wearing the blue cashmere jacket and the flannel trousers with their respective labels which, although hidden, attribute the manufacture of my clothes to Cucci, Rome. Each time I enter this house I must face the problem of becoming present because before me, since I stand on the threshold not knowing what to do with my feet and hands, unable to adjust the expression on my own face, reduced in my own eyes to a reflection, is that spectacle which does not ask permission to exist, exhibit, place itself on earth. And she rules over it with her twenty-five years of glitter. A quarter of a century. These light-years she has been the star.

Sitting on a black leather stool—now—or pacing quickly and nervously—immediately—over the black and white chessboard rug, my mother doesn't realize that I've come in. She lights a cigarette, she is dressed in black lounging pajamas, buttoned to the neck with wide sleeves embroidered in gold with tarot figures. Her complexion is a blend of old ivory and newborn light. Her black eyes draw back, tense, before springing with claws of spontaneous mockery, anger or laughter. And now that she's greeting that newspaperman being introduced to her, she uses her most ancient and powerful weapon: she stares at him, she challenges him to withstand her eyes with an irony suspended between eventual acceptance and rejection, even though she already knows—even though we all know—that the man will lower his first and she will have that victory, at least. Claudia could not live without a daily victory.

Without the recognition of her victory. When the newspaperman lowered his eyes, my mother had already moved her face slightly, she had transformed it into the mask of her customary victory and is looking at the lens of the photographer from *Life*, that old man with the short and graying beard who is disguised in tweeds and proclaims his professional distance with all the indifferent wrinkles of an Anglo-Saxon face: that is, with the mask—also—of cold simplicity. *Life* will do a cover story on my mother in three months; Claudia's look while she poses is the same as a minute ago, as if she had taken advantage of the unknown newspaperman to try it out and now obtained, without the usual wait which time, competition, or the law of compensation forces on the rest of us, immediate compensation and recognition. That look, now, wants to be free: Claudia recognizes in the photographer a professional and respects him. Nevertheless—then that relaxed tension, that foreign permanence, are not entirely gratuitous—while the camera's shutter snaps once and again, my mother continues deceiving herself, refuses to resign herself to enjoying the taste of her victory and poses, poses, poses today for a cover which will come out in three months because, besides the recognition of today's victory, that of each moment, she loves and fears the time that surrounds her, escapes her and she can only capture it today, one more time today. One more photograph, one more movie, this very day, so that her future time will always be the present time of her beauty. I admire her tension and her devotion; her complete command in front of this Leica is equal to the demands she makes on herself in front of a Mitchell in the Churubusco studios or Cinecittá.

Like me, all those present have been stopping, looking at her, with glasses in their hands and cigarettes hanging stupidly, in defeat. For the publicity agents, such a wonder is their doing alone; their credential. Claudia hugs herself and she's a dark panther; dangerous and tender. The newspapermen, avid, fearful, observe their permanent source of news from a distance; the eight columns (or the column, simply) are an institution created by and for Claudia Nervo. My mother laughs falsely, throws her head back, caresses her neck; her hands and all her skin, the color of white roses. The sad set designer knows there isn't a set capable of obscuring Claudia's presence, of overwhelming or evaporating her under a mass of paper maché. Claudia leans her chin against her closed fist: young, gratuitous, intense. The director of the movie, his bones shrinking, accepts the purely functional role of his work in a Claudia Nervo movie. She places her arms akimbo and, standing, crosses one knee over the other; she's a heron. The costume designer thinks how much the perfect model would cost and the obligation of paying her fees; a justice and a gratitude which cannot be mentioned. Claudia cuddles up in an armchair, unreachable, fetal, creator of herself. The seven, eight, twelve girls who surround her are obscured despite the youthful exaggeration of their clothing: the white boots, the hip-hugger pants, the childish skirts, the extravagant hats, African hunter, Flemish bishop: they pose too, like satellites, isolated, conscious of themselves, their abandon and their nearness, attempting to reproduce my mother's gestures with all the ineptitude of mere idol-worship or envious youth.

Claudia sits up with the languor of a dream come true, a dream of open, shining eyes, which predict their own nightmare; the photographer keeps shooting, nervous toward the end, annoyed that the guests have moved away, leaving an empty space around my mother. He shouts in English that he doesn't want isolated photographs, but rather shots of Claudia in motion, at the cocktail party, surrounded by people. The waiters have stopped moving with their trays full of hors d'oeuvres and drinks and now my mother's gesture is unmistakable, she steps over the immediate situation, she leaves it behind and raises her arm shaking it, pointing her finger at me, at me who sees only the black pajama sleeve that slips down to her elbow and reveals the beautiful Hindu bracelet, the golden serpent which, like all amulets, distinguishes and enslaves its owner.

17

I move, incredulous, toward my mother. Toward the palms of her hands, open and in front of her, as if she were welcoming a prodigal son who was also an enchanted prince. Oh mamma, mamma, it's true, you're calling me, drawing me to you, only you look at me, none of these people do; they don't know of my existence, or don't talk about it. You have hidden me well. And now, from the center of your world, you call me, me who so determinedly and so inopportunely came to this precise and purposeful cocktail party you're having, to announce the filming of your new movie . . .

"Come over here, handsome. We missed you."

It's not me Claudia's looking at. Behind me—they're all looking at him—the actor who's to be her leading man in this famous movie walks into the drawing room. The movie and television cameras buzz louder and that faceless man, smelling of lavender, comes up to her, bends over, kisses my mother's clasped hands and she stands up and both stand, arm in arm, in front of me, hiding me, and I move to one side.

The Kidnappers

> . . . personality is an unbroken series of successful gestures.
> —Fitzgerald,
> *The Great Gatsby*

The car had followed me from school. I realized a car was following right behind me but I wasn't worried because I had a normal and peaceful life. I'd only leave grandmother's house to go to school and I'd walk back alone every day because I never had many friends and I wasn't very good at sports. I liked to walk alone on the streets of Guadalajara, which is a breezy and crystal-clear city, with clean air that tastes of sudden rains and nearby lakes and which neatly outlines everything: the streets, the gardens, the people who are quiet and cunning and speak in a roundabout way.

"Pick him up, hurry."

I hardly resisted, because I didn't understand and because, before, everything was permitted, grandmother would spoil me and I would climb up on a stool and reach to the highest shelf where grandmother kept the jars of cocoanut candy and paper-wrapped cubes of sugar which your teeth sank into so comfortably and then grandmother would say: "A mouse has been here" and nothing else: they lifted me into the car and the woman who smelled of perfumed fox said:

"To Mexico City, quick, there's no time to lose."

She pressed me against her and said that she was my mother and I raised my eyes and found, more then, since it was the first time and a surprise, my own child's face turned into something else, into lips that kissed me and then separated from me to say to the man who was driving:

"What a holy fit his father's going to have."

I had always spent those hours under the window awnings, protected and useless, with the growing, warm euphoria of that solitude which was just like happiness. Houses of Jalisco: everything that was familiar, that quiet image, that commonplace, the thick walls, the striated roofs, the balustrades, the whitewashed outer walls that sheltered mule drivers stopping under the rain to light their crackling cigarettes and construction workers at midday when they'd eat tacos and drink tejuino and take their siestas. And the dark pious old women who would file like powerless witches from one church to the next, pursued by the ubiquitous devil, and the lines of little dark girls, dressed in blue satin, crowned with fading lilies, who would wait for the Archbishop, black and scarlet, the Bacchic Primate, to pass. The hewn stone facades and the niches on the sides of the wooden vestibule reserved for Saint Francisco Xavier and Saint Luis Gonzaga, and the narrow artisan's quarters which were hidden away at one side of the house.

All this, and more, when you'd walk through the carriage porch into the patio of arched corridors surrounded by rooms and salons; here, in these rooms, you'd find opaque paintings of mustached ladies with transparent gloves and hyacinths in their black hair; of old women with lace mitts and green eyes; of men in high black hats, cravats, frock coats, watch chains and calling cards in their gloved hands; of little wax girls, pale and starched, with hoop-skirts, funeral coifs, roses on their bodices and their hands devoutly clasped, wearing the same lace mitts as the old women who still weren't dead; of little boys dressed like national heroes, with false sideburns, plumed three-cornered hats, tin plate swords and military gloves stuck between belt and jacket. All this, to the boundary of the bare mustard-colored bedrooms, wardrobe and washstand, rocking chair and copper bed with its mosquito net and wood slats, everything, everything led to a final sense of devotion, to the absence of touch. The murmured, secret devotion and touch of these willful shadows, and this voluntary withdrawal which transfig-ured the goings-on in the street, the threats of the outside world, into a final receptacle of subdued desires.

And if the whole house in Guadalajara was this warm blind breast, there, under the awnings, was the absolute niche of devoted separate-ness, of protective isolation. I would cuddle up, stretch my legs, withdraw into myself again, hugging myself, fearful that this euphoric heat of the womb could not last, and there I would spend hours.

But when everything became talk about kidnappers, the kidnappers are on the loose, they must be the gypsy women, the witches, the Weepers, the burglars with their skeleton keys, the bandits who cut off little boys' fingers, wrap them in tamale skins and sell them in the market, the circus owners who make them into clowns, train them to be quacks, disfigure their faces and make them carry trunks so that they'll be dwarfs and then exploit them in the traveling sideshows; it must be the Boogeyman, the faceless Monster, the necessary ghost of these peaceful and dark houses; when the season of the kidnappers arrived, as punctual as the celebration of the Immaculate Conception, I left the awnings, too close to the windows and long hands, and went under the bed, already lanky and bony at the age of nine with big black eyes and olive skin and delicate features and straight, blond hair, secluded now by those four curtains of tattered bedclothes, and equi-distant from the four copper legs, so high that I could sit up straight there as on an ecclesiastic chair, during kidnapper season, with my paper tissues and the little chamber pot filled with water.

Those were the good times. I would tie one tissue to another or knot one at a time, roll them into balls, wet them and sculpt to my delight. That's how the mountain ranges, palaces, witches and owls, crowns, angels were born; damp and flexible, stiff and dry, they were the masters of their low, dark palace, their city of darkness, which could also be a shining ballroom when I'd gather grandmother's wooden candlesticks under the bed. These new creatures of paper and cloth were manipulated by the serious little boy I was, smiling when grand-mother would shout don't you go hiding on me, what mischief are you up to now, lunch is ready, your father's angry, come out Mito, don't think you can scare me, the Weeper's coming to get you, it's Boogey-man kidnapper time, where are you?

I want you to know all about it. This is my story.

In and Out of the Enchanted Grottos

All camp objects, and persons, contain a large element of artifice.
—Sontag,
Notes on Camp

The people who stayed in the drawing room after the press confer-
ence—mamma's secretary and the leading man—are trying to chat
amiably and continue to eat peanuts and chopped liver sandwiches
although their real concern is for the voices that do or don't reach
them from the bedroom. I'd prefer not to be here, in the bedroom, but
rather downstairs, in the drawing room, thinking that she's not arguing
with me and that I, like the secretary and the actor, am sitting eating
sandwiches and pretending while the voices get louder and fade off,
and the two of them would like to listen but politeness makes them sit
there as if my mother and I were not arguing in the carpeted bedroom,
decorated in shades of brown.

The tenor of Claudia's voice doesn't at all fit in with the room's
fastidious orderliness. I always think that such an earthshaking and
glass-shattering voice—wagging tongues say it's a sergeant's voice; I,
who wish to ascribe a secret to it, have imagined that it's the voice of
a self-conception—should reach the ear accompanied by some form of
disorder, obvious, physical, visible in the things that surround it.

It's not like that, and right now, without ceasing to embarrass me
with her look and conceiving me with her voice, Claudia moves
toward me, tidying up; she smoothes the bedspread with her hands,
flattens out a crease in the rug with her silk slipper, goes to that final
threshold of her beauty, the dressing table where everything is in its
place . . .

"Who said you could use it, eh?"

"It was a mistake, that's all. Since I have one like it, I thought it was
mine."

"Some excuse! I don't mind you using it, but I do mind you bringing
it back in rags."

"You talk as if I had lent it to a beggar."

"Look at it and tell me if I'm wrong."

"I'm the only one who wore it. I swear. I used it. You use things and
they wear out, right?"

"Stop annoying me. I try to be nice to you. I said you could wear it, just don't bring me back a rag. And if you're too stupid to take a hint, I'm telling you now you're rubbing me the wrong way by wearing it. As if you didn't have your own things."

"As if you weren't the one who paid for them, you mean."

"I don't mean anything. And keep torturing yourself, if that's your bag."

"I'm telling you, I made a mistake."

"You keep making mistakes and I'll end up with a closet full of rags."

"I'm the only one who wore it."

"Stop buzzing in my ear, you sound like a broken record."

"Just me. They're my stains and my sweat, mine . . ."

"Enough, Mito. Stop arguing. Keep it, it's all yours."

The whole time, we looked at each other: between us is that pearl gray cashmere sweater, thrown on a cream velvet chair, and the tone of our voices, which I don't know how to immediately transcribe, which only exists after some passage of time, is high and piercing. But as I loathe them, or don't know how to write them, I avoid the exclamations, the gruff signs that the secretary and the leading man will be adding to our argument, down there, while they chat and pretend and eat chopped liver sandwiches. We didn't look at each other: I talked to her about that sweater and she moved around the room without looking at me, tidying things up and looking, also, toward the sweater, but only when referring to it: her with those incredibly practical, efficient gestures, as if in that way she recuperated from the nervous fatigue of a vain and calculated public engagement.

She comes from a land of cattle owners and revolutionaries, horse riding people, who have to fight the extremes of their climate; people who know how to cut wood and walk on the shady side of the street. Those things. I sometimes think that my mother's public life is like her winter in the North; the extreme cold justifies extreme gestures which, being a defense, are accepted even though their intention is theatrical: this I've seen on the streets of wintry cities. The cold is another excitement, more of the mind and the mask than of the senses; it stimulates certain attitudes of violent elegance during the moments you put your coat on, go out on the street through the revolving doors of a hotel, stand before the sidewalk spectacle and order a taxi. In the cold, with a luxury hotel as our background, we can be an acceptable mixture of Greta Garbo and Boris Godunov.

And her private life, like a summer in the desert, where her defense is not in the sensual relaxation to which heat treacherously invites us, but in that practical precision which eliminates superfluous movements. You shouldn't drink cold water in the heat, but rather steaming hot coffee. Level off the temperatures of the body and the atmosphere. As she's doing at this moment.

"Stop arguing. Keep it, it's all yours."

I pick up the sweater.

It makes no sense, this time, to press it against my chest, sniff it with my eyes closed. This time, it's useless.

I go to the door of the bedroom and open it. I open it so those two persons can hear me down there, in the drawing room, where I'd like to be hearing myself when I stop, clutching the sweater, and shout:

"I hate you."

I can't decide whether to say it out loud again as I run down the marble staircase. All this could be a repetition—a rehearsal—of something. I'm silent because I keep repeating it under my breath while I button my jacket and see my reflection in the mirrors, tainted on purpose to make them look like antiques. Repeating and inventing. That she had to talk about that sweater I returned to her a week ago, so as not to mention the real reason for her anger. Why didn't she call me on the phone when she got the sweater back? Or if she preferred to tell me face to face, why didn't she summon me, like other times, knowing that not caring about the nature of the meeting, I would come happily? She knows, she knows, and now she used the sweater as a pretext to get angry without telling me that I came at the wrong time, that I could have picked any other day of the week, except today, the day of the press party. I cross the hall without looking toward the drawing room, where the secretary and the actor stand up when they see me go by. I wanted to see the face of that man; to see, at least, if he has a face and not only a fragrance of lavender. I stop as I open the front door. No, they didn't stand because of me. They were waiting for me to leave so that they could go immediately to Claudia's bedroom. No, this too I'm inventing. On the threshold the warmth of the house, home, meets the dry and sudden cold of the night. No. They haven't moved.

I reach the parked Lancia, get in and turn the key.

"Who are you?"—I start the car and throw the sweater to one side, not looking at her yet, only sure of her presence and her perfume inside my car, and her bare arm brushing my shoulder. The lights of the other cars coming down Avenida de la Fundición blind me, immediately.

"Bela."

I stick my head out of the car before joining the row of vehicles looking for a shortcut between el Ángel and las Lomas.

"Do I know you?"

"No. I got here just a month ago, not even."

What did it matter. The actor would go up or she would come down. It was the same thing. The secretary would be, once more, the go-between. That procuress with her eternal two-piece suit and her powdered face and her short hair, that excrescence of the freedom which my mother, somehow, conquered for all of them. Ruth, faithful as only that parallel procreation can be, not a mirror but the incubus, the intimate, the fat dog or the well-fed rabbit.

"Where did you meet her?"

"In Italy, last summer. While she was making a film."

"Did she choose you?"

"No. I think she accepted me. Like the rest."

Yes. She would lead him up the marble steps, already bound, both of them certain of every act of this ritual fatality, this expected routine, like the order of the streets. I drive around the traffic circle toward Masaryk, come to a stop, and fear that the clashing lights, the traffic light and the bank and pastry shop lights and neon signs, will reflect on the windshield the face I don't want to see.

"She trapped you, you mean."

"No. She attracted me. I was spending my vacation in Positano and one afternoon I saw her come out of the sea. I was lying on the beach. She shook her hair and looked at me in that way, you know . . ."

"And you lowered your eyes."

"Yes."

"Of course."

They must be in front of the door. Ruth will tap delicately, like a courtesan, with her knuckles, "May I?" and her hand will open the door which I now imagine as a heavy, black, wooden door, with old hinges and an iron grille, as I also venture, almost laughing, to give the faceless man a name: Buridan; I will call him Buridan and I will hide under grandmother's bed to mold him with two wet tissues and I will read the forbidden stories of the queen in the Tower. I will pierce

24

them with pins while they moan and breathe heavily on top of me, on the mattress.

"Then you don't know the game."

"Silly. What attracts me is discovering it."

"But you can't break the rules, you can't . . ."

I close my eyes and she says to me: "Be careful." She puts her hand next to mine on the wheel. I forgot to put on my driving gloves. I take my hand, the one next to the girl's, off the wheel. I look for my gloves on the seat, without looking at her. I find them and put them on, with my teeth. She wants to help me and if I let her, if I accept her hands on mine, it's because the actor, Buridan, has entered the neat, efficient tycoon officelike bedroom. I see the surprise in his false look, the one I have just invented as if I had a pencil and could draw the features of all those men at will. And then erase them. Their surprise. Tomorrow I'm going to laugh at it with Claudia. Oh, what a good time we'll have tomorrow. I'll tell her what I imagined and, in tears of laughter, she will say yes, that was how it was. She will hug me and the two of us will keep laughing and kissing.

"Which rules?"

"I don't exist."

It was like entering an operating room. A bare hospital where the image of health is the same as that of sickness; where the surgeon is the executioner. What a laugh, Claudia, Buridan, the fool who doesn't know you, the fool who thinks this will be like the others, the ones who came before, they told him your fable, inventing it in self-defense, he enters your neat, clean, sacrificial cell, the cage of a lioness disguised as a nun, your cloister, white like the labyrinths of a hospital.

"And if you acknowledge me, you're going to stop existing, Bela."

"You're joking. I figured you were weird. When you came in this afternoon and I asked who you were, they all answered me in a whisper. As if you were a secret or something. But I liked you."

What did the fool expect to find? A remake of the movie set? Delilah reclining on a mountain of skins, fanned by two Persian eunuchs, protected by Saracen guards, contemplating the dance of twenty Nubian maidens, dressed in peacock feathers, turquoise diadems, mother-of-pearl brassieres? Oh, Buridan, the gate to the seraglio opened and you expected Theda Bara. Now you'll know, you poor thing, that my mother devours because she doesn't allow for illusions and she castrates because her life is more violent than your slow dreams, you miserable, perfumed, faceless turtle.

"I am a secret. Didn't they explain? Claudia Nervo doesn't have a son. And especially a twenty-nine-year-old son. People would start figuring."

"Bah. She has no age."

"They all start with that line. They all say the same, in the beginning."

A neat operation. Without chloroform. Precise, like the diligence of the surgeon's knife. Mathematical, like the incision. Perfect, like the extraction. Impeccable, like the stitches. And all without chloroform. It was Baudelaire who compared the act of love to a torture or to a surgical operation. The streets of Mexico are palpitating, faceless Bela, because they are completely empty. Look along the Paseo de la Reforma, now that we're going around the Ángel traffic circle, and tell me if you see a sign of life in this desert, tell me if you see your outdoor cafés, your hustle and bustle. Tell me if you see something other than some eels in their American tin can automobiles, like you and I who don't look at each other so that we are better able to invent our faces: do you want to give me her face, which is yours? Don't let me down, Bela. Tomorrow you'll know the real game, the closed and implacable one. If you're the newest arrival, you will get the choicest morsel. Fit for a cardinal or for a sexton, *chi lo sa?* And then you'll laugh at me or cry at remembering me. Now do you see? I'm preparing you for the revenge, by refusing to speak directly to you, by using you as a part of my distraction and my monologue. Distraction and monologue: aren't they the same? Like my chloroform.

"Where do you live?"

"In Insurgentes."

"Guillermo."

"Oh. They told you my name too."

Now she laughs, Bela, laugh in that happy, free, affectionate way, announce your face to me with your independent ragazza's laugh, the laugh of a little bird who flies from August in Positano to January in Cortina to October in the *boites* of Via Veneto to April in . . . No, Bela, you've never been to Madonna dei Monti. In the spring. Have you?

"And you, where do you live?"

"Here?"

"No. That I already know. In Italy."

"I'm a Roman. In Parioli."

She travels up and down the seven hills and elegant Parioli and around curves, up and down its big windows and high stoops and modern apartments and its *vita* without the *dolce*, provincial and parochial, where nobody speaks anything but Italian and forms, taste, setting are acceptable only in one's memory, present but past, never in the vulgar and offensive irruption of the newly invented. Schifoso Fellini who turns Botticelli into Mandrake the Magician. *Tu quoque,* Narda? The operation is over. Buridan-Lothario, defeated and bald, will be lying face down on the immaculate bed, where only Marguerite de Bourgogne has dared to part the sheets after surgery, and not to rest, but to preclude the postmortem exhibition. The operation took place without removing the blankets, without undoing the bed. There lies Lothario, Buridan, Samson, in as much intimacy as in any motel, flaccid and defeated on the respected sheets. The deflated leopard skin hangs on his body. His fez has fallen to the floor. The Queen's henchmen wrap him in his own skin. Pick him up. Throw him into the Tiber. Before his hair can grow. What comic strips, what *fumetti* . . .

"Do you read the *fumetti?*"

"Hah. I spent two years modeling for them."

"Ah. You work. You're not one of the rich ones."

"Nò. Claudia paid for my ticket."

"What? You owe her something?"

"No. She gave it to me, understand?"

Now it's my turn to laugh. So would Claudia in that moment and I with her, not seeing them. Ruth would be behind the door, or spying through the keyhole, or perhaps behind the mirror if, as I have come to suspect, Claudia yesterday or some day accepts that imaginary proposition of Ruth's: that the mirror be a reflection in the bedroom and a screen in the adjacent dressing room. I congratulate myself: I've resisted the temptation of looking at Bela and we're already on this monotonous avenue which, they say, begins on the Rio Grande and ends on the Guatemalan border. What a lot of jungles and deserts, God what cacti and silent walls: what unconsecrated spaces, waiting for the air to become a temple. No, excuse me, I'm not usually so nervous. I'd prefer to sketch my impressions in another way. But how, on this night of all nights and already so close to my apartment, without having looked at Bela, without having imagined the real truth of what has happened in my mother's house tonight, during the forty minutes we've been rolling through the streets of Mexico? If I could only go slower and make this story longer. Perhaps I would deny it. There are other moments and other stories which demand a pause. I'll get to them sometime and perhaps someone will listen. Perhaps Bela, if she doesn't fall into the trap. If she hasn't fallen already. No. I should have met her before, when I lived in Italy, before she knew anything about Claudia. Before stopping the car in front of the apartment house where I live, on Insurgentes Sur, before Félix Ceuvas: far from my mother's territory, at the other end of the city. Next to a supermarket. Before opening the door without having looked at the girl.

"Did you have a good trip?"

I get out and her voice follows me while she, in turn, opens the door and displays the bare toes of her feet, her gilded, flat sandals:

"Just great. So exciting. All my friends went to Fiumicino, you know, as if they were saying good-bye to me forever . . ."

Her white pants, her legs and her knees.

"Come to Messico. The end of the world. They gave me baskets of fruit and wine, records, *gelsomini*, what are they called here?"

"Jasmine."

The tails of the jacket she's just put on. A peajacket, from the US merchant marine, except it has shiny new buttons . . .

"All my friends, can you imagine that? Sandro Costa and Pierluigi Montale and Giancarlo d'Aquila . . ."

She doesn't need, in the end, to show her face. I guessed it because I feared it. She shows it as she steps out of the car, banging the door shut and repeating:

"Giancarlo Adelphi."

She reveals her immodesty, her black thick hair, obviously dyed, perhaps a wig, her arched, false eyebrows, purposely, imitatively painted, like the bow of her lips and the false mole on her cheek. She smiles so that I'll recognize myself in her again, like I recognized myself in the woman with the perfumed fox fur who kidnapped me from grandmother's house. Disguised as Claudia and then disguised as me with that name on her lips, denying all my singularities, invading my property, making fun of my identity, plunderer, Weeper, kidnapper. Heartless.

I lunge at Bela, stop before her happy and pitiless eyes, raise my hand and let it fall on the crust of false paint and whether she screams or cries or falls on her knees, I don't know, I don't care. I run to my

28

house, cross my threshold and realize what it is: the border of my private country, my holy place.

My enchanted grotto: that's how I wanted it, as I see it tonight, panting, leaning against the door of this vegetal cloister of mine thought up by me built by me: my nature. It has grown like a jungle; that's how you wanted it; I wanted you and nobody else to see what I've achieved thanks to you, via an old photograph of Sarah Bernhardt's apartment and an old copy of Wilde's *Salomé* illustrated by Beardsley: my continuity is here and I am grateful to the cold fatigue, the nervous sweat that makes me stop on the threshold and feel like another object, devoured by the ends of the liberated line: serpents on all the scarlet silk walls: here these pure and free lines intertwine, finding all their combinations, all their conjunctions, all their fusions. There is a violation which liberates when two lineal ends meet, without beginning or end: untied knots, knotted parallels, thin and breakable opaque glass pistils, lead-encased lamps which are closed flowers and opened fruits, jewel, marble, and bead curtains, like strings of rosaries between the living room and the corridor, screens of swans and skinny dancers, whose ribs are visible between the spaces of my apartment. Lead spiders hung from a dropped ceiling of carved boxwood. Here I am isolated. Here I return, like the Incas, to renew my energy; not to the bare house of the gloved families, not to the rival territory of my mother, not to that nebulous model you offered me: only in this space I renew myself. Near my Tiffany lamps and my Guimard furniture. Exhausted, I can only look: I surrender through my eyes to the appeal of the embossed Lalique plates which adorn the mantelpiece near the dining table, filled with twisted ashtrays, illuminated by long and flowing electrical pedestals and lamps hidden behind charcoal-shaded petals, graduated from their intense base to their pale opening. Silver bowls where dry algae swim. I drink in my setting of Turkish stools and divans sunken beneath the weight of painted silks and Persian rugs, pearl-crusted cushions and throw pillows of untouchable satin. The cloister surrounds me; my fatigued trembling receives it without salient angles, without floors, walls, windows; I am part of the matter of this Baroque cancer, of this unprogrammed, curvilinear and flamboyant proliferation, in which objects swim before me like polyps, amoebas, jellyfish, rebel cells of an organism free to devour itself. The lines jump out of the water frames: Salomé has picked up

Johanan's head to kiss his dead lips. Claudia is the gypsy Salomé of purple nipples and ruby claws. I, the masturbated terror of that cold and beardless old man-boy. Bela, all the translucid brides in the midst of the gregarious abundance of monsters. You, head of the Baptist, creator of his own lake of blood and swooning lilies. You, undulating melody, river of names in flames: Saint John gave us our names, like you mine. Names of all that surrounds me in this conquered grotto, of all that adds up to the substance of glass and lead, wood and iron: peacock and sunflower, sea urchin and jellyfish, ivy and grapevine fermenting in their prisons of silk and plaster. I do not want to touch anything. The whole setting permeates even my nails and fingertips as it does the long, wild, perfumed black hair of a woman. Everything grows: I move from the threshold that tries to warm me: passing is passion. But the besieged walls look for the refuge of holy ramparts. One draws a circle and the epidemic cannot enter. The holy place isolates me and continues me: the profane remains outside.

Here I fall on the divan, cut off, like all beings, bees and mice, ants and spiders, bats and night monkeys, who need a hole to survive. To sleep, defeated.

I will sleep alone. Under the old photograph of a saint devoured by secret illnesses, by a time-eaten life. I will sleep under Nadar's portrait of Baudelaire and like him I will be afraid of sleep as one is afraid of an enormous pit. I will sleep alone, near the reproduction of the painting of Sarah Bernhardt in her apartment, accompanied by a tame grey-hound. And between the two, I will dream of the undulating, per-fumed world of women, brilliance in motion . . .

The White Telephone

> . . . And one fine morning . . .
> —Fitzgerald,
> *The Great Gatsby*

"Did I wake you up?"

"Of course not. I went to bed early and I've been up and around for hours."

"Early . . ."

"Right after you left."

"And now what are you doing?"

"I already told you. Everything's in a mess and we start shooting on the second. Ruth is up to her ears in work and we still have to pick out some twenty new getups to bowl over those hicks in Europe. You know I bear the weight of the nation's honor on my shoulders . . . I don't have to tell you: before, Mexico was Pancho Villa, now it's me."

"Then you're going soon?"

"Honey, where have you been! The breakdown's ready, they found the locations in Italy, I have the plane tickets in my pocket."

"The same old thing."

"Yes. I don't see what you're so surprised about."

"Only ten more days."

"Exactly. Now tell me what you called for . . ."

"Mamma, it's just that yesterday . . ."

"It doesn't matter. Nothing happened."

"I wanted to apologize. That's all."

"Precious. You see me spinning around like a black whirlpool, but I think of you more than you realize."

"Really?"

"Believe me, darling."

"Oh how I'd like to be near you right now."

"I do too, I swear."

"You know, if I could only strain myself through the telephone wire and give you a kiss . . ."

"Lick me, you mean."

"Mamma . . ."

"You don't kiss wounds, you lick them."

"Yes, anything you say. But I didn't hurt you."

"What? What do you think you were shouting when you walked out? And what about those poor people downstairs who were all ears for the occasion?"

"And how about you? As if I were some photographer; what am I saying, at least you say hello to the photographer; like one of your servants, carrying trays . . ."

"Who forces you? You know my professional life is one thing and my private life something else. Busybody. You're always asking for it."

"What did you do when I left?"

"Are you stupid this morning? I went to sleep. How do you think I felt after your little performance?"

"That's right, you already said so. Forgive me."

"What for? I'm not the kind to bear grudges."

"Yes, I know. But . . . but if I had come back a half hour later to apologize . . ."

"You would have found me in bed, with a sleeping pill inside me."

"You were alone."

"No. Ruth gave me a massage while the pill was taking effect. Hmmm! You should have seen how fresh and lively I was when I woke up."

"How I'd love to be with you."

"There's no time today. I've emptied all the drawers. This place looks like a battlefield. And you know how I hate disorder."

"Let me come by for a while."

"No. It's your fault."

"Why?"

"I already told you. For coming yesterday without asking, when the place was full of people. If you could have waited just a little, today you would have found me alone."

"I've noticed you've been alone for several months."

"I'm recovering, darling."

"Don't make me laugh."

"At what, you?"

"How exclusive you're becoming. Do you forget that we've been happily together for twenty years?"

"Sure. And look, I'm still in one piece."

"Oh, mamma, what need is there . . ."

"Need? That's a slave's word, honey. Myself I'll take luxury . . ."

"Please. I didn't call to fight."

"You'd have a lot of training to do before you could match me in a fight."

"You're right. I only said that to convince myself."

"About what, darling?"

"That last night doesn't matter."

"Believe me, I don't know what you're talking about."

"That actor, the one who smelled of lavender."

"Guillermo. Guillermito. Mito."

"Don't laugh."

"He's all yours, Herod."

"Don't laugh, I say. You don't know what . . ."

"Here's Ruth. Good-bye."

"What?"

"Master Guillermo?"

"Yes, Ruth?"

"At seven forty-five Madam sent for me. She was in the bathtub. I wrapped her in her terry cloth bathrobe. She asked for cinnamon tea and I went to order it while she dried herself. Madam got into bed and took a barbiturate with her tea. I gave her a massage. She slept from eight thirty on, twelve hours straight."

"Bravo. That's fine, Ruth. Thanks."

"Got it straight, honey? Don't think you're going to hold me up with your fantasies all day long. Tell me something nice."

"I'm sorry."

"Now what's wrong?"

"I don't know. I almost wish it were true, so that we could laugh today."

"Who can understand you. Good-bye."

"No, wait, not like that. Tell me how you would have treated him."

"For God's sake! Whom?"

"The one with the lavender. Lothario. Buridan. Samson. Saint John the Baptist. How. Please, for a laugh. That's all I wanted when I called you, to have a little laugh together . . ."

"Oh darling, to you nightmares must seem like miracles."

"Go on, tell me."

"Let me see . . . Yes, it seems that this blockhead goes around thinking he can share star-billing if he first costars in bed. And I'm telling you, that man hasn't been born yet. But let's give him his little illusion, after all, man doesn't live on cake alone."

"Yes, mamma, what would you do?"

"Suppose this poor prig imagines that I'm just like in the movies . . ."

"Yes, yes . . ."

". . . and that I dress like Cleopatra and sit on the bed to wait for him, with two Nubian slaves. Done up with a crown and very blue eyelids. And a cape of precious jewels and peacock feathers, how does that grab you?"

"Oh mamma, I adore you."

"Stop laughing. Let me go on. So this little fella comes in and it's like Valentino, you know, the silent movies, the tango and all that. Rolling his eyes, his hands over his heart."

"Mamma, stop, you're killing me."

"He falls on his knees. Devour me! he cries. And rushes toward me as if he was trying to win the Australian crawl."

"And then?"

"I slowly take off my cape, and underneath I'm wearing long johns."

"What?"

"A rough one-piece shirt, like the ones my grandfather wore, itchy as cactus, buttoned down to the ankles . . ."

"And then, and then . . ."

"What do you think? My blacks grab him and beat him to a pulp. Curtain."

"Mamma, if only it was always like that."

"It is always like that, puppy, you just don't see it. Don't worry about me. And Ruth has your allowance, don't forget. You'll get your check every month as usual, while I'm away."

"But you haven't told me what happens to Buridan afterward, when the servants stop whipping him."

"Ask Bela. Good-bye."

"Mamma . . . Claudia. Answer me. Mamma! Answer me! Don't hang up! What did you say? Swear to me you told the truth! Mamma! Swear it isn't true!"

Domestic Life

> *Il songeait un peu à se sauver dans un convent* . . .
> —Huysmans,
> *Là-bas*

Then I won't go out at all today. The dogs irritate and bore me, but I say I need them to keep myself occupied. Pharaoh, the Great Dane, has been lying next to me all during the telephone conversation. His sadness is respectful and only after hanging up do I feel him near me, lying at my feet, his head on the floor; now he raises it, moving his ears nervously. But his tender sad brown eyes do not lose that terrible remoteness which people, always false, always insistent upon attributing human forms and moods to these innocent sages, would like to explain as the presentiment of memory in dogs. I stretch my hand toward him from the chair. Pharaoh licks it mechanically. Poor Pharaoh, with neither memory nor destiny. His remoteness is only that: a disdainful sadness, not to be compared with nonexistent happiness. As a puppy, yes, he would play, slip, disappear among the curtains, fight with the fringes of the furniture and drapery. That happiness was pure as his old sadness of today.

Perhaps I'm the guilty one. I've accustomed him to so much company, for nine years now, ever since Claudia took me out of boarding school and said that I could live alone in an apartment. She didn't exaggerate when she said "alone." I had always besieged her, crying, making myself unbearable, telling lies about how they treated me at boarding school. She waited for me to be twenty-one and, as a birthday surprise, she handed me the keys to the apartment. She never understood why I wanted to leave boarding school and I, perhaps to make fun of her, but also out of understandable compulsion, filled my new home with dogs. As I could have filled it with stamp collections. Old magazines. Sausages, girls, flags, or lead soldiers.

Of course, Pharaoh was nothing more than a ball of fur, the smallest among a beautiful pack of Afghans and sheep dogs, among the ridiculous court of Pekinese and Chihuahuas which I went on demanding, not only to keep me company in this then cold place of white, low ceilings, with walls painted black and orange in the style of the moment, not only to make it inhabitable, but also to make Claudia realize how I replaced her, ah, and each time I asked her for a dog, she not only had to be aware of my existence, but also of my intention to fill the place with a dozen dogs.

One alone would have been enough to offend her. But she isn't capable of accepting an offense of this kind. No sir. Each dog was delivered by the store, a friend, the veterinarian—anyone my mother could get hold of—just to satisfy my whim. Not even that minimal relationship, indebtedness, was established. Claudia did not intend to buy my gratitude with her presents. All that my demands got me were dogs and not the trace or intention of Claudia's subjugating me because she gave me presents. With or without them, it would have been the same. Their continued presence only provided, conventionally, for any absence: I could make believe the greyhound was the impostor, or the terrier the reincarnation, of any nameless soul or meaning that wanted to inhabit their bodies.

The dogs' illnesses and meals filled my days. The arbitrary selection of those who would sleep in my bedroom. The whim, also, of taking only one out for a walk on Insurgentes to the sunken park, where the maids would hide to neck with their boyfriends and the children would play statue. That didn't matter anymore. All that remains is my

35

impression of the court, of them following me inside the apartment, while I eclipsed my first compulsion with the second: to redecorate the place with all the art nouveau bric-a-brac that was wasting away in the less frequented antique shops. But this floral delirium was only in homage to you.

My poor witnesses, today dead, escaped, lost, faithful, and proud, only at times roguishly independent in an attempt at mischief or betrayal—bite, sic'im, growl, howl, Pharaoh—who, I confess, could scare me, into running to my bedroom, closing the door behind me, and remaining against it in the dark, blocking the way, with the heavy and cold smell of a mastiff in the hallway, perhaps about to lose his transitory incarnation, to recover an ancient, forgotten, unreproducible visage.

The smell and the death of the dogs. The death struggles. The contained fury of sexual heat. The escapes. The weary return, the scratched or wounded skin, afterward full of clotted scabs. The long howls when they knew that one of them would not return anymore. Intuition, the impenetrable restlessness when Claudia would go on a trip or return from another: the dancing agility of some, the threatening growl of others, the funereal howling over the loss of one of them, which could also be that of recovery.

Maybe because of that I began to forget, to abandon them.

She chose them.

She sent them to my house.

They were hers although I asked for them.

The records, I bought.

I myself set up the Garrard stereo and distributed the speakers in the rooms.

I began to spend entire hours in Margolin, drawn by the shiny covers; pretending to be making a deliberate choice, although my intent was to buy everything, take the whole record store home, begin with the Gregorian chants and end with the Mazatecan chants. The music became an eternal return within each temporal progression. Eight, nine records a week were barely sufficient to nourish that turntable which I later duplicated with a permanent magnetic tape, connected to the apartment's lighting system: to come in, turn the light on and hear, from the back of my cave, an Irving Berlin ballad or a Handel oratory, became another defense, as if the original, dogs and décor, were not enough. My image was this yellow kimono, these bare feet, this face, firm before the mirrors, unsure outside them. This young man who caresses the records, protects them against dust, walks around listening to the music among Ottoman puffs and snake frames, among Beardsley drawings and carpets of flowing Grecian frets, listening to those voices,

Hier ist die Grüft

and, followed by the dogs, by all the solitary dogs who ask in vain for my caress or attention, I think of Bethlehem and Golgotha, in the bare cloisters of the beginning and the end. The pack follows me and I light a cigarette looking at myself in the mirror and I hum and the dogs whine, get up on their hind legs while I change the cigarette for a lump of sugar and, letting them observe me, I suck it slowly, moistening it first and then letting it dissolve on my tongue.

They follow me, day after day, in this season of rain when I lose interest in the outside world, but the only thing they can expect of me is that I'll open the door to the pantry for them and order the cook to serve their steaks and canned food. When they're thirsty they go to the bathroom. I've left the door open and the bidet full of water. And the rest of the time they follow me around the apartment, sad, defeated, without the opportunity of trying themselves or myself: if they have it, that strength will become stunted in the end.

And if they dare to bark, like now, I will continue humming the oratory as if I didn't hear them; and if they all stand in front of me, looking at me in that pained way, disillusioned, and one begins to bark, and another imitates him, and the third howls, and in the end they all look like coyotes, with their snouts raised to the sky and their yellow eyes half-closed, I will run, no, I will go slowly toward the amplifier and turn it to full volume, till the voices of Bach's Easter Mass suffocate and overwhelm that chorus of melancholic, shrill barking of dogs who are no longer looking at me, who seem to be conspiring by increasing their howls while the music rises, and I turn all the sound knobs, looking for the highest and shrillest tones, of total, intolerable volume . . .

Not now. Now only docile, domestic Pharaoh licks my hand when I hang up. I no longer listen to the records. The dogs are no longer here.

Another Visit

I open the door and am afraid to recognize her. And she herself, as soon as she raises her head and sees me, turns her back on me and lets her glasses, on a silver chain, fall.

"What do you want?"—she says to me with an impatient voice.

"You told me to come by for my check yesterday." I stop to fix my tie. Ruth throws a bathrobe over an object on the bed.

"Why don't you knock first. Where did you learn your manners anyway?"—she waves her arm in Ruth's direction, who is sitting on the edge of the bed with papers on her knees, while Claudia turns her back on me and leans her elbow on the dresser—"Ruth, you have the check."

"Yes, it's ready." —I wonder if those squeaks are part of her voice. The woman gets up and walks toward me and perhaps she isn't as disagreeable as I've wanted to imagine her: tidy and gray, efficient, with her hair neatly combed and dyed mahogany black. Short-sleeved blue sweater, pearl necklace, Scotch plaid skirt: a secretary who knows the limits: low key, soigné, never offensive elegance. I take the check and put it in the jacket pocket, next to my heart.

"The best boarding schools, the most expensive high school in Switzerland, and nobody taught you to knock first . . ."—she stands up but doesn't dare to look me in the face—"What are you waiting for?"

"Am I interrupting something? Because . . . because if not, I'd like to stay awhile."

"Do as you wish."

She still turns her back on me, but she puts her glasses on again, to look over the papers. If I made her uncomfortable, she immediately recovered her poise. Besides, I think she wants to astonish me with her command over figures and business. I didn't know that she herself dictates letters Ruth signs with her name. Letters to notary publics, rent administrators, bank managers, stockbrokers, real estate agents. I believe she's snapping these orders and dictating these names for my sake; and not only to astonish me, but also to ease my mind, to let me know that I'll always be provided for. Yes, I cannot separate her from her material wealth and common sense, her fruits, her nourishment, in the same way the earth cannot be separated from the trees that grow on it or the rivers that run through it: my mother is this proof: she exists.

Nevertheless, she exposes herself to this stinginess of wealth: routinely, she transfers a deposit in the Chase Manhattan Bank to la Banca Commerciale Italiana, invests a sum in real estate and, at the same time, orders repairs in the apartment house she owns on Avenida de los Insurgentes—where I live—and a rent raise—which will not affect me, I gratefully admit—. Ruth serves her a cup of coffee and a piece of unbuttered toast and Claudia hands her a page out of a New York newspaper. While my mother drinks the coffee and chews half of the piece of toast, Ruth examines the financial page with a red pencil and I comb my hair in front of the full-length mirror, adjusting the side mirrors so that I can see myself in profile and from the back. She watches me in the dresser mirror. Her pale, thin, remote face, which I can barely make out, is repeated three times in the mirrors that reproduce me and, in a triple, superimposed image, of quartz and paperweight, the one which returns to the dresser mirror. Would it be possible to have three different mothers? There are tribes that believe in it: man inhabits, in his fetal state, the fragmented matrixes of toads and swans, grottos and abysses before penetrating, by means of a magical contact, the simple, functional, undetermined womb of a mother: the gestation took place in other wombs, similar to a nocturnal and disperse crystal which the mother picked up and put together . . . shrieks, scratching paws.

I whistle softly. I know that she's looking at me, paying attention to me, she's looking for a reflection in mine, no matter how monotonously Ruth intones that litany I'm barely listening to, American Sugar 28⅞, Ampex 24, Brunswick 9¼, Cyclop Corporation 41, Disney 52¼, Falstaff 17⅞, Hilton International 20½ and Claudia asks about the fluctuation of U.S. Government Bonds. What things belong to the earth, what things are manifested because of the earth? Aren't they the forests, the fauna, the oceans, everything, earth? Ruth tells her how much. Claudia laughs and raises a fist: what a military, obscene, political gesture. What a problem, to raise crops from the earth when people think that's the same as mutilating it, plundering it: rape and robbery, vultures. She is saying, although I cannot follow her exact words, that to play the market you need confidential information. But the buzzard also purifies, he's the one who plunders the unnecessary, the garbage and the corpses. It was worth the tip, my mother exclaims; it seems that even though the bonds lose their value the interest rates still rise; it depends upon when you invest; I don't understand a thing. It was necessary to invent a whole myth, a whole faith, a whole reason, to justify the loving cultivation of the earth and overcome the repugnance of murdering it with hoes, multilating it with shovels; of pulling out my mother's hair.

"Tell the gringo to sell real fast. Now's the time. Send him a cable. We'll get Texas back yet."

Tlazolzéotl was the native goddess of death, fertility, and filth; her hands smeared with blood and excrement were also the hands—you only had to strip off her ceremonial gloves—of purification: he who cleans gets dirty. I see her confused and sure, with one foot in the rite and the other in the game. My mother keeps laughing and Ruth accompanies with a low and reticent murmur. But Claudia's laughter grows, and when Claudia laughs it's like an epidemic; I catch it, I, who didn't understand, who didn't listen, lower my head although my arms are still raised, with the comb in my hands, before the mirror; her revengeful Mexican humor is so spontaneous and ferocious that I can picture it, and I describe her:

". . . coming into Dallas in an open car, with all the cowboys on their knees . . ."

"Oh no, that's out" —Claudia laughs, crying . . . "I'll take the land, the oil wells, and the cattle, but those dumb Texans, not a chance. I always refused to make movies in Hollywood. I'm like a torero: speak English? not even to please God: Forget it!"

I take advantage of the moment. I kneel beside her, I rest my head on her bare knees shaken with laughter.

"Have a strawberry?" —she passes the saucer to me and I reject it: nothing makes me sicker.

"How would you get even, mamma?"

"Get them at their own game, like me. Do you know that today I'm going to take three hundred thousand dollars out of the United States?"

Pretext: sit at her feet, on the ground, like Pharaoh, near me, like my dogs. Pharaoh: to sit on the ground, the Egyptians said, means to give birth.

"Let's see, tell me . . ."

"Join the Union . . ."

"What?"

I don't know what I'm saying. I feel all the pains, hugging Claudia's legs which I lightly press together, afraid they will open: we will go, like the Maori women, to give birth on the banks of the rivers, among the reeds. I don't know what I'm saying: Claudia is happy.

"Yes, let Mexico become another state, and we'll send Washington a bunch of senators and labor leaders . . ."

"Wrong again, Mito! We'll make them sell enchiladas on the stoops of Congress!"

"We'll eat away their system with payola."

"Ahah, so you think they won't realize it. No, I say it's through the stomach that we'll win, honey . . ."

From the womb to the river: abandoned to the waters, I could have been something else. Something more than the son of Claudia Nervo: an orphan condemned to the cosmos, I would wander along the rivers and the forests till I found my other destiny: my she-wolf. My she-wolf. Another time.

". . . honey; have a presidential campaign featuring our native food, our meat soup, strawberry pulque, chile, tacos, and fish pies and every one of them will go down on their knees begging forgiveness."

"Human sacrifices in the White House rose garden . . ."

"No, not that! We'll scare the living daylights out of them. Death notices fly in Sonora, and at the end, only us mothers and widows are left after the Revolution."

The children die and are buried at the roadside: they will furtively take possession of the wombs of passersby: they will be reborn.

"How funny you can be, mamma."

"Breeding makes the greyhound. Listen . . ."—she caresses my hand, violently—". . . it's been years and happy days since you've asked me for a dog . . ."

"No. I already have too many."

I hide my face between her knees.

"It must cost you an arm and a leg to keep them."

I open one eye and try to look at her. What is my mother going to do to me?

"I have enough, really. Thanks."

A faint drumming: Ruth, in another room, types up the dictation.

"If I wasn't going around in circles all the time, I'd have as many dogs as you."

"Of course. They need a lot of care."

"More than you give them, honey."

"I couldn't treat them better."

"Come on. Don't you see they're thoroughbreds?"

"Yes, I know."

"Yes, of course. When they find one mashed to pieces on the

thruway in the morning, they trace him and I'm the first one they call. I bought them."

She finishes filing her nails.

"And besides, you forget to take off their collars and they identify them right away."

She begins to put on her makeup with the precision of her business transactions. Little by little the color returns to her face, as if the cosmetics, more than applying color, invoked it. That clean, clear complexion and those high, hard cheeks. The beauty of a face is its bones. I stand up and look at the tips of my moccasins.

"You know it all, don't you?"

"It's not my fault. They come and tell me everything, I sure don't ask."

"And what does it matter to you? They're my dogs."

"Sure."

"Then why do you bring it up now?"

"So that you'll know you're not fooling me."

"And what more do you know? Do you have me tailed by a detective?"

"What for? I know you like the back of my hand."

"What time I go to sleep, what I read, what I eat, when I pee?"

Claudia brings her knees together. She pushes me away.

"You're vulgar and boring, honey."

"You think I have no secrets?"

I fix my hair to hide the blush on my face.

"Maybe. But if I don't know it, it can't be too important."

"Please leave the makeup. Look at me."

On my knees again, on the floor, imploring.

"Get up. You look like a lap dog. Vulgar and boring, I swear. And weak, weak like the little fountain in Navojoa square."

I'm on my feet, straightening the creases in my pants, shaking off the fuzz from the rug.

"Tell me, what makes you say that?"

"Because of the dogs. I already told you."

The pancake restores the tanned color; the two pairs of eyelashes, the intensity of her look. But she doesn't look at me.

"Why don't you go with people your own age? The girls are downstairs and Ruth and I haven't finished yet."

I'm about to answer her, to say that she doesn't know my real secret. I am, perhaps, about to reveal it, only to defeat her. She wouldn't understand. That she wouldn't understand. I laugh and leave the bedroom. I close the door and my smile freezes. I came to ask for Bela. Jokes, arguments, associations: I forgot. And she, for the first time, has asked me to go with the girls. Before, the girls weren't supposed to acknowledge me. And I was never supposed to mention them.

"Do call them 'the girls,' it sounds better."

Formica Sanguinae

> . . . in accordance with divine laws
> —I translate: inhuman laws— . . .
> —Borges,
> "*Tlon, Uqbar, Orbis Tertius*"

I want you to know everything. The first time they only looked at me reproachfully and with a kind of pity. The second time, they all whistled aggressively and someone shouted, "Let's get 'im" and they all took up the rhythmic shout "let's get 'im, let's get 'im." The next time is the last, but I never got to make three goals against my own team. First they gave me center left and then they let me gradually move, unawares, to a corner of the field, near the fence of eucalyptus trees.

"Where have you been?"

The branches are very thin and it's difficult for the nests to stick to them. Like delicate ticks, they don't have time to establish roots in the weak corner between the branch and trunk. You don't have to climb to get them; they fall. Sometimes, only broken little eggs. Other times, with luck, newly born birds. Blind and naked, with necks like poor old men and beaks like millionaires' nails.

"What are you hiding there?"

Behind the soccer field fence, the real country begins, a green fountain that seems to flow from the sunbathed edges of the earth to the basin of the plains. I would miss it climbing up to this plateau of dust: a strangely desired dust. You say:

"I would like to know your country because there it all evens out. The forces of death are equal to the forces of life."

I sneak away between two reeds. Nobody notices, neither then nor at the end of the game.

That time I returned home dirty, my hands and knees smeared with mud.

"There, that's how I like to see you. A real little man."

Delicious fatigue of that field which only I know and is the only one I know. If in the distance other children, in overalls and white shirts, are playing soccer, they don't see me. A thin, tenuous odor leads me through the thickets to that plain which, unknowingly, is emptying, returning its juices to the dust that needs them to maintain that parallel procreation, to return the sand to the face of the sun. There's that constant return which will also be a permanent revelation. As in the books at home, handed down from the dead grandfather to the living father and to myself barely brought to life, in those where to open a page is to enter a labyrinth without further exit than abandoning it: closing the book, forgetting.

"You have to be strong. You don't know anything."

Going out to the world through an anthill. From that yellow mound, lost in the plain, behind the sports field fence, before the other boys' plain, flattened by their feet, where four bushes have been torn out by their roots to mark the goals of the game. A few bottles of beer, one day, among laughter. And that exploration in squatting position, dressed in black shorts and the white T-shirt and the shoes which would finally return muddied and scraped.

"I only wanted to give her a decent life. That wasn't good enough for her!"

"Don't talk about her in front of the child."

And the posters? And the photographs in the magazines: last night in Ciro's, yesterday at the airport, Sunday at the bullfights. And the newsreels. No, never the movies. I didn't know nor did they explain. But in a corner of the closet the spiders have nested. Grandmother never moves the furniture from the wall: one needs this sense of exploration. And to be faithful to all that others cannot share with me: this absence of touch when I bring the smooth little birds, in my father's hat, to the impalpable black widows' dark watchmaker shop, in that corner. Will I dare, ever, to touch the tiny bodies, with throbbing insides? The sticky eyes of the little birds prevent me; the spiders, in contrast, have eyes for the night, bulbous periscopes which seen through a magnifying glass are like the domes of a church or an observatory on the always hidden face of a planet: temples of a riddle. To not withdraw when I hear steps, and then the coal stoves, blowers, stone and clay tools of that bad imitation of a patriarchal life. But grandmother didn't know anything else: pounding mortar and grinders.

44

"Zero in sports. Zero in sports!"

They die a few hours later, there's scarcely time to show them to the spiders and then, with a desperate effort, to rub them with my bare, gloveless hands, keeping back the nausea, closing my eyes and feeling the bitter taste, climbing on all fours to my palate and falling exhausted on my tongue while I rub the smooth little bodies, the clean bones of the wings, and try to forget the tremble of the breakable claws and to count the spaced beats of the belly, the heart, and finally the craw. There's no time. I wrap them in socks, under the bed. My hands would not be enough; they had already lost their warmth.

"I don't want what happened to me to happen to him."

"Sh!"

"Some day he'll have to know."

I put the ants in a matchbox and keep it in the back pocket of my shorts. These blood-sucking insects, drunk with the nearness of the parasite which by giving them pleasure enslaves them: the sweet sweat of the parasite, vaguely insinuated in the zoology textbook: I want to imagine it. Nested with the ant, invoked, rejected by it: a dark and poisonous couple which will now be offered, from a matchbox, to the spiders that could never come near the dying birds.

"Ramírez Nervo! Center left! Where the fuck . . . ?"

Rojas kicked my shin bone and Carvajal ran toward me with clenched teeth and Ortega was foaming at the mouth and couldn't talk and Yáñez threw himself on the ground, pulling his hair, and then he got up when everyone shouted, "Let's get 'im, let's get 'im!", when the whole team fell upon me, kicking, punching, the rabble near my ears which I covered with closed fists, not shouting, not crying, beaten under kicks and grunts and growls until falling face up on the muddy field and making out the gentle murmur of the eucalyptus trees behind the fists and shoes with nails and bloody knees and black elbows and open palms which drummed on my head . . .

"There. That's what I like. A little man. Now you can tell."

I went to Chapala one Sunday, with the little birds inside the matchboxes. Broken and dead, they barely fit in those coffins of card-board and sandpaper. The lake didn't have a real shore. The thick, wavy grass penetrated right to the low waters and if from afar that sandbank looked like a wheat field, a bordering space of fertility, close up, barefoot, with the muddy and warm water near my ankles and the slime caressing the soles of my feet, it was a jungle of canals and reeds. I pushed the boxes toward the little lake, one after the other, prevent-

45

ing them, with quick hand movements, from crashing against the reeds or getting stuck among the grass. Each footfall caused explosions of mud and finally the little boxes departed, when the lake iridesced, goose flesh, another mirror, toward the basalt of the Island of the Scorpions.

Some Smoothie That Jesús

No, I didn't look for her girls. I've always known the names of some. I know that they're not to be mentioned. But now I know one of them. Bela.

This morning, I went back to my apartment without accepting my mother's invitation. I was afraid of meeting up with the six or seven girls. For as many reasons as I wanted to list on my way back to Insurgentes. Fear of the unknown, of course, but more, afraid of a tricky move of Claudia's. And afraid of meeting up with Bela again. Perhaps. And, above all, afraid that those meetings would cut short the week my mother had left in Mexico. And a desire greater than the fears: that the next move would be mine.

Arriving at my apartment, I realize that my hands are empty, like the hours ahead. And, immediately, I have one recourse left: my own satisfaction.

Oh, I'd need counts and castles, ghosts and memories to fill this story with adventures. I am complaining, as Hawthorne and Henry James once did. Back at the apartment, I cannot detect any other incident than this very exciting one: Gudelia, the cook, has gone out shopping and the telephone rings and rings while I open the door and barely across the threshold it stops ringing. Shall I sit down and write about the ladies who play canasta in las Lomas or about those who follow the soap opera on Channel 5? I have the perfect excuse: there is no subject. Besides, nobody has asked to me explore with words an imaginary life I have never publicly insinuated. I am the son of Claudia Nervo: that's my niche, that's my social label. Nothing else. But this, in a new society of dauphins in which we are all, now, sons of somebody, is enough. One no longer knows anybody who isn't somebody because he's the son of the minister, the banker, the newspaper editor. They only ask that we take a course in business administration or disappear discreetly. To be dauphins without devoting ourselves to the most extravagant idleness reveals, I believe, our bad conscience. As the

46

politician keeps talking about revolution, the rich boy must keep pretending he's a self-made man. If not, the peasants will cut our ears off.

What can you do. The morning and afternoon will be long. To-night, I can see my movies again. Meanwhile, Gudelia must be buying detergents in the Félix Cuevas supermarket. The potatoes are boiling in the pressure cooker when I peep into the kitchen. Pharaoh follows me and I don't listen to him. That's how it should be. Gudelia, the cook, isn't in.

I go quickly to my bedroom and open the closet. I have to take a chair and climb on it to reach the highest shelf and there, with my hand in the dark, look for the unmistakable feel of cashmere and pull the pearl gray sweater out from its hiding place behind the hats I never wear in this city. Nor in any other: we seem to save them for going to airports. I don't know why we Mexicans only wear hats to travel on planes. Maybe it's for fear of being scalped in barbaric lands.

I run with the stained sweater and Pharaoh barks after me and follows me through the corridor and kitchen and washroom to the maid's room.

I open the door cautiously; Jesús, Gudelia's lover, cannot be there at midday. The squeaking cot is there and the inevitable wall of pictures and magazine cutouts stuck on with tacks. The Virgin of Guadalupe. Claudia Nervo. The Atlante team. A calendar with the cheap color photograph of the elegant Pueblan Woman. Some yellowing photographs, of fairs and gardens; Gudelia and Jesús next to little wooden horses and near an anonymous fountain; the family group, the rigid and fascinated idols around the poppa with his rainfall mustache.

The wardrobe. I open it quickly. Satin dresses hang inanimately and the hangers knock against each other. Pharaoh growls. Warns. I must caress the sweater one more time and remember how I stole it from my mother's closet and how I slept with its soft fuzz near my cheek. How I kept it, a whole month, under my pillow, always within reach of my fingers. Now I give it up forever. Not without kissing it first, for the last time, and closing my eyes and realizing that there's no longer anything left of the original perfume. No, never again.

In front of the door to her room, Gudelia is standing with her hands in her apron pockets. Pharaoh saw her first and I only upon opening my eyes, with the sweater near my lips. Gudelia jiggles the coins in her apron pocket.

Should I feel ashamed? No, not inside me. I'm the master. But my

47

appearance, more truthful than my feeling, defeats me: I look at Gudelia and blush.

"I came . . . I came to return the sweater," I say without conviction and look away from her.

"It's okay, don Guillermo." And she continues looking at me. "I looked for it all over the place; I even thought somebody stole it." Is she smiling? "If it was your will to give it to me, it must also be your will to take it back."

"No, no. It's yours."

"You must excuse it's being a bit greasy, don Guillermo."

"But you are very clean, Gudelia."

"Yes, I am, but . . ."

"Go on, tell me."

"The truth is . . ."

"Did Jesús wear it?"

"Oh sir . . ."

"Tell me. It doesn't matter."

If I look at her out of the corner of my eye, she has the right to smile.

"It's just that he looked so swell in it."

I can caress Pharaoh's neck, for example.

"Then the grease spots and the circles of sweat . . ."

"What could I do, sir? He had to wear it to work, to show off."

"Easy, Pharaoh . . . And with you, never?"

"Well it's so nice and soft." What a humble giggle. "It even makes it nice to rub against him, begging your pardon . . ."

I can look her in the eyes with dignity. "You keep it, Gudelia. And please forgive me for coming into your room without permission."

"Oh sir, as if the house weren't yours. Who are we maids to protest?"

What am I going to do for the rest of the day?

What, except imagine Jesús, dark and strong, with his narrow forehead, balancing a basket of bread on his head, riding his bicycle and whistling as he displays his bared biceps on the streets, the sleeves of my mother's sweater rolled up, and feels so swell, so swank, so smooth showing off that garment that doesn't even cover his hairy belly, sticking out between the sweater and his trousers? What adventures that Jesús must have, exposed to everybody and everything!

In eight days, Claudia will leave again. Talismans are not enough.

The Absent Lady

Dans l'enfer de son lit . . .
—Baudelaire,
Sed non satiata

I still can't recognize her. I circle around the Diana fountain and only now that I'm driving along the Paseo de la Reforma do I think I'm inventing her again. She is standing beside the stills from the movie and is slowly revealed to me in the snapshots between the windshield wiper strokes. Closer, more certain, more mine: I dare to think that because I see her without being seen, I recognize her, even though this time she appears as herself. She has lost the arched eyebrow and the false mole. Fresh and young, her hair tied in a ponytail, I take possession of her without her knowing. The windshield wipers light her up and switch her off, distant and protected under the awning, they bring her near and fade her away, a full figure and a lean face, they blur her and draw a shining black raincoat and Chanel pocketbook. Rejected and recaptured apparition, she fills my mouth with a sweet anticipation. I stop and blow the horn. She jumps, nervous, smiles, waves her arm.

I invite her in; she moves her head and asks if we can walk: it's just a drizzle.

While I park the car, I remember clearly that the telephone rang again and I admit that I accepted her invitation because I thanked her for freeing me from that lonely afternoon. We would meet—we have met—in front of the Chapultapec theater and I, disillusioned, would have preferred seeing her in her native city, surrounded by those palaces of intense ochre. I see her cross the red, gray, and white Piazza del Popolo; stop between the two churches; greet people, beyond the obelisk and the arch, toward the Pincio; bite her nail at not receiving an answer, hesitate between cafés; finally walk gracefully into the Rosati. Perhaps, together, we could dine at Poldo's and wait for that friendly, mustached Tartar with the shaved head to bring out a good Lambrusco from his wine cellar. After dinner I would take her dancing to 84, or for a walk down the Lungotevere, or for coffee, standing at the bar in any *bartabachi* on the way, or to finish off with a drink amidst the discreet comradeship of the Rouge et Noir: Italo would serve us frozen vodkas and we'd listen to soft piano music. No. We'll return to the café. At this hour of the night it's empty. No: the phantom of the square is doing her rounds, that toothless, frizzled, varicose old hag begs there, day and night.

Bela will speak to me of those lost childhoods, of neat and pale little girls who go and come with their knapsacks on their backs.

The drizzle falls, almost like feathers, on the Paseo de la Reforma. It smells of geraniums and dust settling. One day we're going to miss those turn of the century palaces they're demolishing to put up useless, uninhabited skyscrapers. Bela leans on my arm. It's enough to feel her newly washed hair on my shoulder to not ask her anything.

We walk in silence. Her eyes, black and surprised, question me. No, how are we going to talk about the past. We don't have any.

Bela's hand looks for mine in the pocket of my raincoat and her fingers find the painful root of my nails. Not an attempt to seduce, but rather to play. Or perhaps both are the same thing, but there's a certain happy accent in it which saves seduction from its customary boredom.

I tell her that walking under the rain by her side, I could imagine other probable loves, not only hers. Bela answers yes; she too likes to imagine impossible loves.

"No, not impossible. Probable."

"It's the same thing, *sai*."

Ah. She laughs and says that what's good about imagining many things is that afterward one doesn't settle for the first thing that comes along. Something like that, so that I'll answer saying we only defend ourselves by giving perfection to our dreams, in order to later accept the imperfection of reality.

"Don't be so serious, Guillermo."

"So sad?"

"Kiss me."

She kisses me, smiling, standing on the tips of her black boots: a promise that I want to prolong in her earlobe. She laughs.

"Here they look at you if you kiss on the street. We better walk. But slower."

"I'm sorry. I know I walk fast."

"Where are you rushing to? We have the whole afternoon."

"That's right."

We walk, telling each other about possible loves. I have all these fantasies which I can never decide if they are invented or not: "I couldn't tell you if they were true or false."

I can't tell if it amuses me or makes me sad to talk of those dull facts which once seemed mysterious and exciting. All those afternoons in freezing motels on the Toluca road, all those dates with that woman in the tea shops of the Cuauhtémoc Quarter. The crazy habit of walking, holding hands, on the miserable streets near the Juarez tenements, those streets full of holes and small grocery stores, stoves cooking spicy green corn and the dragging, calm and rapid walk of my fellow citizens. She said that she trusted her friends and that nobody had informed on her because to lose her friendship was worse than losing her love. She'd eat chocolate eclairs in the Duca d'Este, which is not on the Via del Corso, Bela, but on Calle Londres; she'd pretend to have orgasms, I'm sure. She would receive her mail at a neighbor's house and I am also sure that she and her husband would have great laughs together, and celebrate the highlights of a melodramatic life, getaways in the middle of the night, the lover hidden in the dish closet, fearful of breaking plates; getaways, melodrama. The tension of life in Mexico takes place somewhere between the picaresque and melodrama, you know.

"Me too. Sometimes I decide to be honest with myself and admit that they're all lies."

"And then you realize that the imagined is always better than the lived?"

"No. Never. Only that it is different. Tell me about another love affair."

"I can only think of sordid tales."

She laughs again, and again makes me walk slower.

"I'm out of breath. It must be the altitude."

I look at her and she disguises a certain melancholy with the energetic and happy gesture of the people of her country: shoulders raised with resignation, hands stretched out.

"Guillermo."

She cuddles against the lapels of my trenchcoat.

"Tell me."

She would talk like that, with a defenseless happiness that is almost a painful urgency: I caress Bela's chin and understand her, adorable because she prefers being hurt to being forgotten. Perhaps another memory exists, the one we haven't touched, that offers us—where? under those dripping ash trees?—pain and danger as the real enigmas of happiness. Bela hasn't said anything that makes me think of this; but Bela is there, cuddling up to me, and I think of it. Perhaps this will not be true another day and another hour; it is when Bella, the real one, walks beside me, warm and near, and I continue looking for the offensive replica of my mother that I slapped two days ago. Wasn't Bela's imitation only prophetic salvation from something she was supposed to copy to avoid living? I have to repeat to myself that I met her then, not now, seeing her as she is.

"I'll tell you what I like."

She shakes her head and looks at me with closed eyes.

"Go on."

"This. Walking."

"I knew it. The Romans like to know their city."

"Waking up in a good mood."

"Singing in the shower?"

She nods her assent and hides her eyes with a hand, ashamed.

"Men who work at home. They fill it with electricity. They give you energies and emotions which they themselves don't know, *vero?*"

"Bela, Bela."

"There's nothing like being near a man who paints or writes or argues at home. There are no schedules. You live with him and you don't ask him for anything: he gives all the time. Okay, so I ask him to go slow and gentle . . ."

We run across between the stopped cars in front of the red light on Mississippi Street.

"Aren't you tired?"

"No."

"Want some coffee?"

"A little later. Don't laugh if I turn red and shiny like an apple. My peasant blood's beginning to circulate. In December the shepherds come down to Rome from Ciociara, dressed in lambskin coats and fiber sandals tied to their legs with leather strings. They are very red and toothless and always travel in pairs. One plays the bagpipe and the other the flute. It is very strange and very beautiful music."

"I have listened to it. It sounds like a lament, an ancient charm."

"Yes. They walk along the Via Frattina, among the elegant people, holding out their old caps for you to give them a few lira. I see them, every Christmas, and imagine that I could have been like that, a red peasant without teeth and with many children."

"Tell me more."

"No plans, no schedules, nothing! I hate them. On the other hand, I like to be very orderly so that he'll be the one who's a mess."

52

"You're soaking wet and you're contradicting yourself."

"No, no, you don't understand me . . ."

"Let's go to a café."

Now we're crossing the Paseo and I would like to see the two of us, from a distance, standing on the boulevard. The rain's pouring down. We run toward Amberes Street and the Café Viena.

"In Mexico they don't know how to make coffee."

I help her take off her raincoat. I think that it would have been marvelous to be sitting right here, alone, and see her come in, and sit at another table and then study her from a distance and imagine our possible friendship. What would she look like from a distance? Honey-colored hair and suntanned; now, the sleeveless striped jersey. White and black stripes.

"It's simply that in your country they are geniuses at making coffee. It must be the machines, since the beans come from America . . ."

Bela gathers her damp hair in a temporary braid and exaggerates her gestures: *"Cappucino, lungo, doppio, machiato, espresso, semplice, como lo desidera, gentiluomo?* No, it's the way they toast it."

Or her with some other man. Listening to the nonsense that man would be saying to her. He will talk, they will talk. If I were only in his place, if I could talk to Bela, communicate with her, receive her.

Would I have the courage to pick her up, alone, or to get rid of the young man who's with her with insults, if necessary with blows?

I take her hand.

"Why did you go after me?"

"I told you the other night. I like you. You."

"Why did you follow my mother?"

"I told you that too. She attracted me. Guillermo, I don't resist my impulses. What can we do about it? If I had known you first, I would follow you and that's that. Don't make a fuss about it, please."

We ask for two *cappucinos*, knowing that they'll bring a lukewarm concoction topped with cinnamon.

"Are you going to leave her?"

"Dio, Dio, Dio . . . If she helps me with my career, what for? And don't talk as if it were something dirty. You know very well that all this is innocent."

"What do you want me to know? You yourself saw how I was received the other night. As if I didn't exist."

"It's very simple. She wants a court. We need the protection of a great star. Or to feel in the center of things. I don't know. That's enough. I need work and I'm bored with Rome, with modeling for *fumetti*, with seeing the same faces. Living alone in a crummy apartment on Via Margutta. Or one month here, another there, in this boy's pad or that one's. Enough. I like change. And I've met you . . ."

I stop her hand: "Don't put on makeup."

"What's the matter?" she asks me, with the powder case near her nose, not understanding.

"I don't want you to imitate her again."

"I thought it was a good joke for the cocktail party." It fascinates me to see a woman close a powder case: in some, in Bela too, it is the maximum gesture of elegance and sufficiency. "That's all. It seemed to amuse her."

"Anything amuses her."

"Guillermo, we were so happy . . ."

"I'm sorry. I'm sorry, Bela; I'm a spoilsport."

"You're moody, temperamental, but not annoying. Once I lived with a charming boy. But annoying! Always harping on the same thing, that I used up the hot water and he couldn't shave. I bought him an electric shaver and ran him out of the house. No sense in confusing things, eh?"

They serve the coffee and Bela talks and I listen without listening. I vaguely distinguish, in the long hour at the café, the subjects, the names, the feelings with which she tells me about her life. Neither now nor any other day will I be able to repeat them. And it's not for lack of interest. On the contrary: in this moment, a communication exists between Bela and me that I have almost never felt. Bela talks to me directly: she doesn't confuse or mislead me. My gratitude is my tenderness. I have her hand in mine and if she doesn't stop talking or guess my absence, it's because my eyes penetrate hers in order to stop listening to her words and to capture the memory of this presence. The smell of bodies and wet clothes from the couples coming into the café, of cigarette smoke and the syrup on the pastries a waiter wheels back and forth in a little cart, have gone. Who has given me this moment? Bela must know too, while she talks, that this moment will never be important not because it happened now, but because it is only a part of our nostalgia from now on. Neither she nor I, sitting here, looking at each other, with a vague consciousness of the rain falling near our leaning faces, can explain or express our presence; and perhaps, by accepting the disappearance of the moment we are living together, we are conceding to its only justification: its charm. I know that she knows you. I would like to ask about you. Bela laughs:

"Amor-Roma. You get it? Roma-Amor."

And your name comes back to me.

"Let's go."

Of all that you said when I spent those days in the Palace of Madonna dei Monti, tonight I only remember one thing: nothing unfolds, all is transfigured. I wanted to unfold a scene. Prepare everything so the moment would evolve, as it should, toward its culmination. I know which lights should go on as I enter my apartment so that it may retain its fugitive aura. And soft music. The most melancolic Bécaud. The crystal flasks containing the whiskey. The loosened tie. Shoes off. The cigarettes in the dusk. Everybody gets ready in the same way, all the preceding acts are identical: such is the code of chivalry. Only the final act will be different each time, I am thinking now that Bela has dropped her slippers and I lean against her hard thighs and smoke without looking at her and she hums. The final act divides our lives forever.

I don't admit to this gratuitously. And I don't know if Bela waits and understands. I kiss her fingers that caress my neck and try to put her on her guard. There's no way out. Fusion or nuptial song, it will be an act and not a secret. And nevertheless, how to resist her fingers which are still mere promise?

"Isn't promise enough?"—I murmur as I turn to lie face down and kiss Bela's spread hand.

"*Cosa?*"

"No, nothing . . ."

Afterward I'll loathe my lack of imagination. If I only knew how to prolong the moment. If I didn't already see myself in bed with Bela. And afterward; that horrible afterward: the clothes picked up from the floor, the still damp socks, the cold underpants, the wrinkled trousers. Getting dressed again, awkwardly. Putting on makeup. Combing your hair. We haven't died.

We're not extinct yet. I bring her face near mine to kiss her, kiss her like that, open, abandoned, hoping that this passion will satisfy her, that in the kiss she'll find the climax in its announcement and renounce a crude and weak repetition of our symbolic surrender . . . Bela, where do I begin? To kiss, kiss and not die, not vanish. I sink my face between your legs and now I do want to communicate my obsession to you: understand; no, you won't understand what you should know only because you are alive: that you should be unreachable, Bela; that I'll only keep wanting you if I know that to possess you is impossible; that I need to know you're far away for nothing to come between my desire and you . . . don't caress me like that, darling; not like that, please . . . Go away. Come closer. I need you near me tonight to continue desiring you when I remember you tomorrow. I need you far from me tonight so that a tomorrow without you will be unthinkable.

"Let me go to the bedroom."

I pretend not to hear her. I've lost my hands.

"Please. Tell me where it is." ·

"At the end of the corridor. To the right."

"Aren't you coming?"

"No. I forgot. I don't have the key."

"What?"

"The key to the bedroom. I remember now that I lost it."

I deserve that laugh, the first that separates us. Bela's isolated laugh rejecting me with disbelief and ridicule. Still laughing, she takes off her sweater and stands, half-naked, with her hands on her hips.

"I don't care. The couch is comfortable enough."

I pretend not to hear her. I have other things to do. Why did I complain about the lonely afternoon? I walk to the closet and take out the movie screen, unroll it and place it on the stand. I kneel down to pick up the cans. I press a button and the projector appears between two lines of false books with gold spines: an intriguing imitation of Cobden-Sanderson bindings. And Bela is there with her breasts bared and her hands on her hips.

"I'm telling you I don't care!"

I smooth down my hair: won't you get cold there, Bela?, while I pretend to be concerned and look around me in the dimly lit room, as if a key could appear among that artificial heap of ottoman sofas and engravings, records and curtains, tables and countless objects. I glance over everything, squinting my eyes. It's not necessary to describe it again, although you always insisted on describing and redescribing as the only possible joke we have left: inventories, catalogues are the final irony with which one can answer all the weary stories, all the defeated characters, all the empty meanings. Objects, the kingdom of appearances, take revenge on the impalpable, spiritual world that once ruled over us. Velvet and Chinese ink, silk and leather, dust and plaster, glass and varnish, run under my fingers.

I open my eyes. Bela is no longer there. Bela has gone. My silhouette is fixed on the silver screen. There is no other light than the blinking projector: I don't want to be alone, I snap my fingers so that Pharaoh will appear, come near me, settle down at my feet again. The filmless projector throws a cold, intermittent, concrete light. We are captured within an enormous neon sign.

It's the only light. It leads me to the front door and I open it. There's no light on the landing either. Only the projector, from the living room, lights up the whole corridor behind me, to the end where Bela is waiting for me, arms crossed, in front of the open door to my bedroom.

There are only transfigurations. The hot morning surrounds us and denies us: our silence can do nothing against the whole world's slow and exhausting heat. Like that first night, I drive without looking at Bela. The city again, the same city but now turned into a magnesium flash: whitewashed by the sun, this gray and ugly city is now its exposed negative. Feather duster and chamois to clean the cars, lottery tickets, unlit marquees and enormous advertisements for beer and rum: tall houses and small houses, all about to rot.

Bela remains aloof and doesn't look at me either. I imagine her, huddled, a kitten hugging, licking herself. Hurt. Exhausted. I don't know if by an act or by forgetfulness. I don't know. Who's to call us to account?

I stop in front of my mother's house. We continue avoiding each other's eyes and I wait for Bela's first act: to get out or stay, stay mute or speak, speak to say what?

I turn off the motor: "Madam is served."

Unnecessary. How unnecessary to say that and add:

"*Tu es chez toi.*"

And to think while I say it, that, in five days Claudia will take a plane; and I won't see her for eight months.

I get up the nerve to look at Bela.

"Why?"

If earlier I imagined it, now I know. The eyes of her question resolve that enigma. Is pain happiness? And immediately I look at her without having stopped looking at her, as if a second vision were born from the first: yesterday, while we were walking, that cipher was a riddle; today it's a reality. Today it exists to begin to vanish. Yesterday it was tolerable and seductive: a secret. Today it is intolerable and repulsive: a truth.

I swear, first she hugs my neck, crying. And then, Claudia walks out of the house.

Only then the figure of my mother, the most minor details of her appearance, the gloves she's putting on, the panther skin hat, the marvelous beige mink coat—and the heat, the sultriness of this day: is it just my own temperature?—erase the trembling and warm nearness of Bela and incite the desperate acts of my whole reborn body.

Claudia stops at the gate of her house, stretching her hands inside the gloves, with that pose of the sorceress or the mannikin supported by the sumptuousness of its attire, by the real cold of this morning that I'd like to feel as hot. Which perhaps it is: Claudia creates her own climates and takes them with her wherever she goes.

I put my hands through the openings of Bela's sleeves, I feel the immediate shiver down her back, the answer of her grave pink nipples at the touch of my fingers, the moaned protest of her unsatisfied and resigned body, from the scabs of the night and the new juices of the morning: I cover her neck, her chin, her lips with kisses, her whole head thrown back, the violent arch of a face that still can't see clearly, that still has not emerged from the chaos of my shameful pawing, of the cold violence of my hands between her legs while Claudia motionless watches us, continues to watch us when Bela scratches my hand and bites my lips and I shout at her, but not so she'll hear me:

"Stay away from me, you slut!"

Bela represses her complaint. I let go of her. She gets out, disheveled; she stops for a moment facing Claudia; her mouth trembles; she runs toward the house.

I take off without seeing them again. Or if I see them, it's in the specter of dust that the windshield wiper tries, uselessly, to erase: perfume, brilliance in motion, skin like silk paper, pale women drowned in satin: tube of excretions, soft mucuses, lungs bleached with tobacco, pus compressed at the back of the palate, rotten oysters, festering nipples, clots of menstrual blood, nausea of the eternally open carrion, scarless wounds, swollen intestines, green gases, thick bile, long tunnel of shit and infested little eggs and threatening placentas: I would love to see them skinned, like they really are, without deceitful skin, without volatile perfume, a mere compendium of rot, depots of useless semen. Shit on you bitches.

> He wanted to dream a man.
> —Borges,
>   *The Circular Ruins*

You asked me:

"What are you going to do? Where are you going to spend Christmas?"

I shrugged my shoulders and immediately regretted the involuntary rudeness of that gesture. You smiled: "If you can't think of anything better, come home with me."

I think that from then on I imagined that village just as it was, lost behind one of the ridges of the Matese. It's true, I imagined it; the place names of Campania, the nearness of Naples, induce an easy identification with the sun and with a certain ochre color of stone. I wanted to imagine a cold and gray palace which denied its own name: Madonna dei Monti, another picturesque trap in that country of yours, overrun by all the armies of time, and which never succeeds in revealing its true, slight, severe, secret, essence: I am describing you without realizing it.

I remember you like this on that day in December, nine years ago, when I received my mother's telegram. Claudia said there were only three days off from shooting between Christmas eve and Twelfth Night; the truth is she didn't want to leave Paris, she had plans for the Réveillon, she didn't want me with her. It is a horrible and sad commonplace to be the only student at school during the holidays. And not because this boarding school looked like the ones I'd attended before in Guadalajara and Mexico City. I don't know if it was my age, or simply the atmosphere of the school, the beautiful town on the outskirts of Lausanne, the nearness of the lake and other lakeside towns, equally beautiful, but here I secured what I had always looked for: the awning, the hiding place under the bed, the margin of solitary freedom, all the things I thought I had the right to. The teachers were demanding without being inhuman, the courses complex without being useless. Far from the forced memorization which marks Mexican education, here everything had its origin in the student's curiosity, his extracurricular reading; and classes, more than echo recitations by deaf men, were primarily offerings of the student's doubts and the teacher's suggestions. There was time for everything. To wander around nearby places, to travel to France and Italy, to read.

As soon as I discovered the secondhand bookstores in Lausanne, I sank—and sank more money into them than Claudia was ready to provide—into the discovery of what I knew were the equivalents of my secret imagination. Perhaps it would have been impossible for me to read these books before, in their modern editions, but now I recognized them and looked for them with their old bindings, their tired spines, their stained engravings, protected by sheets of rice paper. I had seldom read since childhood and now I filled a gap of ten years each time I entered one of those dusty cellars piled with books, which looked so much like the bookstores and antique shops described in the books I acquired here—*The Wild Ass's Skin, Markheim, The Old Curiosity Shop*—as if, again, a page of the story book opened to offer a glimpse of the following illustration. First Scott, then Dickens and Balzac and Stevenson; especially Dickens and the image that captivated me, of the Cricket on the Hearth and his prodigious world of a fable invented by the father so that the son would never know the true reality: a reality which that little blind boy doesn't need to know.

I bought and read all of it, in the dormitory where from the windows one can admire the vastness of Léman Lake, in the school gardens and sometimes with luck, during the Sundays spent on a rock near Chillon Castle, accompanied by the gentle and cold beat of the waves. My world, during that first semester, consisted of great moments of exaltation in chiaroscuro: a black Thames from which Gaffer Hexam and his daughter would pull out the drowned, at midnight, to rob them; a nocturnal Paris, brilliant like Paquita's eyes, criminal like Vautrin's hands, implacable like the wild ass skin that at each new desire shrinks in the hands of its temporary and condemned owner.

Nobody asked me to account for my weekends. Nobody, since I didn't expressly ask, forced me to join the sailing or soccer teams. And when the fever of my readings didn't point to any other outlet but to travel urgently to Paris to see the lanes and vestibules of that world of pure energy, terrifically resistant to the words Balzac invented, the head of the school gave me a week off, with pleasure: all the students were foreigners and we should be sure to take advantage of our stay in a Switzerland that feels proud to be a strategic center, a haven and a springboard for the visitor.

Back from one of these excursions, I resumed my visits to the bookshops. Inside one that smelled of varnished cedar, I was about to pick the chosen and beloved volume: *Great Expectations*. I had my hand on the spine and my imagination concentrated on its reward: other unforgettable images, which today I know, which in that moment were candies wrapped in colored papers. The old Miss Havisham in her somber wedding day dining room; the meeting of the little boy with the convict on the heath. But another hand rested on mine. We were between two high shelves, in a narrow and badly lit aisle. At first I couldn't see the face of the person who, so delicately but so firmly, guided my hand along the ridges of dust until stopping it, first on one book, then on another. François Villon, Petrus Borel. Guiding me, he remained behind me; his breath was smiling and, perhaps, a little mocking. He left me with the books in my hands and along the aisle I could only distinguish the rapid movement, the wide shoulders. Then, the ding-a-ling of the bell, the door opening and closing.

"Who went out?"

"We don't know him. He isn't a regular customer, like you. Fifteen francs forty. Bonjour, m'sieu-dame."

After all that, we could have laughed so much that night when I read for myself the *Ballade des dames du temps jadis* and, little by little, what my eyes followed turned into sounds and, in the dark of the dormitory, another voice repeated,

Mais où sont les neiges d'antan?

Seen from a distance, unsure of that presence, I couldn't or didn't want to see it clearly: one prefers to give a blurred, collective semblance to the persons one isn't intimate with. We say the Chinese or the Blacks all look alike because we don't wish to acknowledge or accept them near us. The same thing happens with that crowd, that aggressive power, my schoolmates, and it is significant that I could only recognize a schoolmate I hadn't seen all semester, in the dim light, against the light, of a secondhand bookstore and of a badly lit dormitory.

The habit of smoothing his hair, of passing an open hand along his black, straight hair, as if to give the impression of a village Don Juan. Yes, that image could be so obvious: at first sight, the pimp image, if later you don't see that certain premature wrinkles, certain furrows in his cheeks give that Latin lover face a true austerity and melancholy.

I know; I remember and describe it as in one of the novels I was reading then. But that image really was a Raphael de Valentin; and simply to remember that hero would remind me ironically of the Italianized name of the great velvet boa, the decadent feline who forty years ago was the possessor of what you call *morbidezza;* a Puglia peasant transformed into Arab chieftain, tango dancer, pomaded Cossack. Yes, a kind of masculine counterpart of my mother. I thought of him in family terms that night and laughed at this household joke. The laugh froze on my lips. A dignity, not hierarchic like ours, but alive and cordial and adventurous, was in this way offering me its friendship and typifying that remoteness which, imaginatively, I later attributed to a house, to the name of a village, when you invited me to spend the holidays with you.

I imagined a cold, gray village clambering up a slope of smooth stone, in search of the faraway sun and snow. Its aspiration would be the meeting of opposites, fire and ice, which would also fuse in its remoteness. Madonna dei Monti rises from the misty valleys of the wintry Campania toward the cluster of squares and straight streets which so much remind me of certain Mexican towns; Orizaba, especially, for its constant drizzle, the nearness of the mountain, the balconies with painted wood rails. But, the chessboard sketch is immediately lost in the swarm of lanes that were once stairs, stairs which turn into passages, passages which will become tunnels. The shaded Matese mountain range is the geographical crown of the village; the palace, its historical crown.

I wanted to look longer, take in the boy dressed in thick casual green corduroy pants, a thick gray sweater, and suede half-boots. On Saturdays only: a blue blazer with embroidered monogram, flannel pants. They told me:

"He spends his money at the Evian Casino and doesn't come back to school till Monday morning."

I wanted to approach you several times, first to thank you for pointing out the books, then to comment on them. But each Monday I could only watch that strangely refreshed and tired face, with a new wrinkle on the forehead, a deeper furrow on the cheek: aged before your time, rejuvenated, cleaned of some infantile excrescences or fat which we sometimes like to identify with our candor and which are only the final traces of the act that in creating us, violated us. I stopped going to class, on Mondays, to devote myself to watching. I knew what I've just said. Nothing more.

That's why I was so surprised when, the holidays near, you, the very person who had never spoken to me, came over and invited me to spend them at your house, to wait for you at the Lausanne station: Swiss trains run on time: a delay would be a national catastrophe, a loss of confidence; that the steam would rush out whistling between the wheels and surround me; that there you'd be: that you'd throw the cigarette carelessly over your shoulder, without thinking that the stub could burn somebody; that I'd wait for you with my overcoat on, my books under my arm, my two suitcases on the platform; that you'd laugh and cross your chest with your only luggage, the black and yellow striped scarf; that you'd hop on while the train was in motion while I, awkwardly, would run with my two suitcases, trip, reach the last open door, drag my suitcases along the passageway, looking for you: the steady crescendo of the train in motion, beat of bell and dagger, metal in motion, a way of waking up or being wounded: train, dagger, bell, my excitement; that a lit cigarette would hit me on the cheek; that I'd cry out; that you'd be sitting in the compartment, your legs stretched out, watching me innocently; that I would put my things away as well as I could, without looking at you.

"What the hell do you have in those suitcases?"

"Nothing. The usual."

"Come on. Put everything away. You're a great master of routine. Is all the garbage you're dragging along yours?"

"No. My mother bought them."

"Dauphin. Then you too travel without anything, like me. Then nothing belongs to you either, like me."

"Look."

"Your hands."

"How do they look?"

"Spread. Clean. Burnt."

"Look. Chillon Castle. Do you want a banana?"

"No, thanks."

"What are you going to tell me?"

"Everything."

"Do your stories serve any purpose?"

"I don't know. I don't think so."

"That's better. Amuse me."

Autographs

. . . fatal handling of hope . . .
—Borges,
The Terrifying Redeemer
Lazarus Morel

Gudelia returned from the bank unable to clearly explain the problem. The simple fact is they didn't want to cash my monthly check, signed by Ruth in my mother's name. I had to dress quickly and go to the bank. No, they couldn't cash the check. Yes, my mother stopped payment yesterday: no check to my name was payable.

I don't care if I'm dressed this way, fiber sandals, no socks, corduroy pants, a loose sweater, no shirt underneath. I stop for a moment on the sidewalk, the check in my hands, blinded by the glare of the sun. Thinking of these vulgarities offends me. Two new suits. The record shop bill. Gudelia's wages. Cigarettes, gas, food . . . And yet I can't bring myself to tear this greenish slip of paper into a thousand pieces. No, the aggression doesn't consist in preventing me from cashing it; the revenge is this moment of petty and absurd and total dependence: having to remember that a tailor will present me with a bill of two thousand pesos and that I don't have anything to answer with. That to put off the payment I have only one recourse: to remind him:

"I'm Claudia Nervo's son. Please excuse the delay. I'll pay you next month."

And to wait on the corner near my mother's house, now, for her Mercedes to sally forth like a polished tank to the daily wars, the chauffeur in front and she, the lady marshall, in the back with her sealskin coat and black medieval cardinal's hat, hardly visible to me in the rapid, reflected passing of her automobile near my covered Lancia, hidden on the corner, waiting with the motor running to follow, confront, humiliate her wherever she goes, to show my courage.

Following her is enough to feel justified. Two or three cars behind hers, I only make out occasional flashes of her profile and the ecclesiastical form of her head, blurred by the windshields, the car's shining surface, the vague shade of trees, the intermittent sunlight and the reverberating vapor of engines and pavements rather than by this brief distance. I follow her without knowing the route; I mechanically obey the traffic signals but my guide is the Mercedes; I mustn't lose sight of it. And the city surrounds me, perhaps because I don't pay attention to it, and as I don't recognize it, I stop resisting it. Or, by concentrating on my mother's fading silhouette, I fuse her image with the city's: I purify and free it of its uglinesses and bulges and anarchy, to adjust it to a being built like Claudia, out of deliberate style. I return to the old photographs of a wholesome and perhaps plump woman, excessive in her incarnation of fate. I superimpose on them this new figure of prominent bones, outlined like a flame, untouchable and near: like the city should be.

Claudia's car stops in front of a fashion boutique on Avenida Madero. She gets out wearing dark glasses and enters unrecognized. The chauffeur drives the Mercedes to a parking lot and I look for mine, on Bolívar: for a moment, the attendant doesn't recognize me either, in this loose sweater, without a shirt or tie. Immediately yes, he knows who I am and I hand him the keys without a word.

I stop in front of the Iturbide Palace, where the boutique is; I remember the house in Guadalajara. The baroque stonework, the floral excess which is the counterconsecration of our fear disguised in good taste, reticence, quiet tones; the pendulous styles of our architecture and our lives are another revenge, another blackmail. I cross the street and enter this rosewood box through glass doors heading straight for the velvet curtain, without paying attention to the bowing heads or the look my sandals, bare neck, and chest deserve.

Behind it, that black and gold brocade dressing gown, those black furs confining her neck, the sleeves, the long flowing A-line skirts, like the ceremonial tunic of a Czar, are reflected seven times in a rhombus of mirrors.

Claudia stands in the perfect pose. The dressmaker stops working and looks at me; Claudia looks through me: I am not tolerated, I am not welcome.

"What is this, a persecution?"

I refuse to look at her: I can talk to her in the seven mirrors with my back turned: "I'm returning the check. It bounced."

Claudia shakes the black fur cuffs. "Yes, it's worthless."

"Why?"

"Guess."

"I don't know. Do you want me to say I've behaved myself, like a good boy? Okay: I swear to you I've behaved myself."

The dressmaker, kneeling, with her mouth full of pins, resumes her work. What a capacity for becoming invisible.

"You upset my system, darling. You don't respect me."

If I sit down, I'll lose authority; if I continue looking at the mirror, she'll end up devouring me: I am surrounded by seven Claudias: glass ruins, prison of mirrors.

"You told me yesterday morning that I should look for them, get together with them."

Will she forgive me? She opens her arms and watches the dressmaker's operations at her feet, pinning the fur on the skirts.

"Look for them. All of them. Not one in particular."

I plop down on the easy chair, with my face in my hands.

"She looked for me. Believe me. I thought you wouldn't mind. You told me to look for them; I . . ."

"You can't resist a single temptation, can you?"

I set my hands on my knees. "Look who's talking."

"You don't see the difference. I would be weak if I resisted temptations; you're weak because you give in . . ."

And her supple body, which assumes all the traditional postures of elegance before mirrors, denies with its physical fantasy—feet wide apart, bare, together, on tiptoes; arms in the air, stiff; look over the shoulder, pretended surprise, static joy—the sententiousness of her words. Everything in me stretches, like a double arch, to acknowledge the impossibility of revenge and to suspect, to suspect . . .

"You knew I would look for you, right, mamma?"

"Dream on, if you like."

And she's no longer the same. I've touched her. I've surprised her. No, I've only touched something alive in her. I won't loosen my fang: "The rest doesn't count. If I had cashed the check today, I wouldn't have had a pretext for seeing you" —I laugh softly.

Feet wide apart, bare. "You're getting into deep waters, Mito. Into my territory. You're exposing yourself."

"Did you blackmail me to come looking for you here?"

Feet together, on tiptoes: "Who knows?"

"Did you want me to see you again, but like this, and not like the other day, with glasses, dictating those . . . ?"

Now she's next to me, standing, and I'm sitting and her hands don't dare touch my head when I lean it against that bright aggressive material, against her slim hips, and Claudia, at last, touches my face with her hands and I hug her waist and press her body against my cheek.

"I love you, mamma." We don't look at each other, we don't move, the dressmaker goes out quietly. "I thank you for being as you are, for

66

treating me like this . . . I thank you for separating me from my father . . ."

"Mito, Mito . . ."

"Don't you know that they didn't love you?"

"What does that matter? Poor slobs. I left them in a daze."

"They said nasty things about you in secret; they thought I didn't hear, that I didn't understand . . ."

"They were right. I made them miserable. I made them feel that the world didn't end inside their four walls. Your father figured that what he'd offered was tops; who could want more? Why, he'd given me his name and his home. It wasn't his fault."

"Yes, yes, you would have died there, you would have died young, mamma, in that boring, stodgy place."

"Are you kidding? There or wherever you say, I would have been myself. They just couldn't follow me. I'm telling you, darling, I'm ready for anything. Whoever wants to can follow me. I don't think I ever rejected anybody, really. People can't keep up with me, that's all."

"Not me."

"That remains to be seen."

"Claudia . . ."

I raise my face: she's there, all of her, mine.

"Claudia, that's it . . . Would you like to take a walk with me along Paseo de la Reforma? How about it? I'll buy you a coffee. You and I, together, alone . . ."

She laughs and stops caressing me: "It isn't necessary."

She turns her back to me and looks at herself in the mirrors: she whirls around and makes them whirl.

"Guillermo, the secret is knowing how to get into my life. I make it harder for you because you're my own flesh and blood, the only one."

"Let's try, please." Standing, I follow her to the middle of the room; but I'm afraid to touch her now. "It can be so much fun, going where everybody else goes, hiding, you know, incognito."

"Give me a cigarette. That's not the way. It's too easy."

"You too think we're acting?"

The smoke destroys her face. "What you want you can save for my movies and go see them with lots of handkerchiefs; I guarantee an hour and a half of crocodile tears. As for the other, darling . . ."

"Yes?"

"The other is performed in Ixtapalapa every Good Friday. Or in Oberammergau. Have you ever been to Oberammergau?"

I shake my head and again feel that I have useless hands and feet.

"Here or there, it's the same. You go every year and everything is repeated but nothing is repeated. You know how that story's going to end but it's as if you didn't know. That's the Passion, precious. That doesn't make you cry; it just changes you, understand? But don't make that face. It's okay."

She slowly undresses, in front of me, smiling, without asking me to close my eyes or look away: a camera would suggest the whole thing with a close-up of my face. She unbuttons the dressing gown and comes out, svelte and marvelous as she is, without an inch extra, light and majestic when she's again dressed in the simple red wool A-line and putting on the black hat before the mirror and caressing the seal coat that I place on her shoulders.

"Let's take a walk together. Come. Learn one thing, darling. If you don't succeed in getting something, take it easy, don't eat your heart out, and the thing will come to you."

She takes my hand and pushes aside the crimson curtain and we say good-bye to the employees in the store and now we're on Avenida Madero, arm in arm, smiling, as if everything had been resolved: this would be the climax, the dream come true, walking together, going to a café, talking for hours, telling each other all that we have never been able to say: no longer repeating our phrases of bribery, hate and love: recognizing each other.

But the dark glasses are not enough.

They follow us.

Murmur.

Draw near.

Put their heads together.

Point with their fingers.

Who is the first who gets in our way, smiles idiotically, asks my mother if she's really she; who's the second, while she lets go of me, smiles and denies, tries to keep walking; who's the third, when she stops looking toward me, laughs, accepts the first piece of paper offered, scribbles her name, tries to move on? Who's the fourth, the fifth, the tenth, when she signs and signs autographs, leaving me behind, exposed to the elbows and rushing and jokes and compliments that I hear around me, "look at the crow's feet," "she's extremely well preserved," "I cried so much in her last movie," "I have an album full of her pictures," "she'll do in a pinch, eh," "doesn't she look a bit masculine to you?", "she's a goddess," "doesn't turn me on," "the most beautiful woman in the world" . . . ?

I reach out and can no longer touch her.

I wave my hand, up high, to tell her I'm there and I'm helpless against this instant mob that's surrounding her.

A policeman comes over; the chauffeur stops the Mercedes; the policeman clears the way; Claudia gets into the automobile amidst cries of dismay.

I stay behind and watch the car drive off. The policeman disperses the people who then go their way, bumping into me because I've remained motionless, they excuse themselves, murmur, and seem annoyed at brushing against me.

That same afternoon the new check arrived. The doorman took it up to the apartment and said that the chauffeur had brought it. Gudelia handed it to me and offered to cash it immediately; I reminded her that the banks close at one and as always, when she can't be useful to me, she hung her head and shrugged her shoulders, as if I had offended her. Then I have to come over to her and put my hand on her shoulder and tell her it's not her fault. And, if she persists in feeling hurt, I have to give up some old clothes so that Gudelia can give them to Jesús. Gudelia accepts them smiling and tries to kiss my hands and I'm the master again. I don't know what I'd do without Gudelia. She liked the old turtleneck I gave her; giving it to her was no sweat off my back. But the sweater was. Without Gudelia, I'm sure, the apartment would die of cold and disorder. Gudelia and Jesús and the creaking cot. That's something at least.

The check is nothing. It should have been cashed immediately and disappeared into that invalid circulation. Now, it will be necessary to keep it until tomorrow and to allow it, simple paper, to represent my monthly allowance of eight thousand pesos for this whole afternoon and night; to continue having a value beyond that of the expected time between its expedition and its cashing. I don't know where to put it and I even accept the temptation of framing it, hanging it between my books and drawings in the living room. One check, at least, should have that luck. A check for posterity, a "work of art": many people keep their first payment for eternity. And they might not have the security of receiving another. I do. Claudia will not let me die of hunger.

Another hero would do the same as I at this moment: go out on the balcony with the check in his hands, ready to tear it and throw it into the street; Lafcadio would do it. Would you do it? I stand there, with the check in my hands, imagining a walk with my mother along Paseo de la Reforma; a long conversation in the coffee shop. The tailor is waiting for his two thousand pesos.

It's not the first time I undress slowly, with the windows open, feeling the draught behind me. They say that the climate of Mexico City is treacherous: hot in the day, cold at night. But an air current couldn't do more than my imagination, never. It all consists in imagining the first chill, the first indomitable sluggishness and then dragging myself into my pajamas, turning down the sheets, getting into that deep, welcoming, ancient, copper bed.

"Gudelia, I don't feel well."

"Shall I make you a cup of tea, don Guillermo?"

"Yes, tea and aspirin."

In all my schools, first in Guadalajara to get out of sports, then in Mexico City to see if she'd take me out of boarding school to stay in her house for a few days, it was easier to play tricks. They'd say that hiding an onion in your armpit is enough to give you fever. Besides, I tried to avoid what the other kids liked—games—and nobody could believe that I wanted to live with my mother—poor little thing—. They thought I was telling the truth about my complaints and headaches.

But the bed, immediately, has given me peace. I always associate it with reading, with the fattest novels, the ones you reserve for colds and convalescing. I just thought of Lafcadio and I take the volume which is on the night table, leaf through it at random, looking—just as spontaneously?—for the paragraphs that are underlined.

"Here it is, sir."

"Thank you."

"Shall I put it on the little table?"

"No, on my knees, please."

Her washed, black hair brushes my lips. "Like the little boy who plays hide and seek, who doubtlessly doesn't want them to find him, but who wishes, at least, to be looked for, he got bored."

"Oh I'm sorry!"

"It's nothing. And, Gudelia . . ."

"When I say unmotivated, I mean gratuitous. Evil, what we call evil, can be as gratuitous as good."

"Yes, don Guillermo."

"Don't go out today. I don't like to be left alone when I'm sick."

"Whatever you say, sir."

"*Si tu vas à Naples, tu devrais t'informer comment ils font le trou dans le macaroni. Je suis sur le chemin d'une nouvelle découverte.*" I close the book and my eyes. Will I be subtle or crustacean, for God's sake? And which of the two is it worth being? How can I think that out of the blue Claudia will call me on the telephone!

"Did you call, sir?"

"Has my mother called? . . . Don't look at me like that . . ."

"She sent a letter, that's all."

"What letter? What's the matter with you? Why haven't you given it to me? No wonder you people never get anywhere . . ."

"What do you mean what letter? The one I gave you."

"Ah. The envelope with the check."

"You must know."

"Sorry, Gudelia."

"Do you want me to call your mother?"

"No. No."

"Do you want me to call the doctor? If I call your mother, she'll tell me to call the doctor. It's one or the other, sir."

"I feel better now. Leave me."

As if a fever was enough. The time I escaped from the boarding school I had to jump over the fence. I cut my hands to pieces on the broken glass which was supposed to keep thieves away and, I then realized, to prevent children from escaping. The fence was high and I had to plant my hands on the glass to lift my weight, jump and run with bloodied hands, the teacher blowing his whistle, running after me down Calzada de la Verónica. He never thought of jumping into a taxi and catching up with me. He must have thought his duty was to pursue me on foot. We all have our codes of chivalry. I left him behind, puffing. I ran and ran: to get to my mother's house at eleven in the morning, see her wake up . . . She wasn't in, or they just didn't let me in, but there was her car, you could hear laughter and murmurs, from the room with the closed curtains. Her evening hadn't ended. I was afraid to wander alone on the streets and I went back to school to have my hands healed. I wanted to throw that in her face. And today she dared to say that there was no melodrama in her life, only passion. Compassion? For myself.

"Call her, Gudelia; touch my forehead; tell me if I'm not sweating;

tell me if I'm imagining things; call her before it goes; tell her I feel very bad."

"But she's only going to send the doctor."

"Do as I say."

I press the book against my chest. I've managed to make my heart beat irregularly and my legs freeze. If only I could stay like this till she gets here. Lafcadio Wluiki. If only I was able to sleep with all the doors open, to rescue a little boy from a house in flames before pushing to his death a stranger who travels with me on the train; if only I could tear up all the secret photographs of my life once other people have dared to poke around in my drawers. And then declare that I'm the murderer when nobody is accusing me, when someone else has already been captured in my place . . . *J'étais affamé de merveilles.*

Ah, one Christmas she took pity on me and I missed my beautiful chance. But at the age of thirteen, what weapons does one have? Sneaking barefoot, in the night, into the bedroom of the man who lived with her and, with a smiling secrecy that I've never had since, crossing the bed with threads, from one post to the other, from the head to the foot, in straight and diagonal lines, creating a bogus spider's web of almost invisible filaments, thick but light, woven and inter-woven like the drawing of airline routes over a world map, and waiting behind the door, with a hand over my mouth, for the man to wake up into the nightmare I had prepared for him. Or filling the water tanks, when I hear him go into the shower, with the dirty water from the laundry. The last Christmas with my mother.

What does she say, Gudelia? That she's going to come? I don't believe you. That I should wait for her? But didn't you tell her I'm sick? That I'm making it up? That's what she said? That I'm making it up? You're lying. You're a lying little broad. Claudia would never talk to you. She would send the message through Ruth. She does talk to me, see?, she does me that favor. If you tell me that Ruth told you my mother would come to visit me, I would believe you. And you know what I would do? Don't you have any imagination, Gudelia? Do you think your sighs, your timid orgasms, don't reach my ears some nights, and others as well? Don't I hear them amplified, jumping like crickets on the walls of our bedrooms and halls? Don't you invent them to satisfy Jesús? Don't you delay them so that they're so quiet, they enter my fantasy almost inaudibly? Let's ask ourselves why I tolerate this indecency under my own roof. We too could laugh together, you and I. It would make you laugh to see me jump out of bed as soon as you tell me my mother's on her way: strip off my fever like Claudia, this morning, stripped off her Byzantine monarch's robe and let me see her; dress and go out into the street, into the approaching night. Leave her flat.

"Where is Guillermo?"

"He went out, Madam. He said he'd be back late."

"The lover is alone with all that he loves." Those words you read with a flat voice, almost scornful. You said that the romantic wanted to signify an interior solitude and love and that then his pain was almost satisfactory. The terrible thing, you said, is that today those words are true in another sense; we are alone with all that we love outside of ourselves. We can no longer console ourselves with thinking that we can invoke it when we are inspired. The beloved is there, before us, outside of us, challenging us to touch him, to accept him as a material presence, to take a risk and live with him. We are alone, not with nostalgia, desire, oblivion, or the feeling of the beloved, but with his serious, measurable proximity: we have succeeded in giving body to all our illusions; we have attended the incarnation of all our ghosts. We have turned into matter all that moaned, walled in and invisible, between the heavens and hells that the world has annexed. And you ended: "We have no choice but to disguise the visible ghosts, to make them tolerable and allow them into our living rooms." ("The mystery of the world is not the invisible, but the visible.")

Yes, now that I walk under this insistent drizzle, with my raincoat lapels raised—Bogart style—along the deserted streets of the city, along the broken sidewalks of the Roma Quarter, to where anything but intention has led me, at ten o'clock at night, I wish that Claudia was only my imaginary creation. But if she has come to the apartment, to my false sickbed, to take care of me and touch my frozen forehead, she should do it as in certain movies of hers, with aigrettes and bustle; with a long train and a low décolleté and puffed sleeves, she should for the first time step into my transformed room, my beautiful turn-of-the-century grotto, like a D'Annunzio heroine, like a Bernhardt, a Duse, a Lillian Russell, a Carolina Otero. I am here, passing the bakeries and drugstores of Saltillo Street, only to prevent a figure different from that one, the beloved one, the one with the hourglass figure, from entering that cloister.

"Don't move, mamma. Don't let me come near you."

"I've never been here before."

"Yes, once."

"But it was another place. You certainly have changed it."

"I did it for you."

"Do you think I'd like to live like this, darling?"

"No, Claudia; quite the opposite. I don't want you to recognize yourself in anything; not in a decoration, nor in a mirror, nor in a man, nor . . ."

"Oh, darling, don't try to fool me. You know I only want to last."

"Here?"

"No."

"With me?"

"No."

"Can you imagine something better?"

"No."

Each negative is like a light that goes on and off—or like a darkness that defeats and affirms itself: between them there's not even time to twinkle your eye—. About to welcome her with a touch, I stop and throw myself, face down, on the wide sofa and its many silk and velvet cushions. I react, in this bright darkness, in this gloomy brilliance, and I wheel the serving table over to her: café, cognac . . . ? I quickly kiss her cheek and turn my back on her. I run to my room and lock myself in. Claudia has rushed to my side and I run from her, I leave her alone in that room of another time, that grotto of silk and wood panels, of scarlet screens and majolica candelabra, that stage of serpentine cabinets and twisted, slender lamps like wild flowers and thick curtains and lecterns standing on undulating pedestals, that gallery of objects of wrought glass and lead encased lamp shades. I leave her so that, a decoration, she disintegrates like the malignant hags in Pushkin and Henry James, in the secret museums that don't charge admission. Then, mummy of dust, I will be able to contemplate her among the other objects: she fell into my trap. She ceased to exist outside of me. I possess her without the need of desiring or touching her.

I scratch my nipple. I caress my armpit. The diabolic weakness of Baudelaire's eyes, in Nadar's photograph, watches over the angelic strength of my solitude. I contemplate Sarah Bernhardt, reclining on her Turkish divan, with the loose slipper and the dog at her feet. I possess them without the need to desire or touch them. I am going to think it, to free myself. I am going to let one thought creep in: perhaps Claudia is a fool. Absent, I could repeat for her Baudelaire's words: foolishness, *la bétise*, always preserves beauty; it keeps the wrinkles away; stupidity is a divine cosmetic that protects our idols from the ravages of thought. I will think of the central and obsessive figure of my mother standing in a great white pit that fills the empty stage. And I, in the wings, who am I? I caress myself slowly and see myself freed of foreign desires, alone in my enchanted grotto, about to turn into desire itself: *putto*, immaculate angel who will take neither husband nor wife, disinterested cherub. I open my legs in a great Y of egoistic freedom; childish and sick. I hide from the mirrors which invoke me and only offer me the disguise of the world that will never recognize the angelic character of my solitude. I open wide the doors of the closets. I will be as the world wishes to see me, aloof, ideal, dressed by Cardin: I brush my fingers along my fitted jackets, my silk and cambric shirts, my patent leather slippers with silver buckles, my Spanish cape, my velvet top hat. I dress for the mirror. I will live and sleep, Baudelaire, before a mirror, I will be the perfect, unemotional dandy whose artifice allows him to survive the illusions, *survive the illusions*, that you dreamed. I will live and sleep.

"Miss Ruth says that your mother doesn't want to be bothered just now, but that if you wish she'll send the doctor. And did you try the thermometer."

"It's okay, Gudelia. Tell her it's not necessary. I was only tired."

"Would you like something else?"

"Let me endorse the check. Cash it early tomorrow."

"Yes, sir. Good night, sir."

My autograph. My name?

Name of the Game

> "Play!"
> —Fitzgerald,
> *The Great Gatsby*

There won't be any light tonight. We must hurry. I want you to see the house.

A low, gray sky hastens his announcement. The maid is an old woman dressed in black, all in black, with black stockings. She lights the fire in the living room without looking at us. She murmurs: *"Piove, piove."*

Outside, the garden we must visit before night falls. I stand next to the window and push aside the muslin curtains. It's a garden of yellow dead leaves: a dog scratches among them and the bare trunks are the fig and laurel trees. The lemon tree. The dry geraniums.

Come. Don't stop. There's no time.

The old woman smiles and says that she'll serve dinner at nine. You and I, from the garden, stand looking at the beheaded statues on the terrace.

Can't we come closer?

No. That side is closed. It belongs to an uncle.

Does he ever come to the palace?

No. Never. He's satisfied knowing that his wing is condemned. It was all he inherited and he wants to give himself the luxury of being capricious about it.

The terrace is brick; the statues, perched on the balustrades and in the ochre niches of the wall, speak with the gesture of their broken hands, of their fixed postures. Not a single head is left, only bodies of heightened color: remnants of white, aggressive black, plaits and more plaits of absent and total colors, denying and fusing one into the other, united and separate. The drapings of mythical clothing, the nakedness of ceremonial flesh, black and white, belong to the dead half of the planets: I repeat it to you now: to the half without light, without eyes, without head, that lies in ambush in every corner of the palace of Madonna dei Monti. The palace itself is the other face of the mountain which shelters it among the cliffs and ravines. There is no sound other than that torrent which springs from the peaks of the Matese and descends, becoming a stream of debris: from the kitchen windows you throw nut shells down the ravine. That part of the palace is the original buttress: a great smooth wall grounded in the depths.

Wall and ravine separate us from the other world, that of the stone caves carved into the mountain and turned into houses. The little boy comes out on that balcony, on the other side of the torrent and the piles of garbage. He begins to shoot. A pause. He has eagle eyes, rapacious pupils sunk into the tender insolence of his white face, his straight, dark head. He aims, from his balcony, toward the open kitchen window where we breathe the cold air and think we are admiring those vertically cut masses. You scream. He couldn't fail with that beast of prey look. You scream. You lift your hands to your throat and fall on the table, the pets, the pasta, the immediacy of the kitchen abandoned by the old woman in black who has gone down to the village: "You didn't warn me. I don't have any food."

76

I don't move. I exchange looks with the little boy with the rifle. The rapaciousness of his eyes doesn't change. But the blushed cheeks twitch, he throws down the rifle and runs, mute and nervous, into his cave-house. You get up laughing and do a dance step.

Your arms extended, you slide down one of the slopes that go from the courtyard up to the main terrace of the palace. A slimy stucco lion rises in the center of that patio. You sit at his feet and offer me a bottle of pills.

Vitamin C. You've got to prevent colds in this humidity. The campanile rings five times. People go down to the village by the ancient passages. The palace is on the peak, but the nearness of its details distracts and obsesses me. Only now, descending, do I realize there's a forest of television antennas and, further on, those white sparks, that steady blue glare on the scaffolding of a modern edifice.

It's the first apartment house they're building here.

The solderer's torch goes out. You look at me mockingly; your silence is mocking.

I don't want to go down to the village this time.

You shrug your shoulders and we go back to the palace. You point out the plaque at the entrance of the front door. Historical monument: out of bounds for all troops. PC 1st BR HQUS 387 Engineers. I begin to lose confidence. I let you go first, in front of me, I being your guest, in order to watch you again. The long scarf wraps around your neck and falls down your back; the thick sweater barely shines, as if it absorbed the humidity; the legs, in contrast, move in that dry and elegant way; the scuffed boots step down hard on the tiles. What are we going to do together? I instinctively raise the lapels of my jacket; I already know that the cold inside the palace is worse than on the streets. And watching your self-possession, your confidence, the fox's step that precedes me like a shadow, I again feel the awkwardness of my movements, the unconfessable torture of communication, the unhappy desire for solitude. My whole negation is in your way of walking. In your way of existing. Stendhal, Italy: the man who fascinates will be forgiven.

I follow you along the corridors of blackened arches. You kick open the double doors. You walk in and I follow you. I stop. I listen to your breathing; then your confident steps in the dark, finally the crashing of ivory balls.

Do you want to play?

No . . . I can't see a thing.

One, two, three abrupt knocks. I sneeze.

Come. Follow me.

That light barred by poplars and Venetian blinds reaches as far as the walls of the great uninhabited sitting room, corroded by the dampness which comes down from the ceiling and rises from the floor, without completely erasing the hazy whiteness of the frescos. Old weapons which nobody uses. Helmets. Flags which signify nothing. Mutilated and empty pedestals. Fat rosy angels, who want to announce with their bugles the triumph of a forgotten glory: the glory of these objects, these painted ruins of weak lines, of tepid yellow, pink, and blue bathed in dissipated whiteness, covered with that discolored cream which makes it all distant: I want to imagine the ironic conception that, upon celebrating some particular feat, or the simple abstract majesty of the ancient house and its inhabitants, predicted its eventual collapse, its fatal decline in time.

The painter had placed, on the line, the color, the atmosphere of these frescos, a seed of destruction that must have grown, like mushrooms encrusted in live skin, as his work, and the theme of his work, aged. The fat-cheeked *putti* blow their bugles, fly over the mound of weapons and standard-bearers with a nostalgia of glory which is also an announcement of oblivion and misery. I feel, before the frescos, a remote pain and anxiety: empty salon of games and consecrations and inside it a little boy my age, you, here, and I in that house of the absent touch.

You draw near the fresco and light a match: you scrape it over the cherub's face. You deform it. You smile watching my quick and timid gesture of defense.

Historical monument. Out of bounds.

I don't know why they preserve it. It's been more than half a century since they lived in it.

But you live here . . . Well, from time to time . . .

Yes. I had to force them. I told them I was going to die of cancer and that I wished to end my days here. That they understood. They thought there was a certain grandeur in the image. The dauphin returns to the palace to die. They would have liked that conclusion very much. A good reason to keep up the fiction. It never ceases to be offensive. My death considered as the last historical date of the palace. As if nothing extraordinary has happened since Garibaldi. Then, yes, the troops entered, set up quarters, tore the curtains and stained the furniture. Not during the last war. It was an aseptic office of the Americans.

You light another match and go to the darkest wall. Your hand revolves, illuminating that second fresco.

As a little boy I strutted back and forth here dressed as a *balilla*. I looked like a grotesque dwarf in that child's black uniform. Since this is the largest room in the palace, I used it to practice the soldiers' march.

Other angels, pulverized by the light of a broken pointillist: brush stroke, created and destroyed by that willfully false light penetrating them with a thick transparency: an applied, savage, slow work, of construction and destruction: a final form, not perceptible to the naked eye, of fetus and corpse, uterus and tomb: what is an angel?

My own rebirth. Oh, it was a family of condottieri, they received the lands as payment for their services in some make-believe wars, they built the palace with the spoils, they even became popes . . .

Another mound, another college. Announced by the fetus-angels, by the corpse-cherubs who blow their jazz trumpets over the stack of objects stuck to the wall, in bulk; the pasteboardlike photographs of women with hourglass figures.

Can you imagine anything more vulgar? Grandfather squandered his fortune on roulette. He went to Monte Carlo, lost, returned, humbled himself before the family, asked forgiveness, recovered his good spirits, sold some land, returned to the casino. As a little old man, he was frightfully stingy.

The old tray of cracked lacquer: rose buds, false violets, cancerous pineapples; the silver teapot; the covers of illustrated magazines; the outstretched and moth-eaten wings of a bat; rooster crests; wine corks; Coca Cola caps; yellow condoms; hogs' heads, amputated, bleary-eyed, pale despite their purple spots, buzzing slightly with a stench of big-bellied, shiny, greenish flies; the profiles of silent movie vamps, Francesca Bertini, Italia Almirante Manzini, Pina Menichelli, Giovanna Terribili González: their velvet profiles kiss the white mask of the statues, the switched heads, the marble matter eaten by a nameless pox.

I run to the grillwork windows, pin my eyes to the gratings brushed by the whiteness of the poplars, I want to pass through that whole filigreed barrier to see the landscape of mutilated statues on the terrace, to know that the heads have grown on again, no longer of stone: now of rags, now protective sorcerers of the seeds: scarecrows with sleepy

79

eyes and mended mouths from which tongues of grass peer out: only the end of the evening, the lost speed of the sun, the curfew bell of the barracks.

Your hand caresses my shoulder, behind me. Guglielmo, there's something contaminating in childhood. We are too close to our own origin.

The fur bedspread had fallen to the floor. I felt a nakedness as cold as this new morning which announced Christmas with a light drizzle. But I wasn't cold. The pink rag girl doll—or boy doll—continued sleeping, sprawled out, next to me. Perhaps I was holding it all night. I don't know. The stitches were a bit loose and on its rag head, missing painted features, there was something I couldn't remember. The cotton-filled arms and legs were twisted all around me; the paint on the rag was fresh: I noticed it on my stained hands, chest, stomach.

I raised my eyes. Over the headboard, instead of the usual religious picture, one of the silent movie vamps, again, her mouth half-opened, showing her retouched, bright lips, she hid her breasts with one hand and caressed her neck with the other: that poster, worn on the edges, newly varnished, was the daily victory—the eternity—of that old actress. This act of adoration was enough for Francesca Bertini to retain forever the present time of her beauty. Hail Francesca, full of grace: I knelt on the bed and clasped my hands near the leopard skin which covered the body of Bertini. And blessed is the fruit of thy womb . . .

You repeated your name from the stone frame of the door which connected my bedroom to yours. You were naked and drying your head with a towel.

"Have you seen what a horrible day it is? *Buen Natale, caro. Beato tu*, in your country Christmas comes with cocoanuts and palm trees."

You shook your head till water came out of your ears: you wrinkled your nose while you looked toward the landscape hidden behind the drizzle.

"I've never seen a white Christmas here. Every year, rain and mud. Just as well. Nobody thinks of coming to keep me company."

"Not even your mother?"

"Never. She's extremely busy with her fashion boutique. She sews and sews. Besides, I would forbid it. *Beato tu;* you're far from home."

I rested my chin on my knees. "No. My mother is in Paris."

"Ah. You didn't want to spend the holidays with her either."

I nodded yes and you offered me your hand. I got up from the bed, guided by your hand. You wanted to lead me immediately to another place; I felt it in the urgency of your hand.

"Wait. Let me get dressed."

"No. It's not necessary. The old woman has gone to celebrate with her relatives. We're alone in the palace."

"I don't know."

I knelt again on the bed and Bertini looked blessed art thou amongst women: it's true, the artist had painted the false tear between her lashes: one-eyed.

"I didn't sleep well. I prefer to spend the whole morning resting."

"Okay. We'll see each other at lunch. I'll make it myself. We have enormous strawberries for dessert."

"No, thank you. Strawberries make me sick."

Are the shutters tightly closed? Can anybody see us? It doesn't matter: darkness begins to take shape within the darkness. I am far away, behind the door of that cloister of yours, the one with the twin frescos, the renaissance wall and the one you yourself made with those objects. I look between the cracks. Now you have filled that great naked room of yesterday with all those dilapidated chairs, lined with a velvet that seems torn off the backs of rodents, fed by that straw which emerges, almost crackling, to scatter itself on the floor.

I spy on you.

You have put on that black and dusty Napoleonic jacket, with enormous lapels of dead brocade; that's all you're wearing while you move around your family's cloistered salon, you bow courteously, you convert courtesy into angry pride, you do those gavotte steps, like a faun: your jacket and your bare feet make me imagine a God Pan in Versailles. King, where is your court? I spy on you.

They wait upon you: the life-sized dolls, all in pink rags, all featureless, all badly sewn, filled with that cotton which spills from their cracks like the straw from the bottoms of the broken-down chairs: I spy on them through that material darkness of hurriedly stitched fabrics: I spy on the crooked white wigs which give them a drunken air: I spy on the ballerinas' slippers with heavy tips that overwhelm those flaccid white-laced cotton legs still more; I spy on the hoop-skirt frames that cover them. And in one or another, the excessive filling in its stomach, the belly swollen with cotton that fights to break loose of the stitching, emerges like bloodless larva.

Yes. I too would like to feel it. I swear.

Invoke, like you, that slower than slow music, that slow possession of a rhythm of pins strung into this semblance of flesh. But those pregnant dolls are pincushions, have been created with thimble and thread; they're meant to be tortured, to dance, like you, the young king in the old jacket, the ridiculed and naked monarch who whirls with the potbellied doll in his arms, the virile emperor who can take those limp princesses without asking their permission, throwing them on the floor, uncovering the entrance you yourself made.

I came into the room, like you, a master of the dark, I said your name: I voluntarily interrupted you and you looked at me with that serene and inevitable panic one must feel in ill-matched combat with the shark, the tiger, fire, the plane crash: the moment when terror becomes a resignation that can be the highest moment of our happiness: there's nothing left to overcome.

You moved away from the doll, rolled over, ended face up, with your legs open and arched, leaning on your elbows. And the child-birth—I'll never know if I could say it was that—was of the being who returns each time he forgets it, who has died before, and will always die, now and then, not to seem like a monster: you sweat, twist around, slowly, under the gaze of the fat angels and the silent screen vamps, of the art you inherited and the art you created, to finally say what I didn't want to hear.

Don't touch anything, Guglielmo.

Get up, please, get up.

I want to survive, Guglielmo. I am looking for the way, the only way I know. Swear to me that while you're here you won't touch anything.

But it is now, from now on, that I do want to touch.

Don't distrust me. Understand me. Desire, plead, kiss, but don't consume . . . Only that is touching. Consuming.

This carousel of beheaded statues and rag dolls, cancerous moldings and cover-story-actresses revolves: there's a rotation of lunar objects, of drums and flags, of hogs' heads and rooster crests; there's a new statuary, a new decoration, a new serpentine Grecian fret, a relief of damp plaster, of which I am becoming part . . . I face you. You're not there. Or you are in the night which separates us: your face is the night. How am I going to reward your pity, your abandon of that caramel-colored toy, what prize am I going to give a body, turned, in the middle of my stay, into the vanished presence which contains and invites me to come out of my own skin? I feel hungry. I remember the supper the old woman is making for us. Or the lunch you yourself are going to make. And immediately I reject the promised satisfaction. I'm not sure I understand you. To consume is to consummate is to touch is to sin. I follow your steps without touching you, without knowing if you're before me along those unlit arched corridors which you know by heart, my only guide the touch of the damp stucco, the broken Grecian frets, the cold knobs, the soft walls, the rusty knockers, the unsilvered mirrors, the engraved, intertwining cornucopias in the tunnel leading us to the inhabited wing of the palace while I think I am following your steps and perhaps I am only hearing mine which stamp the rooms with something that is already your command: honor and secrecy, service and patience: love of myself, when finally entering that freezing bedroom and smelling its retreat of furs, rugs, and closets opened for the first time in many years; distant love, daring to touch the headboard of the iron bed, the leather cover of an ancient desk; consolation of that absence rescued by a twin sense of narcissism; quick and fatal undressing of myself in that solitude without light or color, in that little hell of the bedroom you have reserved for me; slow immersion into the bed covered with furs; new encounter with the place of my body, the campaign against my own skin, the war against the hiding places of all that I am and am not permitted to be: beautiful darkness, veiled love, prize of heat, piety of the sheets: marvelous ardor of a forbidden touch, endless passion of my unsatisfied body, unknown grace of exhausted sleep. The lights will never return, tonight.

"Please, watch out . . ."

"Don't worry. There's not an Italian who isn't an ace at the wheel."

"Go slower, please . . ."

"What time did we leave Naples?"

"Thirty-five minutes ago, I think . . . It's too . . ."

"With luck, it'll be sunny. And the sea will be there. A pretense of summer."

"Let's go back to the palace."

"I can't stand it anymore. Enough. At this speed, we'll be in Positano in twenty minutes."

"We're not in any hurry, please, please . . ."

"Enjoy the scenery and stop being afraid, Guglielmo. Aren't these cliffs beautiful? They feel like reaching the sea, like rushing, like us."

"At least blow your horn on the curves . . ."

"To feel safe? It wouldn't be any fun. Let go. I'm driving the car. Let go, I tell you! Are you very frightened?"

"Yes, I'm very afraid; please; this highway has no fences!"

"Do you think my father had fences when he flew over the Libyan desert? Do you think anyone promised him he would return safe and sound?"

"Your father is dead, I'm not . . ."

"Idiot. Who told you he's dead? They never found his body. He might return any day now, God willing! Then they wouldn't nag me with those stories about his heroism. Hero! They all know the Italians ran like rabbits! The old man must have taken advantage of the war to stay with some whore in Tripóli and save himself forever from tradition, the family, my devoted mother, a broken-down palace . . ."

"Watch out! He's on top of us!"

"Eeeeh . . . That was close . . . *Ciao, cretino.*"

"Don't laugh!"

"I'm not laughing! I'm transfigured! I want to survive, I already told you!"

"You want to survive? You want to survive? Where? Splattered on one of those rocks? At the bottom of the sea?"

"God willing! *Magari!* The mountain itself is constantly falling into the sea, don't you see?"

"I don't want to. It's a sharp fall; look . . ."

"Don't look!"

"Don't look, don't touch, don't . . . I feel sick. I've had it. Let me out!"

"They'd run you over. The peasants don't walk the highway to Amalfi. They walk up there, with the goats, among the rocks."

"Put on your lights, at least have pity . . ."

"No."

"Have pity . . ."

"No! Only when I see other lights flicked on us. Poor devil. Don't you realize that I want to survive? How many times do I have to repeat it?"

"I too want to survive! Stop! Let me out!"

"This is the only way: a transfiguration and another and then another. Guglielmo, if time captures you it kills you. It begins, it develops, it ends. If you're transfigured, you only pass from one state

84

to another, always incandescent, like the statues in the palace. Don't touch! I'm driving the car!"

"Those lights . . ."

"It's Positano. Relax. They're the lights in the houses. We've arrived. Don't you feel different? It's the adrenalin, the adrenalin, the adrenalin . . ."

You've asked for a plate of strawberries and you eat them in bed while I listen to you and far from you, standing, I push aside the window curtain in our hotel room and look toward the nocturnal beach of Positano. You ask me, laughing, not to let myself be fascinated by the sea: poets who didn't want to be loved, but rather remembered, have drowned there. I say that I'm not looking at the sea, but at the beach. It's true: that girl rides, now, at night, identical with the night, over the sand. I would like to ask you if you know her. You should listen, from afar, to the rhythm of the hoofs on the sand, because you say, while you eat, naked and sleepy and nevertheless tense and covered by the bronze from the morning sun, that I should avoid windows that face the infinite. I sob pitifully. You behind me, that feminine vision before me, I, divided, impaled, pained and with a desperate desire to be alone and to dress and to walk along the beach and, maybe, make out the face of the girl who, every day, at unexpected hours, rides a horse and looks toward the islands of the sirens. You guess, you make fun of me: you say I always need mediators; you say that you will teach me—if we have time—to see things without the need for sacraments. I offer you an angry face that thinks it's responding to your mockery. I would like to laugh at your stupidity and I can only stammer that you don't understand anything, that I'll always need them, you or that girl who rides along the beach facing the Tyrrhenian Sea. You watch me affectionately, Giancarlo, almost sympathetically. You close your knees and wipe your mouth with the sheet and insist on offering me those strawberries which make me sick. The bedroom smells too much of fresh whitewash. You say that the true vision will restore the original couple; the free vision, without mediators. Because we run the risk of confusing the mediator with the half we desire and then the vision escapes us. I don't understand you. You sigh and make plans for the next day. We will go by boat to Amalfi and we will eat in a restaurant on the bay. You make up a menu of white wine, tortellini, and frutti di mare. You say that you'd like to get drunk on sambuca; a pleasant, heavy high. Superstitious: neither more nor less than three grains of toasted coffee floating in that viscous liqueur. Friends, Guglielmo? Brothers? Even though it be temporary, *caro*. Brothers born of the same mother. Apollo and Dionysus, who, during the winter only, shared their oracle. Delphi. Twins, Guglielmo: Apollo, god of the sun, and his antagonistic pal, Dionysus, the conductor of souls. I look out and the girl on horseback has gone away.

Wherein It Is Declared and Related

> I solemnly declare . . .
> —Dostoevski,
> *Notes from Underground*

Ruth is sitting at the counter in Sanborn's on Niza Street, drinking American coffee. There's an empty place next to her. I take it. First she doesn't pay attention to me. She has a *Newsweek* opened, propped against the container of drinking straws. Then she looks at me without recognizing me. Finally she laughs, pretends to choke on a mouthful of coffee, covers her mouth with a paper napkin, and laughs again. She says she imagined me in bed, with a fever; she winks an eye. We talk and Ruth declares:

"No, there's nothing to be surprised at. Our relationship has been stable for some time now. Claudia no longer feels the need of imposing herself on me. She knows that I love her a great deal and that I do what she wishes. You don't remember her when she was still an insecure woman. Basically, she was afraid they accepted her too much for her beauty and at the same time rejected her personality. Now she knows that they're both the same thing and she no longer worries. Perhaps she owes me something. Yes, that; I proved to her, in the beginning, that I could stand all her violence and rudeness without losing my esteem for her. You probably don't remember all those scandals; she'd arrive late on the set, she was moody, she'd insult the director. God knows what else. But she would have never exhausted her violence if she hadn't had me at her side, putting up with it, every day of my life. No, don't think I'm a masochist; I'm not even unselfish. I give your mother something important, but she gives me something even better. I can't imagine who would be interested in my story; it's very common; an everyday disillusion, not worth the trouble remembering, really. You know how the families and the men are here. Anyone would say they have an understanding at the woman's expense, she always gets the worst end of the deal. It doesn't matter. What I learned with Claudia is that a woman can be free of her loved one and continue living. No, don't think I'm going to tell you something silly, that your mother made me forget my troubles and I've been keeping that old love alive for fifteen years as if . . . No, look. Claudia almost hits me, almost drags me around her room shouting at me. 'Well, what do you want? Do you want to be a sinful and devout little nun? Do you want to forget what happened and at the same time remember it as if it hadn't happened? Look, Ruth, nunneries have never been anything but lesbian brothels and don't think I'm going to play along with you. In my house there are no cells. This cage is made of pure air. If you stay here, you're no longer going to believe that you'll never again be all you were when you first fell in love. You're going to hurry up and forget that with age you can be more or less, but never exactly what you were then. With me there are no pasts. Everything is happening right now.' You see? With Claudia there isn't that terrible temptation to get sentimental or nostalgic, because her whole life is the present, understand?, the present but not apart from her. She doesn't name things that happened, never. They are a part of what she is, now. Don't believe her if she talks to you about something that's already happened. It's a story she's just invented: it's part of her present. Sometimes I think that because of this, people call her immoral, because she doesn't try to justify the past, like almost everybody else. Maybe so. Maybe your mother has made all us women a little freer, a little better. Why not? I'll accept that. My life is borrowed, just like the maids who pay their four pesos to see her in the movies. What do you want? It's enough for me. Only I don't look for what Claudia Nervo offers in her movies. Love and beauty and danger. For me your mother is strength. I prefer this borrowed strength. Alone, I would be very weak. All the strength that I could summon alone would be nothing. To live through your mother is everything; much more than I could imagine, really. I have everything I need and I like things. Well, the necessary things, of course. But why does a person have to suffer for having what's indispensable? A washing machine, a car, a good stereo. Imagine if we'd be left without that. Could you live without those comforts? As Claudia's secretary, I have more than I need; a trip abroad every year, magnificent hotels, the best restaurants. And all the rest. See how she takes over, how she makes fun of it all, how she outdresses the smartest.

How can I complain, Guillermo? I imagine myself a typist in an office or a saleslady in a five-and-ten and it gives me the jitters, I swear. And Claudia? Well, she always has in me an average member of her audience and at home, don't you think that's something? No, I'm kidding; it's much more than that. Your mother has shown that in Mexico a woman can live according to her own morals and fantasies. Don't you think that's something? You don't know what it was like twenty years ago. . . . Look, I do everything she does. Really. Only that I prize my modesty. Claudia knows it and I think she thanks me for it, well, common people like me . . . You know. Besides, with Claudia you get to know things, the real inside stories. What more do you want? That's another satisfaction I have, another enticement: knowing enough to keep it to myself. Don't look for her, Guillermo. Claudia will appear when you least expect it. She knows her game."

Gudelia has come up with the morning mail. I sort out the bills—the bulk mail—and separate them from the correspondence—a single letter—I recognize the envelope and am puzzled. He only writes on special occasions, a week before my birthday; sometimes, a few days before Christmas. But now we're in September and my birthday is in July. He's read the newspapers. He knows Claudia will be going in two days.

"Here things are the same as always, I get older and older and almost nothing amuses me. Sometimes I go to the movies, but I don't like what they're doing today. Why do people have to suffer and see ugly things as if real-life suffering wasn't enough? But they're making pretty Mexican movies in color and you don't have to read the subtitles. My eyes have gotten very tired. I tell your grandma that it must be from so many years of checking invoices and keeping bills up to date. With all the petty thievery there is, it costs twice as much to be honest. You c_n see the years on me more than on your grandma. Maybe because she can't get any older. She has almost completely lost her memory, she forgets everything. Imagine, sometimes she gets confused and thinks I'm her husband, I mean the grandpa you didn't have the good fortune to know. I've had to drop tennis on doctor's orders. I went for a checkup last month and it seems like the old machine has a few more years to go, provided I take things as they come. I was a lion, my boy. I traveled the whole Republic when I was a salesman; there's not a town in the Bajío I don't know like the palm of my hand. Now it's time for me to rest at home. I had a stone in my liver but your grandma knows about herbs and that got better by itself. In any case, I have to take some pills for high blood pressure after each meal. You know how flushed I've always been. Bad sign, high blood pressure. But now even my hair is fading on me; from red it's turned to gray. The dentist looked me over and is trying to convince me to get a whole new denture, just like that. What do you think? Some of my friends have done it and at first they look very strange. But then you get used to it, like everything. As always, your grandma keeps your room ready, just as you left it. Sometimes people come around to make a deal to buy the house, but you know I'll never do that. There are too many memories, good and bad, but memories all the same. And I don't know how mamma would feel if she had to leave. Maybe I'll change my mind when she dies. If we hadn't lost you, everything would have been different. Laws don't have anything to do with reality, son. If I were a judge, I'd first make sure of the truth in each case and I'd let my sense of right and my human feelings guide me. It would be another story entirely. But that's how things are; no luck. That fight wore me out good. I haven't been the same since. I feel empty and only the hope of seeing you some day keeps me going. I'm telling you the same as always, man to man, this is your home, the day you get tired or need a change of air. There are pretty girls here who are dying to meet you. I'm not imposing, you'll know when you need us and then don't hesitate or go and believe we're people who bear grudges. Maybe you'd like to see your old schoolmates again, the ones you played soccer with as a kid. They've all turned out well, nice decent people, like Ortega and Yáñez for example. I know that deep down you're good and if I was ever strict it was for your good and perhaps it's helped you somehow. Remember that your roots are here and that sometime in your life you've got to return to them. It's like the sap of the trunk, you understand. Maybe you'll gain something. At least, the strength of confronting things that in any case are part of your life."

No; among the bills is a letter from Bela. I misplaced it; it comes in an ordinary, thick white envelope, stained with fingerprints and without a return address.

"You didn't understand anything, nothing at all, you thought I wanted to take something away from you, *beato tu,* you don't understand anything, I wanted to give you something, give you, give you, you didn't understand me, you fool, you are a disgusting menace, I'm telling you, you are stupid and monstrous because you no longer have anything to do with life, you can no longer see what the rest of us are, the men and women who don't play your horrible solitary game, you are as proud as you are foolish, you don't deserve me, you don't, I'm telling you, you don't deserve my kisses and my body and all my joy, for you I would have done anything that night, you only had to ask me and I would have given it to you, you deceived me, that evening you made me believe that two people could live together without sacrificing their own fantasy, you made me believe we could be together without becoming one, each of us separate and complete but the two together, you prepared and opened and moistened me for nothing, you are a monster, I'm telling you, there's nothing for you to do here, you're like some pretty words that don't serve any purpose, you are a horrible night full of light or a horrible day full of darkness, you will continue threatening me as long as I live and you make me think that I may find you again, with another face, disguised, ready to prevent my beautiful contact with all that really exists, my cup of coffee and my shepherds of Ciociara and my songs in the shower, you are not an annoyance or bad habits or irritation, you are stupid crime, you are the crime that doesn't kill, you are a torture and I was open for you, I am not a mirror, I don't know how to look at myself in mirrors, nobody can live in mirrors, I know how to be embraced, calm and trembling in the arms of a man, I know how to caress and wait and smile and thank, I am full of verbs, I don't have names or hard ideas, I have senses, they were for you, for you, I would have followed you in your lies if you weren't so foolish, if you knew that there are lies that bring you close to the truth, not you, not you, you only want lies that isolate you, I don't understand you, I only desire you, you don't deserve me and I still desire you, you, you, before it's too late, before you invent something that separates us forever, something more than what you've already done, I prefer you like this, now, when you're only beginning to make me suffer and not after, when you'll be worse than now, when you can't even give me suffering, I don't know why I'm writing this, yes, I do know, there's something worse than you, in this house, I prefer you because I know what you are, not something that also threatens me in this house, with your mother, you don't deserve me, you have humiliated me and now you must save me, you must save me by accepting what I can give you, before I believe that you and your mother are together in all this . . ."

I am drinking a campari-soda, calmly, in the bar of the María Isabel Hotel. I say "calmly" because the racket those guitarists are making is so great that it cancels itself out, it abstracts itself and lets me sit here, alone, with a glass in my hand and a tray of guacamole tacos on the table. Loneliness is only in these places, not in my beautiful grotto, not in my beautiful receptacle of all the company I want. This is how I want to feel, sleepy and remote, in the midst of all the ghosts of this city, near the social climbing slaves that inhabit it, up close to the ugly, silly, corny women and the ridiculous, loud, joking Don Juans who come here to tell each other about filthy love affairs and crooked business and obscene puns. They all smell of Yardley's lavender and they have just got their first three-button jacket with narrow lapels. They all have purple faces and thick mustaches. They wear dark glasses and silver rings. Their suits shine like airplanes. They look at the manicured nails of their chubby hands, scratch their fat buttocks. I drink, plug myself in, bend over to listen to them. "Hey, Nacho, ever hear about the broad who wanted to be like the Constitution so they'd violate her every once in awhile? Ah, Chihuahua. That reminds me of another. Drink up, pal, the drinks are on me. Listen, no sweat, I'm not hungry yet: I still have some fuel left in the old tank. Then let's see who lasts longer. You talk big but when the time comes to separate the men from the boys . . . How about one for the road? Let me warn you that my wife does yoga and I take judo lessons. You got to defend yourself, right? Come on, where's the waiter? Lousy service. What kind of a cathouse is this? No, we're going right now, but first we've got to get in tune, right? You ought to see those fat broads. Yeah that's right, you've already been. Every two minutes they ask me when you're coming back. My old man this and my old man that. We have what it takes, right, old buddy? Ah but tonight the drinks are on me, yes sir. Just remind me when the time comes and it's as if I had five in a row, not bad, eh? Shitty broads, that's what they're good for. The right to the first night, how about that? They knew how to live in those days. Now you have to ask their permission and they still complain about doing you a favor, miserable broads. Think what you like, but I haven't missed a trick yet. I never miss my target. What'll you have, baby? Whammo! What? Hell no, he's by himself, let him come over here. . . . What? Really? Her son? If they send her to me, she won't get back to the corral in one piece. You can sure pick up some trophies there. Ay mamacita. I'll roll the cape over that big fat broad . . . Psst. Let him look. He's just the son of the bitch . . . What are you looking at, kid? Don't like our faces?"

Erinyes

> Would I find La Maga?
> —Cortázar,
> *Hopscotch*

The first floor drawing room is transformed. A week ago, during the cocktail party, I couldn't see it or describe it. It was the same house on Avenida Fundición. The same. Now, as I walk through, I realize that the room exists to be described, not lived in or dramatized. You will say: to be consecrated descriptively. You always say that the external world should avenge the negation of the years, that supposed psychological profundity that takes pleasure in denying the only reality, surface reality.

Now I remember you because this white light, in extreme contrast, demands it of me. The room seems photographed with 4-X film: white light like lime and bone, dessert and milk, which granulates everything and pursues all the edges until it banishes them from the suddenly all-embracing contours. A lemon body. The inside of the maternal womb must be like this: an illuminated placenta, like this gallery where the details of decoration escape, dissolved by a damp powder, by a solar reverberation of the figures which are set against the light and are, because of it, black silhouettes. They pose, still and suffering: by the door frames, on the threshold of the closed garden, against the sliding glass doors. On the furniture: open hands, eucharistic cups, trees of leather and rosewood.

Only two paintings compete with each other and against the white mist. The Fernando Botero I've always understood. It's the pink and malignant Gioconda, infantile and plump-cheeked, indigestible, chubby, stuffed with unmentionable candies, facing the José Luis Cuevas painting: a Marquis de Sade who waits by the dying fire upon the secret demands of his family. The wife, cross-eyed and powdered, weaves; the children, in wide, loose baptismal gowns and coifs, suck their fingers; the paterfamilias looks upon the scene beatifically, a hydrocephalic, big-bellied gnome, with wasp eyes and a gargoyle's profile: he pries into the *pot-au-feu* King Henry bequeathed to all Frenchmen, while his tight, clandestine clothes, the green frock-coat and ochre pants, creak.

You said this, not I, who only understands these things thanks to you and then repeats them like a parrot: in Cuevas' painting de Sade presides over all the slogans of household corruption: a chicken in every pot, get rich, man was born free, back to nature, honor your father and mother, pay the church its tithe, obey your government, feed the hungry, educate your children, respect the laws, accept the judge's verdict, to each his own, and remember that love is a many-splendored thing. Cuevas' de Sade, ochre and green and black, resists the invasion of this light, evenly spread only because it's uncommon; it doesn't reach this room with the evolutional sign we wish to attribute to all living things. This light has not traveled through the strata of air and fire, the combat of molecules, the cloud filters or earth mirrors that we know. This light is refracted from an incandescent, bizarre quartz, no touch or vision precedes it.

Uncreated, it illuminates from its own center the labyrinth through which I am walking, the salon of my mother's house, bare and as arbitrary as its characteristic suppression of the arbitrary.

Clean dropped ceiling, projected like an empty de Chirico square.

Raw cement walls and white mosaic floor.

Pedro Friedeberg furniture: receptive hands.

Volume dissolves in space and the angles flow toward the concrete, visceral, corrosive, acid, thick, self-wrought light of plaster, self-sculptured to that dagger and diamond point of brightness sufficient to prevent any color, form, or gesture from escaping its contrast. Everything fuses within it, nothing establishes the loathed harmony, the previous meaning, hardened in the idea. The light and figures beg contemplation. They violently invite sensorial amplitude and relaxation. They are the opening through which the new touch, the new vision, the new smell can penetrate, and also the new sound which is part of the light and explodes in the loudspeakers with the melancholy of a well-earned rest, the beautiful fatigue of an energetic spending of all the senses in the voice of John Lennon.

You've got to hide your love away.

The neo-Elizabethan lament of flutes, electric guitars, and tambourines.

Love will have a way.

The evanescent spirit of that satisfied appetite, of thigh and onion, beer and lace, eiderdown and wild boar, grape and sword, belch and sperm.

I need you

And you, whom I think they call Vanessa, leaning against the foggy glass door of the garden, your arms open and the palms of your hands leaving their traces on that damp morning crystal: Vanessa in the white hood and black leather harlequin suit and yellow boots: cold juggler with a colorless face, no eyebrows, white lipstick and long stockings brightened by orange diamonds: are you the first or the last? Your stiffness is already a· concession, but you, the so-called Ute, your chin resting on your knees, nestled in that seat which is a powerful hand, you are the oval of the Flemish virgin whose long hungry hair hides behind the raised legs and the wide bell-bottom pants, a possible golden seed, a fetus transformed by Midas's touching your sleeveless, stone-crusted coat: your bare arms, tanned Ute, oh beauty, do you come from the deep heavens or do you rise from the bottomless pit? Your suntanned skin is near the blue skin of Paola, standing, made up like the moon and disguised as the original Dietrich, the eternal Galatea: silver top hat, silver lamé pajamas with the plunging neckline that stops at the pubis and the coccyx; motionless, you surrender to the gesture of your blue nakedness and like Lola-Lola, you wound one beauty to duplicate the other: morality and poetry are alien to Hermione's isolation, in her inquiring pose: natural, without makeup, with snub nose and freckles, she wears the frock coat of the gallant king, the cap of the drugged detective, the knickers of the imprisoned aesthete, all in Scotch plaid, like the cape Hermione waves on the night of the ripper, this night of mortal combat between tea and biscuits. I imagine you, the so-called Hermione, killing the king with his own golf clubs on the green fields of Erin, mesmerizing the neighbors on Baker Street with a quiet violin, making the obese poet burn his extra pounds in a perpetual race, *aller-retour*, of tandem bicycles between the Mayfair palaces and the Reading gaols. You would be my favorite,

Hermione, if your masculine garments were less innocent, if they rushed me to an amphitheater, a clinic, or an execution; if, in short, behind you, while I walk along the gallery, I didn't anticipate the gothic profile of Kirsten, wrapped in Gobelins, in curled brocade slippers like the feet of a sultan, with the red straw cardinal hat and the icon of the Prophet Elijah dividing her invisible breasts: Kirsten, martyr of the north, oral myth of the Celts, mortal desire of the Germanic legends, secret heresy of blue eyes which turn into the imprisoned snow of your black pencil fjords: the brocade tongues cover your ears, sensual Erasmus, they tie under your chin, tempestuous beauty of the terror, and only Iphigenia, high-cheeked native girl, dark and negroid, dares, in this snake dance of mannikins, to mark the rhythm of the music so that her dress, an enormous green, black, and white tennis scarf, waves with a sway girded to the hard, totemical body, which emerges in the dark arms and vanishes into the white boots: sweaty, smelly, prunelike, you will be beautiful in the secret corner of her coldness.

I walk among them, while they look at me as what they are: the ever-renewable chorus that accompanies Claudia on her trips, her work, her vacations.

Only one is left out. I'm missing only one. The one they offered me. The one I fear. The one who fears me. Who thinks she knows. Who must know and accept and forgive so that she'll never think of revenge. The one I wanted to disarm giving her the names of goodness instead of the lashings of anger. At the end, at the end of the grotto, behind the fantastic guard of Vanessa the juggler and Ute the virgin and Hermione the policeman and Kirsten the martyr and Paola the angel and Iphigenia the totem, must be that humble prisoner, the newly arrived, the one who's still not acquainted with the pageants and functions of her sisterhood, the one who still doesn't clutch the whips or carry off the food.

Bela, the Italian girl, who again copies the eyebrow and lip, hair and eye lines of my mother. Sitting at the end of the drawing room. Hidden by the seven veils of the seven vestals who begin to laugh when I approach Bela, simple in her Mondrian dress of straight lines and colored squares.

The laughter grows behind me.

Hidden Bela, defeated Bela, Bela in the arms of the leading man who there, on the long white sofa, caresses her and smells of lavender. Lothario in his absurd patent leather suit. Buridan caresses Bela before being thrown in a sack into the Seine. Samson who still doesn't have an identifiable face. Now even less. Now that he's only the spoils.

Bela lets the actor kiss her but looks at me idiotically. The chorus of boisterous laughter rises, rises like the barking of my dogs when I raise the volume of the record player. The six women dissolved by the white light turn their backs on me, laughing. They all point toward the garden. Toward the other figure in the other light that moves toward us, toward the chorus of women who laugh and tremble with fear and hate and pleasure. Toward the couple embracing before all the world, exposed and resigned: Bela and her anonymous companion. Toward me, who is once again an awkward reflection, an intruder.

We all look toward the garden. We all try to overcome the barrier of fog that separates us. We all think that the natural light, the sunlight that illuminates her, is a false light and her own.

Claudia stands off in the distance, laughing, in the garden.

My mother, in the distance, triumphs. Her transparent muslin dress, her embroidered bust, her ostrich feather boa, all the foam and green tide of her remote elegance, makes the girls' clothing look old.

We all look toward the Leonora Carrington triptych on the wall at the end of the salon. It is on the altar that was its destiny: an open cemetery, of spikenards and weeping willows, stretches behind Claudia and I don't know if the real cemetery is the garden where the real Claudia is watching us, or if the false Claudia of the garden is the real Claudia of the triptych, the Claudia in black skin and bats' wings. I don't know which of the two is the head of the ravenous dog who knows how many surround him: the live men who could be, at the razor's edge, lions and wolves.

Claudia disappears, laughing.

(I will spy on her through the keyhole and I will see her spying, wrapped in a bronze-studded cape and kneeling, on the object on the bed: the black mouse in the glass tube. Covered with metal, Claudia observes the rodent: one can't be sure if that glass tube contains air or water or is a vacuum. Claudia and the mouse hypnotize each other, she covered with false coins, the mouse paralyzed by the foreign element: they look at each other and I try to hear my mother's incantatory murmurings, I kneeling outside her bedroom, a penitent before her closed door, listening to her murmur yes, one must observe a lot to change other people: look at them, look at them, look at them, she murmurs to the prisoner mouse, she smiles, asking him: "Who are

96

you?", Claudia laughs and stands up, the copper disks knocking against each other, light bell chimes, Claudia paces before the painted black mirrors, the mirrors that have ceased to reflect, and the mouse scratches the glass prison, this materialized air which lets him see everything and touch nothing, Claudia murmurs, "I'm sick of seeing myself, sick, sick" and she kneels in front of the rodent again, fixes him with the big eyes of a close-up without spectators, murmurs to him: "But I'm not tired of being seen. When I'm tired, you'll change. Look how I look. Look how I look at myself. Look how I look at you." The black mirrors surround her. Claudia's face looks for itself in a painted, blind mirror. The rug. I hadn't noticed the rug, covered with desiccated animals, dead birds, pumas and falcons, monkeys and humming birds, covered with masks, tiger and buzzard masks: Claudia puts on the eagle mask, caresses the dried body of a monkey, invokes while she paces, disguised, before the lightless mirrors, lulling the gummy monkey, invokes as I do, from the other side of the door, praying, before the keyhole, my eye would like to look at itself, my ear hear itself, my touch feel itself, I want to be two, you and me, when my eye can look at itself, I will be you to be me, you must look at me in my name, you will be the look of my look, the name of my protection.)

I can't tell whether it's the eighth or ninth martini; I lost count a while ago and all the colors, musics, materials, revolve at the same time in an elusive memory of the present.

> My love said to me,
> a hero you'll be . . .

They have all danced and are dancing. Bela, now or before, tore herself crying from the arms of the actor who is now playing the fool dancing with Iphigenia. The black or Indian girl or whatever she is has wrapped him in the great sporty foulard and the little faceless man, with whom I haven't exchanged a word, tries awkwardly to follow the girl's gliding movements: all that is natural in her is hapless imitation in him.

> . . . if you bring me the rose
> of loooove . . .

They are all dancing and, little by little, surrounding the actor. All except Hermione, who is sitting next to me, fanning her face with her Scotch plaid cap.

Hermione is a quiet spot: I tell myself this when I accept one of her cigarettes and reject the feeling of complicity I do not want to acknowledge: perhaps Hermione is not like the others. She has been telling me that in Dublin her family would get drunk and that then all of them—mother, father, children—would sing Irish Republican Army marches and recite old ballads.

> Let Erin remember the days of old
> Ere her faithless sons betray'd her . . .

The time came when they only communicated musically: they'd sing for breakfast, sing hello, sing the news from work, like *Les parapluies de Cherbourg*. Hermione grew tired and found a job in London with a high-fashion photographer. Then she discovered she could take care of herself.

"The notorious sensitivity of our time is only the old reality of narcissism. I concentrated on being the faithful reflection."

The girl photographer armed with a black and portable reservoir. A camera dedicated exclusively to capturing the moment of the new fauna, the ballad singer and the beat poet, the priest of pot, the rock groups, and the male models. Her albums of photos, she told me, were only of men and of strictly naked men. Thorax. Manes. Details.

"You know. Whatever infuriates the Establishment before they pin your British Empire medal on you."

Young boys with medals on their chests. Kittens licking their nipples. Dead pigeons on their stomachs. Streamers coming out of their navels. Lizards sleeping in their armpits.

"Crazy and eternal success. But Claudia doesn't let me, you know."

"No, I don't know."

"Don't you find that there's something very masculine about her?"

"Gossip."

"Here. Dry yourself."

Out of one of Hermione's many Edwardian pockets came the handkerchief and I rubbed it on my stained pants.

"I already lost count."

"Let me get you another. . . . That was what fascinated me."

The five women have closed in on the actor: a perfect circle: holding one another: him in the center. The prey. I don't know what they're doing. I try to follow Hermione.

"I just had to take a picture of her. She'd be the only woman in my collection. Can you imagine the fury?"

"Whose fury?"

"Of all the women excluded, dear. The most beautiful stable of virility in the United Kingdom and only one woman. Claudia. The final touch. Who's who?"

"I'm surprised she hasn't let you."

"Here. Would you like a bib with your martinis? I'm very stubborn. I pursue her like an Eumenide. I've climbed the roof of the house. I've inserted a miniobjective through the keyhole. Nothing. I never catch her naked. She protects herself like a lioness."

"Oh I see; she knows you'll leave her when you get the picture."

"She's a wretch. Once, on the set, I had the camera hidden in my bra. Claudia insulted me and undressed me in front of everybody."

Hermione snatches my drink and throws it on the floor, shouting:

"Stop getting drunk! Help me! I don't want what they're looking for! I want to take a picture of her!"

The actor has fallen on his knees. The five madwomen dance around him, enraged.

I need a witness, witness.

And the light has lost its original charm. I cannot invent the usual words of my enervated monologue before that look of impotence with which Hermione begs for complicity.

That look as repugnant as the thick atmosphere of tobacco and sweat and spilled gin which has taken hold of the drawing room. A rancid air surrounds us and I want to get up to open the stained-glass windows and I realize that the sun has set.

The spectacle of the five dancers should fascinate me but I don't see the joke.

Chicago City,
that's what the sign on the freeway reads.

The actor fell asleep some time ago, while they continue dancing around, their garments no longer as elegant and sensational as in the first hours.

How does it feel
To be on your own

I think it's Kirsten who tears off her Byzantine locket and throws it in the face of the defeated Lothario.

"Damn hag," Kirsten murmurs and looks at me.

"Witch" Vanessa strips herself of the hood and reveals the shaved skull which now sways mechanically, like a robot: like Brigitte Helm in *Metropolis*.

"Filthy hetaera" Paola goes through the top hat with her fist.

I grope, in the sudden darkness and dizziness of my senses, for the cocktail shaker. Hands confuse me, push, make me fall on all fours, at Hermione's feet. The breathings, sweats, worn perfumes, surround me, enclose me, circle around me: if I could see, I would know that the six manipulate me: they join their heads in a circle over me and far away the actor snores and stirs and stops snoring. I can hear, not identify.

"Mercy, mercy."

"Your mother."

"The whore."

"The egoist."

"The cruel one."

"The witch."

"Tell us."

"What do you know?"

"Give us a weapon."

"Satisfaction."

"Don't you love us?"

"We'll reward you."

"We'll feed you."

"We'll whip you."

"Speak."

"Don't you know who you are?"

"Pick one."

"All six."

"Why did she let you come here?"

"And I try, and I try."

"Why did she hand you over?"

"Do you know who she handed you over to?"

"To terror and cunning."

"To fury and rebellion."

"To lies and blasphemy."

"To revenge and quarrel."

"To intemperance and fear."

"To pride and defeat."

"To the titans and the Tartar."

"To the air and the mother."

"*La cochonne.*"

"The bloody bitch."

"*La mignotta.*"

"Have you ever heard her moan?"

"Cry?"

"Ask forgiveness?"

"Do you know what she does at night?"

"In the day?"

"Why do you let yourself be humiliated?"

"Tell, tell . . ."

"What do you know?"

"Free us."

"I can't get no satisfaction . . ."

"He's drunk."

"It's a long time."

Already blind, I want to be deaf. My hands are deaf and will protect me, as the darkness obstructs for me the images of the six women and only smell, treacherous and persecuted, refuses to conspire, flees giving me the running mascara, the smeared pencil, the stale perfume, the bare feet, the damp necks, the erased eyebrows, the disheveled hair: finally, them, painted black bodies, dogs' heads, vampire wings, blood-shot eyes, brass-studded scourges.

"Tell us."

"Who is she going to banish?"

"Who is she going to sacrifice?"

"Who?"

I cover my sex with my hands, but it doesn't matter; they stand me on my head, open my legs in a Y, put my head in the martini pitcher, stick flowers in my asshole, in the midst of their howls and canticles, and I see, upside down, the image of the triptych, men exposed on the treetops, pecked at by the birds and my mother, young and naked again, receives from a golden boy, with bird claws, a white flower with a black root. I close my eyes. I will be her partner. I will complete her. We were a couple. The first couple. Mother and son. Behind the couple, suffering, afflicted, the snake-haired women howl. (I will rush up the stairs. The howls come from above. Ruth is in front of the door to Claudia's bedroom. She opens her arms and blocks my way. The howls are glasslike. I want to go in.

"No."

"What's wrong with her?"

Ruth shrugs her shoulders. "She stopped smoking. She said she was bored of seeing the world through a smoke screen and she stopped smoking."

"But why is she howling? Let me in!"

"No. She has to scream. She was smoking three packs a day. The body is demanding its poison."

Her long uncontrolled look contradicts the explanation:

"But the danger is that when you stop smoking, you feel a terrific hunger. She is pure will power. She doesn't smoke and doesn't eat. She howls. Let her be. Don't be silly."

Behind the door, Claudia pulls off a pearl necklace: I hear it, that I can hear, as they roll, as those drops from the immaculate shell knock against each other, how Claudia screams behind the door, how she tells of a life I do not want to know: I prefer you empty, hollow, a white pit in the center, and not have to listen to what you're saying, mamma, if those girls only knew, you're telling them, not me, right?, let them know what you're shouting about, your loves, your ambition, your humiliations, where you came from, whom you deceived, what repugnance you felt, how coldly you calculated, what do they know, they who still want to look at themselves not knowing that you're sick of seeing yourself on the screen and in magazines and newspapers and soap and instant coffee commercials, what do they know about how much you paid to stop being an object: how you were an object to stop being one, so that nobody could handle you; how you begged so you wouldn't have to beg again; how you debased yourself to reach pride; you talk of cold rooms and hot jewels, you talk of vulgar men and bounced checks, you talk, behind your condemned door, howling, not knowing that I'm listening to you with my head on Ruth's shoulder, you laugh at yourself, you tear up old pictures of your youth, you say that you didn't know how to dress, you say that you had a cook's handwriting and you learned, through sheer will, Sacre Coeur handwriting, you say that nobody knows how much gossip, how much abuse you put up with, you say that you dragged yourself to ask forgiveness of those who couldn't give it to you, you accuse yourself of venting your anger on those who didn't deserve it, you say you were able to be free by being a slave, you talk of remoteness and distance, I don't even remember which, I don't talk about it, confess what's ailing me? never! there it stops being called pain, who wants to know my past?, keep guessing, as long as I don't remember it, it won't exist and if you have made me suffer I won't tell you nor will you see me in my hole licking my wounds, who hasn't offered me the whole sky to give me not even a piece of cloud?, and I don't hold a single grudge, and I haven't told stories about anybody, but this, yes, the man hasn't been born whom I cannot scorn, there's not a clay stud whom I haven't cracked: you shout that you have a pair of nuts like no cheap stud has, not a one of them, you are only an imagined man, the one who can only be invented to be dreamed about, your nonexistent partner, and for me, hugging Ruth, as it happens, in front of your door, listening to you, asking you, what surprise is in store?, all that I have left are premonitions, I believed in so many places that weren't mine, how many times I kept quiet, how I've swallowed words, and been surprised, surprised at knowing what I could stand, surprised at how many things were in me that I didn't know, I don't even remember now, the worst is what I guess at my own risk, the worst is that I can commit all the sins except loneliness, all except that, not loneliness, not loneliness before my face in the mirror, my face on the screen, my face in the magazine, any crime, any license, any cruelty not to stay alone with the mirror: the pearls roll, I hear them, Claudia speaks of dead, old men, seduced once by that mirror: you were them, mamma, they weren't themselves, all the painful pity of your body couldn't convince them that they were anything but your reflection, you closed the doors, you withdrew, you painted the mirrors of your bedroom black: so that nobody sees himself in you anymore. And I, who only think and live to get you back. And I. You scream again. Places. Names. Men. Jewel. Weekend. Concession. Contract. Insult. Check. Whim. Plea. Automobile. Suicide. But not loneliness, not loneliness.

"But the screams are coming from the roof!"

"Forget about them." Ruth hugs me so that I won't move. "It's a rehearsal."

"Who's on the roof?"

"I'm telling you they're rehearsing for the movie."

Claudia moans empty behind the door. Empty, she says she wants to be hollow, she says her hands aren't enough to create something new, she says they can barely substitute some things for others. I smell the spilled perfumes. I smell burnt horsehair. There are footsteps on the roof. Steps that drag a body and stretch it out in the sun. They are offering it to the buzzards. Mice scuttle over my head.

I don't know if it's the sudden blast of sun on my eyelids that awakens me, or the rustling of the curtains she opens, violent but exacting, to let the sun into this messy drawing room which I begin to make out as I rub my eyes. I still can't recognize Claudia's distant voice but I already know that the six girls are lying in the corners of the room, weary and defeated, and that my mother, who I still can't see, is talking to them: she is far away and her voice is even further than her. A stubborn murmur and half-baked, sleepy protests.

". . . and you can give me back my rags . . ."

"No."

" 'No' is what the Devil said and see where that got him."

"You gave it to me."

"And I'll take it back just like I gave it to you."

"What's in it for you?"

"My pleasure and that's more than enough."

"Claudia, please."

"Leave her alone."

"If you don't like it, get out. You're here because you want to be."

"Liar. You need us."

"I need to breathe and to taste guacamole from time to time. Period."

Paola gets up slowly. The lamé suspenders hang from her waist, but her naked torso is not attractive without the hide and seek game of the lost décolleté. And she raises her hands to her temples.

"Tomorrow I'm taking the plane back."

"With luck you'll get there safe and sound, you poor dear. You'll be better off if you die while the dying's good."

"Don't worry, I'll get there fine. I'll get out of this hell of yours and go back to where I belong, my house in Milan, where they treat me like a queen, not like here, not . . ."

"Why, you were as bored as a turtle on Lent. Some nerve. You'd do better to crash, I'm telling you. Your place is in heaven, you fool."

"Claudia . . ."

"I'm hustling you out, get it? Or do you want me to print it in the Alamos Gazette?"

"It's better alone . . . ," Paola stutters.

"Alone? Try to go it alone, dear. You'll be splendid, comfortable, beautiful, unrapable . . . and in any case you'll end up on your knees begging someone to keep you company. Who do you think you are?"

The rest gradually raise their heads, the uncombed and bright little heads, looking at Claudia as I do, finally seeing her, standing among our ruins, incredible Claudia. It's a new day, and time, which has stained the rest of us so much—"what day is it, please?"—has not touched her, bright and cold, dressed in blue, sleeveless—"woman and her clothes, an indivisible totality"—: the silver-threaded dress comes together in a great knot on her chest, an enormous bun which picks up the sparkles of mamma's flesh and those of the sun in the garden: silver and blue, Claudia with her hair down and neatly combed and the little ribbon holding it like an ocean wave in a still photo.

The young ruins gradually picked themselves up, sore from the night and the floor and the sofas. Hermione with her man's cap down to her ears. Ute with her bell-bottom pants fallen and wrinkled. Kirsten, the beggar, with the Gobelins cloth thrown over her shoulder. Chilly and bleary-eyed Iphigenia: the yellow eyes of the blacks.

"Aren't you going to thank me?" Claudia shouts at Paola. "I'm letting you go. You can get off the boat. Take your junk and scram!"

And the rest look at each other and Paola with tears in her eyes. I can't stand it and yet I stay there, in a loose corner of this edgeless room. Claudia is not addressing me.

"Please." Paola hangs her head and rubs her arms.

"What's so hard for you, then? Go back to your hicks and fend for yourself." My mother crosses her arms.

"They're not going to take me back. I broke with everything to follow you. They say I am dishonored . . . that's what they say."

Claudia's snicker: "Honor and love have never gotten along. Where they offer you moralizing is where you find hate. It's no use. You already know that if I accept one, another has to leave. You're all a pain in the neck."

"Let her stay!" Hermione answers the snicker.

Claudia arches her eyebrow: "Only I stay. You pass. I last."

Ah, the eyebrow. Like in the movies. What a laugh. If she only realized I am laughing. And that, immediately, I stop laughing. That I cannot make fun of her. Calm, elegant, fresh, with her arms crossed and her eyebrow arched.

"I'll think about it, brat. You look too good in last year's clothes, but if you don't make the sacrifice, one of you has to. More than five at a time gets on my nerves. And there's not enough cake to go around."

Hermione shrugs her shoulders: *"If that's the case . . ."*

"No, not you" jingle Claudia's enormous earrings. "You're the only one who doesn't inherit anything from me. It's the others who handle my things and think they own them. Ah, but how they like the left-overs,"—my mother laughs motionless. "My clothes and my men. Keep talking, numbskulls, after all, words don't kill. And don't lose hope: I'll keep passing you my used goods. I like to have my garbage dump close at hand, so don't worry."

"You're not so young any more"—Ute laughs, with a belch; she steps forward and stops, dizzy; her hands look for the support of a chair.

"And you, yankee pup, there you are, under the table like a bitch, waiting at twenty for me to sweep my zombies' crumbs your way."

Claudia says it without emotion but caresses her neck and smiles.

"Forgive me." Ute plops down suddenly. "Forgive me, Claudia."

"Listen, I'm not the Holy Father to be going around handing out absolutions." Those hands on her hips, Claudia the guerrilla fighter. "Forgive yourself. And get it straight that I'm not afraid of old age. I'm afraid of wasting myself. But where there's a will . . . No, puppies, you'll see me at eighty yet, with my dog collar, all dressed in black and flourishing a gold-headed cane to drive away the boys who say "it's her, it's her" when they see me go by straighter than a Prussian general. Why go on?"

She turns her back on us, looks at the garden and crosses her arms again. You're betraying yourself, Claudia; that impatient heel tapping.

"No. None of you have to go."

She laughs and caresses her hair. Tics, Claudia. I'm watching you.

"Of course you'll all go when your time comes, like the others. When you get married or die. Let nobody say I'm not a good mother."

Don't look at us, Gorgon, don't take away our lives without killing us first, don't give us the still death of your look.

"It's not necessary. We're one big happy family. Bela is going to go."

They all look at each other, humiliated and satisfied. The imposed clothing hangs on them like talismans. Like a new pig skin. Claudia turns on her heel and looks us in the face: at all and at nobody.

"Enjoy yourselves. Where is that fool?"

They look at each other; one—I don't remember her anymore—dares to look at me.

"I don't know"—Iphigenia grunts. "He was asleep on the floor. He must have gone."

Close your eyes, mamma. Don't ask for me. I have come, isn't that enough? I have been your witness and I will never inform on you. I am invisible, the way you want it. Do you think I'm so weak? No, you know what I'm capable of.

"Does anybody else want him? This time I'm not forcing him upon you. Once was enough. No? Then don't touch him again. Nobody is to speak to him. We're leaving on Friday."

This Is the Truth

I knew they were there. Maybe it was the smell that revealed them. I'm probably inventing, I'm trying to blame smell for something that is the responsibility of another sense which I'm afraid of acknowledging and accepting. Chekhov says that when we die, five of our senses stop functioning and another ninety-five begin to live. And one of these is telling me that I'm not alone in my bedroom. That other presences sniff and throb in the dark, around the bed, among the curtains: only an aura. But it's the smell of dry metallic blood. Of scars that won't heal. Of damp curly hair. Of red anuses. Of black paws.

I don't move. I don't try to take my hand out of its warm hiding place between my legs, my arm out of its shelter under the covers, to light the night lamp, the violet and blue lead-encased lamp which is next to the headboard: I imagine the books on the same headboard, the inevitable books, *Les Caves du Vatican, A Rebours, The Picture of Dorian Gray, The Quest for Corvo, Cardinal Pirelli,* as if their own fictitious existence could dispel that of the other, immediate, fiction: mediate it. It's useless. I don't try to without first imagining the rhythmic spasm of the livers and intestines and hearts that accompany the beating of my own. I imagine, and can't, the bedroom full of sun, before this permanent darkness, barely interrupted by the noises, never by another light, takes over.

The needle, very far away, scrapes on the record label. Did I forget to turn off the stereo? That's all it is. No. I didn't forget. I forgot to close the living room window: is the filmless projector purring and making the reels turn and look at themselves in a painting of white and empty light? The water in the bathroom; the gas flame; the refrigerator motor; a telegram slipped under the door?; is the maid snoring? at night, I know it, I tolerate it, she lets her lover in, does the cot in that bare room creak?; and when I reach one hand under the bed to find my slippers, the other toward the bureau to find a cigarette, next to put the light on, I swear it, I touch near the bed and under it the moist flesh, the foamy animal lips. Under the bed: water and tissues, damp cardboard. Don't hide, brat; the kidnappers are coming now.

I smell them, I feel them. They are all there, invoked by loneliness, sent to keep me and threaten me with their low growl, which grazes the ground, the ground of Persian rugs and parquet and glazed tiles, and sniff among the hidden places of my furniture and my flesh.

I turn on the light. I'm not dreaming. I'm not deceiving myself. Never. All is true.

I let them die, get lost, run away, destroy themselves.

I closed the door to the bathroom. Lavatory: *l'abbatoir*.

I denied them food and I scolded Gudelia for the first time when I found her giving them bones. She cried.

I saw them come back wounded from their nocturnal escapades and I let the wounds from other fangs and claws become infested.

I put up with scabs and mucus and almost the rabies, almost the rabies . . .

I turned up the volume of the record player to the point of driving them crazy with their own barking.

I let them loose in the middle of the street, I threw them out of the car into the traffic, to the wheels and brakes, and there they stayed, for days, their bellies split open.

I was their surgeon. I amputated their tails and paws and let them bleed to death.

I have only one dog left, Pharaoh, obedient and faithful and lonely. He doesn't reproach me for anything. Terror has tamed him, faithful and affectionate Pharaoh. I spoil him and attend to his wants. His red collar is beautiful, adorned with bronze studs. Long, tired, with his prominent rib cage, he knows how to keep me company.

I stay with him after turning off the projector and without putting the lights on in the living room, I draw near the open window of my seventh floor and peer out into the night of Mexico City.

There's a breeze, it's a bit cold.

The automobiles head up toward San Angel and Coyoacán, the taxis go downtown empty. A neon *charro* hat and jumping lasso advertise a nightclub; a colorful rooster, a restaurant. If there were some kids on the street during the day, they now sleep; those poor kids who try to sell the last copy of *Extra* can't possibly be kids, but they are the only life on the street, with their poorly shaven heads and black, bare feet with rose-colored scabs.

The murmur of the trees: you can see their tops, from here, waving in black masses. Further on, night-covered light reflected on the streets and windows. The still ashes of the volcanos. The darkness.

The curtains wrap around me, standing by the window. They hide me, like a monk's cloak, they protect me.

The Swallows

> . . . the party was over.
> —Fitzgerald,
>   *The Great Gatsby*

The snapping flashes, the firing squad of photographers, the dense row of cameras blind me and I am far away, trying to make my way through, while Ruth steps out of the first car and gives orders to the porters, and from the trunk and rack and the inside of the car come the twenty odd pieces, all in blue leather, hat boxes, jewelry cases, plastic and silk garment bags, the *nécessaire* and the mink rug for the night flight over the Atlantic. The jewel case remains in Ruth's hands; also the nylon folders with passports, tickets, travelers' checks, smallpox certificates . . .

Claudia steps out of the Mercedes wearing her ermine-lined green gabardine coat and her hair braided in the green and gold turban. She poses against the door of the car and enters the long airport tunnel, followed by the pack, sometimes at a slow pace, other times, quick, playing with the reporters' breathlessness, and the illegibility of their notebook scribblings: I let myself be carried along, sometimes near, sometimes far from her, from Claudia who toys with her dark glasses as she walks. Ruth has stayed behind, attending to the baggage and transactions . . .

"How does it feel to be a star?"

"It's something that burns in silence, but burns slow."

"Is it true you're going to take diction lessons?"

"Diamonds aren't parrots, mister."

"What's your favorite fashion?"

"The one that only my mirror has seen."

"Do you prefer men or women as friends?"

"Women, if all men are like you."

"What kind of man do you prefer?"

"The one I most easily forget."

"What is pleasure?"

"A way of accepting things."

"Do you have many enemies?"

"All the people who owe me a favor."

"And many friends?"

"All the people who are still expecting a favor from me."

"What do you feel about being a mother?"

"That I have what you lack."

"If you hadn't been Claudia Nervo, who would you have liked to be?"

"A Claudia Nervo fan."

"What is a good movie?"

"The one the spectator thinks he dreamed when he's leaving the theater."

"What's your opinion of the public?"

"That it's going to last longer than me."

"Time, Claudia, time . . ."

"We have to let it cool us off but not harden us."

"Would you like to be fifteen again?"

"Yes, to lose my innocence again."

"What age do you declare in your passport?"

"Mister, do I look like I need a passport?"

"Have you destroyed many men?"

"I've won all my medals in self-defense."

"What's your opinion of Mexican men?"

"They love themselves too much."

"And American men?"

"They love their mammas too much."

"And the Italians?"

"They think they're sultans, but in my harem, I rule."

"Do you believe in sincerity?"

"It's the least obvious form of hypocrisy."

"What has been your biggest mistake?"

"I haven't made it yet. It would be to answer your question."

"Have you ever thought of suicide?"

"Me? And how will I read the commentaries?"

"Come on, Claudia, tell us how old you are."

"One day more than yesterday, the same as you, you virginal prune."

"What do you use to preserve your beauty?"

"Hay and pumice stone."

"Are you going to miss us?"

"There's nothing like Mexico."

"What do you think of Fellini?"

"Divine, simply divine."

"Did you like making a film with Buñuel?"

"Snails and spiders stole the show from me."

"Aren't you thinking of retiring?"

"Where to?"

"Are you very rich?"

"One hundred million red corpuscles worth."

"What's all that you're taking in your suitcases?"

"The *Encyclopedia Britannica.*"

"Is it true this will be your last movie?"

"Can't you tell? Well you're wrong."

"Romance with the leading man?"

"I haven't read the script yet."

"In Rome will you ask for an audience with the Pope?"

"That's a very old joke. The Calvary is more beautiful than the Cross."

"How much is your wardrobe worth?"

"A little less than the hanger . . ."

Near and far away, pushed, elbowing my way through, I hear her say these senseless things, things capable of intriguing the newspapermen, of providing them with copy, but also things which, in some way, bear witness to her immunity to a flattery she seems to accept, a flattery she rejects, smiling: fame is water thrown on that burning pyre which cannot be consumed as long as she doesn't give up something that goes beyond fame: fame continues being a step toward something . . .

"I'm her son . . ."

The guard lets me into the VIPs' waiting room, solitary, cool and almost underwater in its greenish light which screens the smoked windows.

I look instinctively for a dark corner, next to one of the ornamental palm trees in a flower pot, almost afraid that someone, coming in, would guess, like a horse, my nervous fear.

Perhaps I shouldn't have come. Perhaps I should return another day to this same place to pronounce a sad and sleepy monologue. I don't remember, no, I can't remember which of the two, in this moment, should feel offended; whose turn it is, at this moment, to resume the aggression or give the first show of affection; I can't distinguish, waiting for her here, between the love and hate which she and I owe each other, between the rejection and acceptance that tie us together like Siamese twins: I no longer know which should inflict the wound and which kiss it. Like a bad chess player, I don't know if this is my turn. Or which piece to move.

I laugh absentmindedly, looking outside, toward the pad of rever-berating concrete dotted with resting airplanes. A grotesque world, as grotesque as the interview I've just witnessed, will resolve my dilemma without asking my permission, without respecting my feelings . . .

"You believe everything they tell you," Claudia laughs behind me. "My legend has grown because I've pushed it. What am I complaining about?"

I watch her take off her gloves and throw them on a sofa. I look at her out of the corner of my eye, turning my back on her, not knowing at what point to resume this relationship of such solid outbursts be-tween such prolonged absences. I've lost the thread.

I murmur, in the dark. "I think it's disgusting, disgusting . . ."

"Don't be so sensitive, darling. I understand more than you think. Would you like a drink?"

I don't want to look at her. I've lost the confidence of youth, if ever I had it. "That poor idiot, that greased-up nothing. With that you create your legend?"

"Not all of them are prestige movies. Sometimes you make a bomb. The important thing is to know how to present it with a lot of fanfare. You can live off that for a century."

I'm afraid to look at her, like a drunk is afraid to look at himself in the mirror when he wakes up. "And the girls . . . they take the first thing . . ."

"I'm telling you again, precious. The first act was so sensational that at curtain time the show goes on, even if the theater is empty. I picked the right stage: Paris. And the actor: Gombrowicz."

"Oh, I don't want to listen to you. I wish I were alone. And there isn't any famous actor named Gombrowicz."

"He acted in the convents and on the borders. He was a Polish Jesuit who fled after the war and finally settled in Paris with his clan. You know the Jesuits; you studied with them. They have to know the world to defend the faith. They go out into the wind exposed and then they don't want to catch pneumonia."

I cover my ears for a moment, to block out her laugh.

"Gombrowicz ended up being a snowball in hell. Or an orchid in the North Pole. Whichever you prefer. I figure that after escaping disguised as a railroad worker, he believed that the cassock was the disguise. In the cassock he only lived; in railroad worker's suit he saved his life. Or perhaps he thought he had already fulfilled his obligation to be a martyr."

I begin to move around, incredulous, to assure myself that Claudia is there and telling me these things.

"And I, not to be less, disguised myself as a Pueblan woman on our national holiday and went to the altar of the Guadalupe Virgin in Notre Dame so that all the Mexicans would see me. Nobody got scared; the altar was already covered by a Saltillo serape."

"You, the Pueblan Woman and the Virgin. The most holy trinity in skirts."

"And there was Father Gombrowicz."

Now it's my turn to laugh. "Telephone calls, waiting rooms, long waits in the hotel lobby. The smitten priest."

"No, you don't know this story and if you interrupt me, here is where we part. I didn't ask you to come."

"I'm sorry. Then, you seduced him?"

"Wrong again. Our little typist. Her Indian blood showed through that twelfth of December and she decided to confess her sins right there and then. The saint got into her and she kneeled before the priest. I was green with envy. Ruth turned pious on us, out of pure nostalgia. If she had found a lost mariachi, she would have fallen in love with him, too. Not a chance: the Virgin stayed in her sackcloth, but the priest was willing to listen to our Ruth. First in the church, then in the parks, until the holy man settled down in our suite at the George V."

There she is, telling me this story I didn't ask for, this story which she's surely inventing, which is probably true, but crude and simplified like a cartoon. And nevertheless, she herself, Claudia, the narrator, does not physically enact what she's telling me: she is this faraway cathedral of demolished laces, this intertwined ascension of something which I can only make out as two arches of a fleeting brilliance, destined to meet in some dark crown, there, in the unbreathable air of this valley. Or in the jet's pressure cabin. Yes, perhaps she's no longer here, and that's why she talks:

"By then, Ruth had gotten back to normal. She no longer wanted to see him and that only upset the little father more."

One step, only one step, Claudia, and the illusion vanishes. You're there and your way of lighting the cigarette is hard and ugly.

"It was I who had gotten used to the coming and going of that pained and serious young man with the clean-shaven face, and to hearing the rustling of his cassock."

The frozen daiquiris are waiting on the table. By picking up the drink, I can turn my back on my mother.

"I would come back from the set exhausted, go to bed, and hear the footsteps and the rustling of the cassock."

And her hand has taken my arm. Before I could realize it.

"Then I realized one thing, Mito. Or rather, I asked myself a question."

She makes me, by imperceptible force, face her.

"Who is looking for me? Have you ever asked yourself that? Have you never felt that somebody, without your knowing, is looking for you? . . ."

And all that vague and sweet fragrance, of perfume and carmine, comes up from her lips and her breasts and her ear lobe. . . .

"Yes . . . I feel it all the time. And I control myself, I keep myself back . . ."

The separation is immediate, light, predictable.

"That's where you and I are different."

But if Claudia turns her back on me, her hand takes mine and squeezes it. I don't want to see it like this, like a stage direction; I can't help it. This whole story looks too much like *découpage*.

"The nearness of the priest made me think I was at death's door, that I was dying in bed. Priest and death, like night and moon. And I refused to die without having completed myself. I felt afraid of dying and above all afraid of dying of fear, or of exhaustion, or mere annoyance."

She leans her head on my shoulder and I don't know how to move my hands, which squeeze the snowy crust of the glass.

"I was about to break down, darling. I wanted to call the priest so that he could listen to me and give me absolution."

She closes her eyes.

"I felt nervous, tired; it was my first movie in Europe and I didn't have the same prestige I had in Mexico. It was like beginning again. The director didn't give me my place, I spoke French badly and came third in the credits. I was going to let myself be beaten."

It's the first time I feel her smaller than myself; the first time she raises her face to meet mine and offers me the temptation of caressing her chin and keeping her features still. . . .

"I was going to resign myself to peace and tranquillity. To let the priest come in and see this, a death because of fear, annoyance, and exhaustion, and absolve me from those same sins. And they all lived happily ever after. But, Mito, I reacted like a panther."

I put my free hand on the nape of her neck.

"If they give me absolution, I die. I accept that the priest is the priest and that his profession is to absolve me; and then I accept that I want to live and die in peace."

I think I'm going to hug her. But I don't know where to put the glass, how to get rid of it; I grope for the table. . . .

"Nonsense. The creaking footsteps and the rustling cassock on the other side of the door had to be more than that. Everything has to be more than it seems, or life wouldn't be any fun."

How could I believe that there was a tenderness in that hoarse voice meant for me?

"Just like that: passion and sanctity instead of peace and tranquillity. Ruth had only warmed him up. Perhaps he thought Ruth was calling him, because it was dark in the bedroom."

She realized it before I did and she herself moved away from me, got up again, to be above me. I describe objects and movements. It doesn't matter. The words we say to each other have nothing to do with our presence and our movements.

"Did people find out?"

I offer her a drink and she rejects it with a wave of her turbaned, braided hair.

"They had to find out. He went everywhere with me, frocked. To the set, to the races, to Maxim's, to Deauville . . . It seems like another era."

"Yes, it's a Bonnard poster. *Tous les soirs*. France-Champagne. A lot of photographs, surprise and admiration, the movie director's new attitude, fame?"

I said it with my best face of wronged dignity. Who am I accusing of being melodramatic and grotesque? Only then I made my mother into a figure of triumphant dignity: neither as far, nor as near as the one I imagined a moment ago.

"It didn't last long, but it wasn't enough. The bishop took away his cassock and poor Gombrowicz stopped being fun. In civilian clothes, even his face changed. The pain made him poor, weak, and ugly. Without his friar rags, the secret simply became fear."

"And the passion became annoying. You passed on to him what you were afraid of."

"Just like that. You can see that I don't stop and think. All that I know, I know like that. I don't know. Yes, perhaps that's all I wanted. . . . The other actress in the movie asked me to introduce him to her, to see if she could repeat the coup. I became the sweet little father's manager. I set him up in a hotel room, a rather modest room . . ."

"A very delicate detail."

". . . and first the actress, then a society girl and then a model; they all began to call me for introductions to the *défroqué*. Gombrowicz became a kind of passport to fame. He put the cassock on again. His second glory was to feel like a rebel. By the time I left Paris he was only an agent provocateur. A caricature of himself. But the girls never abandoned me from then on, nor I them. In my fashion. Now you see I'm not shortchanging them. In fact, I give them much more than they give me. A court for me and sure publicity, eroticism of sorts, and the best clothing in the world, for them; well, even if the affection and the rags are secondhand."

"And Gombrowicz?"

"He still has some success with American hags. He makes them feel they really are in Paris. He offers them instant French vice. My movie came out and the audience felt it was about to attend a religious orgy. At the snap of a finger."

She has to snap them so I won't doubt her presence.

I drink the daiquiri.

"Did you go to bed with him?"

"You're so off the track you're not even offensive, my love. Gombrowicz had power as long as he looked for me. Once he finds me, he's dead. Just like my girls' boyfriends. Nobody interests me when he stops looking for me. No, I too knew how to control myself, like you, but still in possession. You've got to know how to have things without wasting them. You, darling, don't even have them for fear of wasting them."

Now that the moment has passed, I have to come near her, awkwardly, not knowing how to hug her, like a kid: "I would like to understand you, mamma. But I'm happy enough that you let me keep you company for a while."

"We're not going to see each other for seven months."

"That's why everything you tell me today will be the only thing I'll remember in all that time. . . ."

"Listen, precious. Sometimes I think you're pulling my leg."

"Why?"

"Because all you do is repeat lines from my movies. You know them by heart! What you just said, I said around '45. As if it mattered what they make me say in the movies."

"You're a star."

"Oh, come on, Mito."

I don't know if I should admit a victory or proclaim a defeat. We are parting again, this time, both at the same time: a time seen while it is happening, like getting to a party we had just left, the attempt to recover it only a bitter return. And Claudia says, remote again:

"No, darling, none of this is free, that I'll tell you."

She says this when I can no longer get her back. She says now what she should have said in my arms: "We all need compensations, of course. . . . We all have to choose. . . . Well, make believe this is all the letters I'm not going to write you: Make believe."

But I have—I think I have—the last move, the letter.

" 'I don't know if you are truly happy. But I consider it my obligation, as always on the days of family events, to send you my regards and repeat to you . . .' "

"What's that? What are you reading?"

" '. . . and repeat to you that this is your home and here you will have the opportunity . . .' "

"Darling! Let me read that letter!"

" '. . . to set yourself on the right road and recover the moral foundation that I wanted to give you . . .' "

"No! Mito!"

" '. . . your father who loves you . . .' "

"Darling, you're killing me. . . ."

"I want to tear it into pieces, right now. . . ."

"Do it, Mito . . . but don't make me die laughing; your father the redhead was never any good at blackmail, only at selling school supplies."

". . . and throw them out the window. . . . Like that. You can stop laughing."

The heat and dry wind come in through the window. We stand a moment, she and I, while all the noises invade this underwater cloister: the jet engines, the confused voices of the loudspeakers. Claudia puts on her gloves.

"Do what you like, I tell you. But don't think I feel obliged to you. I say it to your face. You like to dramatize everything."

"No, look, I couldn't tear up the check."

Ruth comes nervously into the room, with the passports and boarding passes, the jewel case and the mink rug. Claudia nods.

"I hate to disappoint you. I love you but I don't need you."

The doors to the field open. Claudia starts walking. I run to stop her. I take my mother's arm and she smiles at me:

"Don't believe everything I tell you. It's only my legend. Do you think I know why I was born? Do you think I'm convinced that it was only for what you see me do? Good-bye, Mito. Be seeing you. Knock on wood."

I know that I mustn't cross the threshold. She can, with overloaded Ruth behind her; not her: she puts on her dark glasses, finishes putting on her gloves, goes out into the sun, outside the inclosure, the space restricted to consecrate and protect us—temple, palace, apartment— out to the handkerchief-waving public behind the wire fences, to the airlines employee who hands her a corsage of orchids, to the band of mariachis who play that sad music which accompanies the distant and lost Claudia, Claudia who goes out to meet Claudia, outside the holy places, among the noises and tumult and threats: she waves her hand from the stairs of the plane and disappears.

And Ute and Vanessa, Iphigenia and Paola, Hermione and Kirsten run across the field, like puppets moved by their steel wires, loaded down with cameras and plastic garment bags, hatboxes and bottles of tequila: Ute waves a piñata in the air.

I look at the jet which begins to tremble. The engines create all those layers of undulating and transparent heat. I look along the port- holes, blinded by the sun. There, behind one of them, that distant face leans on a hand and looks at me. Bela and I look at each other for the

118

last time. The stewardess closes the door. The plane makes a full turn
and it's too late.

Silver Screen

To photograph a face is to photograph a soul.
—Godard,
Le petit soldat

Pharaoh does not move from his place when I get up from the chair to
show that this story must end here, and I take the screen out of the
closet, roll it open, and place it on the tripod. I stoop to pick up the
cans. I press a button and the projector appears between two rows of
false books with gold spines: an intriguing imitation of Cobden-
Sanderson bindings. I insert the reel and snap my fingers so that
Pharaoh will come to me. The dog obeys, moving reluctantly, and
again settles down at my feet. I turn off the lights and run the movie.

The worn copy blinks and jumps at the beginning, but then Claudia
appears riding a horse on a South American plain, and her stiff face,
her mask of youth, draws all the light and shadow as she spurs the
horse and there, forever, are her aqueous dark eyes, the only eyes
which by virtue of darkness create light, as if to deny something were
the only way to finally conquer it. And her full, cruel lips twist in a
grimace of hate and her Spanish hat falls on the ground as she brutally
halts the horse. My mother's hair becomes light, waving, a flame of ivy
and algae and snakes; from the horse, she horsewhips the poor drunkard who had been her lover and the scene is prolonged, repeated,
because I have all that was filmed, before the discards and cuts, and this
act of violence is not pretended, it is prolonged as my mother gets off
the horse and adds the force of her boots to the beating and the
drunkard, face down in the dust, raises his hands and begs for pity, not
to heaven but to the director of the movie, and then the assistant and
the boys on the staff stop her, hold her, snatch the whip from her, and
Claudia's eyes are full of sad anger and her lips, of foam, and the
makeup woman comes over and wipes the edges of her lips with cotton
pads.

The film, with the yellow tail that joins the clips, jumps and now my
mother, in another drama, comes down the marble staircase of a
tropical mansion, to the salon where the poor actor, unawares, prepares

a couple of highballs, his gaze lost in the wide sea and the inevitable moon. Claudia stops to look at him without being seen.

This is her image.

Oh yes, this one, above all. Since what does her Gorgon's hair, her lips that almost spill blood, her great eyes of cruel almond, the gothic arch of her eyebrow, the mole on her cheek, the whiteness of a neck on which you guess the secret marks of the night, the proud majesty of her breasts, pleasure and nourishment, mean, except that desire is the root of cruelty? Claudia keeps walking, décolleté, all in white, dragging an ermine fur (in the tropics, Good God!) toward the obvious consummation of desire in destruction. She walks to love, she walks desiring; but only she, and never we, admits that what is desirable is desperately painful. Claudia knows that the desired one must pay for the moments of unsatisfied desire: the other must pay for the time between desire and satisfaction—the only time of our real pain, which is only the frustration of desire—accepting cruelty, relative pain, once she conquers it. But there is something more, and this image of Claudia on the silver screen confirms it: known for her beauty, the Medusa demands to be recognized for her horror.

Magnificent defense, now that the actor discovers her and offers her the glass and she drinks, looking at him, looking at him steadily, bewitching him, preparing what must follow the predicted act of satisfaction that is already worn out in the great imaginary pool of Circe, who has already seen in all of them the potential fate of the hog, the ass and the castrated lion. Before fulfilling the first desire, the second demands its dominion, its countersense: the Beauty offers herself and challenges the prince to discover the Beast, beauty corrupted, the exquisite corpse that hides inside her: the stained and obscene monster who, in turn, contains the certain resurrection of the Beauty. All power is inverted, and when Claudia kisses the leading man, we already know that he'll never understand. That Claudia's life is an endless pilgrimage which never finds the answer of a Lucifer capable of joining her game of mirrors. Exiled, because there is no act of creation without a beautiful fallen angel reflecting my mother's lost beauty when she will be completed in the image of death and will assume the probable horror, she announces it with that infernal tremor when she recovers, thanks to the reflection, the mask of candor and of life.

I understand this seeing her lying on that glossy divan of the forties, opening her arms, Claudia, out of this world and out of its times, Justine, Dragon Lady, Praying Mantis, Belle Dame Sans Merci, Pussy

Galore, enormous lip of flesh and fuzz and clear opaqueness and black salts: you've lost innocence but not nature. And because you know it, you've never said you're sorry. The fall has left you intact: you should have been Jehovah and Lucifer, Gaya and Eumenide, because no one has been able to accompany you either in the creation or the loss of your life. That is your strength. Because of that they cannot judge or condemn you, Claudia: you are as complete and necessary in your hell as in your paradise. Devour him, devour him, devour the mannikin in the white tuxedo with the clipped mustache and a carnation in his lapel, he dares to kiss you without understanding you, mamma, devour him. . . .

I violently caress Pharaoh's neck until the beast lets out a howl. I caress him gently. The scene changes. Claudia Nervo walks along a strange landscape of another era. She's wearing a monastic habit and is climbing toward a castle or a monastery. Angelic voices accompany her. Claudia, moved, stops. A little boy runs toward her from the door of that fortress, that space built to save itself from space and to consecrate space. Claudia kneels down and opens her arms. The little boy who escapes from the temple or fortress reaches the unprotected place of my mother and kisses her. She closes her eyes and caresses his hair, lulls him, protects him forever, saves him, yes, saves him forever from the world and danger. I don't know where she'll take him, now that both walk hand in hand and leave the monastery behind.

Sweet and pretty and faraway, I cry.

Terrible and beautiful and faraway, the dissolves I ordered follow. Claudia, you are the general's mistress and for him you leave your home and walk barefoot toward the twilight with the troops, toward the fade-out, oriental dancer with your adamantine navel, wrapped in gauzes and hashish smoke dissolved in the skies of buzzards who look at you, mute and hieratic among the nets of the native fishermen, and you are, in my editing, the cabaret singer in a false and smoking Macao, the camp follower in a battlefield of cardboard rocks, the army nun in a Lima of viceregal stage props and the queen of the Belle Époque in ostrich feathers; you are the incredibly beautiful young woman, dead on a horse, you are the madam of a brothel of the twenties and the schoolteacher in a lost, sad village, you are the Mayan princess sitting at the foot of the Tajín pyramid and your faces follow one after the other on my screen and there I have you forever: did you imagine, when offering them, that your faces would be for me and not for the priests and colonels and impresarios and chiefs and viceroys and millionaires and spies and two-timing daddies who transitorily kissed and caressed them in my name? The camera didn't rob you of your face: it preserved it for me, your son, the starnapper.

Dissolve, pretty Claudia, my one and only Claudia, dissolve in all the mirrors of my loneliness. I am, I will always be, the fallen angel of your creation, I will film for you and for me the scene which is missing, the forbidden scene, the one which really steals away our soul.

My story ends here. In this solitude. No one can continue it. No trespassing. I don't want to know the rest; nobody should. But solitude tells me that I'm not alone. That there's something else. I deny it. I am the narrator. I have the power of life and death over this story. I refuse to continue. I forbid you to continue reading. As on the screen, the words "The End" are inscribed here. All the rest should not be seen, should not be read, there's no gain in it; there's only risk, the tedium and confusion of the intermissions. I want to stay here, the day Claudia flew to Italy, seeing the former youth of her movies.

I look and—I can't help it—I think. Between frames, a certainty is established: I only know that I won't know anything. At some moment—I'd like to pinpoint it—I gave up the knowledge of my mother. I didn't want to admit what I knew. And perhaps, it's that all this time I've been writing a book I'll never write. And a book doesn't refer us to a meaning: a book is. A book isn't made for us to recognize ourselves in. It's simply a book, supremely indifferent to us. But besides, if my life is in a certain way a spectacle, then some eyes will know how to discover the absolute similitude—maybe, confusion— between what they see and what they read. Claudia passes over the screen and there is not, for me, a difference between the space and the thought. I will never know more. The mystery of the world is the visible.

Card Tricks

> . . . faithful to the ancient terror . . .
> —Borges,
> *The Widow Ching, Pirate*

I don't understand how I could have imagined it differently. It's a poor, sad, Italian town. They said it was supposed to be happy, that the south takes the cake. Because it doesn't know any other customs. The teen-agers in the dim, leaking poolrooms. The shoemaker and the bakery, the shops with boxes of chocolates and dusty, old and old-fashioned hats. And some modern things come, gratify, resign. The families get together in the bars to watch television. At the movie house, the posters announce double bills of the labors of Hercules and coming attractions: spaghetti westerns. The hero, naked under his lion skin, armed with a Winchester, always surrounded by violence and love, palaces in flames, bar brawls, tigers and horses, identical women, Barbarellas of Crete and Arizona. A loudspeaker on the street, in the rain, transmits the film's dialogues to the indifferent townspeople. *Sono Ercule: nulla me resiste.* And the statue in the square, facing the railroad station, repeats the slogan on the pedestal of that bronze veteran: *Nulle resiste ai bersaglieri.* We are cut in half. The first man, the true one, the all powerful, the one who could conceive himself, must have been androgynous, to fertilize himself and give birth to his first son. There is no other reality to genesis. The people walk close to the houses, in the rain. The apartment building has been rented: the clothes hung out to dry, stretched between the windows, are getting wet. I'm back.

You push me and then I do feel the terror. No longer that fabricated one, of my dogs and their possible aggressions. No: the physical terror of feeling less than a known and catalogued animal: the other being, born of the original labyrinths, prematurely: blind because I don't have to see, mute because I don't have to talk: smell and touch: skin and claws, cold scales, vibrating external ears, webbed hands, tapir, anteater snout; new joints, different rhythm: of the toad or chameleon, necessary to survive, escape, climb, jump. It would not be a big jump; first I raise my chest to the wall of this dry canal and immediately try to lift myself up. You stop me. Your hands touch my shoulders again, to prevent my escape and health. I smell and touch. The burnt air. The dry tar. The pulsating lubrication. My knees, scraped when I fell. My hands, weak when I scratch. Health and escape: jump back to the platform, run feverishly through checkered labyrinths, iron staircases, connecting tunnels and exits which invite and tempt me and I am almost buried in this matrix of spasmatic nerves: Port de Clignancourt, Porte d'Orléans. If only I could escape. These are the last trains. We'll return to the hotel. Tomorrow you'll take me to Orly. Today, your arms prevent my motion of salvation; you hug me and murmur that there's no time. I have time to look at you again though: the scarf rolled around your neck, the sweat on your face in this nocturnal subway. There is no time. You don't have a watch; you don't own anything. But the station clock warns us. You repeat what you said a moment before pushing me toward the rails: exactly one minute between the train that comes out of la Cité and the one that leaves from Odéon. Exactly one minute. I yield. Your arms and chest feel that I yield and begin to walk: you push me: to run; only a minute between the two trains. Saliva fills my mouth, spills from my lips; I don't have to see, only run at your side, into the tunnel, pass and forget the entrance lights and the warning that again stops me, without my daring to sob. Danger of death. Public works. I turn around again to see the station we're leaving. St. Michel. And your punch throws me to the ground, between the shining rails of the labyrinth's mouth. Do you want to die? Run like mad, like the dickens, like a bat out of hell, like a house on fire, into the grotto, further and further in, toward the center of the urinary, dripping, porous earth, full of placentas of carbonized stone and electric stalactites: avoid cables, rifles, walls: run breathless, tearless, blind, spilling your saliva and your mucus and your urine: don't touch, don't look at what you shouldn't, let smell guide you, running, tripping in the dark, between the cold steels which should guide you, now, in the center of the corridor: don't fall, get up, scratch me if you want, but don't stop, there's no time! To stay forever in the matrix of the earth is to become gold: all extracted metal loses the chance of being so; gold is a mineral that has lasted a long time; all veins would be golden if nobody touched them, if they let them gestate and last, masters of the time of silence. I only know how to swallow; the air is metal, the saliva is my veins, the sweat, the smoke of my corridors of smell and trembling: I have a body: danger tells me so: nails, when they tear them off; eyes, when they puncture them; penis, when they cut it off: a small boy in the bathtub. Danger: bat ears hear it without seeing or touching it. I already said it didn't matter to be blind and mutilated: I hear the whistle blast, the rapid pulse behind me and my swollen legs, paralyzed by varices, occlusions, gangrenes, embolisms they didn't know about: your hand, your arm: don't leave me. The trains are going to cross each other. Cross us. Odéon. Ulysses had a beautiful trip. *Visitez la Grèce.* 700NF, *tout compris.*

I would follow them. At a distance. The highway is very wide and you can follow far behind another car without losing sight of it. The scenery would not distract me from that concentration. I would not read the names of the towns. I would not stop at the service stations. I would wait outside Orvieto, in my car rented from Hertz in Rome. I would imagine them paying the sexton of the Duomo to turn the light on the frescos in the chapel. All those men have their backs to us. There is an impenetrable sodomy—you say—in the murals of the Creation and the Apocalypse: all turn their backs on the ancient terror of dying and being born, but Signorelli turns fear into sensuality, the same as us. Amber and blue, the lights of the two acts are identical; the solitary achiever does not require portents or contrasts.

I would wait for them. I know where they have to go. Where I want to take them. Is there another place? Only this landscape, that I will not want to look at—cultivated and gentle, nourished, like those who are still to be born, by the wind which disseminates the myriad possible creatures all along the calm rivers, to the heights of the castles in ruins, to the depths of the misty valleys, to the twining of the grapevines—can hide its negation where the two of you must stop.

The car must be parked in front of some walls covered with wild leprosy. It must go up a hill, past the iron gates, and afterward go down to the park designed like all Baroque parks: a symmetry still more extravagant than the architectonic insanities hidden among the laurels of India. They will lie in ambush as they have done for two and a half centuries, ready to jump on their prey. The monsters of stone and marble, the dragons and demons of the mad prince who decided to materialize his nightmares, the enormous porcelain elephants, the houses like masks: the two of you must enter by that door which is the gullet of the Succubus, into that cloister behind the angry eyes of the Demiurge: you will have to tremble when you see me. No, he wasn't a madman, says Leonor Fini: he was a Prince Orsini who put his Saracen prisoners to work.

I walk toward the front of the symmetrical garden. I flatten the gravel. I get wet in the high grass. I am gray, distant, mimetic, at one with the order of the garden and the disorder of the sculpture. I have been recalled, with rings under my eyes, from the yellow copies of a silent movie, from outside the selected frame of the painting. I bring, like the symmetry of the garden, the logic of the diagnosis to the proliferation of the illness. I have arrived without the two of you knowing and being able to defend yourselves, like the cancer disguised as health which settles in the midst of the benign cells without resistance, apparently identical, insipid, inoffensive.

The two of you will know that you should implore me, that I'm the master of this power over you: the power of intercession.

In the world one can be a thousand different things. One can stop being a man and open up to a new knowledge. To know that a man can be, in a very short time, only a curious and bygone intention. The creatures of Bomarzo, which are still nothing, are, despite everything, a blurred, imperfect, tired announcement of the other realities awaiting us. I walk, wanting to be a ghost, dressed in black, with an umbrella hanging from my arm.

I would kill you.

I would kill you to enact the first murder. I would kill you if you didn't implore me. She cannot be yours without my consent. Not yet. In our world that is forbidden. You must ask me that favor so that I can refuse it, so that you will remain suspended on the edge of passion: it would be intolerable for you to give her up, it would be impossible for you to keep her. I can help you. I can hand her over to you, if I want. You should kneel down to ask me to, to tell me she is mine and that I should surrender her to you.

And she should kiss me and implore me, also, to let go and forget you so that you can be hers.

I will be the judge. How do you two think one pays for someone else's suffering when one finally has love at hand? Will you not know how to keep back the seed, return it to the body itself, as I do? Will you not know how to reject satisfaction so that love never dies, so that this trembling and this power of the skin which I feel here, before the two of you, in the cave of the gargoyles of Bomarzo, will be eternal: terror and pleasure and desire without solution, without meeting, forever in love with its unreachable, voluntarily distant opposite?

The cypresses, the damp plaster, the wet earth, the bodies separated and laid out toward one another, without ever touching: this is the only epiphany that we three can permit: the three of us will be perfect, we will be mother, brother, son, wife, lover. We will all say No to say Yes. We will all forbid each other and watch over each other. All that brings us together kills us. All that separates us makes us live: love is distance and separation.

Don't you understand me? Don't you accept me? Then I have other weapons. Cain's. Oedipus's. I will invoke the elements. With a hand I will draw the storm over the garden of the monsters, with the other I will raise the dust of its bed; wrapped in mud and water I will corner you in the bottom of the open mouth of that baroque Demon where you look for refuge, not knowing that I have assumed the powers of the fallen angel, of God's double.

You have traveled with the top down, as another challenge: to the rain, the wind, the earth. The oils, the mascaras, the pancake, are not enough. You are standing there, with the pride of danger in your whipped faces; you don't know that my hand too is nature and danger: my hand and my words. Twins: the two dressed in English trench coats, cheap thriller kind, very snug at the waist.

But I alone will pull off the scarf so your straight, damp hair will fall on your shoulders. Ah, you are my own statue: I can disfigure you and humiliate you, just as the crazy designer of the park thought he would deform the live models whom he turned into a pure dream of stone. I can pull off your false eyelashes so that your eyes stop shining and are really those of a fifty-year-old woman, gloomy, distrustful, tired, resentful. With my hand I can erase the false color of your thin, dry lips like the mouth of the clay piggy banks of our poor Mexico that works with its own earthen body, cooking, varnishing, decorating it. I can put my hand into your hair, next to your neck, tangle your bleached snakes; I can rip your dog collar so that he'll get a good look at the tortured fat of your double chin, the wrinkled nerves of your neck: I can reveal the scars on your temples, your skin stretched like a funeral drum, the turkey skin of your arms, the purple paps of your breasts, the soft fritters of your belly. I can shake off the perfume of the foxes. I can expose you. I can unveil you. I can show your last soul, the one the cameras, the flash bulbs, the shutters haven't stolen from you. I will make my way, tiny and terrible as I am, among the sands of your deserts, the creeping vines of your jungles, the petals of your flesh: I will be your parasite, hidden in the bottom of your womb, I will nest in you again to intoxicate you with my sweet sweat. You will be my shroud. You will be the alcove of my death.

You will implore me. You will ask my forgiveness. There won't ever have been loneliness or humiliation, distance, hate. I will be again, forever, inside you: you will promise me that, this afternoon. You would like to get me back. You are the Weeper, the kidnapper: again you keep me in you, conceive me in you; I am your seed. And preserved within you so that you'll no longer be able to deny me your company, your heat, your attentions, we will wait: he will come too, he will come in and be with us. The three of us, always the three of us, alone and united forever.

Tell him. Implore him. Ask my forgiveness.

Force me to be quiet: can you go to bed with your own mother, Giancarlo? Look at her: Here she is: she's mine. She's everybody's. You don't know her. The general and the priest, the impresario and the political boss, the viceroy and the millionaire, the spy and the two-timing papa have all kissed her. Take her if you want. I tell you that you will just be one more: the young love that her autumn wants to devour.

Don't look at me like that.

I thought I had lost my eyes and they are blind; they don't look at me. All the palace decorations should surround me, should disguise me because I am part of them and in only that way can I see it all, I who have been left eyeless: I am the stucco lions and the beheaded statues, the garden of dying fig trees and dry geraniums, the torrent and the campanile, the teapots and the trays, the mirrors and the beds, the ramps and the arched corridors which lead me, again, to the condemned room where the final act unfolds, where everything is murmured, where the most violent gestures and words become spectrally weightless and withheld.

I have become a decoration without ceasing to be myself: everything is decoration. Illusion: the deserted palace. Lie: I walk sorrowfully through these corridors filled with people, squads of potentates, processions of beggars: there is no more space in this place than when I first saw it, by myself: out of bounds: the troops have returned, the esplanade is full of spirited cars, polished steeds, steel donkeys, Percheron buses, mare limousines, colt sports cars: announcing this tense, showy, bored crowd which strolls around the courtyard and up the stairs and in the rooms and passages of the palace of Madonna dei Monti.

Every disguise is here: mandarins and Pharaohs, Flemish infantry soldiers and gangs in blue-jeans rub elbows; Oriental slaves and Bourbon courtesans rub thighs; Chicago gangsters and Florentine condottieri, shoulders; Arabian eunuchs and English lords, cheeks. Under the sudden sun in the courtyard, waiters pass around trays of Coca Cola and ice cream sodas, Dr. Pepper and Seven Up: chorus girls in white satin spangles, cowboys all in black, drink them, like the Spanish noblemen who take their hands off chests, theirs and others': the low necks and pregnancies of the First Empire, the flight of gauzes and rapiers, of starched gorgets and tight skirts, of feather capes and Hussar coats. An orchestra of wigged, frock-coated Negroes, well swathed, well-powdered, in laced slippers and white stockings, plays the fife and the rebec, the lute and the psaltery, and the fat mamma, the ash-colored grandmother of musicians, the one with the carrot-colored hair and the Lent lips, sings "Positively, 4th Street." An Italian bandit, dressed like Marcello Mastroianni, offers me frozen hot dogs from his brass tray. I push him aside to keep moving, among the rockettes with aluminum stockings who go up and down the entrance ramps with mutilated breasts and fly swatters in their hands, humming "Embraceable You." In the drawing rooms they continue offering malted milk shakes to the men in shirt sleeves, tapered shirts by Tripler's, New York, and to the women who drum on electric machines, noiseless, in Prussian blue varnish, with their hands gloved and sapphires strung on their gloved thumbs and fur hats and violet pince-nez. The men in over-the-calf socks and tergal trousers argue, unroll sheets of paper covered with numbers, curves, years; all the walls have been garnished with nails, covered with diagrams and shiny, glossy, flossy photos: lean models, perturbed models, surprised models, models who balance on the edge of a tenement wall, models who are paralyzed on the Gobi Desert, models who dance in front of the Washington obelisk, models who smear themselves against the walls of Harlem, models without lips, eyebrows, eyelashes: pure eye and mouth models, suspended, flattened, open-mouthed, orgasmic: Bert Stern. The men cross their arms and stop speaking. The little blond man, with owl eyeglasses and thin bangs, adjusts his drip-dry jacket and points with a magisterial rod to the products placed in a row on the cement picnic table disguised as wood; he praises pink, steel, Titian, China orange, silver temptation, golden dream nail polish; iridescent, striated, breakable, carved bottles of perfume; powder cases, wafer-thin, square like screens, triangular like the divine eye; powder puffs of humming bird feather, turkey tail, orchid petal, wasp membrane, bee cunt; blue cacao and red snow brushes and pencils; jelly and spray deodorants; the creams of sperm and dust, of volcanic ash and baby mucus, of harelike cornea and frozen strawberry, all the potions of beauty, the love potions, the plastic retorts, and the little blond man's singing voice and the heavy breathing of the painter who's describing parabolas with his cane and the silent chorus of the women who drum on the machines.

The sound is different in the dark corridors; I look for the salon, the real, the only one, along the passages where psalms and prayers, complaints and belches, farts and brayings are intoned by all the homunculuses in broken silk and discolored bowler hats, in ceremonial coats and striped shirts, with black cigar butts and ripped pants seats, with jingling hoods and faceless cowls; all the little women with cracked skin and matted hair like ground asparagus, uterine poisons and fattened armpits, wine cellar bellies and long clay nails; all the children with spurs and humps, sun albinos, open-mouthed morons with bulbous eyes, dwarfs who still don't know they are, condemned in order to be born, little hog buttocks, scorpion and walking stick sexes, crustaceans with corn hairs, blind between hide and flesh: kidnapped circus jumpers, the children of the Boogeyman and the Weeper, those with their mouths split to laugh in circus tents, those with their eyes pierced to cry in the streets, those with their fingers cut off to be wrapped in dough; they cut capers in the dark corridors of the palace, they moan and howl their greasy, snively, bratty, pesty, beggarly, and overpraised music: the music of the poolrooms, invaded now by the sixty or seventy couples who keep time to the Big Beat without moving their feet, shoulders and arms, other prayers, other charms, plea for orgasm, exorcism of anguish: face to face, colt and salamander hair, the tight pants of the boys in striped shirts and velvet suspenders, the old-fashioned sailor pants of the girls in kaleidoscope sweaters and black leather suspenders: the perplexing dance of separation, the touchless dance, the musicless dance: they dance to the beat of the little grunted, hungry songs, of the little coxcombs in the corridors. All the lights of the discotheque revolve: panther skin.

And behind, the condemned door.

The dancers do not look at me. I pass among them, the faithful in the hour of the Muezzin, to open the doors to the salon of the frescos.

All the lights blind me.

White, polar, icy, like Midsummer's Night: the glowing light which bathes her, erases her features. She is a body. A marvelous.body, a metal statue. Her suit: infinite pieces of stained copper. Her face possesses the whiteness that the light, hissing like an Indian snake, wants to give her: grains of light which fix on her hair, eyebrows, lips, eyes, eyelashes, and fuse the rest of her flesh into the albino air of this cloister without paintings, of this whitewashed interior of the egg, whose center she occupies, her body, her copper suit, her noise of metal disks knocking against each other.

She, there in the center of the stage, and you disguised, Murat, King of Naples, whip and boots, Napoleonic jacket, brocades of dull gold, rusted braids, tight, white pants which reveal your excitement. You run the game. She occupies the center. The girls, the margins, behind the scenes; ah, but how they make themselves felt, how they hover, with all their insignia bared, each with her secrets exposed, the bronze-tipped whips, the bat wings, the coal-black skin, the dog masks, the wigs of snakes and the suits, the dresses, the dolls' pink stockings, the mannikins' rustling hoop skirts, the white slippers, the bows, the ballerinas' lead tips: how they make themselves felt, how they howl on this island of wailings and dawns, in this sealed salon shaken by a breeze which must be born from the movements, leaps, birth-giving contractions of Ute:

"Her name is Thetis and she was born by the sea, born of the sea, is the sea which is the girdle and belt of the world."

And Vanessa: "She is the night and the wind fertilized her: she gave birth to a silver egg."

And Iphigenia: "Her name is Rhea and no one can escape the hallucination of her bronze drums: she is sitting, playing before the cave where you enter the world. No one can escape."

And Paola: "She was born from the chaos and danced without other company than the solitude over the sea: she didn't have earth to rest on."

And Hermione: "She fertilized herself so as not to be alone. She fornicated with the phallus of the wind, the bitch mother, and gave birth to the serpent and with the serpent she devoted herself to orgasm and the serpent thought he was the true creator but she showed him, she showed him . . ."

And Kirsten: "She crushed his skull with a kick, she kicked out his teeth and exiled him to the black caverns of the black world. Watch out!"

They fix me with their red looks, they jump like trained beasts when you make your own whip thunder, you push them aside, you protect my mother, you receive from her the white flower with the black root, you kneel down, you kiss her fingers, Claudia's twining coppers, you conclude the speech:

"The story doesn't end where people think. Penelope and Telemachus were not content with just hearing Ulysses tell them his adventures. We should have guessed it, a dissatisfied mother and son listen to the song of that fantastic voyager who with his odyssey humiliates, excludes, and dominates them."

You circle around Claudia, you circle around my mother with your ready whip: you protect my motionless mother, with her silver eyes to hear you better: the star is listening to us with the vibrating hair of waves and lost sails.

"Don't they also have a right to accident and risk, to fortune and lies, to adventure?"

To eat us better: speak, Claudia: "Resentment corrodes me. Your father is very old. I want you to go out and travel in his name, I want you to resume the travels of this old man. Return to the island of wailings, to the coast of Istria guarded by my wolves and rapacious birds. And there, in that palace which is the original residence of the storm, in that open labyrinth, in that cemetery of willow trees and woodpeckers, on that isle purified by the blood of pigs, you will find your brother, who is my son."

They howl behind their cardboard masks; you whip them: they moan, they cower, they shrink and protect each other while Claudia says: "One brother relieves the other"—and you continue: "Telemachus sinks into Circe's bed. Telegonus, son of Ulysses and the witch, resumes the abandoned pilgrimage, the return which is the start: he travels to Ithaca, to the denied home, to consummate the substitutions, to close the true chronicle."

The girls get up, fly, crawl. Claudia opens her arms and closes her eyes. The six furies cover my mother with the gold and blue cape, crown her with the heavy engraved metal, draw the intangible halo around her dark head, sprinkle her soles with cold roses, help her to mount the horns of the moon, fall on their knees before her, murmur while she screams:

"I cannot reject my son!"

"Ark of the covenant . . ."

"He is my real suitor!"

"Consolation of the afflicted . . ."

"The real, the young Ulysses has returned!"

"Morning star . . ."

"The one who left for Troy!"

"Tower of David . . ."

"The one who enjoyed himself with enchantresses and witches while I wove, waited, unraveled what I wove, grew old!"

"Mother of sinners . . ."

"And now you, the young one comes through the doors of the rustic palace to avenge time."

"Mother of God . . ."

"Murder all the old, bury all the impotent, dissolve the legend."

"Holy mother . . ."

"I am the mediatrix."

Ute and Vanessa, Paola and Hermione, Kirsten and Iphigenia drag the wrinkled, rubber, gray rag doll to the center of the stage; the six hold its flaccid extremities against the floor; with the black iron dagger you approach that grotesque figure with the white beard and china eyes, the girls pull off his tin, pronged carnival crown, you thrust the dagger into his side and they fall eagerly upon the corpse, and pull newspaper and cotton, feathers and sponges, smoking horse guts, its little bird heart, divine shit out of its side, and with these new offerings crawl to the feet of my motionless mother, her arms crossed.

Claudia's sergeant voice explodes: "Pesty old man. It was high time."

You hang your head: "The myth was defeated. And they all lived happily ever after."

You fall on your knees, embrace my mother's legs, kiss her thighs.

The six furies shout: "Happily ever after! Happily ever after! Happily ever after!"

The wind opens the windows. Stage thunder resounds in and outside of the room. The little blonde comes in the window, dancing the Watusi, moving her slender legs, letters and numbers woven on her white pants. On one leg, the name: Bela. On the other, the telephone number: 844393.

The short man, the gnome, comes out of the shadows to take over. I've seen him before somewhere; I recognize his boots and riding pants, his turban, his mustache and the little silk beard, the viperish eyes, the monocle, the leather and metal gadget supporting his Prussian head and stiffening his broken neck: "Cut. Okay. That was beautiful, *ach so.* Print it. Kill the five thousand. Leave me those two thousand. Gaby, look at this frame. Where did I leave my viewer? Ach. Mahoganny, have the extras ready in an hour: beggars and dancers, in the next room. We have to have everything ready for that scene. Jenny, you take charge of the pillows; we have to strip two hundred; pillow feathers in the palace, snow outside the palace: with that scene I'll run the company bankrupt. They don't know that I'm not using it in the final editing, ach, ach, ach. Producers exist to go bankrupt and end their days in a Chinese laundry, ach, ach, ach. Bilbao, have the horses ready for the ballroom scene. Tiger, give a cigar and a glass of champagne to each beggar. Now, shot sixty-nine, shot sixty-nine. Claudia alone in the room. First camera on the crane; an easy fall, easy now, to Claudia's great C.U. Second camera, dolly toward Claudia. Third camera. Arriflex in hand panning Claudia, a full turn, three hundred and sixty degrees. Have the boom ready. What did they say? I am not a tyrant. A half hour for coffee. Kill the beast!"

The icy reflectors, the glowing arches, go out, one by one. The six girls take off their dog masks, throw down their whips, leave sighing. Only two spots. One on my mother's face. Another on yours. They go out slowly like constellations, remotely, like Andromeda's light. Neither of you moves.

The light disappears. You disappear. The set is dark. And empty. . . .

Another possibility: cannibalism. But if I kill her to eat her, where will they bury me and who will watch over me when I die? Besides, the murder would be an act. I alone have nostalgia for her: abulia, disappearance. Must all be a desire of the past or of the future? And she is the mistress of the eternal present. That is the true struggle. . . .

Don't look at me like that. Why do you two look at me like that?

Why do you protect her?

Why do you let her humiliate me with her look and her words?

What do I do but look out of the hotel window toward the Via Veneto and think that this autumn will not look like any other, that the styles will change, that people will stop listening and dancing to this music, that all the cabarets will close their doors, that all the movies will be filed in a film library?

The music, the voice of Ornella Vanoni, emerges from the bars and discoteques. *Io ti daró di piú.*

"What are you going to tell him? Of what are you going to accuse me? What are you going to say about my life and loves? What? I dare you!"

No, I won't say anything. My only strength is silence. But you have to say it, your arms around her in this suite in the Hotel Excelsior, in this room which smells of old carpets. A service. A feat. A long wait. Chastity and secret and pity. I would give them to you too, mamma, I would give them to you.

"You're going to keep on giving me the same as always, darling. You're charming and ephemeral. Don't worry. I don't have dreams. I've lived them all."

"I want to live with you."

"You must return. And to return, you must first go away. I don't want you to tear your eyes out. I'm reserving something else for you. We all have to change from time to time, so as not to die of boredom. I mean it. To avoid wasting away, which is the only thing that makes us old. Not sudden blows, not changes."

I say there is no light in the garden of porcelain and gravel. I say that I don't see. I say that I can't see that slow, cruel kiss, as prolonged as my blindness is gradual. I don't know how to see. Little by little I realize the unaccustomed disorder in the suite my mother and Giancarlo occupy in the Hotel Excelsior. I didn't want to see that messy bed, those damp, perfumed sheets. I didn't wish to look at all the details of atrocious intimacy, the cord of the electric shaver on the floor, the brocade bathrobe on a chair, the box of Kleenex on the night table, Giancarlo's tie on a lamp. And the smells of mentholated foam, deodorant, Vétiver and Bandit, toasted bread and coffee residue slip my attention.

"Brother," Giancarlo murmurs when he stops kissing Claudia.

A sun bleeds on my corneas as I move away, without turning my back, my hand raised and my arm threatening, withered, damned, wanting to kill my likeness with the stucco jaw of a smiling dragon, surrounded by alder trees which moan from the cemeteries of the islands. He was mine. He was the only one who was mine. The King is son of the Queen.

Io ti daró, molto di piú, molto di piú. Ornella Vanoni sings, this fall, from all the juke boxes of Rome and I walk down the Via Veneto looking absentmindedly at the boutiques, imagining the undulating, perfumed world of women, brilliance in motion, trying to remember a girl who was riding a horse along Positano beach at unexpected hours.

I stop in front of the Cucci show window and cannot see the clothes on display. My look cannot go beyond the reflection. The reflection is me: a man of his class, his time, his space: of a condition defeated beforehand by a kind of chosen fatality. And by a renunciation which has sketched this vague frown, barely visible in the dimness of the glass. I close my eyes before the moment passes: the one that lets me remember some words shouted behind a door. Claudia has stopped smoking. Claudia says her truth for a minute. And I have refused to recognize it. I haven't refused to investigate the mystery of a painful and lonely struggle. Claudia defeated the fat men in the Hotel María Isabel bar; how could she fail to defeat me? I want to tell myself that in my abstention there has been respect; I must admit that to really get close to her would have meant losing my precious fatalism and the indulgent tone of pity for me that goes with it. The pain that says its name stops being pain.

The summer is long and the sidewalk cafés are full. Rome has the color of a burnt beach. The girls have returned, suntanned, from the coasts, and have put on their little boots and mini skirts. The boys stroll like peacocks and try to be fascinating enough to be forgivable. But I, behind my black glasses, have to look among the tables for the pale and fat-cheeked face of a prostitute, the violet grimace and dark wink which knows how to single out the foreigner without allure but with traveler's checks. I take a seat next to her. I have seen Claudia defeated. I have seen Claudia changed. . . .

Bela wrote to me. I returned to Italy because Bela wrote to me. *Beato tu.* Taking it easy in your apartment. And your mother in Rome and in full regalia, followed everywhere by *paparazzi*. Oh, what great clothes she's ordered. And how generous. I took her to Princess d'Aquila's boutique. I myself modeled the numbers. Your mother bought them all and recommended me very warmly, as if I belonged to her, like a daughter. The Princess had to invite us to dinner. Only she and her son. Did I ever tell you about him? He's a *bravo ragazzo*. Full of fantasy. He charmed Claudia. They are inseparable. Sometimes they invite me out with them. Rome in September, Guglielmo. Have you ever been in Rome in September? Yes, Bela. How the summer takes its time in dying; what golds, what ochres. The beauty doubles itself; each palace, each piazza, each monument exists twice, as if it invoked a friendly ghost. *È proprio bello.* Yesterday we walked around ancient Rome, from the Pantheon to the Piazza Campitelli, where the city again opens up to the Forums. We sat down to have an espresso on the Via del Teatro di Marcello. The waiter was a chattering Sicilian; he didn't recognize your mother. She thanked him for it. *Beato lui.* She laughed with him. We laughed a lot, all of us. We never admit inferiority. We all descend from the Caesars, *accidenti!* The waiter couldn't be less: ancient Sicilian nobility, eh! Nobody walks around with his coat of arms on his face. With a lot of words, a lot of lip, as you people say, we provide the proof of our ancestry. Oh, how he talked. Descriptions of Taormina; his childhood, army days; school; love. That's what he told Claudia: only moments of love exist, not love. Look: he looked at Giancarlo: you must love your son a great deal, madam; one can see right away that you're a good mother, but you only love him in certain moments, *ma soltanto per un attimo, vero?* We laughed ourselves to tears, Guglielmo. That is the truth. These are the things one can touch and enjoy. The September sun. A delicious cup of coffee. The beauty of Rome. Our laughter. I understood. I left them alone. They walked to the Campidoglio. The stairs are full of cats. Did you ever realize how many cats there are in Rome? Yes, Bela. You and I know why. They told us. Everything has a rational and historical explanation. Rome was the great warehouse of grain in the empire. These got filled with mice. In Rome cats are holy, they reproduce and increase and the people protect them. There are people who live alone with an army of cats, especially spinsters who didn't get married just to be able to take care of so many cats. Claudia and Giancarlo didn't pay any attention to them. They are so happy, busy with preparations, the movie, the wedding, the publicity. They went, I believe, up to the Roman she-wolf's cage. The one who founded us. *Ciao*, Guglielmo; *ciao, ragazzo; auguri!* . . .

I came out of the clinic in December. The month of rest only sharpened the hunger of my profile. I don't recognize myself. My clothes look big on me. I look in the mirror and I have too much shirt, no neck. The coat and scarf cover me in that weak way. But I am no longer delirious. Now I can think rationally. And you have taken pity on me. You've come to the sanatorium a few times, at the end of the convalescence, when the sun is out, to push me in the wheelchair, to wheel me around the garden of gravel and cypresses in the sanatorium on Via Camilluccia, high, exposed, dominating the panorama of Rome. We've hardly said a word. But you don't fool me; you less than anybody.

Your care is false. Your interest, that I accept the situation without protest. That I don't create problems. Your mission, to take me to Paris where I'll take the direct flight on Air France to Mexico.

All is well.

Yes, I would have gone quietly, too. The sanatorium calmed me down. I needed to be alone, without reading or thinking. I'm positive I could have caught the plane alone, at Fiumicino, and transfer without danger in New York. All that care, and precaution, wasn't necessary. Who knows what the two of you saw in my face that inspired so much pity or distrust. It wasn't necessary for you to take me to Paris and to bother taking me for walks; to hurry my recovery, they said.

Immediately your care began to bother me, your hand helping me when crossing streets, your arm leading mine, as if I were blind or handicapped. No, I'm still not physically incapacitated. My weakness is different. I feel shrunken from the inside, although the new roominess of my clothes tells me that outside, too, I've lost weight. But my illness is different. You should know that. And it has to be reborn and erupt now when, I don't know if with premeditation or carelessly, you lead me to the St. Michel subway station after seeing, in Studio de la Harpe, the movie my mother filmed in your rented palace.

It's past midnight and you don't have the right to drag a weak, sick man into that hurried, vulgar, indifferent crowd. It's as if you were drowning me, exposing me to the danger of falling and being trampled to death; it's a worse dread, not physical, but an impalpable horror of being with others, of losing myself, of not being seen anymore as I am. I am losing you; I cannot move forward; I reach out to touch you, again. I am sweating, pushed against the tide by all the people who look for the exit while I try to find the entrance, reach you, occupy that jammed spot in the second-class car. You could buy first-class tickets, right? My mother is rich. Why have you dragged me into the midst of this commotion, why have you filled me with cold sweats, trembling legs? Why have you brought me here, to enervate me, to scream at you?

"Pig. You told her all my stories. I told them to you alone, she didn't have to know about the spiders and the ants, the house in Guadalajara, my hiding places; those stories were for you. Fool. She's with you because she can't be with me, she doesn't love you, she has to put you in my place, you will be as I have been. . . ."

Nobody's around now. We are alone in the subway station. You can come over to me and take me by the collar and say:

"You're wrong. You don't want to understand how that story ended."

"I've heard that before, liar; it can't be applied to us; Penelope doesn't exist, Ulysses doesn't exist; we all end up with only Circe, turned into hogs. . . . You'll go to bed with Bela, with Paola, with . . ."

"*Sei cretino, caro.* You don't understand anything. The rest didn't happen. There is another climax. Ulysses doesn't tie himself to the mast. He listens to the song of the sirens and gives in, because the sirens have warned him: he shouldn't go home, there his wife's infidelity and death by his son's hand await him. Ulysses never returned, *cretino*, Ulysses stayed on the islands, with the sirens, eternally young, eternally sensual. . . ."

"Let go of me. I don't want to listen to you anymore. Go back to Claudia and be happy. Tell her to give you my monthly check. You can buy dogs and records. Tell her to be afraid of me. Tell her I'm going to take my revenge, tell her . . ."

Then you throw me on the subway track, then I fall on my face between the rails, then I scrape my knees and you pick me up by the collar and speak to me with your lips over mine, with your eyes inseparable from mine:

"*Cretino*, and if I succeed in humiliating her?, and if I act in your name?, and if I break her and transform her and offer you her in all her weakness, behind her aggressive words and false strength?, and if I extract her whole story, bit by bit, and afterward tell you about her loves, her deceptions, her ambition, the repugnance she's felt, how coldly she's calculated?, if I surrender your real mother to you, naked, maskless, insulted, finally revealed by an imagined man who offers her the last surprise: the surprise that, despite all appearances, I don't reflect her?, and if your mother finally admits that one flees loneliness only to find humiliation?, do you want to see her like that, do you want me to give her back like that?"

Then you tell me that there's only one minute between trains and we must run, we must race, we must overcome the danger of being crushed by two trains crossing halfway in the tunnel, we must expose ourselves to expose her, we must find out who wins the game.

Holy Place

> How different you look, how changed.
> —Cortázar,
> *Circe*

I believe that was my last pleasure. But one gets used to everything. To loneliness. To love. To death. To indifference. All we do is complain about the only thing that keeps us alive: habit, frustration. We are not self-sufficient. Almost no one is. Almost.

I'm exhausted. Still, I asked for that final excess. Where could I go, back in Mexico, but to her abandoned house? I had a key. I went in, sniffing the stuffy air of two months' enclosure. There was no light: the curtains were gathering dust; the furniture had linen shrouds. But I wasn't looking for this.

Upstairs, the bedroom: for the first time, I listened to how the floor creaked as I went in. The order in which Claudia left it. The cosmetics arranged on the glass table. The shutters of the mirrors on the dresser, closed. I opened them. I again repeated myself three times, angular and slender, smelling the closeness.

Next to it, the enormous closet and everything my mother left: the wardrobe that I also open, also sniff, finally caress, finally brush against my cheek, finally kiss.

I stayed near that clothing for a long time. First standing. Then, with a growing pleasure, letting myself go, voluptuously, sinking into the dresses, coats, foxes and ermines and chinchillas which still hold her perfume, the same as my kidnapping, the same as my childhood. Finally, sitting on the floor, among her shoes which I also caress, which I also press against my cheek and my eyes, which I also kiss; my mouth is satin, jewelry, and vinyl, my tongue, calfskin and crocodile, my palate, glacé silk.

I understand, surrounded by her objects; she lets me see myself as something else; she lets me see myself as her. I get up, with difficulty, laughing; seven thousand suspected witches were burnt in the square at Logroño, five hundred during three months, in Geneva. They will all find out. The duke of Lorraine will ride with his bloodied daggers until there's not a woman alive on his lands; little girl, adolescent, young woman or old. Only me. Me, informing. Me, disguised.

It fills me with fever to undress here.

I won't look at myself in the mirrors. Not yet.

I will poke into the bureau; everything I want is there; the brassiere that I hook at my back, the lace panties, black stockings, garters, satin slippers; the jewel case is there with some forgotten trinkets, jade rings, aquamarine earrings, the amethyst necklace, silver bracelets, another topaz necklace: ice on my badly shaved throat, cold on my chest, my wrists; I deform the panties, the bra hangs on me, slips down my increasingly prominent ribcage; the growing hair on my legs goes through the stockings. Her wig. Her eyebrow pencil. Her eye shadow. Her false eyelashes. The cheek mole. The carmine for the lips. The Hindu bracelet, the golden snake.

What will I tell them when I inform on her? What, when I see her go to the stake? That what's terrible is to know the witch is innocent and for that she is guilty? That we couldn't live without her and we can't live with her? No. Will it be enough to show myself like this, show that I am her, that she usurps my identity, that she has turned me into what the mirrors reflect: into this prince of mockery, into this puppet smeared with cosmetics, into this dry Christmas tree cluttered with costume jewelry, into this ravenous dog who can no longer hold himself up on these high, gigantic heels, stilts, and falls scratching the glass, falls with the empty jewel case in his hands and with it claws the mirrors?

She must be exterminated. Not even the judges are safe. She fascinates them in the act of judging. The lord ceases to distinguish himself from the serf. Both desire love and deserve consolation.

Face down, I look at the mouse that's looking at me from a glass tube. . . .

I growl. They don't know how to run the movie. They mix the reel, project the copies backward, everything is cacophony and the confusion of twisted film, scattered on the floor, crushed. I growl to protest. Jesús sticks out his leg and kicks my snout. My growl becomes a whine. I rub my paw over my snout. I scratch myself. I'm still not used to it. I lift my gentle, brown eyes and look reproachfully at the strong, dark man sitting, sprawled, on the chair and serving himself cognac in the plastic glass with which I used to rinse my mouth. Now he pinches Gudelia's ass and Gudelia laughs and slaps him and falls on his lap. Jesús has put the cashmere sweater on again; she, that red nylon négligée which also belonged to my mother and which Gudelia has decorated with spangles and tricolor bands from the fairs.

They neck and with his elbow Jesús knocks down the Tiffany lamp

141

in scarlet lead casing. The slender flowing bodies of my engravings contemplate the petting of these two stocky, congested beings, who will never be able to tell the difference between the mouth and the anus. Gudelia flips off her slippers and I watch them for a second; maybe they'll get tired some day; I look away: I prefer to see what's left of my apartment, the tapestries torn from the walls and used like rugs, the Lalique plates filled to the brim with ashes and butts and wrinkled packages of Elegantes, the walls thumbtacked with color pictures and cutouts from magazines and photographs taken in the Villa de Guadalupe. The Chinese tables heaped with clay pots, paper napkins, bottles of beer and tequila, leftovers of greenish tortillas and warmed-over kidney beans, odors of hot chile and Indian fricassee.

Jesús gets up and washes his hands, cleans his sex in the fountain of algae. He whistles, his pants down and dragging. Gudelia yawns and walks barefoot toward the record player. She puts on a selection from *Rigoletto*. I get up and go to the bathroom, to the bidet full of water. The trills of the soprano fill the house. *Caro nome* . . . I drink quickly, I lick it up, and lick my lips. They're going to forget my dinner. I do well to say my dinner. I will continue calling it that. They won't make me lose everything, forget everything. They won't. What does it matter. What matters is that they're getting drunk and fornicating and listening to music and forgetting me, my hunger. And now they're fighting.

In three leaps I'm in the room. Jesús buttons his pants and cleans his nose with his fist and throws the record on the floor; Gudelia cries and calls him a big bully; Jesús calls her a son of a bitch and puts on a bolero. Gudelia cries. Moon that breaks, over the darkness, of my solitude.

I am trembling on the threshold of the room. No. I should make myself invisible, I shouldn't make myself felt. Jesús doesn't only kick; sometimes he takes off his belt and beats me hard. Better for me to lie down in the bare corridor—the carpet almost caught fire one night—and repeat to myself those precious names, fabularia, fascinatrix, femina saga. Ancient lady educator. Persecuted mistress of antidotes and charms. Did you know? In her, opposites fuse: you are I; we are all someone else. Sometimes I go to sleep thinking these things. This life isn't so bad, after all. If they'd only remember that I'm hungry. That I can smell better than ever; that the vapors of the grease and acidity of the kidney beans they've left on the table reach me; that this is stronger than me, that I have to run to the table, reach up, hold myself there with my front paws and stick my snout into the pots while Gudelia cries and Jesús attacks me with his belt and I growl and would like to bite him and I can't; I'm too tame. I only know how to sniff and whine and lower my head and hide in a corner, behind the stained curtains, smeared with fingerprints.

Jesús yawns and takes off the sweater. He gives Gudelia a slap on her butt and she laughs again and bites her nail.

I'm hungry. I'd like to eat. Even though I feel cold afterward.

I look with my moist eyes at the abandoned and broken painting of Sarah Bernhardt in her apartment, with a dog at her feet. *Mon semblable, mon frère.* Elvis Presley is now in the frame of the Baudelaire photograph.

I would give anything for a plate of strawberries.

"Take it easy, eh; don't get so riled up."

"Oh Chucho, you know I'm your woman, why are you always looking for a fight? The music's swell, I mean it, really. It's just that the boss's music seemed a lot classier."

"Come here, honey."

They put out all the lights.

I sniff around me: it's the smell of the wet celluloid, of Claudia's movies. I don't want to sleep. We know that sleep is the photograph of death. When I sleep, I only see a dead girl next to a dead horse on a dead beach.

Afterward, everything will be better. Ruth will take charge of bringing me good steaks from time to time. I, grateful, will lick her hand. How strange. Now I know. Ruth uses a rubber mask, a little, wrinkled one. Her real face, a monkey's.

She will say to me:

"Poor dear."

But I won't complain. Even a dog knows that pleasure can be divorced from consciousness, but not from fate. And perhaps fate will afford me another show. Each one of us has thought so much of the others, each of us three. Perhaps that circulation of tones, looks, movements—those moments which have linked our three appearances—will still be referred to and recalled in the future. And then, one day, they might come to this house and decide to make love in front of me. We animals have always been faithful witnesses of sex. Swans, panthers, dogs, we can look upon the mater-matter, paradox of the untouchable violation. The two of you could give me that satisfaction. I imagine you between the sheets of my bed, as within an immaculate shell. I imagined the tortured kisses and caresses of the man who was my brother, on the body of the glowing, sick woman who was my mother. Their bodies joined on my bed will reverberate like two crystal glasses. And my twin will want to tell me that the true myth, the one that picks up the threads of all the rest, tells that at Delphi, Apollo and Dionysus, born together, will also share a common death. But I will defeat them. Not because I decide to draw them to me to take advantage of their ecstasy and then jump, bite their faces, plunging my incisors into their jugular veins, no. Only because, brothers, it takes time to abandon our mother's womb, although she strained to give birth to us: we thought that to come out of her, to abandon her, was to die. Nine months is a century. And he, now, in her arms, will not want to abandon life, will want to remain buried in her and will be afraid of death just as both of us, before being born, were afraid of life.

Not I.

That is my victory. A dog knows how to die unsurprised.

José Donoso: HELL HAS NO LIMITS

translated by Hallie D. Taylor and Suzanne Jill Levine

For Rita and Carlos Fuentes

1

La Manuela forced open her bleary eyes, stretched briefly and, twisting away from the sleeping Japonesita, reached for the clock. Five to ten. Eleven o'clock mass. Sticky films again sealed her eyes as she put the clock back on the box by the bed. Half an hour at least before her daughter would ask for breakfast. She ran her tongue over her toothless gums: hot sawdust, and breath like rotten eggs. From drinking so much new wine to hurry the men out and close early. She felt a shiver—of course!—she opened her eyes and sat up in bed: Pancho Vega was in town. She covered her shoulders with the rumpled pink shawl from her daughter's side of the bed. Yes. Last night they came to tell her. Be careful, the truck had been seen around, his snub-nosed red truck, with the double tires on the back wheels. At first La Manuela didn't believe it because she knew that, thank God, Pancho Vega had other interests now, near Pelarco, where he was hauling grape-skins. But later, when she had almost forgotten what they said about the truck, she heard the horn by the post office on the next street. He must have honked it for almost five minutes, that hoarse, persistent horn, enough to drive any woman crazy. He always honked like that when he was drunk. The idiot thought it was funny. Then La Manuela went to tell her daughter they better close early, why take chances, what happened last time might happen again. Japonesita warned the girls to finish up quickly with the customers or send them away: remember

149

last year, when Pancho Vega came to town for harvest and invited himself in with a bunch of roughnecks, all of them full of wine . . . there might have been bloodshed if Alejandro Cruz hadn't arrived in the nick of time. He made them behave in a civil way, so they got bored and left. But they said that afterward Pancho Vega was real mad and went around swearing: "I'll screw the two of them, Japonesita and her fag of a father . . ."

La Manuela got up and started to put on her trousers. Pancho might still be in town . . . Those hands, hard and heavy like stone, like iron, she remembered them all right. Last year the beast got it into his head that she had to dance flamenco. He heard that when the party warmed up with the new wine, and when all the customers were like pals, La Manuela would put on a pretty red dress with white polka dots, and dance flamenco. You bet! Big brute! Think I'd dance for you, just look at you! I do that for gentlemen, for my friends, not for stinking bums like you, stuck-up peasants who think they're big shots because they have a week's pay in their pockets . . . their poor wives in the shanties, breaking their backs over laundry so the kids won't starve to death, while the sports are out drinking wine and punch and even hard liquor . . . no sir. And since she had one too many, that's exactly what she told them. Then Pancho and his pals got angry. They started by barricading the place and smashing bottles and smearing the bread and cold cuts and wine on the floor. Then while one of them twisted her arm, the others pulled off her clothes, and trying to force her into the famous flamenco dress they ripped it in two. They had begun to molest Japonesita when don Alejo arrived, like in a miracle, as if they had invoked him. Such a good man. Why he even looked like the Good Lord, with his China-blue eyes and his snowy mustache and eyebrows.

She bent down to fish her shoes out from under the bed and sat on the edge to put them on. She had slept badly. It wasn't just the wine, which made her feel bloated. But also, God knows why, don Alejo's dogs had been howling all night long in the vineyard . . . She would be yawning all day long, with no strength for anything, and pains in her legs and back. She tied the laces slowly with double bows . . . if you got down on your knees, there, way back under the bed, was the suitcase. A cardboard job, with peeling paint and white mouldy edges, held together with rope: in it was everything she owned. And her dress, or rather what was left of her lovely dress. Today, when she

opened her eyes, no, wrong, last night, when they told her Pancho
Vega was in town, God knows why, she was tempted to take the dress
out again. She hadn't touched it for a year. Who does she think she's
kidding with her sour wine, dogs, rib pains? She had insomnia!
Quietly, so she wouldn't upset her daughter, she bent down again,
pulled out the suitcase and opened it. A total loss. No use touching it
even. But she did touch it. She examined the bodice . . . hey, it's not
so bad, the neckline, armpit . . . it can be fixed. I'll sew the whole
afternoon in the kitchen so I won't get stiff. Fiddle with the skirt and
train, try it on so the girls can tell me where it has to be taken in since
I lost six pounds last year. But I don't have thread. Tearing a strip from
the end of the train she put it in her pocket. As soon as she served her
daughter breakfast she'd drag herself to Ludovinia's to see if she could
find the same color red thread among her odds and ends. Or something
like it. You can't be choosy in a town like Estación El Olivo. She
pushed the suitcase back under the bed. Yes, Ludo's, but before going
out she better make sure Pancho was gone, and if he really had been in
town last night. After all, the honking might just be a dream, like for
the past year when she sometimes thought she heard his rough voice or
felt his brutal hands, or it could be that she only imagined last night's
honking, remembering the horn from last year. Who knows. Shivering, she put on her shirt. She wrapped the shawl around her, put the
dentures in and walked out into the patio with the dress on her arm.
Raising her little, wrinkled raisin face, her black and hairy old mare's
nostrils flared as she detected the unmistakable aroma of the new
harvest in the cloudy morning air.

Half-naked, carrying a sheet of newspaper in her hand, Lucy came
out of her room like a sleepwalker.

"Lucy!"

Lucy's in a hurry: new wines are so treacherous.

She locked herself in the outhouse that straddled the sewer at the
end of the patio, next to the chicken coop. No, I won't send Lucy.
Clotilde's better.

"Hey, Cloty!"

. . . with her stupid face and skinny arms deep in the soapy water
of the wash tub, surrounded by the reflections of ivy leaves.

"Listen, Cloty . . ."

"Good morning."

"Where's Nelly?"

"In the street, playing with the neighbor's kids. That woman is so good to her, knowing what she is and all . . ."

Poor, unlucky whore. That's what she said to Japonesita when they took Clotilde in a little over a month ago. And so old. Who would want to go upstairs with her? But drunk, at night, flesh starving for other flesh, for any flesh that's hot and can be bitten and squeezed and licked, they don't know or care what they go to bed with—dog, hag, anything will do. And Clotilde would work like a dog, never complaining, not even when they made her haul the Coca Cola crates from one place to another. Last night she had it bad. The fat yokel was eager enough, but when Japonesita announced that she was closing up, instead of going with Cloty to her room he said he was going out to vomit and he never came back. Fortunately he had already paid for his drinks.

"I want her to do an errand. Don't you realize that if Pancho's around I can't go to mass? Tell Nelly to check every single street and to tell me if she sees the truck. She knows which, the red one. I can't miss Sunday mass!"

Clotilde dried her hands on her apron.

"I'll go right now."

"Did you start the fire in the kitchen?"

"Not yet."

"Then treat me to a few coals so I can make the kid's breakfast."

Squatting over Clotilde's stove to scoop some coals onto a flattened tin can, la Manuela felt her spine creak. It's going to rain. I'm too old for these things. She was even afraid of the morning air now, afraid of the morning most of all, afraid of so many things, the way she coughed, the bile in her mouth and the cramps in her gums, the early morning when everything is so different than at night when she's cradled in the sooty brightness of the carbon lamp and wine and dancing eyes, the conversations of friends and strangers at the tables, and the silver that falls dollar after dollar into her daughter's purse, which by now must be good and full. She opened the door to the big room, set the coals on the ashes in the stove and put on the kettle. She cut a loaf of bread in half, buttered it, and while she got the saucer, spoon, and cup ready she sang soft and slowly:

> . . . then dawn brought the day
> your boat left the bay . . .
> And now I dream
> Aaaaaaaahhh me . . .

She might be old but she would die singing, and with her feathers on. In the suitcase under the bed, besides her flamenco dress she had an old moth-eaten feather boa. Ludo had given it to her years ago as a consolation because some man had ignored her . . . just which man it was I don't remember now (one of the many who made me suffer when I was young). If the party got lively, and if they pleaded with her a little, it was no sweat off her back to put on the feathers even though they made her look like a scarecrow and didn't have anything to do with the flamenco number. Just to make people laugh, that's all, the laughter all around me and caressing me and the applause and compliments and lights, come have a drink with us honey, whatever you want, anything you want, just so you'll dance for us again. Why be so afraid of Pancho Vega! Those thick-browed, rough-voiced brutes are all alike: the minute it gets dark they start pawing you. And they leave everything smelling of engine oil and garages and cheap cigarettes and sweat . . . and at dawn the wine dregs souring in the bottom of the glasses on the seven dirty tables, the lopsided, scratched tables, everything too clear, too glaring this morning and every morning. And there's a puddle by the chair where Clotilde's fat man had been sitting because the lout spit all night long—an abscessed tooth, he said.

The kettle started to boil. Today without fail she would talk to Japonesita. She was too old to be fixing breakfast every morning after working all night, with gusts of wind blowing into the parlor through the cracks in the loose siding and where the shingles had fallen from the earthquake. Clotilde was having such poor luck in the parlor that they might as well use her for a servant. And Nelly for the errands, and when she grows up . . . Yes, let Clotilde bring them breakfast in bed. What other work could she expect at her age? At least she wasn't lazy like the other whores. Lucy returned to her room. Now she'll get back into bed, the slut, and spend all afternoon between the filthy sheets, eating bread, sleeping, getting fat. Of course, that's why she has so many clients. Because she's fat. Sometimes a real fancy gentleman comes all the way from Duao to spend the night with her. He says that he likes to hear the swishing of her soft, white thighs rubbing together when she dances. That that's what he pays for. Not like Japonesita who even if she wanted to be a whore, poor thing, she's so skinny she'd never make it. But as a manager, Japonesita is tops. There's no denying it. So efficient and thrifty. And every Monday morning she takes the train to Talca to deposit the profits in the bank. Heaven only knows how much she's hoarded. She never tells me, even though it's as much mine as Japonesita's. And what good did it do them, Japonesita is such a miser that no one gets any good out of it. She never buys herself a dress. A dress! Why, she wouldn't even buy another bed so that we can each have our own. Like last night. La Manuela didn't sleep a wink. Probably because of don Alejandro's dogs barking in the vineyard. Or was she dreaming? And the honking. In any case, at her age, sleeping with a pubescent female was no fun.

She put the saucer and bread on top of the steaming cup and walked outside again. Clotilde, scrubbing away, yelled to her that Nelly had gone to look. La Manuela didn't answer or thank her. Instead, coming over to see if Clotilde was doing the other whores' laundry too, she raised those thread-thin eyebrows, leered in mock passion, and warbled:

Havanaaaaaa for a
Niiiiiiiiiiiiight

2

The house was sinking. One day they realized that the sidewalk was no longer even with the dirt floor, but higher, so they tried to check it by installing a stone slab, with two wedges, in the doorway. It was no use. As the years passed, the sidewalk, God knows how, rose almost imperceptibly, while the floor kept sinking. Maybe it was from wetting and flattening it so much for dancing, or from the yokels grinding the floor into a dirt pit with their stomping feet. The stone slab, which was slowly wearing away, had never been level and now its cracks collected burnt matches, mint wrappers, scraps of paper, toothpicks, lint, and buttons. Sometimes grass sprang up around the edges.

La Manuela stooped in the doorway to pick up some scraps. She was in no hurry. It was still a half-hour before mass. A harmless half-hour, not a care in the world according to Nelly's report: not one truck, not even a car in the whole town. It was a dream, that's all. She couldn't even remember who told her about the truck. And the dogs. Why would they be running loose in the vineyard now, when there's not so much as one bunch of grapes left to steal? Okay. Five minutes to Ludovinia's, a quarter of an hour to find the thread, and five minutes for nothing special, to drink some tea or to stop and gossip with someone on the corner. And then, her mass.

Just to make sure, she looked up the street toward the poplar grove that marked the edge of town, three blocks away. Not a soul in sight. Of course. Sunday. Even the kids, who are always screaming their heads off, playing ball in the road, are probably waiting for handouts at the chapel door just in case some rich man's car drives up. The poplars trembled. If the wind blew any harder the town would be invaded by yellow leaves for at least a week and the women would be sweeping them all day out from everywhere, the street, the alleyways, doors and even from under the beds, to gather them in heaps and burn them . . . the blue smoke hovering in putrid clarity, creeping catlike against the adobe houses, coiling into the cavities of crumbling, weed-infested walls, the blackberry thickets devouring them and devouring the rooms and the sidewalks of the abandoned houses; blue smoke in eyes that smart and tear with the street's dying warmth. In her jacket pocket la Manuela's hand grasped the piece of dress like someone who rubs a charm to urge it to perform its magic.

Only a block more to the station, the end of this side of town, and then Ludo's house just around the corner, always cozy and warm with the stove lit since early morning. She hurried past the houses in that neighborhood, the worst in town. Very few were occupied because the coopers moved their businesses to Talca long ago; now, with the good roads, you could get from the country to Talca in no time. It wasn't that the other side of town, where you have the chapel and post office, had better houses or more people, but after all, it is downtown. Of course, in better days this was downtown because of the railroad station. Now it's nothing more than a pasture divided by a line, a dead traffic light, a cracked concrete platform, collapsed among the fennels under a pair of crazy-looking eucalyptus trees, an antediluvian thresh-ing machine on whose rusty orange iron the children played, as if with a tame dinosaur. Further on, behind the mouldy wooden shed, more brambles and a canal separated the town from don Alejandro's vine-yards. La Manuela stopped on the corner to look at them for a moment. Vineyards, vineyards, and more vineyards, as far as the eye could see, all the way to the mountains. Perhaps they weren't all don Alejandro's. If not, they were sure to belong to his relatives, his brothers and brothers-in-law, or at least his cousins. All of them Cruzes. The network of vineyards converged around the houses bordering the town, surrounded by a small park, but a park nonethe-less, and a conglomeration of iron works, dairies, coopers' shops, sheds and wine cellars, all belonging to don Alejo. La Manuela sighed. So much money. And so much power: don Alejo, when he came into his inheritance over a half-century ago, built Estación El Olivo so that the train would stop right there and pick up his produce. And such a good man, don Alejo. What would become of the townspeople without him? Word has it that the gentleman is now going to see to it for sure that we get electric light in town. So cheerful and not at all pompous, considering he's a senator and all. Not like the others, who think a harsh voice and a hairy chest give them the right to insult a person. But who can match a man like don Alejandro? It's true that in the summer, when he'd come to town to hear mass with Misia Blanca and they'd meet by chance on the street, he'd pretend not to see them. Although sometimes, when Misia Blanca wasn't looking, he winked at her.

Ludo served her tea and pastry. La Manuela settled into a chair next to the stove and began rummaging around in the boxes filled with pieces of ribbon and buttons and silk and wool and buckles. Ludovina couldn't see the contents anymore because she was so nearsighted. Almost blind. And la Manuela had told her so many times not to be a dope and to go buy a new pair of glasses. But she never did. When Acevedo died, the moment before they sealed the coffin, Ludo almost went crazy and wanted to throw something in that would accompany her husband through all eternity. The only thing she could think of were her eyeglasses. Naturally. She had been Misia Blanca's servant when Moniquita died of typhus: the missis, desperate, cut off her blond braid that was down to her knees and threw it into the coffin. All of Misia Blanca's hair grew back. But for imitating her, stupid old Ludo lost her eyesight. For Acevedo's sake, she said, he was always so jealous. So that she'd never look at another man. When he was alive, he wouldn't let her have friends of either sex. Just la Manuela. And when they kidded him by reminding him that no matter how things seemed, la Manuela was still Japonesita's father, the cooper just laughed in disbelief. But Japonesita grew up and there was no doubt about it: skinny, dark, bucktoothed, with stiff hair just like la Manuela's.

With the passing years Ludo had become forgetful and repetitive. Yesterday, Ludo told her that when Misia Blanca came to see her she brought a message from don Alejo saying that he wanted to buy her house, funny isn't it don Alejo mentioning that he's interested in my property again but I don't see why and I don't want to leave, I want to die here. And on and on. It's no fun gossiping with her anymore. She didn't even remember what stuff she stashed away in all those boxes, packages, bundles, tubes that she hid in her drawers or under the bed or in corners, covered with dust behind the dresser, stuck between the wardrobe and the wall. Why, she's forgotten everything, everything except don Alejo's family, she knows all their names right down to his great grandchildren. And now she can't even remember who Pancho is.

"What do you mean, you don't remember. I talk about him all the time."

"You talk about so many men all the time."

"You know, that big hunk with the mustache and the red truck who came to town so much last year. He used to live outside of town but he went away and got married. Then he came back. The one with the coal-black eyebrows and the bull's neck that I thought was so nice when I was younger, until he came to the house that time with his drunk friends and was such a pest. That time they tore up my flamenco dress."

No use. For Ludo, Pancho Vega didn't exist. La Manuela felt like leaving, like throwing the tea and boxes of thread on the floor and going home. Stupid old woman. All she had left in her head was a soft lump. Why talk to Ludo if she didn't remember who Pancho Vega was? She poked around in the box so that she could find her thread and leave. Ludo remained silent while la Manuela searched. Then she began to talk.

"He owes don Alejo some money."

La Manuela looked at her.

"Who?"

"The one you were talking about."

"Pancho Vega?"

"Yeah, that one."

La Manuela wrapped the red thread around her little finger.

"How do you know?"

"Did you find some? Don't take it all."

"All right. How do you know?"

"Misia Blanca told me the other day when she came to see me. He's the son of the Vega that passed away who was don Alejo's head cooper when I worked for them. I don't remember the boy. Misia Blanca says that this what's-his-name wanted to be independent of the Cruz family and when don Alejo found out that he was looking to buy a truck, even though it had been a long time since the boy had been in town and his late father had passed away and Berta too, he told him to come around, this kid, and he lent him some money, just like that, without a signature or anything, so that the boy could pay the first installment for his truck . . ."

"So he bought the truck with don Alejo's money?"

"And he hasn't paid him back."

"Not a cent?"

"I don't know."

"He hasn't been around for a year."

"That's why."

"Scoundrel!"

Scoundrel. Scoundrel. If he came around to bother her again, she could say: Scoundrel, you swindled don Alejo, who's been like a father to you. Then, telling him that, she wouldn't be afraid. Or at least, as afraid. It was as if the word would help her break open a hard and sinister scab of Pancho's, that would still be hard and sinister, but in a different way. What a pity all that honking was just a dream . . . then why fix her red dress? She uncoiled the thread on her finger. What was she going to do all afternoon? Rain. Her bones told her so. Go see Ludo? Why? If she spoke to her about Pancho Vega again she was sure to say:

"You're too old to be thinking about men and traipsing around. Stay home and relax, woman, and wrap your feet up, don't you know that at our age the only thing a girl can do is to wait for death to carry her away?"

But death is a woman like herself and Ludo, and among women things can always be arranged. At least with some women, like Ludo, who had always treated her that way, without ambiguities, the way it should be. Japonesita, on the other hand, was all ambiguity. All of a sudden, especially in winter, when the poor thing got so cold that she'd shiver from vintage time until the pruning season, she would start saying that she'd like to get married. And have children. Children! And yet here she is, over eighteen years old and she hasn't gotten her period yet. Amazing. And then Japonesita would say no. She didn't want to be pushed around. And since she owned a whorehouse she might as well be a whore too. But let a man touch her and she'd run like mad. Of course, with that face she didn't have much choice. La Manuela had begged her so many times to make up her mind. Ludo said that she'd be better off getting married, because if nothing else, Japonesita was a hard worker. She should marry a real stud who would get her glands worked up and make love to her. But Pancho was so rough and so drunk that he couldn't excite anyone. Nor could don Alejandro's grandsons. Sometimes, in the summer, they'd get bored with their country homes and with doing nothing and they'd come in for a few drinks: unshaven, four-eyed, quiet, but very young and so busy thinking about their exams that they'd leave after barely drinking anything and without getting involved with anybody. If Japonesita were to get pregnant by one of them . . . no, of course she wouldn't get married, but after all, the child . . . Why not. That was one destiny.

They didn't understand her, la Manuela told herself on the way to chapel, the red thread wrapped around her little finger again. She was going to take the dress in here, at the waist, and there, in the back. And if she lived in a big city, you know, where they say they have carnivals, and all the fags go out dancing in the street all dressed in their finery and having a great time and no one says anything, she would dress up fit to kill. But the men here are all stupid, like Pancho and his friends. Ignorant. Someone told her that Pancho carried a knife. But it wasn't true. When Pancho tried to hit her last year she had the presence of mind to feel the brute over: he wasn't carrying anything. Idiot. They talk against poor fags so much and we haven't done a thing to them . . . but when he grabbed me with the other men and squeezed me hard, with good intentions of course, who's going to stop and think how ugly or how old a woman is. And him so mad because a girl's a fag, heaven knows what he said he'd do to me. Well let's see, scoundrel, swindler. It makes me want to put the dress on right in front of him, just to see what he'd do. Like if he were in town right now. I'd put on my dress and go out with flowers behind my ear, with makeup and all, and everybody in the street saying hello, Manuela, my, you're looking swell today sweetheart, want me to come along . . . Triumphant. And then Pancho, real angry, runs into me on a corner and says you make me sick, go take that off, you're a disgrace to the town. And just when he's about to hit me with those paws of his, I faint . . . into the arms of don Alejo, who's passing by. And don Alejo tells him to leave me alone, not to bother me, that I'm decent folk and after all he's just a tenant's son while I'm the great Manuela, famous throughout the province, and he throws Pancho out of town for good. Then don Alejo lifts me into his car and takes me to the country and puts me in Misia Blanca's bed, Ludo says it's all smooth and pink, simply lovely, and they go get the best doctor in Talca while

Misia Blanca puts compresses on my forehead and gives me smelling salts and tells me look, Manuela, I want us to be friends, stay here in my house until you get well and don't worry, I'll lend you my room and anything you want, just ask, and don't you worry because Alejo is going to throw all the bad people out of town, just wait and see.

"Manuela."

A crossing. Her feet in a mud puddle in the middle of the street. A white mustache, vicuña cape, China-blue eyes under the hat brim, and behind, four black dogs in single file. La Manuela drew back.

"Heavens, don Alejo, how can you come out on the street with those beasts. Hang on to them. I'm getting out of here. Hang on to them."

"They won't hurt you unless I tell them. Easy, Moor . . ."

"They ought to lock you up for walking around with them."

La Manuela was backing off to the other sidewalk.

"Where are you off to? You just stepped into a puddle."

"I'll bet I catch cold. I was on my way to mass, to obey the commandments. I'm no heathen like you, don Alejo. Look at your face, you look half-dead. I'll bet you've been out on a spree, at your age, haven't I told you . . ."

"And you, you must be going to beg forgiveness for your sins, you shameless . . ."

"Sins! Wishful thinking! The spirit's willing, but look how skinny I am. A Saint: Virgin and Martyr . . ."

"Haven't they been saying that you've got Pancho Vega under your spell?"

"Who said that?"

"He did. You better watch out."

The dogs stirred behind don Alejo.

"Down Othello, Moor . . ."

Water soaking her socks, cold pant-legs stuck to her shins. She hadn't felt so near collapse in years. As she walked up the slope toward the next sidewalk she kicked at a pig to make him move away, but she slipped and had to lean on him to keep from falling. From the other side she called to don Alejo:

"Watch out for whom?"

"For Pancho. They say you're all he ever talks about."

"But he never comes to El Olivo anymore. Didn't I hear that he owes you money?"

Don Alejo chuckled.

"You know everything, you old gossip. Do you know, too, that yesterday I went to Talca to see the doctor? And do you know what he told me?"

"The doctor, don Alejo? But you've never looked better . . ."

"You just finished telling me I looked half-dead. And you're going to be half-dead too if Pancho catches up with you."

"But he's not around."

"Oh yes he is."

The honking then, last night. No, she wouldn't go to mass. And she wasn't in the mood for smart alecks on the street. It was too cold. God would forgive her this time. She might catch cold. At her age, the most sensible thing was to get into bed. Yes. Get into bed. Forget about the flamenco dress. Get into bed, if Japonesita didn't have something for her to do, God knows she's always yelling at her to do something or other. Last year Pancho twisted her arm so hard he almost broke it. Now it was hurting her. She didn't want to have anything to do with Pancho Vega. Not a thing.

"Don't go yet, woman . . ."

"Sure. You're not the one he's going to hit."

"Wait."

"Then tell me what you want, don Alejo. Can't you see I'm in a hurry? My feet are wet. If I die you'll have to pay for my funeral because it'll be all your fault. And nothing but the best, ah . . ."

Don Alejo, followed by his dogs, was walking a little ahead of la Manuela on the other side of the street and talking. The last call for eleven o'clock mass. He had to shout to make himself heard because he was near the Guerreros' wagon, full of kids singing:

> It's raining,
> it's pouring,
> the old man is snoring . . .

"Well, don Alejo. What do you want?"

"Ah, yes. Tell Japonesita that I have to talk to her. I'll come by this afternoon. And I want to talk to you, too."

La Manuela stopped before turning the corner.

"Will you come in your car?"

"I don't know. Why?"

"So that you can park it in front of the door. That way Pancho will see that you're with us and won't dare come in."

161

"If I don't bring the car, I'll leave the dogs outside. Pancho's afraid of them."

"Naturally, since he's a coward."

3

Miss Lila looked at Pancho Vega through the window grille, but in spite of the things he was saying she didn't lower her eyes; she had known him too long to be shocked. Besides, it's good to see this big clown again.

"Why you're just like a sailor now, Pancho, only on land, what with your truck and your freight trips: a woman in every port. I'll bet poor Emita never sees hide nor hair of you. Being married to you must be torture."

"She's not complaining."

This time Miss Lila blushed.

"And you, Lilita?"

He tried to take her hand through the grille.

"Cut it out, silly."

Miss Lila motioned toward Octavio who was smoking in the doorway, gazing at the street. Pancho turned to see the object of Lila's fear but seeing only his brother-in-law he shrugged his shoulders. The inside of the shed, whose far end functioned as the post office, was empty except for don Céspedes sitting on one of the bales of clover stacked at the other end. The old man got off his bale and leaned on the doorpost opposite Octavio, to watch the street. Across the road, a few people were hanging around the other shed, the one that was a chapel on Sundays and a party meeting place during the week. It, too, belonged to don Alejo and was even smaller than the post office shed, but this didn't upset the religious ceremonies: the present chapel space was more than enough for the parishioners, especially after harvest when the outsiders and the owners' families would leave. Pancho turned around and lit a cigarette.

"Did the priest from San Alfonso arrive?"

Don Céspedes shook his head.

"They probably had car trouble."

Octavio slapped the old man's shoulder.

"Don Céspedes, you old fool. That priest was probably sleepy this morning and stayed glued between the sheets. They say he danced all night long at old Wooden Heart's house in Talca . . ."

Miss Lila stuck her head out.

"Atheists! You'll go to hell for that."

Pancho laughed while don Céspedes took his hand out of his cape and crossed himself. Octavio went and sat on a bale. Don Céspedes looked at the sky.

"It's going to rain."

He followed Octavio and sat higher up on the pyramid of bales, dangling his dark, dwarfed feet, deformed by scars and dirt in their muddy sandals.

Through the grille the conversation continued.

"Didn't you sleep with Japonesita last night?"

"Me? Not me. I haven't been there for a long time. I'm not wanted there."

"Well, you do overdo it . . ."

"The worst part is that I'm in love."

Miss Lila said sure, Japonesita was a good girl and all, but is she ugly, and no taste at all in clothes. She looks as if she came from an orphanage, with those baggy pants down to her ankles that she wears under her apron. Of course, it's strange that she does that kind of work, since everyone knows she's a decent girl. Yes, yes, she inherited the house from her mother, but she could sell it. When she was a kid, Big Japonesa sent her to school. It was right here, in the shed, before don Alejo bought it. Anyway, my little sister told me that, even though the other girls and the teacher, too, were nice to her, she'd run and hide in the station until school was over and Big Japonesa never found out, and Japonesita never went out to play or anything and wouldn't even talk to anybody . . . All the decent folk feel sorry for Japonesita, such a queer little thing. And for the time being, Miss Lila keeps an eye out for Japonesita so that she can greet her as nicely as possible whenever she sees her on the street. It's only fair, isn't it?

"Yes, but I'm not in love with her . . ."

Miss Lila looked confused.

"Who is it then?"

"It's la Manuela . . ."

Everyone laughed, even Lila.

"Pigs, bums. You ought to be ashamed . . ."

"It's just that she's so cute . . ."

The couple began to whisper again through the bronze bars. Don Céspedes got down from the bales again and stationed himself in the doorway, looking at the sky.

"Christ! Here comes the rain . . ."

The people waiting near the chapel door took shelter under the eaves, plastered to the wall with their hands in their pockets, behind the curtain of rain that fell from the tile roof. The Guerreros' horse was soaked in a second; the Valenzuelas, who had just arrived, waited for mass in their Ford. Don Alejo came running into the post office, his four black dogs behind him. He brushed the water off his cape and hat. The dogs shook themselves violently and Octavio climbed further up to avoid being soaked too. Then they pranced around the shed, making it seem too small for the four of them.

"Good morning, Céspedes."

"Good morning, boss."

Don Alejo glanced at Octavio but didn't greet him. He saw Pancho from behind: the conversation had come to a halt, but he still had his back turned.

"It's good to see you, Pancho . . ."

When Pancho didn't move, don Alejandro motioned to his dogs, who got up from the floor.

"Othello, Sultan . . ."

Pancho turned around. He raised his hands as if he expected to be shot. Don Alejo called his dogs before they could attack.

"Here, Moor . . ."

"Some joke, don Alejo . . ."

"You could at least answer when someone speaks to you."

"People shouldn't make jokes like that."

Octavio looked at them from the top of the bales, near the cross-beam that supported the roof. Don Alejo walked through the store-room toward Pancho, surrounded by the leaping dogs. The only things alive in the whole place, where even the lime on the walls was brown-ish, were the blue of don Alejo's eyes and the red flames of his dogs' slavering tongues.

"And how about your little jokes? Do they seem so trivial to you, you ungrateful bum? Do you think I don't know why you came? I got you a job hauling grapes, but a few days ago, I personally called Augusto to tell him to take it away from you."

"We'd better talk somewhere else . . ."

"Why? Don't you want people to know that you're an ungrateful

164

scoundrel? Besides, it's raining and I don't want to get any wetter, the doctor told me to take care of myself. Don Céspedes, could you do me a favor and run to the butcher, the one just down a ways, and tell Melchor to send me a few good scraps so these dogs will quiet down. And who's that?"

Octavio quickly jumped down from the bales. He cleared his throat while he dusted his dark suit and adjusted the tie that had slipped inside his shirt. Pancho answered.

"Octavio, my brother-in-law."

"The one who works at the gas station?"

"Yes, sir. At your service. Me and Pancho are buddies, you can talk in front of me . . ."

The restlessness of the four black dogs, their magnificent tails, and pulsating throats, filled the shed. Don Alejo's deft eyes withstood Pancho's black look, forcing it to stay fixed under the shadowy eyelashes. He read those eyes like a book: Pancho didn't want Octavio to know about his debt. The wind rustled through the shreds of old letters tacked to the wall.

"So you don't care if I call you an ungrateful scoundrel just as long as we're alone? In that case, you're a filthy coward as well."

"That's enough, don Alejo."

"Your father, God rest his soul, wouldn't let me talk to him like that. Now there was a man. The son who was going to take after him! I lent you that money for him and he's the only reason I haven't had you put away. Get it?"

"I didn't sign anything."

The dogs, sensing don Alejo's fury, stood up, teeth bared, growling at Pancho.

"You lying bastard."

"Here, I've brought you the five overdue payments."

"And do you think that will satisfy me? Don't you think I know why you came? I can see under that layer of grease, I know you as if you were my own. It's obvious, they canceled your freight contracts. So you've come with your tail between your legs to pay me, so that I'll get them back for you. Give me the money, you ungrateful bum . . . give it to me, I said . . ."

"I'm not ungrateful."

"What are you, then, a thief?"

"All right, don Alejo, cut it out, that's enough . . ."

"Give me the money."

Pancho handed him the wad of bills, warm because he had been clutching them in his hand in the bottom of his pocket, and don Alejo slowly counted them. Then he put them under his cape. Negus licked the toe of his shoe.

"All right. You still owe me six installments, and I want them on time, you understand. And listen, I want you to understand something anyone less stupid would already know: I pull a lot of strings, so be careful. You're not getting away with anything just because you didn't sign a piece of paper; if I gave you some freedom it was to see how you'd act, although knowing you like I do, I should have known better and let you sweat it out by yourself. Now you know. Next time tell me you can't pay me on time, act like a man, and then we'll see what I can do for you."

"It's just that I didn't have the time . . ."

"That's a lie."

"It's because I haven't been in the neighborhood, don Alejo."

"Another lie. When are you going to break that damn habit? They told me you were seen several times in your brother-in-law's gas station on the north-south road. Would it have done you any harm to drive the mile and a half here or to the outskirts of town? Or don't you know the way to the house where you were born?"

No. He didn't want to have anything to do with that house or with this lousy town. It pained him to give his money to don Alejo. It meant recognizing the old link, and being chained again to everything he had managed to forget for a while, like a person who whistles to forget his fear of the dark; for five months he had the strength to not pay him, to resist him and save the money, to dream about using it for other things as if he had the right to spend it. It was a little extra money for the house that Ema wanted to buy in that new district in Talca, the one with the houses that looked alike, only painted different colors so that they don't look alike, and when Ema wants something there's no stopping her. Fortunately, Pancho didn't spend much time at home now with all his jobs, sometimes he even preferred to park the truck on the side of the road and sleep there. That's why, she was always saying, that's why I need the house, I almost never see you and how do I know what you're up to, the child and I should have some compensation. . . . And when I take to bed with my ulcer, a fire that burns me here, an animal that roots and gnaws and tears and sucks me, here, inside, and I can't sleep or talk or move or drink or eat, or hardly even breathe; sometimes when everything is hard and cramped and I'm afraid the animal will bite me and I'll burst, then Ema takes care of me, and I look to her because without her I would die and she knows it. So she takes care of him as if he were a moaning, repentant child, but she knows he'll still do the same things the same old way. That's why Pancho needs the house. Sometimes he drives by the neighborhood in his truck to see how fast the "For Sale" signs are disappearing. Now there are no more pink ones left, just blue and yellow, and Ema wanted a pink one. What are a few hundred dollars to don Alejo?

"So why don't you call don Augusto back so I can have those good freight routes again?"

"What was so hard about settling your accounts with me, if the freights were so good?"

Pancho didn't answer. The rain was running the puddles together in the road: impossible to cross. The priest arrived and the people went into the chapel. Pancho didn't answer because he didn't want to. He didn't have to make excuses to anybody, much less to this pompous ass who thought that just because Pancho had been born on his land . . . They said he was don Alejo's son. But then they'd say that about everybody, Miss Lila, Japonesita, and God knows who else, every blue-eyed peon for miles around, but not me. I'd stake my life on my old lady's virtue, and my eyes, they're black and so are my eyebrows, sometimes they take me for a Turk. I don't owe him anything. As a boy his work was driving a tractor and later he learned, on the sly, to drive the car, stealing it from don Alejo with the help of the gentleman's grandsons who were the same age . . . That's all. Learning to drive was all that he owed don Alejo. Plus the last payments for the truck. Until his debt was settled, keep it quiet. Let Ema wait. Maybe another neighborhood like that one, and then everything he wanted, freedom, being on his own, not having to make accounts to anyone . . . that'll be the last of this lousy town for me. But the old man had to say I was behind in my payments in front of Octavio. So that later Octavio might mention it and Ema's stuck-up brothers . . . no, not Octavio, he's my friend . . . the rest of them, yeah, they'll gossip about me all over the place.

"So? What was so hard about it?"

Don Céspedes came back with the scraps. The dogs whined eagerly, licking his feet, his hands, jumping on him, all but knocking him down.

"Throw them a scrap, don Céspedes . . ."

The gory hunk flew and the dogs leaped after it, the four of them falling together in a clot on the floor, fighting over the piece of meat that was still warm, almost alive. They clawed at it, trampling it into the floor and howling at it, bloody snouts drooling, pimply palates, yellow eyes flashing in narrow faces. The men stuck to the walls. The meat devoured, the dogs began to dance, not around don Céspedes who had fed them, but don Alejo, as if they knew that the man with the .cape owned the meat they ate and the vineyards they guarded. He caressed them—his four dogs, black as wolf shadows with their bloody fangs and heavy ferocious paws of the purest blood line.

"No. Not until you pay me the remaining installments. I don't have any reason to trust you. I'm old and I'm going to die and I don't want to leave any loose ends . . ."

"All right, whatever you want, don Alejo . . ."

The floor was a crimson swamp. The dogs sniffed, snorting in search of something to lick. Pancho Vega clenched his teeth. He looked at Octavio, who winked at him, don't be upset, pal, just wait, we'll straighten this thing out between ourselves. But boy, this old rooster was tough. They heard the church bells.

"Aren't you going to mass, Pancho?"

He didn't answer.

"When you were little you used to help during the services. It made poor Blanca very happy to see you so pious, such a pretty little boy. And those long confessions, we almost died laughing . . . How about you, don Céspedes?"

"Of course, boss . . ."

"See? Don Céspedes goes to mass."

Pancho looked at Octavio, who shook his head.

"Don Céspedes is your tenant."

And he swallowed hard so that he could add:

"I'm not."

"But you owe me money and he doesn't."

True. Better not start anything now. Better go to mass without arguing. Can't do me any harm. When I'm home on Sunday, Ema dresses Normita in her sky-blue coat with the white fur and tells me to come with them to the eleven-thirty mass, which is the best one, and I go because it makes no difference to me and I like to greet the neighbors, sometimes I enjoy it and even look forward to it, other times I don't, but I always go because we look so elegant. I'll go with don Alejo, he's watching me from the door, ordering me to go. But Pancho couldn't help saying:

"No. I'm not going."

Octavio smiled, satisfied at last. But before leaving, don Alejo turned.

"Ah. I almost forgot. They told me you've been talking about la Manuela, saying you're going to get her or something. Don't let me find out that you've gone to Japonesita's to bother them, they're good people. You've been warned."

He walked out followed by his dogs, who splashed across the muddy road and waited under the eaves behind the sheet of water. Don Céspedes, hat in hand, held the chapel door open: the dogs entered with the ringing of the bells, and behind them, don Alejo.

4

Japonesita couldn't guess at first why don Alejo wanted to speak to her so urgently. When la Manuela gave her the message, she was surprised, the senator would always drop in without warning like a man in his own home. But soon she realized that so much protocol could mean only one thing: he was finally going to tell her the result of his efforts to bring electricity to town. He had been promising to get it done for a long time. But the answer to the request was always put off from year to year, who knows how many now, and it was never the right moment to approach the authorities. The Commissioner was always away on a trip or we're already spending too much on another area or the secretary of the Commission belongs to the enemy party and it would be better to wait.

But last Monday, as she crossed the Place of Arms in Talca on her way to the bank, Japonesita met don Alejandro on his way to the Commission. They stopped on the corner. He bought her a bag of roasted peanuts, a present he said, but while they talked he ate almost all of them himself, crushing the shells which stuck to the hair of his vicuña cape as they fell, there where his belly protruded a little. He said this time for sure: everything was ready. He had an interview with the Commissioner in half an hour and he was going to throw the Commissioner's neglect of Estación El Olivo back in his face. Japonesita had wandered around the square waiting for don Alejo to return with the results of the momentous interview. Then, since she had other things to do and it was time to catch the train, she had to leave without seeing him. All week she had waited for him to come into town, but he didn't even pass through, not once. She resigned herself to wondering, and more waiting.

But today's the day. Finally. Japonesita stayed in the kitchen after lunch, while all the whores crawled back into their caves and la Manuela took Lucy to her room. Instead of adding another log to revive the remaining cinders in the stove, she kept creeping closer and closer to the fading fire, burrowing deeper and deeper into her shawl: my bones are blue from cold. It was already getting dark out. The rain kept coming and the water slowly covered the brick stepping stones that Cloty had placed across the patio. On the other side, facing the kitchen, Lucy's door was open and Japonesita watched her light a candle. From time to time she looked over to see what they were laughing about. The last outburst, the loudest yet, was because la Manuela, with his mouth full of hairpins from the modern hairdo he was giving Lucy, couldn't help laughing and scattered the pins on the floor, which kept the two of them on their knees quite awhile.

There was still some light outside. But it was reluctant, and too feeble to defeat the kitchen's darkness. Japonesita reached out to touch one of the burners: a trace of heat. All this was going to change with electricity. This awful weather. The water invaded the kitchen through the adobe wall, forming a mud that stuck to everything. Maybe then she could stand the aggressive cold that seized her body with the first winds, cramping and squeezing it. Maybe the humidity would stop mounting from May to June to July, until by August the scummy mildew seemed to completely cover her body, her face, her clothing, her food, everything. Electricity would bring the town back to life as in the days of her mother's youth. Last Monday, while she waited for don Alejo, she wandered through a store where they sold Wurlitzers. She had often stopped at the window to look at them, separated from their colors and music by her own reflection in the glass. She had never gone in. This time she did. A salesman with colorless eyelashes and translucent ears waited on her, demonstrating, wooing her with pamphlets, assuring her of long-term guarantees. Japonesita realized that she was going through the motions without really believing that she could ever buy one of those wonderful machines. But she could. As soon as the town got electricity she was going to buy a Wurlitzer. Immediately. No, sooner. Because if don Alejo was bringing her the news today that he had received permission to install the electricity or that he had succeeded in signing an agreement or document, she would buy the Wurlitzer tomorrow, Monday morning, the one with the most colors, with the painting of a turquoise sea and palm trees, the biggest one of all. Tomorrow morning she would talk to the boy with the colorless lashes and ask him to have it delivered. Then, the first day the electricity went on in town, the Wurlitzer would go on in her house.

Better not say anything to la Manuela. She would only have to mention the project and he'd go crazy with excitement, jabbering, anticipating, not a moment's peace, until she'd end up deciding not to buy anything at all. He was undressing in the room across the way, to try on the red dress by candlelight. At his age he was no longer afraid of the cold. Just like my mother, may she rest in peace. Even on the worst days, like this one for instance, she'd always wear a low-cut dress, big and fat, her heavy breasts like bulging sacks of grapes. At the neckline's V where her breasts began to swell she always carried a tiny handkerchief, and while she was chatting or drinking from her enormous wine bottle or making the best pastry in the world, she would take out her handkerchief and dry the almost imperceptible drops of perspiration that always broke out on her forehead and nose, and especially around the low neckline. They said that Big Japonesa died because of some liver thing, from drinking so much wine. But that's not true. She didn't drink that much. My mother died of grief. Grief because Estación El Olivo was going downhill, because it was no longer what it used to be. All the talking she'd do to don Alejo about the electricity. Nothing doing. Then they said the paved road, the north-south, was going to go right through El Olivo, and that would make it an important town. As long as she had hope my mother thrived. But then they told her the truth, I think it was don Alejo, that the road would only come within a mile and a half of the town, and then she began to lose hope. The north-south is silver-plated, straight as a knife: with one slash it cut the life out of Estación El Olivo, nestled in a cozy bend of the old road. They didn't ship the freight by rail anymore, but by truck, on the road. Now the train came through only a couple of times a week. Scarcely a handful of townspeople were left. Big Japonesa remembered, toward the end, how in the old days the midday summer mass would attract the most sumptuous wagons and carriages in the area, and the elegant young men from the country would meet at sunset in front of the post office, on purebred horses, to pick up the mail that came by train. The boys, so proper during the day when they escorted their sisters, cousins, or sweethearts, let their hair down at night at Japonesa's house, which never closed. And then just the road construction men came, traveling the mile and a half on foot, and then not even them, only the common laborers from nearby, the tenants, the peons, the outsiders who came for harvest. Another class entirely. And later on, not even them. Now the trip to Talca was so short that Sunday was the slowest day—you could be in the city in no time, and it was useless to try and compete with houses like Wooden Heart's. Not even electricity, she used to say, not even that, she was always complaining about so many things, about the fire in her stomach, monotonously, softly complaining, bloated and hollow-eyed toward the end. But no, never, nothing, in spite of don Alejo's telling her to wait just a bit more but one fine day she couldn't wait anymore and she started to die. And when she died we buried her in the cemetery at San Alfonso because El Olivo doesn't even have a cemetery. El Olivo is nothing but a few run-down houses scattered by the geometry of vineyards which seem on the verge of swallowing them up. And what's he laughing about? What right does he have to ignore the cold that's shredding my bones?

"Father!"

She shouted it from the kitchen door. La Manuela stopped in the lighted frame of Lucy's doorway. Thin, small, she looked like a teenager, standing there in the doorway with one hip gracefully turned out and his face outlined in the dark. But she knew that body. It didn't give off heat. It didn't warm the sheets. It wasn't her mother's body: that almost material heat that she had crawled into as if it were a cauldron, sinking into it, drying her moldy clothing and her bones and everything . . .

"What?"

"Come here."

"What do you want?"

"Just come here."

"I'm busy with Lucy."

"I'm telling you I need you."

La Manuela, covering himself with the flamenco dress, crossed the lake in the patio as well as he could, paddling among the fallen leaves from the grape arbor. Japonesita sat down again by the dying fire.

"So dark here, child. Is this a wake?"

Japonesita didn't answer.

"I'm throwing another log on the fire."

He didn't wait for it to catch fire.

"Shall I light a candle?"

What for? She could spend the whole afternoon, the whole day in the dark, like now, without the slightest nostalgia for light, although she would long for a little heat.

"All right."

La Manuela lit the candle and after putting it on the table near the potatoes, put on his glasses and sat down to sew by its light. Lucy's room was dark. She would sleep till dinner. It was easy to kill time that way. Five o'clock. Still three hours till dinner. Three hours and it was already dark. Three hours before night, before work.

"I'll bet no one comes tonight."

La Manuela stopped. He held the dress up against his body, the neck with his chin, the waist with his hands.

"How does it look?"

"Okay."

The rain stopped. In the henhouse they heard Lucy's turkey ruffle his feathers arrogantly: the payment of one lover who didn't have anything else to give. The dress fit perfectly.

"I'll bet no one comes tonight."

"You know that Pancho Vega will come."

La Manuela pricked her finger with the needle and sucked it.

"Me? That Pancho Vega's coming?"

"Of course. Why else are you fixing your dress?"

"But he's not in town."

"You told me last night you heard the horn . . ."

"Yes, but I don't . . ."

"You know he's coming."

Why deny it. The girl's right. Pancho will come tonight come hell or high water. She picked up her dress, the ancient percale, warm from the fire. The whole damn day raining like the devil and she fixing her dress, and herself. Let's see if he's the man he says he is. He'll regret it. If anything happens tonight, the whole town will know, everyone, even the dead, we'll see how much he likes saying things about poor fags. La Manuela laid the dress down and put the candle on the wash basin, below the piece of mirror. She began to comb her hair. So little left. Barely four strands to slick across my skull. I can't do any hairdo with it. Those days are gone.

"Listen."

Japonesita raised her head.

"What?"

"Come over here."

She moved to a wicker chair in front of the mirror. La Manuela took hold of Japonesita's lank hair, squinted both eyes and looked at her, you have to try to look pretty, and began to untangle it—what good is it being a woman if you're not a flirt, that's what men like, silly, that's what they come here for, to forget the scarecrows they're married to, and with your hair this way, look, this is how you do it, now it looks nice, with a bit falling over your forehead and the rest up in what they call a beehive; and la Manuela untangles it for her and here they put a ribbon, don't you have a pretty ribbon? I think I have one stuck away in my suitcase, I'll lend it to you if you want, I'll put it right here. Last summer I saw one of don Alejo's granddaughters with her hair like that, see how nice you look with it this way, don't be silly, take advantage of it . . . look, this way . . .

Japonesita calmly gave in. Yes. He was sure to come. She knew it as well as la Manuela did. Last year, when he tried to take advantage of her, she felt his sour breath on her cheek, in her nostrils. Under her father's thin hands, which occasionally grazed her face, the memory pressed on Japonesita. He had seized her with his brick-rough hands, his square thumb, the corroded, oil-stained, wide, flat nail imbedded in her arm, hurting, a bruise that lasted over a month . . .

"Father."

La Manuela didn't answer.

"What do we do if he comes?"

La Manuela put the comb down. In front of the mirror Japonesita's hair was as smooth as an African's skin.

"You have to protect me if Pancho comes."

La Manuela threw the hairpins on the floor. That was the limit. Why did she keep playing the fool? Did she expect her, la Manuela, to stand up to a hulking brute like Pancho? She's got to realize it once and for all and stop telling herself lies . . . you damn well know I'm just a hopeless fag, no one ever tried to hide it from you. And you're asking me for protection: when Pancho comes I'll run and hide like a nervous hen. It isn't my fault I'm your father. He didn't make the famous bet and he didn't want anything to do with the whole affair. What could he do. I've asked you I don't know how many times since Big Japonesa died to give me my share so that I can go, where I don't know, there'll always be some whorehouse where I can work . . . but you never wanted me to go. And neither did I. It was all Big Japonesa's fault, she had convinced him—that they would make a fortune with the house, what did the girl matter, and when Big Japonesa was alive the girl didn't count because la Manuela liked her mother . . . but it's been four years since they buried her in the cemetery at San Alfonso because this lousy town doesn't even have its own cemetery, and they'll bury me there too, and in the meantime, here sits la Manuela. Not even a floor in the kitchen: plain mud. So why should Japonesita bother her? If she wanted someone to protect her, she should get married, or get a man. Why he wasn't even good for dancing anymore. Last year, after that Pancho thing, his daughter bawled him out saying she was ashamed of being the daughter of an old fairy like him. That of course she'd like to go somewhere else to live and start a new business. But that she wouldn't because Estación El Olivo was small and everyone knew them and were so used to them that they didn't even notice. Not even the children asked questions because they were born knowing it. There's no need for explaining, that's what Japonesita said, and one of these days the town is going to go up in smoke and you and me with it, this shitpile of a town that never asks questions and that nothing ever surprises. A store in Talca. No sir. No restaurant, no cigar stand, no laundromat, no warehouse, nothing. For us El Olivo, to hide in. . . . Okay, okay, you crappy girl, then don't call me father. Because when Japonesita called him father, the flamenco dress over the washstand looked older, the percale threadbare, the red faded, the stitches showing, horrible, inane, and the long, cold, dark night reaching through the vineyards, clutching, choking this spark that had been cultivated in the deserted town, don't call me father, empty-headed bitch. Call me la Manuela, like everybody else. And you want me to protect you! That's all I need. And what about me, who's going to protect me? No, one of these fine days I'm packing my wares and leaving for a big town like Talca. I'm sure Wooden Heart will give me a job. But he had said that once too often and he was sixty years old. He went on smoothing his daughter's hair.

"What am I supposed to protect you from? Don't be a fool, go to bed with him. He's splendid. The best stud around and he has a truck and everything and he could take us for rides. And since you'll have to be a whore someday . . ."

. . . let him have her. Tonight's the night, even if there will be bleeding. With Pancho Vega or anyone else, she knew that. But today it's Pancho. For a whole year she'd been dreaming of him. Dreaming that he beat her and raped her, but in that violence, beneath it or within it, she found something that beat the winter's cold. Last winter, because Pancho was cruel and brutal and had twisted her arm, had been the warmest winter since Big Japonesa died. And la Manuela's fingers, touching her head, patting her cheek near the ear while fabricating a flirtatious curl, they weren't so cold . . . he was a child, la Manuela. She could hate him, like a minute ago. And not hate him. A child, a little bird. Anything but a man. He himself said he was very much the woman. But that wasn't true either. Anyway, he's right. If I'm going to be a whore I may as well start with Pancho.

La Manuela finished doing Japonesita's hair up in a beehive. A woman. She was a woman. She would get Pancho. He was a man. A poor old queer. A fag who was mad for parties and wine and rags and men. It was easy to forget, sheltered here in town—yes, she's right, we better stay here. But then Japonesita would suddenly call him that and his own image would blur as if a drop of water had fallen on it and then he'd lose sight of herself, himself, myself, I don't know, he doesn't know, he can't see la Manuela anymore and there's nothing, this anguish, this helplessness, nothing else, this enormous blot of water in which he's shipwrecked.

As he gave the finishing touches to the hairdo la Manuela sensed through her hair that his daughter was warming up to him. As if she had really surrendered her head so that he could make it beautiful. This kind of help he could and wanted to give her. Japonesita was smiling.

"Light another candle so I can see myself better . . ."

He lit it and set it on the other side of the mirror. Japonesita softly touched her own reflection in the piece of mirror. She turned around:

"Do I look all right?"

Yes, if Pancho wasn't such a beast Japonesita might fall in love with him and they'd be lovers for a while until he left her and went away with someone else because that's the way men are and then she'd be different. And maybe not so stingy, thought la Manuela, not so tight with my money, after all, I work hard enough to get it. And maybe she won't be so cold. A little pain or bitterness when the brute leaves, but what did that matter, if she, and la Manuela too, would feel easier.

It was one of those nights when la Manuela felt like going to bed: bundle up, take a pill, and, another day. She didn't want to see anybody because she had given all her warmth to Japonesita, leaving herself with none. Outside the clouds chased around the vast sky that was beginning to clear, and in the patio the kneading trough, chicken coop, outhouse, everything, even the most insignificant object acquired volume, flinging precise shadows over the water wasting away under

176

the speckled sky. Maybe Pancho wouldn't come after all . . . it was probably one of don Alejo's jokes, him being so fond of jokes. Maybe not even don Alejo would come in this cold—he himself said he was sick and that the doctors were pestering him with examinations and diets and treatments. She touched her dress, wilted over the dirty potatoes, and in the silence she heard Lucy's snores from the other side of the patio. She saw herself in the mirror, over her daughter's face which gazed at itself ecstatically . . . the candles, on either side, were like those of a wake. Her own wake would have light like that, in the parlor where she used to dance when the party's warmth had melted the harshness of everything. She was going to remain in Estación El Olivo forever. Die here, a long, long time before this daughter of hers who couldn't dance but was young and a woman whose hope, as she looked at herself in the broken mirror, wasn't a grotesque lie.

"Do I really look good?"

"Not bad . . . for an ugly thing like you . . ."

5

They put a jar of wine, the very best, in front of him, but he didn't even taste it. While he was talking, Japonesita removed one of the pins that held her hair and scratched her head with it. The dogs were lying on the mud sidewalk, growling near the door from time to time or scratching at it so hard that they almost knocked it down.

"Easy, Negus . . . easy, Moor . . ."

La Manuela also sat at the table. She poured herself a glass of wine, the kind her daughter reserved for special occasions and never let her drink. Cloty, Lucy, Elvira, and another whore were drinking tea in a corner where the wind, blowing in through the cracks in the doors and roof, wouldn't get them. Pour me some more. No one's coming tonight. They were yawning. She'll probably close up as soon as the gentleman leaves and then we can go to sleep. Elvira, change the record, put on "Bésame Mucho," no no, something better, a happier one. Elvira wound the Victrola on top of the counter, but before putting on another record she started to clean it with a rag, straightening the pile of records next to it.

Don Alejo brought bad news: they weren't going to install electricity in town. Until who knows when. Maybe never. The Commissioner said he didn't have time to bother with anything so insignificant, that it was El Olivo's destiny to disappear. Not even all of don Alejo's influence combined with that of the whole Cruz clan could convince the Commissioner. Maybe in a couple of years, but he wasn't making any promises. Come back then and we'll see if things have cleared up any. It was the same as a flat no. And that's what don Alejo told Japonesita, in no uncertain terms. He tried to convince her that it was logical the Commissioner would think that way, he gave her reasons and explanations even though Japonesita didn't utter a single word of protest—yes, well you see, child, there are so few coopers left, a couple, I think, and so old now, and the rest of the people, as you can see, are so few and so poor, and the train hardly even stops here anymore, just on Mondays, so you can get on in the morning and come back in the afternoon when you go to Talca. Even the wine cellar at the station is falling down and it's been so long since I've used it that not even the smell of wine is left.

"Even Ludo told me this morning when I went to ask for red thread, before I met you, don Alejandro, that she was thinking about moving to Talca. It's only natural, what with her Acevedo buried there, and mass every day, and her sister and all . . ."

"Ludo? I didn't know that. How strange that Blanca didn't say anything and I saw her just a while ago. How is Ludo? Is the house hers . . .?"

"Of course, Acevedo bought it for her when . . ."

Then la Manuela remembered that Ludo had told her that don Alejo wanted to buy it from her, so he knew very well who the property belonged to. She looked at him, but when her eyes met the senator's she looked away, and glancing at the whores she motioned them to come over by the stove. Lucy settled herself between Japonesita and don Alejo and she offered him the wine again.

"Don't you dare turn me down, don Alejo. It's from the vintage you like so well. Why even you don't have any of this left . . ."

"No thank you, dear. I'm on my way. It's getting late."

He picked up his hat, but before getting up he lingered a moment and covered Japonesita's hand with his huge one. She dropped the hairpin in a pool of wine on the table.

"You ought to get out of here too. Why do you stay?"

La Manuela was burning to take part.

"That's what I keep telling her, don Alejo. Why are we staying here?"

The whores stopped murmuring in the corner and, as if expecting a verdict, looked at Japonesita. Huddled in her pink shawl, making the slow steady motion of negation with her head that la Manuela knew.

"Don't be silly. Go to Talca and set up business with la Manuela. You have plenty of money in the bank. I know because the other day I asked the manager, my cousin, about the state of your account. I wish it were mine . . . that's what he told me, a lot of holdings and a lot of debts, but Japonesita has it all cleared up. Buy a restaurant, for example. If you don't have enough I'll ask the bank for a loan and I'll endorse it for you. You'll have the money in a couple of days, everything arranged among friends, people you know. Cheer up, girl, can't you see, this isn't living. Right, Manuela?"

"Certainly, don Alejo, help me convince her . . ."

"Why ask him when all he wants is to fool around?"

"The money belongs to both of you, in equal shares, that's how I see it. Isn't that how Big Japonesa left it?"

"Yes. We would have to sell the house . . ."

Don Alejo let scarcely a minute elapse.

"I'll buy it from you . . ."

His eyes were turned down, staring at the hairpin floating in the wine. And on the back of the generous hand that sheltered Japonesita's golden hairs flamed. But she, la Manuela, was very sharp, and he wasn't going to fool her. She had known him too long not to realize he was plotting something. She had always wanted to catch him at one of those shady deals his political enemies accused him of. Of course, when they elected him deputy almost twenty years ago, he sold the voters a lot of cheap land, on long terms, here in Estación, because this town is on its way up, there's a big future here, in these parts, and the people started painting and fixing their houses, because naturally, values were going up around here . . . yessiree, not even a sewer, and barely a couple of streets of flattened ground. What do you want to do to us now? Don't you think you've done enough already? What's gotten into your head now, want to buy the few houses in town that aren't already yours. Don't come around telling her, la Manuela, stories. Don Alejo didn't come to tell them the bad news about the electricity, he came to offer to buy the house. His blue eyes had sparkled at the mention of Ludo's house. And now this house . . . he wanted to take it away from them, hers and Japonesita's house. What did it matter if don Alejo made them jump through hoops and lose all their money, as long as they went to live in Talca!

"You don't like this business, you never liked it, not the way your

179

mother did. I'll get you the money tomorrow if you want, and we can draw up the sales contract at the notary's, if you decide. Give her a little push, Manuela. I can help you find a convenient locale in Talca, a good one, a really good one. Are you taking the train tomorrow?"

"Yes. I have to make a deposit."

"Well then . . ."

She didn't answer.

This time don Alejo stood up: the kernel of light in the neck of the carbon lamp fluttered with the cape's motion. The dogs began to pace around outside, thirstily smelling the air of the room through the door hinge. La Manuela and Japonesita followed him to the door. He reached for the latch. With his other hand he put on his hat; it shadowed his face. He spent a few moments talking to them, repeating that they should think it over, if they wanted they could talk about it again another day, he was at their service, they knew how fond he was of them, if they wanted the house appraised, he knew an honest authority and was prepared to pay the appraiser's estimate . . .

When he finally opened the door, went out into the air and the stars, and closed it again, the Wurlitzer behind Japonesita's frowning eyes shattered into a million pieces. She and the town faded into darkness. What did it matter if everything went downhill, it made no difference as long as she didn't have to move or change. No. She'd stay here, surrounded by the things she knew, surrounded by this obscurity in which nothing happened that wasn't a degree of slow, invisible death. No. The electricity and the Wurlitzer were nothing more than mirages which for an instant, a blessedly short one, made her believe that something else was possible. But not now. Not a hope remained to grieve her, even fear was eliminated. Nothing would ever change, it never had, it would be the same forever. She went back to the table and sat in the chair warm from don Alejo's cape. She leaned over the stove.

"Lock the door, Cloty . . ."

La Manuela, who was walking toward the Victrola, stopped short and turned abruptly.

"Are we going to close up?"

"Yes. No one's coming now."

"But it's not going to rain anymore."

"The roads are probably filled with mud."

"But . . ."

". . . and there's a frost coming."

La Manuela went to sit on the other side of the stove, and also leaned over it. Cloty put "Black Flowers" on the Victrola and the record began to shriek. The other whores disappeared.

"Why don't we think about what don Alejo said?" she said.

Because suddenly she saw that don Alejo, just as he had created the town, had other plans now, and to carry them out he needed to get rid of Estación El Olivo. He would tear down all the houses, he would wipe away the crude mud streets and cow dung, he would reunite the adobe of the thick walls with the land it came from and he would plow that land, all for some incomprehensible purpose. She saw it all. Clearly. The electricity would have meant salvation. Now . . .

"Let's leave, daughter."

Japonesita began talking without looking at la Manuela, scrutinizing the gray-headed coals. At first it seemed as if she were only singing softly, or praying, but then la Manuela realized she was talking to him.

"Stop the record, Cloty, I can't hear."

"Will you need me?"

"No."

"Well, goodnight."

"Goodnight. I'll close up later."

They were alone in the parlor huddled over the stove.

". . . let well enough alone. What would we do in a big town? People laughing at us . . . no friends, living in another house. Here there'll always be peasants who are horny or who feel like getting drunk . . . We won't die of hunger or shame. Every Monday when I go to Talca I get back to the station early to wait for the train so people won't look at me—sometimes I wait for over an hour, sometimes two, and there's almost no one at the station . . ."

When Japonesita started talking like that la Manuela felt like screaming, it was as if his daughter were drowning him in words, slowly encircling him with her flat voice, that monotonous singsong. Damn the town! Damn the girl! Believing things were going to change and his life would improve because Big Japonesa made him her partner and house proprietor after the bet that, thanks to him, she won from don Alejo. Of course things were better then. Even the carbon lamps gave off more light, not like now with the rains starting and oh, my God, four months of feeling ugly and old, when I could have been a princess. And now don Alejo offering to help us so that we can go to Talca and start a business, the two of us happy, no troubles, she'd like dry goods since rags was something she knew about, but no, the girl would start in talking and never stop, like now, slowly building a wall around la Manuela. Japonesita turned the screw to put out the lamp.

"Leave it alone."

She stopped for a moment but then continued turning the screw.

"Fuck you, I said leave it alone. . . ."

La Manuela's scream startled Japonesita, but she kept turning down the light, as if she hadn't heard. Even if I yell I don't exist. Until one fine day she, who could have been the princess of the whorehouses from Chanco to Constitución, from Villa Alegre to San Clemente, princess of all the whorehouses in the province, she would kick the bucket and the old woman of death would come to carry her off forever. Then no trick or lie would convince the stinking old witch to let her be for a little while longer, why do you want to stay, for God's sake, Manuela, let's go, business is much better on the other side, and they would bury her in a niche in the San Alfonso cemetery under a stone that would say, "Manuel González Astica" and then, for a while, Japonesita and the girls from the house would bring her flowers but then Japonesita was sure to go somewhere else, and of course, Ludo would die too and no more flowers and no one in the whole area, just a few spitting old men, would remember that the great Manuela was lying there.

She went to the Victrola to put on another record.

Black flowers
of destiny
in my loneliness
your soul will tell me
I love yooooooouuuu . . .

La Manuela stopped the record. She put her hand on the black turntable. Japonesita had stood up too. In the center of the night, far away, on the road that led into town from the north-south highway, a horn swelled, a hot, insistent, red flame that got closer and closer. A horn. Again. Playing the fool, the idiot, waking everyone up at this hour. It was coming into town. The truck with the double tires on the back wheels. Honking all the time, now in front of the chapel, yes, honking and honking because he's probably drunk. La Manuela smiled, the fragments of her face neatly arranged.

"Turn off the lamp, you fool."

Before it went out, la Manuela made out a smile on her daughter's face—fool, she's not afraid of Pancho, she wants him to come, she's waiting for him, the fool is eager for him to come, and I'm waiting too, dirty old woman . . . but it was important for Pancho to think that no one was up. And important that he not come in, that he think everyone in the house was asleep. That he knew they weren't waiting for him and that he couldn't come in even if he wanted to.

"He's coming."

"What are we going to do . . ."

"Don't move."

The horn came closer in the night, undeniably closer, as if in the whole vineyard-striped land there was nothing that could stop it. In the dark la Manuela went to the door. She opened the latch. Scoundrel, waking up the whole town at this hour! She remained by the door while the horn summoned and aroused every muscle, every nerve and left them alive and suspended, ready to receive wounds or blows—that horn wouldn't stop. Here he comes, yes, in front of the house . . . her ears ached and Japonesita closed her eyes and covered her ears. But like la Manuela, she was smiling.

"Pancho . . ."

"What are we going to do?"

6

The women of the town agreed not to complain for having to stay home that night, even though they knew perfectly well that the men were going to Japonesa's. The mayor's wife, the police sergeant's wife, the postmaster's wife, the schoolmaster's wife: they all knew their men were going to celebrate don Alejandro Cruz's victory, and they knew exactly where and how they'd celebrate it. But because the party was in don Alejandro's honor and anything that had to do with him must be good, they didn't say a word.

That morning they had seen the three Farías sisters step off the train from Talca: Fat and squat like barrels, their flowered silk dresses girdling their beefy flesh like steel bands; they were sweating from the effort of carrying the harp and guitars. Two younger women also got off, and a man, if you could call him that. The women, watching from a careful distance, discussed what he might be: skinny as a broomstick, with long hair, his eyes were made up almost as much as the Farías sisters'. Standing near the platform, knitting to not waste time, surrounded by kids whom they had to keep scolding so they wouldn't beg from the strangers, they had something to talk about for days to come.

"He must be the queer who plays the piano."

"But Japonesa doesn't have a piano."

"That's true."

"They said she was going to buy one."

"He's an actor, look at that case he's carrying."

"He's a queer, that's what he is . . ."

And the kids trailed after them on the dusty road to Japonesa's house.

The ladies, back home for lunch, chided their husbands to not forget a single detail of what went on that night at Japonesa's house, and if there were any delicacies, could they possibly save some tidbits for them in their pockets when no one was looking, after all, they had to stay home alone and bored while the men would be doing God knows what at the party. Of course, it was all right if they got drunk today. This time it was for a good cause. But it was important that they stay close to don Alejandro so he'd see them at his celebration, and they could remind him offhand as if they really didn't want to, about the land deal, and the barrels of wine he had promised to sell them at a discount, yes, let them sing together, dance, and paint the town red, today it didn't matter as long as they were with don Alejandro.

For months the town was wreathed in green, sepia, blue posters of don Alejandro's face. Barefoot boys ran everywhere hurling flyers or kept handing them out to the same people on the street, while the rest of the children, the ones who hadn't been trusted with the political propaganda, collected them and made paper boats or burned them or sat on the corner and counted them to see who had the most. The campaign headquarters operated out of the post office shed, where the citizens of Estación El Olivo met nightly to revive their faith in don Alejo and to spread that faith by arranging interviews and campaign trips to the neighboring towns and districts. But the real heart of the campaign was Japonesa's house. It was there that the ringleaders met, from there came the orders, the projects, the assignments. Now no one went to the house who wasn't a member of don Alejo's party, and the women, drowsing in the corners with nothing to do, heard the voices that schemed untiringly at the tables in the parlor, buzzing around the wine and Japonesa. Especially during the last month; when approaching victory inflamed the proprietress' gift for speeches and made her forget everything but her political passion, she would serve her wine generously to any visitor whose political leanings were precarious or ambiguous, and in the course of a few hours she'd either resolve his doubts or clear up the ambiguities, leaving him with a keen sense of duty.

The election took place ten days ago but don Alejo had only recently returned to town. Japonesa's salon and patio were plastered with pictures of the new congressman. Only the select few in the district received invitations, the chosen citizens of El Olivo, administrators, majordomos, and vineyard keepers from the nearby estates. And from Talca Japonesa commissioned her friend Wooden Heart to send a reinforcement of two whores, the Farías sisters, so there'd be music, and la Manuela, that funny queer who does flamenco dances.

"It's going to cost me plenty. But why shouldn't I please myself too. This is for the bright future that the pride of our county, that brilliant congressman don Alejandro Cruz, here with us, has promised us . . ."

Naturally Japonesa was pleased with it all. She wasn't a kid anymore, no doubt about that, and the last years had fattened her so that the accumulation of fat around her cheeks stretched her mouth perpetually into what seemed to be—and almost always was—a smile. Her myopic eyes, which had earned her the nickname "Japonesa," were nothing more than two oblique slits under the brows that she stenciled in high arches. In her youth she had had an affair with don Alejo. It was whispered that he had brought her to this house years ago, to a former proprietress now long dead. But their affair was a thing of the past, a legend that gave root to the present reality of a friendship that united them like a couple of conspirators. Don Alejo used to spend long periods of time working either in his country vineyards, not returning to his city home until after harvest, or on the pruning or spraying. So he was often away from his wife and family, which was very boring for him. But at night, after dinner, he'd escape to Estación for a few drinks and laughs with Big Japonesa. In those days she took it upon herself to have a special girl for don Alejo, a girl that only he could touch. He was generous. The house that Japonesa lived in was an ancient holding of the Cruz family and he gave it to her for an insignificant annual rent. And every night, winter or spring, the people from the neighboring area, the administrators and the vineyard keepers, the chief mechanics and sometimes even the smaller landowners, and their sons who had to be kicked out when their fathers appeared, all would come to Japonesa's house. Not so much to climb into bed with the women, although they were always young and fresh, but to amuse themselves for a while talking with Japonesa or downing a bottle or playing a hand of cards in a cheerful but safe atmosphere, because Japonesa didn't open her doors to just anybody. Only refined people. Only people with money in their pockets. That's why she belonged to don Alejo's political party, the historical, traditional, organized party, the party of decent people who paid their debts and stayed out of trouble, the people who went to her house for amusement and whose belief that don Alejo would do great things for the region was as unshakable as Japonesa's.

"I have a right to do what pleases me."

The great pleasure of her life was giving the party that night. And she took over la Manuela almost the moment he arrived. She had thought the dancer they told her about was younger: this one was pushing forty, like herself. But it was better this way because young ones tried to compete with the women when the clients got drunk: a big mess. Since la Manuela came early in the morning and didn't have anything to do until late that night, at first he just wandered around and watched, until Japonesa motioned him over to her.

"Help me put these boughs on the platform."

La Manuela took the decorating into his own hands: not so many branches, he said, the Farías sisters are too fat and with harps and guitars and boughs to boot, you won't see them. If you just put branches up there it's better, yellow willow branches with colored paper that looks like green rain, and at the foot of the platform the biggest picture of don Alejo you can find, framed in weeping willow branches too. Japonesa was thrilled with the results. Manuela, help me hang the paper wreaths, Manuela, where's the best place to put the grill for roasting the pigs, Manuela, peek at the salad dressing, Manuela this, Manuela that, Manuela, check that over there. All afternoon and with Japonesa's every order or request, la Manuela would suggest something that would make things prettier or the barbecue sauce tastier. By late afternoon Japonesa, half-drunk, fell into a chair in the middle of the patio, still shouting orders but relaxed because la Manuela was doing everything so well.

"Manuela, did they bring the strawberries for the burgundy?"

"Manuela, let's put more flowers there."

La Manuela ran, obeyed, corrected, suggested.

"I'm having a marvelous time."

Wooden Heart had told him that Japonesa was nice, but not this nice. So unpretentious, being a proprietress and all. When Japonesa went to her room to dress, la Manuela went with her to help: soon after she came out looking elegant for sure with her black silk dress coming to a low point in front, and all her hair gathered in a discreet but coquettish chignon. The wine flowed as soon as the first guests arrived, while the aroma of the pigs, starting to brown, and of the oregano, hot garlic, onions, and cucumbers soaking in the salads' juices, floated into the patio and salon.

Don Alejo arrived, quite bombed, at eight. During the applause he hugged and kissed Japonesa, whose eyeliner had run either from perspiration or from sentimental tears. Then the Farías sisters climbed up to the platform and the music and dancing began. Many of the men took off their jackets and danced in suspenders. The women's flowered dresses darkened under the arms with sweat. The Farías sisters seemed inexhaustible, as if they rewound themselves after every tune, and heat and fatigue didn't exist.

"Bring out another bottle . . ."

Japonesa and don Alejo had quickly finished the first bottle and now they ordered a second. But before starting it the new congressman carried the hostess off to dance while the others formed a circle around them. Then they went to sit down again. Japonesa called to Rosita, who had been brought from Talca especially for don Alejo.

"See, don Alejo? Look at that rump, feel it, go on, just what you like, soft, pure affection. I brought her down just for you, I knew you'd like her, shouldn't I know your tastes by now . . . Come on, let me be, I'm too old for that sort of thing. Yes, look, and Rosita isn't too young because I know you can't stand them when they're like kids . . ."

The congressman squeezed the proffered buttocks and then sat her beside him so he could put his hand under her skirt. The mayor of Estación wanted to dance with Japonesa, but she told him no, that tonight she was at the exclusive service of the guest of honor. She herself chose the golden slices of pig, watching over don Alejo to see that he ate well, until he got up to dance with Rosita, his mustache stained with sauce and oregano and his chin and fingers smeared with grease. La Manuela walked over to Japonesa.

"How're things?"

"Have a seat."

"And don Alejo?"

"All right. He hasn't said a word."

"Good."

"Did you help yourself to everything?"

187

"It was delicious. All I need is a small glass of wine."

"Drink some of this."

"What time do I dance?"

"Wait until the party warms up a bit."

"Yes, that's better. The other day I danced in Constitución. I had a lovely time and stayed to spend the weekend at the beach. Don't you ever go to Constitución? So pretty, the river and everything, and such good sea food. The owner of the house where I stayed knows you. Her name is Olga and they say she's half German. Which isn't surprising since she's full of freckles, here on her arms. No, I'm from around here, I was born in the country near Maule, that's right, ah, so you've been there too. Hah . . . we're countrywomen. No. I moved into town and later worked with a girl and traveled all the towns in the south, yes, she did well, but don't think it went too badly for me either, just between you and me. But I was young then, now I'm not. I don't know what's become of her, we even worked in a circus once. But that didn't work out at all. I prefer this kind of work. Of course, a girl gets tired of moving around so much, all the towns are alike. No. Wooden Heart is getting senile. Over sixty, way over, almost seventy. Haven't you noticed her varicose veins? And they say she used to have such lovely legs. I brought the dress in my suitcase. Yes. One of the prettiest I've seen. Red. A girl who worked in the circus sold it to me. I guard it like a saint's bone, it's real class and since I'm so dark the red looks magnificent on me. Hey . . . Now?"

"Wait."

"How much longer?"

"About an hour."

"But shall I change?"

"No. It's better to surprise them."

"All right."

"God you're in a hurry."

"Of course. I like to be the belle of the ball."

Two men who overheard the conversation started to laugh at la Manuela, trying to touch her to see if she had breasts. Hey honey . . . what have you got here? Let's have a feel, get out of here you drunk bastard, don't come around here trying to feel me. Then they said it was too much having queers like this around, it was a disgrace, they were going to talk to the policeman sitting in the corner with a whore on his lap, and he'd put la Manuela in jail for being immoral, for being a degenerate. Then la Manuela scratched one of them. Leave her alone.

She could have the policeman thrown out of office for being half-drunk. He'd better watch his step, because la Manuela was well known in Talca and on good terms with the police force. I'm a professional, they paid me to put on my show . . .

Japonesa went to get don Alejo and hurried him over so that he'd intervene.

"What are they doing to you, Manuela?"

"This man is bothering me."

"What's he doing to you?"

"He's calling me names."

"Like what?"

"Degenerate . . . and queer . . ."

Everyone laughed.

"Well aren't you?"

"I might be queer but I'm not a degenerate. I'm a professional. No one has the right to treat me like that. What's this ignoramus bothering me for? Who's he to call a girl names, huh? They brought me here because they wanted to see me, so . . . If they don't want the show, fine, pay me for tonight and I'll go, who wants to dance in this shitpile of a town full of starving beggars . . ."

"Okay, Manuela, okay . . . drink this . . ."

And Japonesa made him drink another glass of wine.

Don Alejo broke up the group. He sat down at the table, called to Japonesa, sent away someone who wanted to sit with them, and sat Rosita on one side of him and la Manuela on the other: they toasted with the newly imported burgundy.

"May you be ever triumphant, Manuela . . ."

"The same to you, don Alejo."

When don Alejo got up to dance with Rosita, Japonesa moved her chair next to la Manuela's.

"The man's taken a liking to you, honey, that's easy enough to see. Nope, there's no one like don Alejo, he's one of a kind. He's like God here in town. He does whatever he wants. They're all afraid of him. Don't you know he owns all the vineyards, all of them, as far as the eye can see? And he's so good that when someone offends him, like the guy who was bothering you, he immediately forgives and forgets. He's either a very good man or else he doesn't have time to worry about people like us. He has other worries. Projects, always projects. Now he's selling us land here in Estación, but I know him and I haven't fallen for it yet. According to him, everything's on its way up. Next year he's going to parcel out a block of his land and he's going to make a town out of it, he's going to sell model homes, he says, with easy payments, and when he's sold all the lots he's going to have electricity brought to town and then we'll be riding high for sure. They'll come from all over, my house, you know, already has quite a reputation, they'll come from Duao, from Pelarco . . . We'll expand and my house will be more famous than Wooden Heart's. Ah, Manuela, what a man he is, I was so in love with him. But he doesn't let himself get tied down. He has a wife, of course, a pretty blond, very ladylike, distinguished I'd say, and another woman in Talca and who knows how many more in the capital. And all of them working like dogs for him during election. You should have seen Misia Blanca, she didn't even buy stockings, and the other woman too, the one from Talca, working for him so he could win. Naturally, we all profit by it. And on election day he even came with a truck and anyone who didn't want to vote was thrown in by force and let's go my friend, to San Alfonso to vote for me, and he gave them money and they were so happy with the whole thing that later on they went around asking when there were going to be more elections. Of course they would have voted for him anyway. He's the only candidate they know. The others just from the propaganda posters while don Alejo, him they really know. Who hasn't seen him on that gray horse of his, on his way to the bazaar in San Alfonso every Monday? And besides the money, he gave the ones who voted for him a good supply of wine and he killed a calf, they said, so they could have an all-day barbecue, and he brought them all back to San Alfonso in the truck again, they all said he was such a nice man, but later on he disappeared because he had to go back to the capital to see how things were going . . . Look how the mayor is dancing with that blond . . ."

Japonesa squinted her eyes so she could see the far end of the patio: when she couldn't see something, she'd tell la Manuela to check and see if the blond was still dancing with the same man, and who was Sergeant Buendía with and were the cooks putting more pigs over the coals, look they might not be hungry now but in a little while they'll want to eat again.

Don Alejo came over to the table. With his delft blue doll's eyes, the earnest eyes of a saint's statue, he looked at la Manuela who trembled as if all her will power had been absorbed by the gaze that surrounded and dissolved her. How could she help feeling ashamed of meeting those marvelous orbs with her grizzly little eyes and skimpy lashes? She lowered them.

"What's the matter, sweetheart?"

La Manuela looked at him again and smiled.

"Shall we go, Manuela?"

He said it so softly. Was it possible, then . . . ?

"Whenever you want, don Alejo . . ."

Her shivering grew more intense, or multiplied into chills that circled her legs and her whole body, while those eyes remained fastened to hers . . . until they dissolved into a laugh. And la Manuela's chills subsided with don Alejo's friendly slap on the shoulder.

"No, woman. It was just a joke. I don't go in for that . . ."

And they drank together, la Manuela and don Alejo, laughing. La Manuela, still swaddled in a blanket of sensations, took short sips, she smiled a bit, gently. She couldn't remember ever having loved a man as much as at that moment she loved Congressman don Alejandro Cruz. Such a gentleman. So suave, when he wanted to be. Even when he made jokes the others made, with their thick, gross lips, he made them another way, with an artlessness that didn't wound, with a smile far removed from the guffaws of the other men. La Manuela laughed, drinking what was left of her burgundy, as if trying to hide the flush that climbed to her plucked eyebrows behind the greenish wine glass: right then, as she raised the glass, she forced herself to admit that anything besides this platonic cordiality was impossible with don Alejo. She had to break this feeling if she didn't want to die. And she did not want to die. And when she set the glass down on the table again she no longer loved him. What for. Better not to think about it.

Don Alejo was kissing Rosita, his hand under her skirt. He removed it to smooth his hair when a group of men moved their chairs over to the table. Of course he had promised to make the sheds near the station bigger if he was elected, certainly, and of course, remember the electricity as soon as possible and the business about enlarging the police force, especially during harvest, because of the outsiders who wandered around the vineyards looking for work and sometimes stealing, of course he'd remember, this victory isn't going to give me a swelled head, don't forget about us don Alejo, we helped you when you needed us, after all, you're the town's mainstay, its support, without you it would die, yes sir, pour yourself a little more don Alejo, I'd be hurt if you didn't, and pour your girl a little more too, look how thirsty she is, why if you don't take good care of her, she's liable to go off with someone else, but as I was saying, sir, all the sheds leak and they're so small, you can't say no after we've helped you, you said you would. He answered stroking his mustache from time to time. La Manuela winked at him because she saw he was trying not to yawn. She was the only one who realized he was bored, humming along with the singing Farías sisters: that isn't any kind of talk for a party. Men are so tiring with their business talk, isn't that right don Alejo, la Manuela said to him with her eyes, until don Alejo couldn't hold back a monstrous wet yawn that displayed his epiglottis and the whole of his pink palate ending in the tunnel of his trachea, and the men, while don Alejo yawned in their faces, shut up. Then, when he managed to close his mouth, his eyes watering, he searched for la Manuela's face.

"Hey, Manuela . . ."

"What, don Alejo?"

"Weren't you going to dance? This is getting dull."

7

La Manuela whirled in the center of the platform raising a cloud of dust with her red train. The moment the music stopped she plucked the flower she wore behind her ear and tossed it to don Alejo, who rose and caught it in the air. The crowd broke into applause as la Manuela dropped panting in the chair next to don Alejo.

"Let's dance, sweetie . . ."

The sharp twanging voices of the Farías sisters took command of the patio again. La Manuela, head thrown back and body arched, pinned herself to don Alejo and together they danced a few steps surrounded by the cheering men forming a circle around them. The postmaster came forward and snatched la Manuela from don Alejo. They managed one turn around the floor before the mayor took her away from him and more and more came from the circle that closed in on la Manuela. Someone stroked her while she was dancing, another rubbed her leg. The vineyard boss of a neighboring estate tucked up her skirt, and when they saw that, the men grouped around her, trying to carry her off, helped raise the skirt over her head, binding her arms as if in a strait jacket. Embarrassed and choking with laughter, they felt her skinny, hairy legs and lank backside.

192

"She's hot."

"She's steaming."

"Let's throw her in the canal."

Don Alejo stood up.

"Let's go."

"We've got to cool her off."

Several of them lifted her up. Squawking trills, and flapping her arms, la Manuela let them carry her off. In the street's light they marched toward Estación's eucalyptus grove. Don Alejo gave orders to cut the wire fences, which after all were his, and forcing their way through the brambles they reached the canal that bounded his vineyards and separated them from Estación.

"One . . . two . . . three . . . heeeeeave . . ."

And they pitched la Manuela into the water. The men who were watching her from above, standing between the blackberries and the canal, doubled over with laughter, pointing at the figure that struck poses and danced waist deep in water with her dress floating around her like a wide stain singing "El Relicario." She shouted to them as she took off her dress and threw it on the bank, she dared them, taunted them, insisting she liked them all each for himself, don't be cowards in front of a poor woman like herself. One of the men tried to piss on her, but she managed to dodge the stream's arc. Don Alejo gave him a shove and the man, cursing, fell into the water, where for an instant he merged into la Manuela's dance. When they finally gave them a hand so they both could climb onto the bank, la Manuela's anatomy startled them all.

"What a stud!"

"Hey, this guy's well-hung . . ."

"Wow, that doesn't look like a fag to me."

"Don't let the women see that or they'll all fall in love with you."

La Manuela, teeth chattering, answered with a laugh.

"I only use this thing to pee."

Some of them went back with don Alejo to Japonesa's house. Some went home without being missed by the party. Others, their bodies heavy with wine, fell among the weeds on the bank or the street or in the station to sleep it off. But don Alejo still felt like celebrating. He ordered the Farías sisters back to the platform to sing, and sat with some cronies at a table littered with leftovers, some cold bones and a greasy knife. Japonesa joined them to listen to the details of la Manuela's bath.

"And he says he only uses it to piss."

Japonesa raised her tired head and looked at them.

"That might be what he says, but I don't believe it."

"Why?"

"I don't know, just because . . ."

They argued about it for a while.

Japonesa became excited. Her swollen breast rose and fell with the passion of her conviction: yes, la Manuela could do it, if she were handled in bed in a special way, you know, with a little care, delicately, so she wouldn't be afraid, yes, Big Japonesa was sure that la Manuela could. The men felt the wave of heat that emanated from her body, sure of its technique and its charms, not quite as fresh as before but hotter and more insistent . . . yes, yes . . . I know . . . and of all the men who listened to her saying yes, I can excite la Manuela no matter how queer he is, there wasn't one who wouldn't have given anything to be in la Manuela's place. Japonesa dried her forehead. She ran the tip of her pink tongue over her lips, which were shiny for a minute. Don Alejo was laughing at her.

"But you're old now, what could you . . ."

"Bah, the older the wiser . . ."

"But la Manuela! No, no, I'll bet you can't."

"All right. I'll bet you I can."

Don Alejo cut short his laughter.

"It's a deal. Since you think you're so good, you've got a bet. Just try and get that queer hot for you. If you manage to excite him and he performs like a man, fine, I'll give you whatever you ask for. But it has to be with us watching, and put some action into it."

Everyone was silent waiting for Japonesa's answer. She motioned to the Farías sisters to keep singing and ordered another bottle of wine.

"All right. But what will you give me?"

"I told you, whatever you want."

"And if I asked you to give me El Olivo?"

"You wouldn't. You're an intelligent woman and you know very well I wouldn't give it to you. Ask for something that I can give you."

"Or that you would want to give me."

"No, that I can . . ."

There was no way of breaking him down. Forget it.

"All right then . . ."

"What?"

"This house."

When the bet was first mentioned she had thought of just asking for a few barrels of wine, the good kind that she knew don Alejo would send her without having to ask for it. But then he made her mad and she asked for the house. She had wanted it for a long time. She wanted to be a proprietress. How would it feel to be a proprietress, me the owner of this house where I started working as a girl. She had never dreamed of owning it. Only now, because it angered her that don Alejo should count on what he called her "intelligence" to take advantage of her. If he wanted to laugh at la Manuela, and at everybody, and at her, fine, then he would pay for it, don't count on her to be reasonable. Let him pay for it. Let him give her the house if he was so almighty that he could push them around like that.

"But the house is worthless, Japonesa."

"Didn't you say that property values are going up here in Estación?"

"Yes, of course, but . . ."

"I want it. Don't try to get out of it, don Alejo. I have witnesses here, and they'll say you don't keep your promises. You build up a lot of hope and then, nothing . . ."

"You're on, then."

While the onlookers applauded, don Alejo and Japonesa touched glasses and emptied them. Don Alejo got up to dance with Rosita. After that they went inside to spend some time together. Then Japonesa wiped her mouth with the back of her hand and closing her eyes yelled:

"Manuela . . ."

The few couples who were dancing stopped.

"Where's la Manuela?"

Most of the women had already paired off with the men they'd stay with for the rest of the night. Japonesa crossed under the grape arbor, whose leaves had begun to shiver in the wind, and walked into the kitchen. It was dark. But she knew he was there next to the black, but still hot stove.

"Manuela . . . Manuela?"

She sensed him shivering near the coals. The poor thing was wet and tired from so much revelry. Feeling that la Manuela was there, Japonesa drew near the corner and touched him. He said nothing. Then she leaned her body against la Manuela's. She lit a candle. Thin, wet, diminished, revealing the truth of his miserable structure, his feeble bones, as a bird is revealed to someone who plucks it to throw into the pot. Shivering by the stove, wrapped in a blanket someone had lent him.

"Are you cold?"

"They're such boors. . . ."

"Like animals."

"It doesn't matter to me. I'm used to it. I don't know why they always do this or something like it to me when I dance, it's as if they were afraid of me. I don't know why if they know I'm just a fag. At least they only threw me in the water, usually it's worse, you should see . . ."

And laughing he added:

"Don't worry. It's included in the entertainment fee."

Japonesa couldn't keep from touching him, as if she were searching for the wound so she could cover it with her hand. They both had sobered up. Japonesa sat on the floor and told him about the bet.

"Are you crazy, Japonesa, for God's sake? Can't you see I'm hopeless? I don't get it. How could you think of such a dirty thing?"

But Japonesa kept talking to him. She casually took his hand. He withdrew it, but while she talked she took it again and this time he didn't object. No, he didn't have to do anything if he didn't want to, she wasn't going to force him, it was just a matter of playacting. After all, no one would be watching close to them, just from the window and it would be easy to fool them. It was just a matter of undressing and getting into bed together, she would tell him what to do, everything, and by candlelight they couldn't see much, no, no, no. Not even if they didn't do anything. He couldn't stand women's bodies. Flabby breasts, excess fat, fat that things sink into and disappear in forever, those hips, those thighs like two huge mountains that fuse together in the middle, no. Yes, Manuela, hush, I'll pay you, don't say no, it's worth it because I'll pay you whatever you want. Now I know that I must have this house, that I want it more than anything else, because the town's expanding and the house and me along with it, and I can do it, this house that used to be the Cruzes can be mine. I'll fix it up. Don Alejo wasn't at all happy when I asked for it. I know why, they say the north-south highway will come right through here, right by the door. He knows what the house will be worth and he doesn't want to lose it, but he was scared that the others heard the bet and he had to put up or shut up . . . and then he said okay, it can be mine. I would bring in performers, you, for example, Manuela, I'd always bring you in. Yes. I'll pay you. For just being naked in bed with me for a while. Just a little

196

while, a quarter of an hour, no, ten minutes, no, five . . . and we'll have a good laugh, Manuela, you and I, I'm tired of those big studs I liked before when I was young, they stole my money and two-timed me with the first woman who came along, I'm tired of them, and the two of us can be friends, as long as it's mine, my house, mine, if not, I'll always be clinging to don Alejo, doing whatever he wants, because this house is his, you know that. But it scares me, even that scares me, Japonesa, the playacting, it doesn't matter, it doesn't matter. Do you want me to pour you some tea, you're shivering, I'll drink some with you, no, I don't like tea, I'll just have some now to keep you company: damn you Japonesa, you're feeding me propaganda, confusing me, you'll see how warm the tea will make you feel don't be afraid, don't be afraid of me, the rest of the women yes but not me, see how good the tea is, in a few minutes you won't be cold. But la Manuela kept saying no, no, no, no . . .

Japonesa put the tea kettle back on the fire.

"And if you were my partner?"

La Manuela didn't answer.

"As my partner?"

Japonesa saw that la Manuela was thinking.

"We'll split everything. I'll sign you as a partner, you too as owner of this house when don Alejo transfers it to me before the notary. You and me, partners. Half of everything. The house, the furniture, the business and everything we'll have . . ."

. . . and that way, as a proprietress, no one could throw her out, because the house would be hers. She could give orders. So many whorehouses they'd thrown her out of because she always went wild when the party got going and her mug hot from the wine, the music and everything, and sometimes the men started fighting because of her. From one whorehouse to another. Ever since she could remember. One month, six months, a year at the most . . . it always had to end because the owner got mad, because, she would say, la Manuela added fuel to the fire by being so scandalous . . . to have my own room, mine forever, with cute pin-ups on the wall, but no: always from one house to another, ever since they threw him out of school when they found him with another boy and he didn't dare go home again because his father had an enormous riding crop that drew blood when he beat the horses, and then he went to the woman's house who taught him flamenco dancing. And then she threw him out, then others, always from house to house, not a nickel in his pocket, nowhere to rest when his gums hurt, those pains he always had, ever since he could remember, and he'd never tell anyone about it and now at forty my teeth are falling out and I'm afraid of spitting them out when I sneeze. Big deal. It was just for a few minutes. I don't like beans but when there's nothing else to eat . . . big deal. Me a proprietress. No one can throw me out, and if it's true this town's on its way up, maybe life won't be so bad, and there's hope even for an ugly fag like me, and then my misfortune wouldn't be a misfortune but would turn into a miracle thanks to don Alejo, and things could be wonderful, singing, laughing, dancing in the spotlight every night forever.

"Okay."

"Is it a deal?"

"But you better not do anything to me or I'll scream."

"Is it a deal, Manuela?"

"It's a deal."

"We'll put one over on don Alejo."

"And then we'll sign at the notary's?"

"At the notary's. In Talca."

He wasn't trembling now. His heart was beating fast.

"And when are we going to put on the show?"

Japonesa looked out the door.

"Don Alejo hasn't come yet, wait a bit . . ."

They sat by the stove in silence. La Manuela took his hand away from Japonesa's, who let go because now it didn't matter, that person was all hers now. La Manuela in her house forever. Tied to her. Why not? She was a good worker, that was obvious, and cheerful, and she knew so much about decorating and clothes and meals, yes, she wasn't bad, better to be partners with la Manuela than with some other man who would make her suffer. La Manuela would never make her suffer, a friend, just a friend, the two of them together. Easy to love him. Maybe some day she would suffer for him, but in a different way, not with that scream of pain when a man stops loving her, being torn in pieces because a man goes off with another woman or deceives her, or takes her money, or takes advantage of her and she, so he won't leave her, pretends that she doesn't know anything, scarcely daring to breathe at night next to that body that suddenly, suddenly could say no, never again, this is as far as it goes . . . she can excite him, she's positive, almost without trying, because inside, without knowing it, the poor thing was already responding to her warmth. If he hadn't she never would have decided to try him.

198

Exciting him is going to be easy. And making him fall in love with her. But no. That would ruin it. Complicate things. It was preferable that la Manuela never forget his place in the house—the queer of the whorehouse, the partner. But business aside, it would be easy to make him fall in love with her, just as easy as, at this moment, it was for her to love him.

"Listen, Manuela, don't you fall in love with me . . ."

8

"That's all that counts, buddy, don't be a jerk: money. Don't you think you'd be as good as him if you had it? Or do you think don Alejo is something special? No, no two ways about it. You're afraid of the old man because you owe him money, period. No, of course I won't tell anybody. You think I want people to know how he treated my sister's husband? In the envelope I gave you there's enough money to pay him what you owe . . . no, pay me whenever you can, there's no hurry, you're one of the family. I'm not a two-faced heel, I won't treat you like he does. The things he calls you, my God! I told you not to worry about it, I'm loaded. People like him make me furious . . . Why should you do what he says and not go to Japonesita's house if you feel like it and pay your bill? Does Japonesita belong to him? Of course, that ass thinks everything belongs to him, but no sir. He can't order you around, or me either, and we'll go wherever we feel like going. Right? Pay him his money and good-bye . . . Come on, Pancho, cheer up, it's no big deal . . ."

The truck went by Japonesita's house without stopping. It turned the narrow corner slowly and went back around the block past Japonesita's house, not honking this time, Octavio persuading him, going around and around the block.

"And what will I do about the freight jobs?"

"Don't worry. Don't you know that all the trucks from around here go by my gas station and I know where the best jobs are in the area? Don't worry. I'm telling you you're not the old man's slave . . . Okay. I'm sick of the whole thing. Let's pay him right now, yes, now . . ."

"It's late . . ."

Octavio thought it over.

"So what, what do I care if they're eating. Let's go."

Pancho spun the truck around in the narrow street and headed the other way, toward the El Olivo estate, past the station. He knew his truck, and on the road past the blackberries and canal that bordered the station he dodged ruts and holes, maneuvering the enormous machine that seemed lighter now that he was going to don Alejo's to wrest from him the part of the truck that still belonged to him.

"We're going to get stuck in the mud."

Octavio opened the window and threw his cigarette out.

"No . . ."

Pancho stopped talking because he was going through a narrow passage of blackberries. He had to move very slowly, squinting his eyes, his head bent over the windshield. To see the rocks and potholes. He knew the road well, but better to be careful anyway. He even knew the noises: there behind the thickets, the Palos canal split into two and the branch that flowed toward Los Lagos pasture gushed through a wooden spout for a stretch. Now you couldn't hear it. But if you went on foot, like he did as a boy, you'd start hearing the noise of the water in the wooden spout right here, passing the crooked willow. This was the road on which he used to run barefoot to school every day in Estación El Olivo, when there was a school. A waste of time. Misia Blanca had taught him reading and writing and simple arithmetic along with Moniquita, who learned so quickly that she always beat him at everything. Until don Alejo said that Pancho had to go to school. And after studying, who knows, the university maybe. You bet. I was the dunce of all times and I never went to the next grade because I didn't feel like it, until don Alejo, who's no fool, realized it and fine, why bother with this kid if he's no good at studying, just let him learn the numbers and reading so they can tell him from the animals and then let him help out in the fields, let's see what we can do with him, why waste time in school if he's so stubborn. Every rock. And further on, the concrete landmark that's always been broken. Who knows how it got broken. It must be hard to break a concrete landmark, but it's broken all right. Every hole, every rock: don Alejo made him learn them by heart, back and forth every day from the estate to the school and back to the estate until they said enough, what good was it doing. But Ema wants Normita to go to nuns' school, I don't want her to be another nobody, like me, who had to marry the first man who looked at me so I wouldn't be an old maid forever—think what I'd be if you had studied a little, why do you say that, you know you liked me the

200

first time you saw me and you walked out on the kid who owned the butcher shop because you fell in love with me, but it would have been different if you'd studied what does studying mean, Mamma, and what are nuns? I want the girl to study something quick like obstetrics, what's obstetrics, Mamma? And he didn't like her to ask, she's too young and what can you tell her, better wait until she grows up. If I want to, if I feel like it, I'll make my daughter study. Don Alejo has nothing to say about it, nothing to do with me. I'm my own boss. Except, of course, the family, like Octavio, who's my buddy so I don't mind owing him and he won't do anything if I'm a little behind on my payments . . . he'll be happy that I'm going to buy a house for Ema. Now I'll pay the old man and leave for good.

The truck wheeled between two plane trees and turned into an avenue of palm trees. Warehouses on either side. And piles of fetid grape pulp beside the dark closed sheds. At the far end, the park, the gigantic holm oak where he used to watch them lying in hammocks and multicolored canvas chairs—watching them from the other side, but not when he was little because he and Moniquita would play together among the giant hydrangea, the two of them alone, and the grownups would laugh at him asking if he was Moniquita's boyfriend and he'd say yes, and then they'd let him in, but not later, when he was bigger: they'd read magazines in strange languages, napping in the faded canvas chairs.

The dogs lunged toward the truck, which was approaching through the palms, and attacked its shiny body, scratching and muddying it as soon as it stopped at the gatehouse.

"Let's get out."

"How, with those mongrels?"

The dogs' leaping and growling kept them inside. Then Pancho, because they made him angry, because they frightened him, because he hated dogs, started to honk the horn like a madman and the dogs leapt higher scratching the red paint that he polished so often, but now it didn't matter, now nothing mattered except honking the horn, honking enough to knock down the palm trees and the oak, to pierce the night from one end to the other until nothing is left, honk that horn, and the dogs howl while a light goes on in the hall and figures come to life among the shadows and in doorways, yelling at the dogs, running toward the truck but Pancho keeps on, he has to, the furious dogs ignoring the peons who are calling them. Until don Alejo appears at the top of the porch and Pancho stops honking. Then the dogs quiet down and run to him.

"Othello . . . Sultan. Here Negus, Moor . . ."

The dogs fell in behind don Alejo.

"Who is it?"

Pancho remained mute, anemic, as if he had used up all his strength. Octavio nudged him, but Pancho remained mute.

"Bah. Coward."

Pancho opened the door and leaped to the ground. The dogs lunged at him but don Alejo managed to call them off while Pancho scrambled back into the truck. Octavio had turned off the lights and the landscape of darkness loomed, the black oak, the palm leaves, the mass of walls, the roof tiles were all suddenly etched against the deep empty sky.

"Who is it?"

"Pancho, don Alejo. Why don't you take care of your mutts?"

"What's this damn racket you're making? You must be drunk to think you can come to my house at all hours making noise like that, you good-for-nothing. You—put the dogs away, go on Moor, Sultan, over there, Othello, Negus . . . and you, Pancho, wait on the porch while I look for my cape, it's getting cold . . ."

Cautiously Pancho and Octavio climbed down from the truck, and trying not to fall into puddles, they worked their way to the porch. At the base of the driveway that circled the estate they saw some lighted windows. They looked in. The dining room. The family gathered around the lamp. A boy with glasses—grandson, don Jorge's son, what's he doing here when he ought to be away at school? And Misia Blanca at the head. White-haired now. She used to be blond, with a long braid she wrapped around her head and cut off when he gave Moniquita typhus. He saw Misia Blanca do it in the stuffy chapel—she raised her arms, her hands grasped her heavy braid and she cut it straight off, at the nape of her neck. He saw her: through the tears that came only then, only when Misia Blanca cut off her braid and threw it into the box, he watched her swimming in his tears, as he saw her now, swimming in the dining room's tarnished glass. Let me have Pancho for a while: she came to ask his mother so he could play with Moniquita because they were almost the same age and the house servants laughed at him because he said he was the boyfriend of the boss's daughter. Now she was like an old lady. She ate in silence. And when don Alejo finally joined them on the porch, wearing his hat and vicuña cape,

Pancho thought he looked so tall, as tall as when he used to look up at him, a boy barely up to his knees.

"What a surprise, Pancho!"

"Good evening, don Alejo . . ."

"Who's with you?"

"It's Octavio . . ."

"Good evening."

"What can I do for you?"

He dropped into a rattan chair and the two men remained standing in front of him. He looked small now. And sick.

"What brings you around at this hour?"

"I came to pay you, don Alejo."

He stood up.

"But you paid me this morning. You don't owe me a thing until next month. What's gotten into you all of a sudden?"

They paced around the U of the porch. From time to time the image of Misia Blanca presiding at the long and almost empty table reappeared, once, stirring her medicine, another time closing the cheese crock, another, crumbling a piece of bread against the snowy tablecloth, all within the framed light of the window. Octavio was explaining something to don Alejo . . . who knows what, I don't want to hear it, he does it better than I do. Yes, let him do it, he won't let don Alejo run all over him like he does me. From a plate Misia Blanca selects a lump of toasted sugar for her medicine. One for her, one for Moniquita and one for you, Panchito, there's a piece of juniper leaf on it, that gives it a special flavor, Misia Blanca likes it that way, well, go play in the garden, and don't lose sight of her Pancho, you're bigger and you have to take care of her. And the colossal hydrangea there in the shade, next to the drain with its dusk-colored velvety bricks, he was the doll's father and she the mother, until the kids caught us playing with the little crib, me singing a lullaby to the doll in my arms because Moniquita says that's what fathers do and the kids laugh—sissy, sissy, playing with dolls like a girl and I don't want to ever come back but I have to because they feed me and dress me but I prefer going hungry and I spy from the flower hedge because I'd like to go back but I don't want them to call me the boss's daughter's sweetheart and sissy, sissy because of the dolls. Until one day don Alejo sees me spying behind the flowers. I've caught you, you little bastard. And his hand grabs me here, at the neck, and I hang from his cape kicking, him so big and me so small looking up at him, like looking up a cliff. His

203

cape a little slippery and very hot because it's made of vicuña. And he drags me through the bushes and I hang onto his cape because it's so soft and so hot and he drags me along and I tell him they didn't give me permission to come, liar, he knows everything, you're a liar Pancho, don't pull away, who's going to take care of her except you, and he pushes me toward the big park and I have to look for her in the briar bushes, and I run and my feet get tangled in the periwinkles but what's the reason for running so hard, she's where she always is, in the hydrangea, in the shade by the wall embedded with shiny pieces of broken bottles, and I find her and touch her and from the tip of my body, after running and breaking through the underbrush, the tip of my body drips something and wets me and then I get typhus and she does too and she dies and I don't, and I'm left watching Misia Blanca and only when her hands lift her braid to cut it off do the tears start because I got well and because Misia Blanca's cutting off her braid. The dining room light has been turned off. This time around she's not there. Octavio's voice keeps explaining: yes, don Alejo, of course, it doesn't matter if they don't give him the cargo, I've already found him some others, yes, very good ones, some brick shipments, that they're making on the other side of . . ."

"Whose bricks are they?"

Octavio didn't answer.

Don Alejo stopped, surprised by the silence, and they did too, Octavio meeting the senator's eyes for an instant.

Was it possible? Pancho realized that Octavio wasn't answering don Alejo's question because if he found out whose bricks they were he could make a telephone call, that was enough to stop them from giving him shipments. He knew everyone. Everyone respected him. He had them all eating out of his hand. But his brother-in-law Octavio, his buddy, Normita's godfather, was standing up to him: Octavio was new in the district and not afraid of the old man. And because he didn't want to answer he didn't. They made a complete turn around the porch without speaking. The park was quiet but alive, and the silence in the wake of their voices was heavy with almost imperceptible noises, the drop that fell from the edge of the roof, the keys clinking in Octavio's pocket, the rustle of the nearly bare jasmine spikes piercing raindrops, the slow footsteps that halted at the house door.

"It's cold . . ."

"Of course. There's a lot of fresh air here."

Pancho trembled at his brother-in-law's words: don Alejo looked at him on the verge of asking what he meant by that, but he didn't, and he started to count the bills Octavio handed him.

"Tons of it . . ."

"What did you say?"

"Tons . . . of fresh air . . ."

Pancho cut his brother-in-law off before he could continue, inspired by his victory. Or was it a victory? Don Alejo seemed too calm. Maybe he hadn't heard.

"No, nothing, don Alejo. Well, if it's all right with you we'll go now and stop bothering you. We're taking up your time. And in this cold. Please give my regards to Misia Blanca. She's well, I hope."

Don Alejo walked to the end of the porch to see them off. Crossing the mud on their way to the truck they turned and saw the four dogs beside him.

"Easy with the dogs . . ."

Don Alejo laughed out loud.

"Get 'em Sultan . . ."

The four dogs shot after them. They barely had time to leap into the truck before they started clawing the doors. As they turned toward the exit the headlights lit up don Alejo's figure at the top of the steps for a moment and then the advancing lights gradually swallowed the palm trees along the lane. Pancho took a deep breath.

"That's that."

"You didn't let me call him a bastard to his face."

"Aw, the old goat isn't so bad."

But he's an operator. Octavio had been telling him that on their way into town and he believed him then, but now it was harder to believe. He said even the stones on the road to Estación knew it. Don't be an idiot the old man never intended to bring electricity to town, it was all lies, on the contrary, now it suited him better that the town never had electricity. Don't be naive, that old man's a shyster. The times he went to talk to the Commissioner were just to irritate him, so he'd never give the town electricity, I know what I'm talking about, the Commissioner's chauffeur is a friend of mine and he told me, wake up, buddy. It's obvious. Think about it. He wants everybody to move out of town. And since he owns most of the houses, if not all of them, what can he lose by having another chat with the Commissioner so that he'll grant him the land the streets are on, it was his to begin with, and then he'll tear down the houses and plow the town, rich, fallow land, and plant vineyards as if the town had never existed, hell, that's what he's after. Now that his plans for making Estación El Olivo an important town have fallen through, because he thought the highway would come right by his door . . .

Leaning over the wheel Pancho studies the darkness because he has to if he doesn't want to topple into a canal or be grafted into a thicket. You have to watch every stone in the road, every hole, every one of those trees that I'm abandoning forever. I thought all this would keep some trace of me, so that later I could think about these streets I'm driving along, but now they won't exist and I won't be able to remember them, because already they don't exist and I can't return. I don't want to return. I want to go on to other things, go forward. The house in Talca for Ema and school for Normita. I'd like to have a place to come back to, not really to come back to, but to have it there in case, that's all, and now I won't. Because don Alejo's going to die. The certainty of don Alejo's death drained the night and Pancho had to clutch the steering wheel to keep from falling into that abyss.

"Octavio."

"What's the matter?"

He didn't know what to say. It was just to hear his friend's voice. To see if he really wanted to be like Octavio, who didn't have a place to go back to and didn't care. He was the best man in the world because he made his own way and now he owned a service station and a little café on the north-south highway where hundreds of trucks passed. He did what he wanted and his wife gave him spending money, not like Ema who took all the money as if he owed it to her. Octavio was a great man, really great. It was a stroke of luck that he married his sister. It was good to have someone to back you up.

"We settled the score. Better not to have anything to do with him. They're a bad lot, pal, I'm telling you, you don't know the trouble I've had with those sons of bitches."

They were coming into town.

"Where are we going?"

"To celebrate."

"But where?"

"Where do you think, old buddy?"

"To Japonesita's."

"To Japonesita's it is."

206

9

Japonesita put out the lamp.

"It's him."

"Again?"

After they slammed the truck doors, a dense moment of waiting passed, so long that it seemed the men had gotten lost in the night. When they finally pounded on the door, la Manuela clutched her flamenco dress.

"I'm going to hide."

"Papa, wait . . ."

"He's going to kill me."

"And what about me?"

"Who cares. He swore he'd get me. What happens to you is no concern of mine."

She ran to the patio. If she made it through this she was sure to die of bronchial pneumonia like all the other old women. Why should Japonesita be any affair of hers? If she wanted protection, let her protect herself, if she wanted to give in to him, let her give in to him, she, la Manuela, wasn't in the mood to save anybody, barely her own skin and much less Japonesita, who called her "papa," papa when la Manuela was afraid Pancho would kill her for being a fag. The best thing was to sneak away and spend the night with Ludovinia, warm in her bed, a nice double bed, no, none of that getting into bed with a woman, now that she knew what could happen to her. But maybe Ludo had some leftover pastries from lunch and could heat them over the coals and serve some tea and they could talk about nice things, Misia Blanca's hats when they used to wear hats, and forget all this, because she certainly wasn't going to tell Ludo about it, she didn't want her to ask questions she'd have to answer. Until this thing let up and faded into the darkness, until she could say to Ludo how do you like that, maybe she could tell her about it tomorrow, how do you like that, the girl finally made up her mind and took him to her room, she's finally come down off her high horse, everything's going to be okay now, and darkness would surround everything until it would be time to go to sleep and she could fall drop by drop by drop into the puddle of sleep that would spread until it completely filled Ludo's warm room.

The light in the parlor went on again. A man appeared in its rectangle. The Victrola needle began to rasp against a record. Octavio leaned against the door frame. La Manuela stepped back, opened the henhouse grid and hid under the water dispenser next to the perch bleached white by chicken shit, and Lucy's turkey began to strut and bristle its feathers, all swelled up and angry. La Manuela tried to warm one of her hands under her shirt but every crease in her musty skin seemed like frosted cardboard, so she took it back out.

Japonesita crossed the rectangle of light, clinging to Pancho Vega.

La Manuela knew they'd soon begin to search the house for her. If only Japonesita were woman enough to keep them busy to divert their virility toward herself, she who needed it so much! But no. They were going to search. La Manuela knew it, they were going to make the whores come out of their rooms, take the kitchen apart, look for her in the outhouse, maybe in the henhouse, wreck everything, dishes, glasses, their clothes, the women, and her too if they found her. That's why they came. They can't fool me. Those men didn't just appear out of the night to rush into the house, go to bed with just any woman and drink a few bottles of just any wine, no, they came for her, to sacrifice her, to make her dance. They knew she had made it plain that she didn't want to dance for them, no more than she did last year when Pancho kept insisting that she had to dance for him, warped bastard, he's coming for me, la Manuela knows it. For the present he settled for dancing with Japonesita. But he'd come looking for her. Yes, I should have gone to Ludo's. But no. Japonesita was dancing, strange, because she never danced, even when they begged her. She didn't like it. She seemed to now. She saw her whirl in front of the wide-open door, glued to him, as if melted and dripping over Pancho, his black mustache hidden in Japonesita's neck. His dirty mustache, the bottom hairs tinged with wine and nicotine. And clutching the bottom of her buttocks, his hands stained with nicotine and car grease. And Octavio standing in the open door, smoking, waiting: then he tossed his cigarette into the night and went in. The record stopped. Laughter. Japonesita screams. A chair falls. They're doing something to her. La Manuela's hand, back between her skin and her shirt, right where her heart beats, clenches until it hurts, as if she'd like to transfer the pain to Pancho Vega's body, because Japonesita screams again, ay, ay, papa, don't call me, don't call me that again, I don't have fists to protect you, I only know how to dance and to shiver here in the henhouse.

. . . But one time I didn't shiver. Big Japonesa's naked body, oh, if I had that warmth now, if Japonesita had it so she wouldn't need other heat, Big Japonesa's naked, repellent, but warm body surrounding me, her hands on my neck and me staring at those things that burgeoned from her chest, as if I didn't know they existed, heavy and red tipped by the lamp light that we didn't put out so they could see us from the window. They insisted on at least that much proof. And the house would be ours. Mine. And me smothered in that flesh, that drunken woman's mouth searching for mine the way a pig roots in a swamp though we agreed we wouldn't kiss because it nauseated me, but she was searching for my mouth, I don't know, even now I don't know why Japonesa had such a hunger for my mouth and she searched for it and I didn't want to and refused, shriveling it tight, biting her greedy lips, hiding my face in the pillow, anything, because I was terrified to see Japonesa violating our agreement, something was beginning to stir and I didn't . . . I didn't want to be sickened by the flesh of this woman who was reminding me that the house was going to be mine for just this simple and ghastly act, that there was no harm done but . . . and don Alejo watching us. Could we fool him? I trembled. Could we? Wouldn't we die, somehow, if we managed to do it? And Japonesa made me drink another glass of wine so I wouldn't be afraid and drinking it I spilled half the glass on the pillow next to Japonesa's head whose flesh was wooing me, and then another glass. After that she hardly said anything else. Her eyes were closed and her mascara was running and her face was sweaty and her whole body, especially her wet belly, stuck to mine and me realizing that all this is monstrous, unnecessary, they're betraying me, oh how clearly I saw it was a betrayal to capture me and lock me up in jail forever because Big Japonesa was utterly reckless with that odor, as if she were preparing a witches brew in the fire that burned in the triangular vegetation between her legs, and that odor took root in my body and clung to me, the odor of that body with its unimaginable incomprehensible channels and caverns, stained with other liquids, inhabited by other cries and beasts, and that boiling so different from mine, my foolish doll's body, depthless, everything on the surface, useless hanging, while she caresses me with her mouth and sweaty palms, her eyes closed terribly so I won't know what's happening inside, everything open inside, passages and channels and caverns and me there, dead in her arms, in her hand that's urging me to live, yes, you can, and me nothing, and on the box next to the bed the lamp hissing lightly near my ear in a long meaningless whisper. And her soft hands explore me, and she tells me you excite me, she tells me I want this, and she begins to murmur again, like the lamp, in my ear, and I hear laughter in the window: don Alejo watching me, watching us writhe, knotted together and sweating to humor him because he ordered it and this is the only way he'll give us this adobe house, with its rat-gnawed beams, and those watching, don Alejo and the others who are laughing at us, don't hear what Big Japonesa is slowly saying in my ear, this is so sweet, honey boy, don't be afraid, we won't do anything, it's just an act to make them believe it, don't worry honey and her voice is warm like an embrace and her wine-stained breath all over me, but now I'm not so worried because no matter how much her hand touches me I don't have to do anything, nothing, it's just an act, nothing's going to happen, it's for our house, that's all, for our house. Her smile stuck on the pillow, etched in the linen. She likes to do what she's doing here on the sheets with me. She's pleased that I can't: not with anybody, tell me, pretty Manuela, tell me not with any other woman before me; tell me I'm the first, the only, so I can have you all to myself my pretty little girl, my love, Manuelita I'm going to have you, I like your terrified body and all your fears and I want to destroy your fear, no, don't be afraid Manuela, no, not destroy them but gently smooth them away to reach a part of me that she, poor Big Japonesa, thought existed but doesn't exist and never has, it never has existed despite your touching and caressing me and murmuring . . . it doesn't exist, stupid Japonesa, don't you understand, it doesn't exist. No honey, Manuela as if we were two women, look, see, our legs wound together, sex in sex, two identical sexes, Manuela, don't be afraid of my thighs moving, my hips, my mouth in yours, like two women when the gentlemen in Wooden Heart's house pay the whores to let them watch . . . no, no, you're the woman, Manuela, I'm the man, look how I'm taking off your panties and loosening your brassiere so your breasts will be bare and I can play with them, yes you have them Manuela, don't cry, you do have breasts, tiny like a little girl's, but you have them and that's why I love you. You talk and caress me and suddenly you tell me, now darling Manuela, now you can . . . I dreamed about my breasts being caressed and something happened while she was saying, yes little girl, I'm making you like it because I'm the man and you're the woman, I love you because you're everything, and I feel her heat devouring me, me, a me that doesn't exist, and she helps me, laughing with me because I'm laughing too, the two of us choked with laughter to cover the shame of our waves of emotion, and my tongue in her mouth and what does it matter that they're watching us from the window, that makes it better, sweeter, until I shudder and am mutilated, bleeding inside of her while she screams and clutches me and then falls, my precious little boy, what a sweet thing, it's been so long, so long, and the words dissolve and the odors evaporate and the hardnesses shrivel, I stay, sleeping over her, and she says into my ear, as if in a dream: my sweet girl, my sweet boy, her words muffled in the pillow. We can't tell anybody, I'm ashamed of what happened, don't be silly, Manuela, you won the house royally, you won the house for me, for the two of us. But swear never again, Japonesa, oh God how disgusting, swear to me, partners yes, but this no, never again because what I'm needing so much now no longer exists, that you and that me I'd like so desperately to call to from this corner of the henhouse, while I watch them dance, there in the parlor . . .

. . . the fists he doesn't have are useless for everything curling themselves up in the faded percale of his dress. Kill Pancho with the dress. Hang him with it. Lucy went out to the patio as if she had been waiting for the moment.

"Ssssttt."

She looked around.

"Lucy, over here . . ."

In the parlor the record keeps repeating.

"What are you doing in there like a brooding hen?"

"Go on into the parlor."

"I'm going. Is anyone there?"

"Pancho and Octavio."

Japonesita and Pancho dance past the doorway, waking up Lucy's face.

"Is she alone?"

"Go on, I said."

What right does that damn whore Lucy have to criticize her because she's hiding in the henhouse? Tomorrow she'll make her pay the money she owes her for a dress, she's been pretending she forgot about it. Since men prefer her, she thinks we have to put up with her. She's here on charity like all the rest. And Japonesita too. So what right do they have? Right to what? Papa. What do you mean papa. Please, it only hurts when I laugh . . . papa. Leave me alone. Nobody's papa. I'm just plain Manuela, the one who can dance until dawn and make a roomful of drunks laugh until they forget their sniveling wives while she, the artist, receives applause, and the light bursts into an infinity of stars. Why think about the scorn in the laughter that she knows so well, it's all part of the men's fun, that's why they come, to scorn her, but on the stage, with a flower behind her ear, as old and knock-kneed as she is, she's still more woman than all the Lucys and Clotys and

Japonesitas on the face of the earth . . . arching her back and pursing her lips and tapping furiously, they'd laugh harder and their wave of laughter would carry her up, up into the lights.

Let Japonesita scream in there. Let them make her learn to be a woman, as they had made her. Lucy is dancing with Octavio, but she's the only one capable of turning the party into something thrilling, because she's la Manuela. Even though she might be trembling here in the dark surrounded by chicken shit that's so old it doesn't even smell anymore. They aren't women. She's going to show them what a woman is and how to be a woman. He takes off his shirt and folds it on the stairs. And his shoes . . . yes, bare feet like a real gypsy. He removes his pants and he's naked in the henhouse, his arms folded across his chest and that foreign thing hanging from him. He puts the Spanish dress over his head and the skirts fall around her like a warm shower because nothing can warm her like those yards and yards of tired red percale. She adjusts the bodice. She smooths the folds around the low neck . . . a little padding here where I don't have anything. Naturally it's because I'm so tiny, a dainty little gypsy girl, a mere child about to dance, that's why she doesn't have breasts, almost like a little boy, but she's not, she's feminine, with her curved figure and all . . . la Manuela smiles in the darkness of the henhouse while she puts the gauze poppy, that Lucy lent her, behind her ear. Do whatever you want with Japonesita. What does she have to do with it. She's just the great artist who's come to Japonesita's house to do her number, she's a fag, she wants to amuse herself, she feels Pancho's heavy hands exploring her that night, like someone who won't explore unless everyone is watching, holding her, yes indeed, holding her and doing it in style. Let them, let thirty men do whatever they want to her. If only I were younger and could take it. But no. My gums hurt. And my joints, oh how my joints hurt and my bones and my knees in the morning, how I feel like staying in bed forever, forever, with them taking care of me. If only Japonesita would make up her mind tonight. If only Pancho would take her away. If only he could make her pale blood circulate through that plucked chicken's body, not even hair where she ought to have it because she's a big girl now, poor thing, she doesn't know what she's missing, Pancho's hands squeezing my pretty girl, don't be silly, don't waste your life, I'm your friend, I, la Manuela, I'm going to dance so that everything will be lively as it should be and not sad like you because you count every dollar and don't spend any of it . . . and the flower in my hair. La Manuela walks across the patio smoothing her dress against her body. So skinny, dear God, no one's going to like me, especially with my stained dress and muddy feet and she removes a vine leaf clinging to the muck on her heel and goes toward the light and before she goes in she hides behind the door, listening, while she makes the sign of the cross as all great artists do before walking into the light.

10

Don Alejo would give don Céspedes all the wine he could drink, drink, don Céspedes, he'd say again and again, that's what it's for, but don Céspedes was a moderate man. Sometimes a small glass before going to bed on the pile of sacks among the wooden barrels cured by harvests and harvests of wine. It was the same wine that don Alejo would sell to Japonesita wholesale, simply because of their friendship and so the poor girl could make a little profit, but not to anyone else, not even if they begged him. Sometimes, late at night, when don Céspedes couldn't get to sleep because of the pains that were always bothering some part of his body, he'd put on his sandals, throw a blanket over his shoulder, walk through the vineyard, cross the Palos canal on a fallen willow trunk, and poking through the barbed-wired blackberry thicket laced with gaps known only to himself, he'd reach Japonesita's house where he'd silently install himself at one of the tables near the wall to drink a bottle of red wine, the same kind that was within easy reach at the gatehouse.

Octavio saw him come in. Japonesita didn't want to dance with him, so while Octavio waited for Lucy and Pancho to finish their dance he called to don Céspedes, who moved to their table. Octavio was going to ask the old man something, but he didn't because he saw that he was sitting rigidly in his chair, staring at one fixed point in the darkness, as if it contained a detailed blueprint of the night.

"The dogs . . ."

"What did you say, don Céspedes?"

"They turned the dogs loose in the vineyard."

They listened.

"I don't hear a thing."

"Me neither."

"But they're out there. I can feel them. Now they're running north, to the Lagos pasture where the cattle are . . . and now . . ."

213

A flock of geese flew over the town.

". . . and now they're running this way, toward Estación."

Japonesita and Octavio tried to listen to the night, but they couldn't penetrate its obstreperous music, nor glean the country's atoms of noise and faraway gusts of information. Octavio poured himself a glass of wine.

"And who let the dogs loose?"

"Don Alejandro. He's the only one who can turn them loose."

"Why does he?"

"When he's in a strange mood . . . and tonight he was. Tonight, when he came to the gatehouse, he told me he was going to die, a doctor told him so. He said strange things . . . that he seemed to be leaving nothing behind because all his projects had failed . . ."

"Greedy bastard . . . if a millionaire like him is a failure, where does that leave us poor people?"

"I'll bet anything he's in the vineyard with them."

"And why does he turn them loose if there wasn't a grape left after harvest and there's no reason to break in?"

"Who knows. Sometimes people come for other reasons."

"Like what?"

"You've got to be careful with the dogs. They're vicious. But they don't bite me . . . why should they bother when there's no meat left on my bones."

Japonesita watched him from the other side of the carbon lamp, gray, remote, like someone to whom nothing can happen anymore; she envied his immunity. Even the dogs didn't bite him. Probably not even the fleas in his mangy straw mattress. Once someone told her that don Céspedes didn't even eat anymore, that sometimes don Alejo's house servants would remember his existence and look all over for him, in the warehouses and sheds, and they'd take him some bread or cheese or a hot plate of food. But then they'd forget him again and who knows how the old man would feed himself, sleeping on sacks in the warehouses, lost among the plows and machinery and bales of straw and clover, on top of a pile of potatoes.

Pancho and Lucy sat down at the table.

"What is this, a funeral . . ."

No one answered.

"Cheer up, pal, if you don't, I'll run off with Lucy . . ."

And he looked at Japonesita to see how she reacted: she was looking at the same point in the dark as don Céspedes. Pancho touched one of her breasts, too small, like a wizened pear, the kind with no perfume, inedible, fallen under the trees. But her eyes. He took his hand away and looked at them. Two orbs lit from within. Each eye flared brightly swallowed up by the translucent iris and Pancho felt that if he leaned over them he would see, like an aquarium, the underwater gardens of Japonesita's soul. It wasn't pleasant. It was weird. If it were up to him he'd let her alone right then and there. But why should he? Because the old man told him to, because don Alejo warned him not to go near her? We're not outlaws, don Alejo, we're as good as you, so don't look down on us, don't think that . . .

"Let's dance, honey."

Lucy closed her eyes and opened them again. But when she opened them she didn't know how much time had passed since she closed them, nor into which fragment of vast, stretched time she was looking. A band of geese passed over. Again? Or was this another part of the same time when she thought she heard them a while ago? The howling of the dogs, some near, others faraway, traced the country distances in the night. A horseman galloped along the road, and suddenly Lucy, who was trying to hear only the bolero on the Victrola, was tangled up in the anguish of not knowing who the rider was or where he came from or where he was going and how long this gallop would last, faint now, very faint, but always galloping further into the interior of her ears until he remained fixed there. She smiled at Octavio because she saw he was annoyed.

"God it's boring . . ."

Don Céspedes yawned and listened.

"That's Sultan . . ."

"How do you know which dog?"

"I trained them for don Alejo, I've known them since they were pups. Since they were born, really. When don Alejo sees that one of his black dogs isn't doing well, that he's getting lazy or tame or has injured his paw, we shut ourselves up, don Alejo and I, with the dog, and he shoots him . . . I hold him so the bullet will hit the right spot and then I bury him. And when the bitch we keep locked up at the far end of the orchard is in heat, we give the dogs a stimulant, and don Alejo and I, we shut ourselves up again with the dogs in the shed, and the beasts fight over the bitch, they go mad, sometimes they're wounded, until they mount her and that's it. He keeps the best pups for himself, but if he's killed only one of the big ones he just takes one pup and I put the rest in a bag and throw them in the Palos canal. Four, he always likes to have four. It makes doña Blanca furious, she says it's not right, but he laughs and tells her not to interfere with men's affairs. And the dogs, even though they change, always have the same names, Negus, Sultan, Moor, Othello, always the same ever since don Alejo was a boy just this high, the same names as if the dogs he kills kept on living, don Alejo's four dogs, always perfect, he likes them savage, if they're not he kills them. And now he's turned them loose in the vineyard. Of course, he was very depressed . . ."

While don Céspedes was talking, Pancho and Japonesita sat down and listened.

"What's that got to do with his being so sad?"

"He's going to die . . ."

"Enough with don Alejo!"

Enough. Let him die. Don Alejo and his charming wife could go to hell as far as he was concerned. Couldn't he and his friend have some fun without having to hear about don Alejo this, don Alejo that. Misia Blanca can go to hell, Misia Blanca who had taught him to read and sometimes gave him sweets that she kept in a tea jar in the pantry. That pantry. Row after row of marmalade jars with white labels written in the angular nun script that he, Pancho Vega, was forever writing—Plum—Peach—Apricot—Raspberry—Chokeberry—and the jars of preserved pears and cherries in brandy and plums floating in yellow syrup. And further on, the rows of white earthenware molds in the shape of castles: apple or quince marzipan, and they always gave Moniquita a castle tower where the candy was clear and sparkling. They can go to hell. Pancho's hand climbed up Japonesita's leg and no one said a word while Lucy's ears scanned the night for another rider to revive her fear. He had paid off the whole debt and the truck was his. His red truck. Caress his red truck instead of Japonesita who smelled of clothing, and the harsh-voiced horn, just like Daddy's voice Normita always said. His. More his than his wife. Or daughter. If he wanted, he could race it down the knife-straight highway, tonight, for instance, he could race it like a wild man, blowing his horn at anything he felt like, slowly pressing the accelerator to invade the depths of the night and suddenly, just because, because don Alejo doesn't have any control over me now, I could turn the wheel a little more, barely flexing my wrists, but enough to make the truck go off the road, bounce and overturn and become a smear of silent, smoking iron on the edge of the road. If I feel like it. And I don't have to explain anything to anybody. Under his hand Japonesita's leg began to relax.

Japonesita was drinking a glass of wine. She wished Lucy would go dance with Octavio so that she could drink it all on the sly. Wine. All the men who ever came to her house smelled of wine and everything tasted like wine. During harvest the wine odor invaded the entire town, and the rest of the year, heaps of grape pressings rotting by the warehouse doors. Disgusting. She had the same wine smell, like the men, like the whores, like the town. What else was there to do except drink wine. Like Cloty, who when she didn't have customers would say, listen Japonesita write me down for another bottle of the cheapest wine you have and then she'd get into bed and drink until she was a total wreck the next day, working like a mule from the crack of dawn, her nose red and her stomach queasy. But I never noticed the smell of wine on my mother. And Big Japonesa was a great one for drinking, everybody knew that. She always smelled of Flores de Pravia soap even though she had drunk quarts of wine in the parlor, and then my mother would light up like a torch and there was no stopping her from talking and laughing and dancing. How did she do it? Her warmth would fill the bed when she'd fall into it and Japonesita would have to undress her, she or la Manuela. Even the tomb in which they laid her in San Alfonso was probably hot and she would never feel that warmth again. Only Pancho's hand, abandoned on her thigh because he was dozing while Lucy danced glued to Octavio. But Pancho was drunk. Like every man she had seen in the house since she was born. And she played among trouser legs under the tables while they drank, hearing their obscenities and smelling their vomit in the patio, playing in the dirty sheets piled next to the wash tub, those sheets on which those men had slept with those women. But if Pancho's hand could excite her the way her mother could be excited, then she could get away from it all, her father told her. Who was that shadow who counted dollars uselessly? The hand moving along her thigh was saying that, because now she wasn't afraid of it and la Manuela had told her, had asked her who are you, and the hand that assaulted her thigh, while the man it belonged to yawned, could give her the answer, this hand that was like the hands of all the men who had come to this house, it wanted to excite her, that blunt thumb with its eroded nail, yes, I saw it, those fingers covered with hair, the square nail advancing and she didn't want it to but now yes, yes, to find out who you are Japonesita, now you'll know, that hand and that warmth from his heavy body and afterward, even if he goes away, at least something will remain from this night . . .

217

"God this is boring . . ."

Then he looked the old man in the face.

"Right, don Céspedes?"

He smiled.

"Hey, Octavio, let's go somewhere else . . ."

Don Céspedes asked him:

"Why?"

"This place has no atmosphere."

It was only then that he realized Octavio was no longer there.

"What happened to Octavio?"

"He went inside with Lucy a little while ago."

He sat Japonesita on his knee.

"Well, I guess it beats eating mice."

She remained stiff. Pancho gave her a shove that almost knocked her to the floor.

"I'm fed up."

He started to walk around the tables.

"Shitpile of a whorehouse! Doesn't even have whores. Where are the other girls? And that beat-up Victrola. Nothing to stuff your gut with even. Let's see . . . Bread: stale. Cold cuts . . . huh, half rotten. And what's this? Candy crusted with flies from the year one. Japonesita, dance at least. Do a striptease. Dance? How the hell can you if you're as stiff as a broom. Not like your mother, she was built like a barn but she was graceful. Like la Manuela, they say . . ."

The same eyes. He remembered from last year la Manuela's eyes looking at him and he looked back at those terrified eyes, shining between his hands that squeezed her neck and her eyes looking at him like glowing orbs with the certainty that he was going to drown that shore of terror in the tides within him. He remained standing.

"And la Manuela?"

Japonesita didn't answer.

"And la Manuela, I said?"

"My father has gone to bed."

"Send for her."

"He can't. He's sick."

He grabbed her by the shoulder and shook her.

"Don't tell me the old whore is sick! Do you think I came to look at your frigid little rabbit's face? No, I came to see la Manuela, that's what I came for. Now, I said. Go call her. I want her to dance for me."

"Let go of me."

Pancho's eyes were scowling, his matted, confused, bloodshot eyes almost blind with rage. Tell her to come. I want to laugh. It can't be all so damn sad in this town don Alejo's going to tear down and plow under, surrounded by vineyards that are going to swallow it up, and tonight I'll have to go home and sleep with my wife and I don't want to, I want to have fun, that nutty Manuela has to come out and save us, there must be something better than this, she has to come out.

"La Manuela . . ."

"You brute. Leave me alone."

"Tell her to come out, I said."

"And I said that my father can't."

"Don Alejo is your father. And mine."

But he looked at her eyes.

"You're right. Madame Manuela is your father."

"Don't call him that."

Pancho burst out laughing.

"At this late date, honey?"

"Don't call him that."

11

"And why not?"

La Manuela stopped in the center of the parlor.

"Put on 'El Relicario' for me."

Back arched, arm raised, snapping her fingers, she circled around the empty space in the center, pursued by her muddy, shredded red train. Applauding, Pancho tried to kiss her and hold her, laughing his head off at this crazy old harridan, this dried prune of a queer, shouting yessir, darling, now the party really starts . . . but la Manuela slipped away from him, snapping her fingers, weaving proudly among the tables before delivering herself up to her dance. Japonesita went over to stop her. Before Pancho slapped her away she managed to murmur:

"Go inside . . ."

"You dumb girl, how much longer do I have to put up with you? You go inside if you want. Right, Pancho? You're spoiling all the fun."

"Yeah, go away . . ."

He dropped into a chair. From there he shouted that now things were moving, why weren't there more people, bring wine, pastry, a roast pig, everything they had, he was paying, to celebrate . . . Lucy honey, sit here and you pal where have you been you left me stranded at this funeral come on over don Céspedes don't be afraid you'll catch cold if you stay so far away and a whore came out to the noise and revived the lamp's flame and Cloty stationed herself beside the Victrola to change the records, staring popeyed at la Manuela. . . .

"Good God, look at this old pro . . ."

In Talca they had told Cloty about la Manuela's dances, but how was she to believe it, the crazy thing was so old. She wanted to watch. They lit two lamps on the table near the platform and then Pancho saw la Manuela's eyes glow, like flames, he remembered them between his hands, and Japonesita's eyes glowed and he took a long drink because he didn't want to see and he poured more wine for Pancho, and for Lucy, drink up everybody, it's on me. He held la Manuela's head and forced her to take a long drink like him and la Manuela wiped her mouth with the back of her hand. Lucy was asleep. Don Céspedes was watching la Manuela but as if he didn't see her.

"Go to it, Manuela my love, go to it . . . Let's make my farewell party a good one. And anyway you're all going to be wiped out, whoosh . . . blown away by you know who. Don Céspedes, you know don Alejo is going to wipe out every one of these ball-busters, just for the hell of it . . ."

In the fields surrounding the town, the vineyards and night were perfectly sketched under the moon: don Céspedes saw it with wide-open eyes. The methodical stripes, the orderly pattern that contained the village of demolished walls, the confusion of this place that the vineyards were going to erase—and this house, this small point where they, together, barely bruised the inflexible night: la Manuela on the platform in her glowing dress must amuse them and kill dangerous, mercurial time that wants to devour them, demented Manuela on the platform: they applaud. They tap their heels on the dirt floor, they slap the lame table where the lamps quiver. Cloty changes the record.

Pancho suddenly becomes quiet watching la Manuela. Watching that thing dancing in the center of the room, all eye sockets, hollows, spasmodic shadows, that thing which is going to die despite its cries, that incredibly repulsive thing that, incredibly, is the party, and dances for him, he knows he aches to touch it and caress it, he doesn't want that writhing thing to be alone there in the center but against his skin, and Pancho lets himself watch and caress from a distance that old queer who is dancing for him and he surrenders to her dance, and now it isn't funny anymore because it's as if he too were gasping for breath. Octavio mustn't know. He can't know. No one must know. They mustn't see him being touched and fondled by la Manuela's contortions and frantic hands that don't touch him at all, letting himself go, but from here, from the chair where he's sitting no one can see what's happening under the table, but it can't be it can't be and he takes one of Lucy's sleeping hands and puts it there, where it burns. La Manuela's dance handles him and he would like to grab her like this, till she breaks, that corrupt body fluttering in his arms and me with a quivering Manuela, pressing her against me so she doesn't move so much, so she stays still, holding her, till she looks at me with those terrified flames and sinking my hands into her hot slimy viscera, clawing, leaving her flattened, harmless, dead: a thing.

Then Pancho roared. After all, he was a man, he was supposed to feel everything, even this, and no one, not Octavio or any of his friends would think him a freak. This was a party! A fling. He had met too many whorehouse fags in his life to be frightened by this ridiculous old woman, and they always fell in love with him—they felt his biceps, they felt the rough hair that grew to where his shirt opened at the neck. He relaxed under Lucy's hand.

The music stopped.

"The Victrola's broken."

Octavio got up to try and fix it. He quickly took it apart on the counter while Lucy and Japonesita watched. It didn't look as if it would work again. La Manuela, sitting on Pancho's lap, gave him a glass of wine. She begged him to go away from here, no, no, the three of them should continue the party somewhere else. What were they doing here. Wasting time, getting bored, eating and drinking badly. Even the Victrola was broken and who knows if anyone would ever be able to fix it. They don't even make those prehistoric machines anymore, let's go, please let's go. With the truck they could go anywhere to continue the party, in a few minutes they could be in Talca and there, in Wooden Heart's house . . . no, let's go, take me away, honey, I can't stand this any longer. I'm dying of boredom in this town and I don't want to die under a sagging adobe wall, I have a right to see a bit of light, I've never left this hole, because they tricked me into staying telling me that Japonesita is my daughter, I ask you, how could I have a daughter when Japonesita is almost as old as I am, we're just girls. Take me away from here. They say that at Wooden Heart's house they have a spread about this time and there's always something good to eat, even ducks if the customers ask for them, and there are singers, I don't know if the Farías sisters are there, I don't think so because they'd be older than me, it's all the same, somebody else who's as good with the harp and guitar as the Farías sisters used to be, may they rest in peace. Let's go now, take me away, look how that cruel girl tells everyone she's my daughter to make me stay, you saw how she treats me, like a servant, her own mother, and she never lets me go out except for mass and to see Ludo. I want to go away with you and have a party somewhere that's fun, where we can laugh for a while . . .

"It's a mess."

"What's wrong with it?"

"The spring broke."

"Listen pal, just leave it and we'll go somewhere else."

"Where?"

"Look at don Céspedes, he looks like a mummy. Wake up, old man . . ."

"Let's go to Wooden Heart's . . ."

They talked for a while and paid Japonesita.

"Where are you going?"

"What's it to you, you mackerel?"

"Where are you going, papa?"

"To whom are you speaking?"

"Don't play dumb."

"Who are you to give me orders?"

"Your daughter."

La Manuela saw that Japonesita said it spitefully, to ruin everything and make them remember. But la Manuela looked at Pancho and the two of them laughed so hard that they almost blew out the lamps.

"Sure, I'm your mother."

"No. My father."

But they were already leaving, la Manuela, Pancho, and Octavio, arm in arm and stumbling. La Manuela was singing "El Relicario," the others singing the chorus. The night was so clear that the walls cast sharp clear shadows over the puddles. The underbrush grew along the path and the blackberry's eternally renewed leaves covered that mass of things with their precise, obsessive, detailed graphic lines. They made their way to the truck parked on the corner. They walked on either side of la Manuela, holding her waist. La Manuela swayed toward Pancho and tried to kiss his mouth while he laughed. Octavio saw it and let go of la Manuela.

"Come on, pal, don't you be a fag too . . ."

Pancho also let go of la Manuela.

"I didn't do a thing . . ."

"No excuses, I saw . . ."

Pancho was afraid.

"You think I'd let this cruddy fag kiss me, are you out of your mind, pal, would I do something like that? Let's ask Manuela, hey, did you kiss me?"

La Manuela didn't answer. It always happened with men like Octavio, why the hell did he have to snoop and why doesn't he clear out of here. He's going to ruin everything.

"Come on, fag, answer."

Pancho loomed threateningly over la Manuela.

"Let's find out."

His fist was clenched.

"Don't be silly, boys, let's get on with the party."

"Did you or did you not kiss him?"

"It was just a joke . . ."

Pancho hit her in the face while Octavio held her down. The blow wasn't well aimed because Pancho was drunk. La Manuela looked around frantically, for the right moment to run.

"It's one thing to celebrate and live it up, but slobbering on my face is something else . . ."

"Stop. You're hurting me."

Standing in the mud, paralyzed by Octavio who was twisting her arm, la Manuela woke up. He wasn't la Manuela. He was señor Manuel González Astica. He. And because he was he they were going to hurt him and Manuel González Astica tasted terror.

Pancho gave him a shove that staggered him. Octavio, letting go, slipped and fell in the mud while Pancho bent over to help him up. And la Manuela, gathering his skirts up around his waist, fled toward the station. Familiar with the street, he avoided the ruts and stones while his pursuers stumbled at every step. Maybe they would lose sight of him. He had to run this way, toward the station, toward the outskirts of El Olivo because there on the other side of the town's limits don Alejo was waiting for him, and he was the only one who could save him. His face ached, his frail ankles, his bare feet cut by the rocks or a piece of glass or a tin can, but he had to keep running because don

223

Alejo promised he would be all right, that he would take care of him, that he needn't be afraid anymore if he stayed near him, it was a promise, almost an oath, and he had stayed and now they were coming to kill him. Don Alejo, don Alejo. He can help me. To the other side of El Olivo. Cross the vineyard like don Céspedes and tell him that first these wicked men try to take advantage of a girl and then . . .Tell him please protect me from the fear you told me nothing would ever happen to me that you would always protect me and that's why I stayed in this town and now you have to keep your word and protect me and take care of me and comfort me, I've never asked you before, I've never forced your word but now I do, you're the only one, you're the only one . . . don't ignore me don Alejo now that they're trying to kill me, I've come running to ask you to keep your promise . . . this way, through the thicket behind the shed like a fox so that don Alejo will defend me with his shotgun. You can kill these sick bastards and no one will say a thing, after all you're a great man, you can do anything and fix it up later with the police.

He crosses the blackberry-covered fence without realizing that the barbed wire is tearing his dress. He crouches beside the canal. Further on is the vineyard: the dirty water separates him from the symmetrical safety of the vineyards. He has to cross it. Don Alejo is waiting for him. The houses of El Olivo surrounded by oaks and a tall pine like a belfry there where the vineyards meet, waiting for him, don Alejo waiting for him with his sky-blue eyes. He has to rest a little. He listens. They aren't coming. He can't go any further. He drops on the grass. Nothing, silence: even the natural sounds of the night have stopped. La Manuela is panting, Ludovinia would say you're too old to be trotting around like this and it's true, true because his whole body aches—oh, his shoulder, how it hurts, and his legs and suddenly the cold of the entire night, of the leaves and grass and water at his feet, if he could only cross this river, but how, how if he can barely move, sprawled on the ground.

"My little darling . . ."

"Now you're really going to get it . . ."

"No . . . no . . ."

Before he could move, the men burst through the bushes and fell upon him like hungry animals. Octavio, or maybe Pancho first, started lashing at him with fists . . . perhaps it wasn't them, but other men who had pierced the thicket and found him and thrown themselves upon him, their hot bodies writhing, gasping over la Manuela who could no longer scream, their heavy, stiff bodies, the three of them one sticky mass squirming like some fantastic, three-headed animal with multiple limbs, wounded and seething, the three fused there in the grass by vomit and heat and pain, looking for the one to blame, punishing him, her, them, shuddering gratifications, excruciating confusion, la Manuela's frail body resists no more, breaks under the strain, can't even moan from the pain, hot mouths, hot hands, slavering, hard bodies wounding his, bodies that howl and insult and grope, that monster of three tortuous bodies, breaking and tearing and raking and probing, until nothing is left and now la Manuela scarcely sees, scarcely hears, scarcely feels, sees, no, doesn't see, and they escape through the blackberry bushes and she is left alone by the river that separates her from the vineyards where don Alejo waits, benevolent.

12

"That's Sultan."

Another bark, further away.

"That's Moor. He likes to lie beside the wall of the blacksmith's shop at night because it gets hot in the sun and retains the heat . . . but there was no sun today. I wonder why he's roaming around there now."

Japonesita had sat down facing don Céspedes on the other side of the lamp's dwindling flame. She turned it down till it was barely a point inside the lamp. She, too, listened to the dogs. She and la Manuela heard them so often last night that they could hardly sleep, but this was different. Because the sky had cleared up around the moon after the rain and the dogs were howling steadily at it, as if they were talking to it or begging it for something or serenading it, and since the moon was too faraway to hear them, don Alejo's dogs kept on howling.

"That's Sultan again."

Everyone had gone to bed. Cloty had left the Victrola on the table in front of don Céspedes, who kept unscrewing, opening, cutting with a kitchen knife that had a greasy wooden handle. They don't make parts for this kind of machine anymore. May as well throw it in the canal. It's no good for anything.

"But we can't get along without a Victrola."

"It won't be long before they put in the electricity."

"They're never going to. Don Alejo came to tell me today."

Don Céspedes sank into his chair, smaller than ever. He pushed the mess of worn cogs, screws, nuts, and wires aside, and slid his glass nearer. Almost empty. Barely a couple of red fingers at the bottom where the flame multiplied its reflections.

"It looks like one of those things churches have."

"What things, child?"

"Those red things with light inside."

Better be getting back. Don Céspedes drank what was left. It was late. Or maybe it wasn't; time had an eerie way of stretching itself, today seemed short, tomorrow endless, and you never knew in what part of the night you were.

"I'm going to Talca tomorrow to buy another one."

"Another what?"

"Another Victrola. From one of those places that sells things sec-ondhand, in the stores here I'll never find one like this that you have to crank. This was my mother's. I know a place where they sell used ones, they don't charge much at all. The gentleman who owns it, I think someone brought him here one night. I'll see if he can make me a good price."

"Negus . . . no, Othello . . ."

They listened. It was easy for Japonesita to sketch the whole countryside in her imagination now, as if, like don Céspedes, she had suddenly acquired the power to roll out the country like a carpet so that it filled her whole head.

"They're restless tonight."

Because the moon's out Japonesita said to herself, or maybe said out loud, or maybe don Céspedes, bent over the stove, said it, or maybe he just thought it and she sensed it.

"Why does he turn them loose?"

"He's in a funny mood. Last night he didn't go to bed. He roamed all night around the walks and under the oak. I watched him from the gatehouse in case something happened, you know how bad people are, so many have sworn to get him. I stayed there without his seeing me, and he kept walking around and around, looking at everything as if he wanted to fix it all in his mind, hungrily, I'd say, until when it was almost dawn Misia Blanca came out and said why don't you come to bed and then before he followed her in he turned the dogs loose in the vineyard."

"Yes. It was dawn when they started barking."

"God knows what's wrong with him."

226

"He's probably worrying about people like Pancho . . ."

"No, this was yesterday."

"It's the same thing. You can't trust anybody these days."

The old man yawned. Japonesita yawned. Tomorrow she was going to Talca. Like every Monday. Now she couldn't daydream about the Wurlitzer. So much the better. Try and be like don Céspedes who never daydreamed about anything, just watching to see if anything happened, alert, hiding in the shadows. Alert, that's all, no Wurlitzers. Just a secondhand Victrola to replace the one Pancho Vega broke. No, Pancho didn't break it. He had left. He was never coming back. Just as well: he left tranquillity behind, no expectations whatsoever, which was better than tranquillity here in Estación El Olivo, until they finally plowed the whole town under. Except her house. No matter what don Alejo said she wasn't going to sell it. No sir. He can do whatever he wants with the rest of the town but I'm staying here, right where I am. Even if less and less people come and everything comes to an end. Endings are peaceful, and if things don't change they end, they always do. The terrible thing is hope. I'm going to Talca just like I do every Monday to make a deposit in the bank. And I'm going to come back after lunch with the week's groceries, the same things I always get, sugar, tea, noodles, red chili; the same things I always get.

Don Céspedes stood up, listening. Japonesita picked up the screws, cogs, the broken spring, and tied them all in her handkerchief to save. You never know when you might need them.

"I have to go."

"Why?"

"I have to go see. They're barking a lot."

Japonesita smiled at him.

"How much?"

"Ten cents."

Don Céspedes paid. She put the money away. She knew everything, she saw everything, everything she needed to see and know. This house. In the dusky adobe walls the spiders nestled in small holes filled with tapestries of pale slime.

"And la Manuela?"

Japonesita shrugged.

"Can't something happen to him?"

"What could happen?"

"He's old."

"He might be old but every day he gets fonder of chasing around.

Didn't you see him leave with Pancho and Octavio? He clutched at the party like a dying man. He was burning up inside. I know him. He's done this to me before. The men buy him drinks, he dances, goes crazy, and leaves with them . . . the wine excites him and they go to Talca and sometimes even further. One of these days something's going to happen to him, I tell myself that every time, but he always comes back. After three or four days. Sometimes after a week of wandering around whorehouses in other towns where they know him, triumphing as he says, and he comes back here with a black eye or a pair of broken ribs because when the men get drunk they hit him for being a queer. Why should I worry! He has nine lives like a cat. I'm tired of the whole thing. And with Pancho's talent for celebrating they'll be roaming around for at least a week. The police know him and don't say anything, they bring him back without telling anyone about it, I give them a few drinks, and it's like nothing happened. But there might be a new policeman, one of those who gets an idea and doesn't let go. And then, a couple of weeks in bed and I have to take care of him. Crying the whole time, saying he's going to die, that he's too old for these things, forgive him, he won't do it again, and he says he's going to throw his flamenco dress away, you saw it, it's a rag, but he doesn't throw it away, he puts it in his suitcase. And then it's the same old story about the men here, the men there, they're all bad because they hit him and laugh at him and then father cries and says what a horrible fate and says what would become of me without my beloved daughter, his only support, and don't ever leave him. My God, don Céspedes! If you could see how he cries! It breaks your heart! And then, of course, after a few months he goes off and I lose him again. It's been over a year now since he did it. I thought he wasn't going to leave again because the poor thing is such a wreck, but you saw what happened . . ."

Don Céspedes was listening to something else.

"What?"

Japonesita studies him, trying to guess what he hears.

"No, nothing, don Céspedes . . ."

She walked him to the door. She opened it just a bit, barely a crack for don Céspedes to slide through. A little wind and some stars filtered in and she huddled in her pink shawl. Then she bolted the door. Rubbing her hands she walked among the tables, putting out the lamps one by one.

". . . three, and four . . ."

She's told them she doesn't like them to light so many lamps when there are so few people, they can't make a profit. The air is full of reeking carbon. Of course, the dance . . . oh well. She went out to the patio. She doesn't know what time it is, but those devils keep howling out there in the vineyard. It must be around five because she hears Nelly cry and Nelly always whimpers a little before dawn. She went to her room and got into bed without even lighting a candle.

Severo Sarduy: FROM CUBA WITH A SONG

translated by Suzanne Jill Levine

The translator wishes to recognize the assistance of Roberto González
Echevarriá, whose knowledge of the Cuban language and the works of
Severo Sarduy has been invaluable.

To Salamandra

CURRICULUM CUBENSE

Feathers, yes, lovely brimstone feathers, heads of marble carried down a river of feathers, feathers on her head, a feather, humming-bird, and raspberry hat in fact, from where Help's smooth orange nylon hair stretches to the ground, braided with pink ribbons and little bells; from her hat the albino cascade falls along the sides of her face, then hips, down her zebra-skin boots to the pavement. And Help, in stripes, an Indian bird behind falling rain.

"I can't go on!"—she shrieks, and carves a hole in the bread crumbs.

"Drop dead!"—Mercy speaking—"Yeah, drop dead, stick with it, kill yourself, go tell the president, go tell the gods, shove it, split into two like an orange, drown in beer, in franks and sauerkraut, fuck yourself. Turn to dust, to ashes. That's what you wanted."

Help pushes aside her locks. She peeps out, Baroque:

> "I will be ashes, but meaningful ashes.
> I will be dust, but dust in love."

MERCY: "*Tu me casses les cothurnes!* (*en français dans le texte*). Shut up. I can't go on either. Wipe away that tear. A little modesty, please. And poise. Stick with it. Take your compact."

The small mirror is signaling. It directs the sun toward the glass skyscraper. On the balcony of the twentieth floor a girl comes out with another mirror in her hand. She hops up and down and moves it around in search of the call.

"Look at yourself. Your tears have made a furrow in the first five layers of your makeup. Make sure they don't reach your skin. Of course for that you'd need a drill. You've lost the asparagus cream. The underlying strawberry is mixing with the layer of Max Factor's baby pineapple. You're graph papered. Vasarelic. Let's sing:

> the ever-absent, ever absent
> gives us evil as a present.

Help, almost singing:

"Yes, that's him. The riddle of riddles. The sixty-four thousand dollar question, the definition of being. Our cupboard's empty. No ham for Tom. No cheese for Jerry. This is how it stands: we stayed behind and the gods went away, they took the boat, they left in trucks, they crossed the border, they shat on the Pyrenees. They've all gone. This is how it stands: we went away and the gods stayed behind. Sitting. Hiding, taking a nap, happy-go-lucky, dancing the Ma Teodora, The First Cuban Song, the repetitive *son*, swinging in midair, like strung-up corpses."

"Shut up. That's what you wanted."

"No. I didn't want this. I asked for life, all of it, with the rattles and the tambourines. I asked for my daily bread and sausage. No go. They sent me the hairless old woman, the plucked, bald, shaven, lonely bitch of death."

"One of your cheeks is showing. It's like the face of the moon: full of craters."

"Rat. Rogue. Frog. May the Being swallow you. Inhale you. May your air conditioning break down. May a hole open all around you. May the Lacanian fault suck you under. May you be absorbed, not seen because unnoticed."

"That's it. I'm leaving. I mean it now. No matter how. They're throwing me out. I'm cornered and with my lance I strike right and left, to and fro, like a Japanese warrior fighting an invisible enemy."

Help moves her head. Golden fringes against the windowpane. Woolen locks. Windmill wings.

"Go away. Unessential. Leave the House. Yes, house with capitals. The Domus Dei. And she nods the way.

Mercy in the Domus Dei

But how could you not be confused? There were thousands. Thousands of little feet. Little worm-eaten hands. Such screeching. Tin plates and spoons. They'd come out looking green and charge against the waves. Siren, and they'd appear. Screeching, and they'd disappear. At the same time. A woman would go to each window. And at each, shake a black tablecloth. The front of the building would disappear behind a curtain of bread crumbs. River of feathers.

"Good morning. I've been phoning and nobody answers."

"Ah," the maid says.

"May I come in?"

"Won't do you any good. She's not in."

"What? After all the time. All the waiting. All the bootlicking and

236

backslapping. I've gone down on my knees in waiting rooms, bounced between the sheets of every minister, bribed doormen."

"Sorry, no."

The maid opens the door wide, as if she were opening her legs, her transparent little box, to the being par excellence. A light erupts from inside: the light reflected from the bald pate of the Great Bald Madame. Mercy contracts all over, turns white, like squid in boiling water.

"Now do you see?"—the acolyte utters hoarsely—. "Her absence is almost present."

By the time Mercy's on the elevator, poor thing, she's screaming at the top of her lungs. A crying little frog face. She mixes up her buttons, bumps against a black man, catches her finger in the door. And so she reaches the ground floor: moaning, bishop purple, cowering in a corner of the aluminum box, surrounded by plucked chickens on all sides, alone with them except for a block of crushed ice and a shopping bag of bitter oranges in one corner.

You ought to hear the cute words the midget doorman saves for lady visitors! He comes out from under his scarlet cap and exhausts the synonymies. With Mercy it's a different story; frozen and all as she is, she kicks him at the first flattery, ties him to the stool with his own belt, presses the button to the roof-garden and launches the echo chamber.

There are mirrors in the hall, and, although threadbare, the Fate just can't stand herself: she pulls out her hogs bristle brush, her orange, diamond-studded eye shadow, the false beauty mark that she places painstakingly on the right corner of her lips so that it rises with each smile, lastly she pulls out her Yoruba necklaces and when she steps out on the street she is something else. To such a point that Help, waiting for her with coupon in hand—good for two mango milk shakes at the Milk Bar on the corner—jumps with joy upon seeing her and waves a handkerchief: she thinks Mercy was received.

"No, I wasn't."

When they turn, slender and symmetrical, toward the building, the windows are already dark. There is no noise. The bread crumbs have bleached the treetops, the black lawn.

"It's like snow!"

Self-Service

"My, we're metaphysical, we must be hungry! Let's go to the Self-Service!"

No sooner said than done. They're off on tiptoes, pressing their tummies, slipping among the shells of rusty cars—their silky hair flows through tin scraps—stumbling, jumping over flattened and spokeless bicycle wheels, over handlebars, moss-covered horns, headlights stuffed with paper, aluminum circles with red bars. Yellow deities. Flavian birds. Stags. They walk among glass, girdled by rain, crowned with frozen orchids from Palm Beach, clean among the dregs, clear-cut as mushrooms upon horse dung, fragrant among the debris of diesel motors.

Following the scaffolds of a construction site—in the foundations, puddles of green water—they walk along singing *Ich bin von Kopf bis Fuss auf Liebe eingestellt,* opening their hungry little fish mouths into heartshapes, tightrope walking on a steel bar.

And behind them, thousands of paper balloons simultaneously light up within squares. Cones upon a red tapestry. And over the buildings, the milky wake of the subway streaks the night. Intermittent blue rhombi.

And off they go, the Flower Girls, the Ever-Present cross another scaffold, another avenue. There they go, under the three-leaf clover of the highways watched by helicopters. Echo tunnels. There, by the escalators, by the rails, where all the trolleys are, a second before the go signal. How speedy!

One potato, two potato, one by one they pick up the potatoes under the table, crouching among feet; she crawls along the gallery of legs, behind a rolling tomato, the paper cup, the bowl of grated beets—little purple strands on somebody's shoe.

People jump over her. Down there, on all fours, entangled in her own wig, soup-soaked Help has fallen with her plate among open tangerines (a spiked heel perforates her jellied egg).

She picks it all up—dirty home fried potatoes—looking up from side to side like a frightened squirrel. She puts on her green glasses. Covers the other half of her face with bangs.

"I want to disappear!"—and she's no longer a squirrel, but a mole: she rolls herself into a ball, and hides her head.

Mercy is now seated, but not eating. She's looking at the food and sobbing rhythmically. She boohoos and blows her nose with a Kleenex. When Help arrives empty-handed—she threw her plate into the garbage can—she shakes her by the shoulders.

"It's nothing," she says.

"It's nothing," she answers.

And they laugh again.

Now both are seated, calm and collected, in front of a celluloid picture window. Not one stain, not one hair out of place, not one drop of tomato sauce on their cheeks. Motionless; their heads, a few inches apart, coincide with the crossing of the diagonal lines in the landscape —blue domes punctured with windows, an airfield: drones and twin engines are taking off—pale hands on their chests. They don't move an inch, but it's useless: everybody's looking at them. They feel on trial.

"Mocking eyes give us the once-over."

"Fingers point to us, put asterisks on us."

Then Help puts her finger to her right temple, jumps up, shaking her mane like a feather duster, clinking her little bells; the girl's all music.

"I have an idea."

She opens a crocodile-skin box that hangs from her shoulder like a canteen on a thin silver chain, and counting them she takes out fifty color photographs. She throws away two which have yellowed, hands Mercy a close-up in black and white, and goes to the end of the dining room with the other forty-seven. From there she starts handing them out, table by table. With each photograph she smiles, combs her hair, introduces herself to the addressee with a bow and doubles his surprise with a detailed description of the picture. Mercy follows her a few steps behind, adding adverbs to the adjectives, curtsies to the bows, cooling the air with an ostrich feather fan, spraying it with balms. At Help's signal, Mercy gives each a little Caridad del Cobre* medallion and a piece of candy.

The first picture is already faded. Help, with her face painted yellow, is in a guayabera shirt and cap, drinking coffee in front of a cardboard tower, or a Mardi Gras float, or a mausoleum lettered in Arabic.

"Here I am in front of the blue mosque of Constantinople, even though you can't see the four turrets. The suit is Empress Ming's,

* The Virgin of the Caridad del Cobre—the patron saint of Cuba.

that's why I have that dragon-painted teacup in one hand and this single-flowered long stem in the other. As you see, my eyes are elongated by means of black lines which, in profile, if it weren't for my ears, would turn into little fishes."

"You forgot to say that these sniveling, bare-assed little boys who are playing mandolins, mouths agape before the lens, are your interpreters."

"My followers. Look at this one. Here I am among the Caduvean or Cadivean Indians, reading Franz Boas with a tape recorder. What the native is handing me is a mask whose general lines correspond to the map of the city. I look good, don't I?"

And thus, she hands out all the pictures. Except one. She keeps the passport size six by eight, in which she is face front, looking slightly to one side, not really serious, in short, her spitting image.

"I don't think we left a bad impression."

"Maybe. But let's go before they change their minds."

"Wait. I forgot my scythe."

Note: The Self-Service is on the ground floor of a Bakelite octahedron. Walls of Coca Cola bottles support a ceiling decorated by a Fall of Icarus in pale pink and gold. From the corners four spotlights move sinusoidally along the walls and sometimes stop on bowls of grated carrots, jellied eggs, or red beets in almond sauce which are imbedded in wicker nooks between the bottles. At each sweep of the light a xylophone arpeggio ascends or descends in the scale according to the altitude of the light beam, and stops on a note when the beam stops on a plate. Since the red beets in almond sauce are practically at ceiling level, the corresponding note is a shriek that turns hoarse when the focus descends in the sinusoid.

The delicacies, like the plates which contain them, are made of plastic.

A New Version of the Facts: Fate and the General

If she entangled him in her champagne locks, if he pricked her with the open brooch of one of his medals, if the cherry tart fell on the Carmelite khaki of his uniform, if he scratched her with a gold braid, if both got entangled, if they held their tongues out of courtesy, if they insulted each other, if the creamed asparagus remained among the decorations of honor, if the Pyrrhic victor invoked the patron saint of artillerymen, the invincible goddess Changó, if she retorted by calling upon the queen of the river and the sky, her antidote and talisman: we will never know.

Let's make a note then on how it stands at this moment: facing the dessert department, among synovial trays and trembling like a burnt butterfly, Help has entangled her hairs . . . No: her hairs are tangled in the aluminum forest that armors a skinny general of the fleet.

There they are—two plumed serpents—cheek to cheek, stuck to one another, their trays stuck together too. Struggling Siamese twins. Bacardi bat, ink spot, double animal, open oyster, a body with its reflection; that's Help and the General.

There they stay, touching at their vertices, extremes meeting. Like a rattlesnake that finds a jiggling, appetizing little mouthful for itself, a pyramidal cupcake that it downs in one gulp, letting loose the scream then, because it's just downed its own tail, and thus disappears and returns to Bald Nothingness.

"But why doesn't the General simply take off his coat?"

Listen to the question that Mercy, and only Mercy, asks.

I: My dear, can't you see that if the General takes off his hardwares, he would be like Lacan's bird painter without his feathers? Like a goat who takes off his black stripes to create a Vasarely with them?

MERCY: I just want Help out of this mess, that's all.

I: She'll get out. She'll go home well-mannered, conceited, chaste.

MERCY: Listen to that! Three adjectives in one breath! It wasn't like that in my day. What today's literature is coming to . . .

I: Yes dearie, three adjectives in a row, but well put. So shut your mouth and swallow.

MERCY: Digressions are not my line, so to the point: what's happened to my friend?

Nothing really, just that this cosmogony-in-the-making simply attracted, sucked in world. As a magnet in a river does to fishhooks, or as a vacuum cleaner in a chicken coop to feathers, so did the binomial Help-General suck in all that was around, and naturally, a black girl and Chinese chick: thus completing the curriculum cubense.

As always, the fourth element, that is, the Unnamable Baldy, was already present. It was stuck on to the third which is always hero-worshipped for its strength, well then, the two that were missing came running. They arrived, twin stones, fish of identical eyes, to get caught in the hair and medals, to entangle themselves in Help Conception of the Universe:

1. an oriental, in white rice powder makeup, prima donna of the Shanghai District Opera,

2. a round-assed, big-titted black girl, very semicircular, very double-breasted, snuggly squeezed into a bright red weave, her hair freshly ironed like a river of creeping vines.

So that, seen from above, in an imaginary mirror which we can place on top of the self-service counter for example (and which is probably there, to see if someone is taking the silverware or hiding, as he passes, a chocolate cookie in his pocket), the group is a giant four-leaf clover, or a four-headed animal facing the four cardinal points, or a Yoruba sign of the four roads:

the white of the wig and the coat,

the China doll of the lottery and the mouth cat cabala

the Wifredo Lamesque black girl

and the last—who was the first:

the red-headed fraud, the Waxen Woman, the Keep-Your-Fingers-Crossed Loner. We come upon them, the four parts of which the wise stud of Heidelberg speaks.

MERCY: Yeah, the one who put the lid on the box.

They're all yours now. Four different beings and four who are one. Already they're breaking loose, already they're looking at each other. How cute!

By the River of Rose Ashes

> In the forest of Havana
> a Chinee lost her way
> and I, a poor lost goner,
> this fair maid did waylay.
> —Homage to the "Shanghai,"
> Havana Burlesque

The moon, the partridge, the fading ferns, the four animals, the wine of the wind, the water of the Almendares: all was set for the rendezvous.

There, among the trunks of violet-striped sugar cane, licking reeds, following the crease of leaves like knives, silvery drivel, the snake jiggled its rattles along with the river's.

And nearby, the red turtle, the one that runs fastest: saddle of the immortals.

Further away, eyes of fire among the black leaves of the redwood tree, the unicorn, with its hemplike mane. And next to him, the forever-on-one-foot, the pink heron.

The earth's murmur was like the clashing of sticks in The Capture of an Enemy Fort, so it wasn't at all strange to see Rose Ashes there. Sewn into that landscape, exercising her Yin right smack in the forest of Havana, she was a white bird behind bamboo, a motionless prisoner among lances. She was reciting the Five Books, singing with her little whistle voice; she looked as if she'd burst like a salty toad, she'd gaze at the moon in silence and recite them over again.

So did the sweet smoke of the Romeo and Juliet, Havana's finest cigar, and clanking medals surprise her.

She did not turn pale; she already was, from so much rice and tea.

Whether she was dressed to receive ambassadors from the provinces in the Garden of Ming; or wearing black slacks and a linen guayabera, as usual, or plain and simply in the state her mother, with one good push, bore her during intermission at the Opera, we'll never know.

Honoris Causa in pool and in the sack—those were her battlefields—the Condecorated, the Glorious One, did thus surprise her. Cushioned by a quilt of moss he crushed sleeping scorpions and orange snails, his step was the Invincible's: pectoral golds, its punctuation. He was the hood master of Seville's processions, the majesty of synagogues, the Galician *aîdos* in forward march. Not a general, but a long-shanked gladiator, yes.

The yellow one shrieked. And with good reason. He kept coming, parting branches, dealing blows, his arms, a double machete, his air, one of combat as he fought his way through the bramble. A Peeping Tom, the licentious rake, and another mystic. But you must admit, the gymnastic arts sure come in handy! Lotus Flower leaps up, and, like the fish that jumping out of water becomes a hummingbird, she flies among lianas. Now she's the white mask striped by shadows of sugar canes, now the flight of a dove, the streak of a rabbit. Try and see her. You can't. Yes! her eyes, two golden slits, snake charmer eyes, betray her. A puckery *caimito* among clusters of *caimitos*. She's mimicry. She's a texture—the white plaques on the trunk of a God tree—a wilted flower beneath a palm, a butterfly embossed with pupils, she is pure symmetry. Where is she? I don't see her. She scarcely breathes. Now, with eyebrow pencil she draws faces on her hands and wiggles them far from her own, to bewilder Mr. Belicose. He, dividing the air with his sword, curses her in alphabetical order.

Rose Ashes becomes a cloud, a baby fawn, the murmur of the river among its pebbles. So they go around in circles, searching each other out with a stare, like two fighting cocks. And so recitation time passes.

The China maid attacks. Changes disguise, throws stones, appears and disappears in the same place, runs zigzag so that no weapon can reach her, erects a stone barrier to make the river run in the other direction and mislead the Enemy; she scats centipedes, squirrels, chameleons, so that they'll bite him as he passes; she imitates the clanking medals, the very voice of her pursuer, or appears as another lecherous general to drive him crazy. One by one she exhausts her scenic resources.

The Slaughterman is ready to fight. For him, her escapes are like the carriages of gold they give an invader to stop him. Around and around his prisoner he goes: it's no longer one, but two swords he carries. With the second knife, the one that bends but never breaks, he opens the underbrush. A Pyrrhic little flute that one!

The finer the Yellow One becomes, the more liquid it gets, the sword you all know, the more fiery; why it's almost two-tongued!

Naturally, with an ally like that, it doesn't take long for Mr. Lecherous to attempt checkmate.

The Forest of Havana is the Summer Palace's forest, and the waters of the Almendares, the Yangtze; Rose Ashes weaves her own figure with lianas and flees, leaving her adversary with that intangible double, that unraveling and moving image.

He subtly approaches from behind; but abandoned by Chola Angüengue, the conga queen of weapons, he gets caught in her loom.

Faraway, the China maid shrieks, and dances the Canton mambo. And he, stuck, here. Still.

Do you smell something? Yes, that's the smell: Cantonese rice with soya sauce. There's something else too: dog urine (it's early); plus: tea. Yes, as you must have guessed, we're in Chinatown.

THE READER: "But, what about that record of Marlene's?"

I: "Well, dear, not everything in life is coherent. A little disorder with the order, I always say. You're not going to ask me to arrange a full-feathered Chinese "ensemble" for you right here on Zanja Street, next to the Pacífico (yes, where Hemingway eats), in a city where there's a distillery, pool hall, whore, and sailor on every corner. I'll do what I can."

And so:

"Chinese atmosphere, girls, come on!"—the Director steps out of a saffron cloud smelling of burnt grass (yes, the same grass you're thinking). He steps out of his pagoda of smoke, pensive, hair greased with sweat, eyes of a jade bulldog—two red balls—hands crossed over his chest (is he reciting the Book?); he walks along a dotted line. He shivers, turns green; the opalescent cloud crumbles in the scenery. He is lime green, a rooster feather, he bristles; a poisonous wind has swept through his nine orifices.

He's inspired. He calmly approaches, looking toward the stage, but in *his* reality he's making his way through battles, he's escaping bats that are Toledan blades, he's crushing rows of ants, and of red dwarfs, he's riding on a tortoise. For us he's taking off an earring; but he's pulling leeches off his ears. Is he fanning himself with his hands? On grass level he's commanding the Waters. Is he scratching his neck? He's trying to get a gorilla off his back, or a troll who's biting his shoulder. The Director, stoned, plays on both waves; he's an amphibian of consciousness, the *mascalzone*.

He's wearing canvas pants, an orange sash at his waist, open sandals, and, above all, a little aroma I'd prefer not to evoke but which is stronger than the stench of badly digested glazed pork.

He stands on the empty proscenium, but feels looked upon. He catches by surprise, between cracks in the stage, sliding, parallel drops of mercury, neon green eyes.

"A cup of coffee, maestro!"—Comes shuffling Lotus Flower by the River of Rose Ashes, her flowered silk bathrobe opened. Through the other stage door María Eng enters, with Dragon Puss, Frog Baby and the Ever-Present Girls, better known as the Fannies: Help Chong and Mercy Si-Yuen, chorus girls of the Shanghai District Opera. The very same who perform a flying somersault through loopholes and splash down inside the castle in The Attack on the Fort, and again, the same who come out butterflies and turn into toads among the leaves of the white water lilies in the Poem of the Barge, yep, that's them. We'll soon see them go through changes, keepers that they are of the secret of the seventy-eight metamorphoses.

To set the stage, now that we're in rehearsal, Lotus Flower sounds her note somewhere between twitched and gurgled (a flute full of beer), but as the naughty *cattiva* doesn't warn anybody in this manner, María, Dragon Puss, and the Siamese twins come running out to Chinese C.

(Outside, the neighborhood's waking up: in the brothel's show window, condoms with beaks, spurs, and comb, with bells; thimbles. The movie house consumptive changes the billboard: today a moonlit bridge beneath pine trees, a face in black and yellow stripes like an Indian fish.)

Gliding in outer space as he was, the Director couldn't take it any longer and, bathed in a sulphurous froth, fell to the floor. María Eng brought in a pillbox of violet salts and a pitcher of orange juice with ice.

The Pekinese flute band had begun the Poem of the Barge's vocal theme, and since once she started Lotus couldn't stop till the grand finale, Help and Mercy popped out of the wings, half-naked, turning somersaults in the air, hummingbirds: they hung their heads back and for a helm used their tails. Sorrel manes, woolen yarn, flame, ribbon of resin, needles, dark green coins, these were the tresses that lamps filtered among curtains imitating curtains of Venetian felt, cardboard walls, bridges, Etruscan birds.

The Divine Ones flew, yes, flew orange-striped, chlorophyll-striped over the stage, suspended by plastic wires the color of the background curtain, the color of the screens in Polynesian brothels and the color of the air a snowy fan displaces.

High up the Smilers howled like castrated rabbits, prayed the salute to the Great Madman and pissed from fear. They looked down at us; little anteater eyes.

Lotus, in a dragon-drawn cart, struggled with a big-headed demon and, singing the Kidnap Aria, crossed northern auroras of stage time. Her face was a flat circle, three stripes under a crown of two facing unicorns.

Over the Cantonese band—two blacks and a Cantonese blowing flageolets—the Empress bends backward in the cart, a bamboo shoot pulled by the river's current.

The Director opened a crack in one eye. He said he had been dreaming of Lotus and that she had been a black kite on gold letters and also a bird pierced by a lance and a great key wrapped in feathers.

His head wrapped in vinegar cloths, feet in hot water, two strawberry ices (for the lack of ice) beneath the two little pockets between his legs which, from the fright, had emptied out on him or were at his bellybutton or God knows where:

"The show must go on!"

The Spaniard knocked on the zinc door so hard that the orchestra stopped playing and the stagehand let go of the plastic wires. (The smell of burnt tea, which experienced noses can detect a mile away, attracts the fuzz.) He let go of the plastic wires, as I was saying, and the Fannies fell to the floor demolishing the flushed parts for which they are so named.

So that, on the stage, all three stared at each other. *Faceba proprio pietá.*

The Peeping Tom's walk, and much more so for being a Spaniard's, does not need captions.

If I were you, Lotus dear, I would have realized by now that it's He who's coming, and instead of sitting there, in your steam bath, weighing yourself, drinking vinegar and washing your eyes with salt, I would have bolted my dressing room door by now. In your present state you'll stay chaste and pure as long as it takes to shake a lamb's tail.

Help and Mercy (*playing canasta in the corridor, already dressed for the Amazon number*):

"Good grief! That's all we needed: God the writer, who sees all and knows all before anybody else does, who gives advice and puts his nose in everybody's business but his own!"

Well, as I was saying before the So Full of Graces interrupted me, Peeping Tom, all the time walking diagonally, appears in slice form. Archimboldesque, he's made of parsley, wood, edible snail when he explores the forest; here in the theater corridor where he advances along the wall, he continues sideways: he cuts like a penknife through shit-stained posters, javelins, lutes with little clusters of hashish hidden inside, Persian pillboxes filled with stones and black butterflies.

He moved so angular and diagonally that Lotus didn't see him when, *comme d'habitude*, she came off the stage leaving the audience in standing ovation, fainting spells, and a rainfall of gardenias.

The *regina pictrix* will now go through the twelve stages of self-absorption. She will unmask herself. She will cease to be Empress Ming; she will be a piece of paint-smeared hide.

When the General, with a bunch of roses in one hand and an extra-fine cigar in the other, threw open the door to the Empress's dressing room, he let out a skinny bald Chinaman, in a linen guayabera and slacks, carrying a grapefruit on a tray.

The Battle Lover went inside without so much as a peep. The Chinaman slipped out.

Like a squirrel, the Spaniard looked here and there, sniffing, poking around, looking for his little Chinese cherry, his lychee. He saw a lace slip hanging from a screen and his mouth watered. He tiptoed near. In one stroke he pulled it down. But he didn't hear a scream on the other side. Nor when he went into the bathroom. He also checked behind the doors and under the bed. Where three calico cats stood on one paw, like pelicans or sea horses.

He lost his patience. It was in the closet where he found a black fitted waistcoat and see-through underpants, television model. Like all generals in a tight spot, this one's digestion stopped short on him (lobster Thermidor, one of the fleet's favorite dishes), became a knot in his throat and another in his belly and he could just about utter the all too familiar "Help me, dear God." He walked out, reread the sign on the door. The Empress. He was just about to leave when he heard the racket. The very irritated Symmetrical Ones were coming, their vocabulary in high voltage, counting the evening's earnings between praises, as follows:

"Your mother doesn't know who your father is."

"Daughter of a thousands jisms and all of them different."

"Monkey vulture crossbreed."

They see Medals Galore and break into a strut, here a hip, there a hip, they dance the Scorpion carnival dance, scarcely touching the floor, as when on the blue rug of the first act they bounce among streamers that inscribe the sign of war, keepers that they are of the Secret of the Bounce.

A Sivaic Band

Aren't they cute? Wrapped in fringed mantillas, hair twisted in Borrominesque helices, falling in sea shells, followed by gold threads like the cars of certain nocturnal photographs. That mallow, that lemon tea lotion, that big wicker basket filled with pocketbooks, pineapples, and *caimitos;* that frozen daiquiri with strawberries they're drinking,

248

they do everything so *mignonnes!* Isn't that right, General? You could eat them up! How tasty, how crispy! Go ahead, have a bite, mate! They crunch deliciously, like little partridge bones. Come on, General, say something to them, paint the town red, remember the old days at the Louvre Sidewalk Café, not to mention the Marte and Belona dance school soirées.

THE GEN: No sirree, I won't say a thing to them.

I: Come on, don't put us on, such a gentleman as yourself.

THE GEN: And why don't you say something to them? To me they're two ugly ducklings, two Peruvian monkeys.

I: Never mind the rhetoric. Throw them something, even if it's only a pebble, a sigh.

The General bent down with the maximum flexion his venerable somatic vehicle allowed. Seen from the rear guard he was like a tricycle or a photographer with his head inside a box camera. From the prow, an adipose grotto: the three layers of his chin, the ovoid of the Thermidophagus veiled in sparkles, upside-down dome. I don't know how you could see from below because I couldn't bend lower than him, but I imagine that a good background for him would be the theater awning, which is decorated with laurel branches in decalcomania, with suns and stars made of silver paper that flies have profaned.

Given the abundance of arachnids, Coleoptera and other neighbors in the place, the General made sure several times that what he was going to throw them was a pebble and not a centipede, spider, or wasp.

The Tiny Feet were already walking backward when in their ringlets they received the homage.

In the twinkling of an eye the cry "Metamorphosis" was heard in G flat, and the Two immediately appear mounted on racing Vespas, at full speed, and armed with Thompson machine guns, two-tongued knives, javelins, flamethrowers, pum-pum guns, hand grenades and teargas bombs. Helmets crown even their helices, all of which is very natural in such a bad neighborhood. What is even more surprising is that each One is supplied with three heads and seven arms. The tetradecapodous and hexacephalous aluminum artifact is a sight to see!

My dear, what a getup! What a Shivaic band! The four femur piccolos tremble under the step of fourteen cornets spitting yellow light, and these under the heads of Tarot Papesses. The albino stream flows through diamonds and clubs.

Help pulls a hair out of this stream, knots it twice and blows upon it, and at the sound of "Metamorphosis!" it turns into a snake that wriggles in the air like a butterfly in someone's mouth, breaks against the ground and becomes a chameleon, toad, giant shrimps. So she populates the square with animals: monkey actors, red antelopes on sun clocks, frightened cranes, camels laden with hydraulic organs, leopards, lynx, bears fleeing from the motor scooters.

Mercy is having a good time, and laughs with a slight hiccup, as if a feather were tickling her bellybutton, until Help starts commanding again and all the creatures, before reaching the sidewalks, are turned into birds and fly away.

The light of the moon comes out as if filtered through an aquarium.

Joined by a bellybutton, Siamese motorcycles, the Vespas duplicate themselves: four opaque triangles. Behind them, a river of metal nuts and rusting tin cans divide an orange and black landscape; they follow its meanderings down empty terraces, aisles of mildewed brass, ashen porticos whose furniture has been bleached by moss.

The Bald Divinities roll along and the squeaking of their tires on the pavement is like that of an orchestra of deaf men, like that of an arm breaking, or a head between cogs. They're moving at top speed. But, do you by any chance think they wobble or wave good-bye? Nothing of the sort: majestic, they wear red scarves, motionless like hanged men's tongues; the air barely grazes their hair . . . Now they throb, contract, swell, and collapse like salty toads, a Maryan toy that nods, that lets go of its rabbi's bonnet, that asks for water in sign language, that unwinds and has hands that trace a dotted line as they move. That stops.

As the heads of saints on a Yoruba altar shine upon the chalice, surrounded by rotten fruit and beheaded roosters, so among horns and crowbars do the heads of the Living-Dead emerge from a luminous plate: white eyes on white faces, peppermint hair crowned by a halo of flames, two thin threads rolling down from broken eyelids and splitting their faces into stripes, Byzantine coins.

They are fluorescent, they are acetylene, they are drums that hypnotize birds, they are helicopters, they are chairs at the bottom of an aquarium, they are obese eunuchs, their tiny sexes among pink flowers, they are piranhas, leprous angels who sing "Metamorphosis, metamorphosis," they are two unhappy creatures who just wanted to escape a retired Priapus. They are forgiven.

What a change, my frog babies! At the green of the traffic light the Divine Ones reappear in normal state. On their Vespas, dressed in leather, they take off noisily, discharging black smoke through their escape pipes. Mounted on those motor scooters and disguised as juvenile delinquents you girls are as sad as the toy horses on a small town merry-go-round!

The Vespa maneuvers explain many things: Lotus, in a guayabera and a Tyrolean hat that hides her bald pate, has already been doing the rounds for quite a while in her zone on Zanja Street, wearing down heels and sidewalk. With night she falls from dollar to peso, bed to cot, whiskey to coffee, and from yes to *sí*. G. sees her go by and stands there as if he were watching it rain. And she, sadistic, smiles at him.

Nevertheless, G. goes wet all over when he sees the Peripathetics coming. Dressed in black leather from head to toe, they adorn the aforementioned helmets with color pictures of Elvis Presley, James Dean pins, autographs by Paul Anka, locks of hair from Tab Hunter, Pat Boone's fingerprints, and Rock Hudson's "*measurements*."

How great they look! Standing on a corner in open offer and demand in front of a Gravi toothpaste poster (Gravi: "the queen of toothpastes") between the giant toothbrush and the pink spiral.

The General comes over. With such publicity, how can he resist?

HELP (*who, in her black leather jacket, is sweating*—average temperature on the "isle" 81 degrees Fahrenheit): Pretty hot out, huh?

GENERAL: Looks like it's going to rain.

(*Giggles from all sides.*)

As to a kingdom of heavens according to its snowfalls and birds, so has Dragon Puss divided the sidewalk into beats. She strolls around the bars and pool rooms in a black bonnet, a belt of rhinoceros hide and a marble tablet in her hands. Sententious, she christens herself The Very Old Man. He indicates with a chalk mark the boundaries of the neighborhood—a Gravi poster, the movie billboard, the shadow of the Chinese laundry's neon sign—he names them according to kind, and then goes around on his bicycle, holding out a little box for taxes. He's a pimp by birth, he's a member of the fuzz. He knows where all the grass and all the numbers are and what they're called. He pushes but neither plays nor smokes. He avoids chance and fire. To control the Illusory is to renounce it—he utters, and so, the master-of-every-possible-science does his rounds selling tickets, joints, and even little envelopes of "sugar" (to support native industry—he says). He psalm-odiously grants Nirvanas.

The initiate call him Heaven of One Hundred Rainbows, Mount of Flowers and Fruits, Face. He enters the smoking rooms singing and leaves in the pipes and samovars an orange cornea like that of the toucan's beak. Donor of Pools of Jade, he disappears; a resinous smell in the air.

G. goes to all those stops, passes through all those concentric curtains, sinks into all those spirals of smoke inquiring after the sense of his being. He searches for Lotus, searches for Lotus, and pays for his "joints" among mocking giggles.

In those sheds of creaking bamboo they drink the most aged wines to his health; they offer him, so that he may have a taste of "hop," the smoking tubes branching from their pipes. He refuses.

"All my alcohols I carry within me."

He has just consummated with the Two—and both together—the bluff that you are imagining. Of course, said fate was perpetuated sadistically and even in his moments of greatest suffocation (which he suffered, dressed as he was in coat and underpants), G. did not halt his interrogation:

G. (*his tins clanking along with his seesawing*): Where is the Empress, my honey-pie, my little moon-shaped fanny?

And the PERIPATHETICS (*in duet*): The Empress is a mirage, a *trompe-l'oeil*, a flower *in vitro*.

And G. (*whipping their waxy behinds*): Ming exists. I've seen her in the forest (and a lash), I've seen her on stage (*and another*).

> Where have you hidden away
> leaving me in such dismay?

And the SMEARED LADIES: Ming is pure absence, she is what she is not. There is no water for your thirst.

Etc., etc.

What an inquisition, my Frog Babies! You must have charged the Spaniard twenty dollars service *non compris* plus hotel and dinner—that steamed cinnamon milk you so much adore—.

EYEBROWS GALORE: Ah yes, some inquisition that was. With the heat and his combinatory mania. He wore himself out in all the Possibles.

I: Well it doesn't seem so. Look. He's heading for Eng zone.

EYES GALORE (*waving big pearl and tortoise-shell fans*): Fine, but what's he going to practice?—and with what?—(*horselaughs*). He's just realized that as we share our zone, since when one wears out her charms contending among feathers, the other refreshes them with new recruits from the show windows, María also shares hers, with Lotus Flower. In María he may find the mediation, the being.

He's now on the other side of the Gravi sign. Sweltering, but in high spirits. He's in Eng zone. From her first round of the night María has left a fragrance of jasmine and water lily; in the dew on the pavement her steps are written, on the show windows the soft brush of her gauze, in the air the mahogany wake of her pearl-braided bun.

Dragon Puss walks by. Behind her, María. G. comes alongside and woos her. He invites her to a daiquiri at the Two Worlds Bar, to another, and then confesses that he's an initiate in the numbers, in the permutations. Thus his fascination for the "theater," and mirrors. He yearns for the double, the symmetrical, the Cartesian devil who comes from the other side of the stage to give himself his reply—you and I—which turns inside out like a glove.

She gets the picture, but says neither yes nor no. She veils her face with her bamboo necklaces. Behind them she smiles. The quiver of the beads is like that of jet black adding beads. Her eyes are like two piggy bank holes, two mechanical lanterns. Now she puts them on high beam; a sailor is approaching.

She leaves with him. She tells G. to wait, "after all, mister is only interested in me anyway," tomorrow is another day.

G. jumped without impulse. Toy soldier. Where was that wind coming from? His stool was whirling. He was out on the street when he felt someone grab him by the arm. It was the waiter. He hadn't paid.

He watches her crumble among letters. Magnified red numbers. Strips of white fabric that are walls. Now she's a Melanesian lute. A bird from the Asiatic tropics on the other side of a river. Of rose ashes.

(*Drum roll*)

It's his footsteps. Military, what else. Does he hear the bagpipes of a march? Does he receive voices of command? María is slipping away from him—snake in water—; and him, after her of course. At full speed. Off he goes. Greyhound after a tin partridge, tiger after a wild pigeon stuck to his own self. His femurs creak. Bloodhound. Tongue hanging out. Wet buck. Strip of scattered hoops. Leaves black lines. Greyhound dog, Shell dragon.

She, there, faraway. He calls to her, puts her together like a puzzle, draws her by joining numbers. Sniffs her—rum, cinnamon, brown sugar—; yes, sniffs her: the Peeping Tom is myopic.

As in a theater when the actor exclaims: "Oh, here is the dawn!" and all the gold spots go on in unison, so, all of a sudden, does the Havana night fall. G., lost. María is that dampness, that absence of birds, the gong at the Opera, its racket—reverberation of tambourines, mildewed cymbals—and the successive shadows it leaves in the air; snakes battling among glass, rotting orchids, typhoon, anis stones growing in bottles, war of Burmese jaguars.

Aporia of Action, María is Desire, the Absence of Lotus. G.: a little blind man being bluffed. He feels around in the void, he's going to touch her, yes, he jumps on her, grabs her.

"Hey, what's up fella? Can't a girl have some peace in this city?"

He had caught the singer at the Picasso Club, who was just leaving the floor.

He sees her again. There she goes. This time it was her. She disappears into the stores, among paper lanterns. A sweet smell of *lukum.* G. zigzags. Follows himself. Propelled photograph, almost whole, it moves, paler, behind his own body, and again, blurred, behind him . . . and again. It's an army. They look at each other in a mirror and step back: dark green, olive faces, grapefruit, dry grass; pyramidal beards of astrakhan, black wool, brown fibered curls; gray cork stains, algae. They see themselves sewn with medals and tricolored bands, ribbons and braids; they see themselves outlined on damasks, on Toledan lace; they see themselves mended with pieces of curtains, gold bees and fleurs-de-lis, tapestries of roses and Flemish apples and serpents. Yes, they take a step backward: with good reason. The honor of the navy!

> Lola, lola
> la la la la
> Ich bin die fesche Lola

"What happened?"

Well, pursuing María and the American, bouncing from screen to screen, G. has ended up inside this *café-concert.* He flops down into a wicker chair—Cantonese girls bring him palm leaves and slippers—and asks for a "cuba-libre." He finally has them: there they are, rubbing each other to music, next to the Charleston band pianola. María, beneath blue oil lamps, her open hands on the *boy's* shoulder, winks at a green-eyed mulatto marimba player. Johnny Smith draws her closer. He's very smiley, red-headed and freckled, wears white sailcloth pants that pinch his little ass and a fluorescent poppy shirt which is why G. can see him despite night and myopia.

The girls who are singing and wiggling and riding painted wood pelicans and cloth bats on the platform in the back are the Baby Faces. My, those girls have changed! You've got to admit, the Secret of the Transformations does outrageous things! Now they're fat ladies with rubbery bellies crowned in hats made of pheasants in a plate of golden fruit, feather boats, merlons. They're the bearded ladies of a Mongol circus. Their four parallel feet tap against the stage boards and raise a yellow dust. They shout: "Lola, Lola." Then Chong and Si-Yuen appear through the side doors—the Tallow Ones do not wish to renounce their former apparitions, so beautiful do they find them, and their show goes on at the Opera—dressed in pieces of red and gold fabric, blond like dolls, burning from alcohol, their blue blue eyes enveloped in black stripes, Klimt's sad muses. They dance a two-step, wrapped in the same garland. Fascinated by that dancing symmetry, G. doesn't see the Roly-Polies open up, let Eng and Johnny through and close again, joining at the middle line, like the shutters of a triptych.

(*Black out*)

HEL. and MER.: "No! We are the Light. We've simply become her absence. Now we're her islands. Look!"

Yes, the ceiling, the floor and the walls are red, blue, and yellow disks that revolve at full speed and cut into each other and light up and go out and are of another red and another violet and explode and cut into each other again. Until the General rubs his eyes.

He flings himself against a wall and goes through it.

He is on the other side.

It is a dark private room, smelling of mentholated Camel smoke. Four black leather sofas in the corners. Mirrors. On a wall lit by a small white lamp, a man is painting. Opposite him—G. sees them reflected—María and *il rosso* are kissing; they sit side by side and look at the wall (where the fresco is gradually taking shape). They caress each other and smile. He shows her his sex, pink and perfectly cylindrical, the glans is a snail or a dome striped in white and the fluorescent poppy of his shirt, like a candy cane or a pinwheel. María touches it with the tips of her fingers. Giggling. Now she shows him her breasts, identically decorated: a yellow spiral starts from each nipple and disappears on her chest; she shows him her navel: painted: the miniature reproduction of a round concave molding. Johnny glues his eye to her stomach to see it. A raging sea takes up almost half the sphere—continuous lines in black ink, like the veins of a tree—where he can vaguely make out a boat. To the right a cliff, foam surrounding the rocks, a sky of red marks.

MARÍA (*very proud*): "Pretty, huh?"

Johnny agrees with a nod.

MARÍA (*professional*): "The original, attributed to Li Sung, who according to our chronology lived between 1166 and 1243, is called "In a boat," and is the leaf of a fan-shaped album, sketched in ink and dye on silk."

JOHNNY: "How I would like to have one!"

MARÍA (*pointing to the painter*): "He's the one who makes them, Little Torture Face, very ancient master in the symmetrical arts of pleasure and horror to the eyes: Chinese Painting and Torture."

G.: "Hey, what's up?"

It's the Mistresses-of-All-Appearance who are taking revenge on G. (cf. blows and lashes during that foolish act, remember?) and they reveal themselves as fluorescent Light. Yes, a great circular neon lamp lights up the room. The turtledoves leap up and dress. G. is exposed in all his deceit: the Peeping Tom was in his Nirvana and, from mere contemplation, had already passed to *praxis da solo*. He was forgetting about Lotus. Or had he substituted the duo with her (and himself as the mister)?

Little Torture Face is now standing (he really does have a scary face: swords for eyebrows; green and orange stripes run across his forehead and circle his eyes, black ones cross his cheeks and nose and turn into flowers; and a tiger mouth).

Now in front of G. he scolds him, waving his paint-stained hands in his face.

"You Peeping Tom, you heel, what the hell are you doing here?"

G. backs up.

And Little Face—"Give me that hand."

He grabs G.'s right hand.

"Here, that'll teach you."
And he tears off a nail.

He knocked on the walls and ceiling. He left a fresh labyrinth on the floor: the thread of blood from his pinky. Cold sweat. A ringing in his ears, a fistful of fig salt on his tongue; rubber legs, vinegar eyes. His night was pierced by green lights like those of the Feast of the Lanterns. Yes, what General can stand the sight of blood? He wouldn't look at his hand, the wet pinky.

He threw himself against a door. An old lady opened it, her face painted white, her lips very red. She kowtowed, and bandaged his hand in a cold compress.

"We were waiting for you," she said, and she brought him a cup of dragon eye soup. G. tried it, and had a whiff of cinnamon syrup along with soaking lye, hot irons, old clothes, and grease.

"I suffer in a laundry"—added the Venerable One—"but believe it or not, I was born with a black jade stone in my mouth, I slept in beds of sandalwood and was an imperial concubine. I strive among soaking underwear but I have drunk the tea of the thousand red drops and the pollen wine of a hundred roses, sap from a thousand trees, unicorn marrow and phoenix milk. Like you, I am expiating here. Come through this corridor. Be careful. Don't dirty the sheets."

G. followed close behind the oriental woman. ("I have fever.") And covering his nose (they were passing between tubs of rotting lye where pieces of blue soap and towels were floating).—"What a plebeian stench!"

"Wait here for me."

It was a room with a counter full of ironed shirts and bags of borax. A calendar hung from a shelf, the picture was a Chinese girl (her face flat, as if they were pressing it against a window) in a bikini, riding a Vespa; a portable refrigerator, a portable radio, a movie camera and a family-sized Coca Cola in an ice bucket bursting from its bags. Written between black marks, down by the wheels, was MODERN CHINA. G. was going to look at the next illustration when a hatch door opened in the floor and the old woman's head came out.

"Come down this way."

The small slimy staircase led him to another dark room. Dampness stained the walls. The Venerable One disappeared. Little Torture Face entered. He wore a purple cap, two gold dragons chasing the same pearl girded his forehead. Dressed in mauve, a flowered scarf of

Japanese satin. Entwined in the scarf, a braid of pearls bearing the eight emblems of the Taoist saints, disappearing behind a belt of tassels.

"Don't try to fool me, General old boy"—and he gave him a quick, violent tap on the shoulder which plopped him on his ass. (Although he looked like a painted goose, Little Face was a black belt in the ring.)

"That's right, don't try to fool me: I know all about it. Don't lose your time answering back. I know alchemy, the sublimation of the vital elixir, the concoction and reduction of cinnabar. How could I not be wise to your tricks? Listen carefully. Just listen carefully: either you stop chasing Lotus Flower or I eliminate you. Get it? I eliminate you. Want me to bury you in ice? Stick burning matches into the soles of your feet? Want me to cut them off with a Gillette blue blade? No? Then take it easy. Lotus and María. Leave them alone. Okay, Gen?

The floor was made of boards and smelled of cat urine. He remembered that the old woman had given him a cup of tea and that while drinking he had fallen asleep. Had many days passed? Was it all a dream? Was he still dreaming?

It was day. What surprised him most was not waking up on the floor, in a stinking pigsty, but rather finding out, in the light which shone through a crack, that what he thought were damp spots was a fresco which decorated all four walls and the wooden door. In it appeared Little Torture Face, the two Fat Ladies, Chong and Si-Yuen, all with shaven skulls, naked to the navel and barefoot, on top of clouds whose edges were like the waves of the round molding. Miss Chong, in profile, wearing a red cape and gold earrings and gazing into space, was pointing to a long-bristled brush, or a fly swat. Little Face was untying a parchment and receiving an artist's brush from Si-Yuen. One Fat Lady held up a red receptacle and a staff with four gargoyles, the other, with her little white feet in the foam, opened her left hand in a U, as if she were outlining a flower, and separated the small pointy and spreading fingers of her right, letting go of coins—or bread crumbs.

Behind the cloud a cliff. Black and fluffy trees, with sharp leaves. A waterfall.

G. peeped into the waters—the crack in the door—. And discovered:

a. that he was in a cellar,

b. that the cellar was the laundry,

c. that in the adjoining room there was a silent meeting of smokers.

Orange smoke. Among tea kettles and blue cups he made out María's head, and those of the little Ophidia Eyes, back in their forms as chorus girls of the Opera (what happened to the Fat Ladies?), covered with stuffed hummingbirds, *guacamayos* and candied pineapples with rubies; also Dragon Puss, the Director, and another Chinaman, thin and wiry like an eel, bald, and mustard yellow. He was in the center of the chorus, standing and naked (yes, he had one, but small and spiraled like a little screw) next to Little Torture Face, in underpants.

The *Biondas* served tea, and politely handed around sugar cubes and small pieces of grapefruit, or *lukum*, or something coated with flour.

Mustard scratched his bald pate, made three bows, and in a faint whistle voice, like a goosed monkey's, he hummed:

"The being of the birds is not the tone of the trills but feathers falling at each change. White, they are other birds in the snow, the signature of the first; red, fish that becomes butterfly when attacked. Another when it changes, goes off course leaving small snake eyes among its old feathers: endows its fraud with a gaze; its joy is to stick itself in the air in front of its blind double, to place the tigers face to face with the Apocrypha.

> Oh, ardent!
> Oh, ferocious!
> Oh, sweet birds!

But G. was not able to listen to more. Opening the body of one of the Fat Ladies in the fresco along the middle line (the navel was the lock on the door), the ex-mandarin woman entered the cellar.

"La Hang medicine! Believe it or not, I know the Books by heart. The gentleman is cured." (*And she pulls off the bandage.*) G. withdraws his hand, like the claw of a boiled crab.

He's out on the street.

Already the screens are opening, the Venetian blinds falling with a sound of sand, the milkmen on their rounds.

The matron from Formosa washes her face. And opens a can of sardines.

G. no longer eats or sleeps. He gets cramps, visions, constipation. He feels looked at (but no grass, no, just coffee, which he takes to perk up, and tranquilizers, which he takes to calm down), he weathers storms in a wine cup—tea he no longer takes—he's all choked up, something's pressing his throat. Are they hanging a rag doll in his image somewhere? Are they sticking pins in the eyes of his photograph behind some door? Is his name in a glass of vinegar? He doesn't know. At night he searches. Absence eats his liver—ontological cirrhosis—. After all it's the poor Mrs. General who pays for the broken plates. With all this nonsense it turns out that Medals Galore no longer rends her homage. She cries behind screens, takes refuge in the cellar with her supply of snuff . . . but no luck. Neither oysters nor Ovaltine in condensed milk: there isn't an aphrodisiac that works. G. remains in the doorhead (or on the threshold, which in this case is the same thing); it gives him claustrophobia.

THE GENERAL: For the Virgin of Covadonga, this is overdoing it! You lie: I've never neglected my conjugal duties. I deliver efficiently and attentively twice a week, Mondays and Thursdays, to be exact.

I: That's what he says. The truth is that Mrs. General . . .

THE (*more and more hypothetical*) READER of these pages: Okay, make up your minds: one version or the other. What I want is facts. Yes, facts, action, development, message, in short. Lyrical message!

As I was saying: For G. the Theater became Mass. Always in the first row. The appearance of Lotus in the Capture of the Fort is the celebration of all the Possibles. In the deceptive, in the ontic, he takes shadow for substance. During intermission he knocks his head against Nothingness. He goes to the dressing rooms and, in keeping with the ancient feudal custom, drops a jade bracelet outside the Empress's door to gain her favors. Always freshly starched, always with his Romeo and Juliet and his jacket, which already displays concentric strata of different blues in its armpits—sweat permits the dating of it like the cortex of trees—and that faint smell of sweet wine with egg yolk, his morning restorative.

He knows the Capture by heart: he yawns during the decagonal ambush, during the dance of the knives and even during the clash between Meng Hai-Kung and the government troops. He weeps when Lotus appears between two *sheng* players, a javelin in each hand, dressed in blue leaves, crowned with two pheasant feathers. In her face fishes sail, black butterflies flee over her eyelids. Two white spirals divide her forehead; two symmetrical fringes, black and yellow, start from her upper lip and sailing around her nose, open like spirals on her cheeks. Two masks resembling her face are painted on her sleeves. A gold cord hangs from the hilt of the sword she wears on her belt. Lotus is here. LOTUS EXISTS. Lighter than the sound of the choral *b*, more delicious than ruby wine and cocoanut milk.

260

Two color sergeants follow her with the blue Flag of the Empire, which bears a letter in its center; behind them the band players: two pipe, two lute, and a *tan-pin-ku*.

Phoenix of the mountain, the Moon illumines her. The Moon is an oscillating lantern; her eyes black darts.

Even after the banquet ginger can celebrate with its seven flavors, and after the rain light with its seven islands: when the acrobats leave Lotus surrenders her best high kung notes. She stands on tiptoe, fills herself with air and emits them effortlessly, perforating hearts and eardrums. She advances with the clashing of cymbals and drum rolls; she steps back and the Queen of Cranes (do you recognize her? can you guess who it is? Take a good look and you'll know—answer two lines below) and the Queen of Falcons (who in the legend is a King, but even metamorphosis has its limits) appear. That's right, you've guessed it, *Chong* and *Si-Yuen*, the Neat Ones, the Mistresses-of-the-Grass-of-Immortality, do battle before Lotus, jump over one another, spin cartwheels, rush on with serrated machetes and bows. Thus they lose their feathers on stage. Behind, Lotus, the Fixed One, smiles, absent, holding in her hand the imperial Phoenix, flanked by two unicorns. There she is, in full possession of her Yin, as you saw her in the forest, remember?

G. *(tearful, il povero)*: Yes, of course I remember, by the ferns, near the Almendares . . .

I: Quiet. Listen to her. She's singing her solo.

G. *(sighing)*: How lovely this all is!

I *(who wakes him up)*: Come down from that cloud and return to reality. The Capture of the Fort is over.

(applause, etc.)

At Home with the General

G. *(angry, purple veinlets furrow his triple chin)*: All I want to know is where she is, who she is, why she doesn't come, where does she hide herself, where.

And he shakes them by the shoulder. Feathers, lice, and spangles come off. Now they're two baldpates.

THEY *(the only girls who, shook up, become two baldpates)*: We can't just say it any old way. She's a secret, she's an appearance, she's . . .

261

The insipid things guffaw, crack up, hop around, they're leap frogs, they're about to come apart.

GENERAL (*confidentially*): I just want you to tell her it's me, the one from the Forest, tell her I go to the theater every day and that (*and his eyes water—are you going to cry? come on, men don't cry—it's really pitoyable*) I can't go on like this.

THE JERKS: We'll tell her.

And so, the big sports put everything in the basket that strikes their fancy, taking advantage of G.'s moment of weakness.

For my room! (*it's Help*). And she grabs an engraving, an ivory fan. Now, graceful, she fans herself like a Spanish girl at a country fair, moving her eyes to the beat, striking her heels against the floor. Olé!

The Other, more discreet, but more jeeringly plays with the angora cats, who run around dragging along ribbons and bells and get caught on the legs of rocking chairs. She prefers the small sphinx heads, hourglasses, stuffed storks, the little jade Chinamen who serve as lamp supports, the big fat angels in gilded wood. She's a Pop initiate, she's quite *à la page*. She's singing, and putting all she can get her hands on into a crate.

G. (*endearingly*): Take everything you want. Tell her to be so good as to look at me.

Oh, this is too much. Look at that. Help is dragging a red marble bathtub mounted on four bronze paws toward the street. What she'll do with it I don't know, because when it comes to taking a bath, only once in a blue moon and even then you have to make her.

Help (*there is no insult worse than the truth*): And you, mind your own business, shithead, this I got for you.

And the smutty creature shows me an enormous porphyry phallus, almost a yard long, that she's taking for her "Pompeian Room." You should see her, she's in it up to her neck. Her Vespa is overloaded and now she's calling for a pickup truck.

The Other, more satiable, is hanging around, chatting with Mrs. General, spinning cartwheels on a Persian rug (which she'll surely take with her) with an albino girl squeezed into a tight red dressing gown—could she be G.'s granddaughter?—. Hurrah! They look like two gladiators.

They sped away, thundering, on their motor scooters. Crossing their fingers they go. They didn't miss a single brooch. They ride in kimonos, and silk hats. They even carry lighted lamps in blue ceramic —battery-run—on their handlebars. Their bags are full of Bibles, paperweights, clocks, etc. The Insatiables didn't leave a thing.

G.: Not a thing! Regard the tables: dust. But not all is lost.

Better said:

When G. saw that all was lost and already in *articulo mortis*, he thought up a final appeal. He gave the Nymphs, on condition that they hand it to her as she came off the stage, a present for Lotus. A smitten heart stops at nothing!

"What was it?"

Well outwardly, nothing special. Just another bracelet, the usual fare, in blue jade, with painted flowers and butterflies, like those the Mongolian peasant women wore. Of course, this one had, besides, an inner device, that would work upon closing the jewel on the wrist, it would spring out two very sharp little razor blades against the inner part of the fist. Yes, just what you're thinking, slit arteries. It's true: G. had ended his parable, completed his parabolic cycle. From Peeping Tom to sadist. He who possesses with the eye possesses with the dagger. He would recognize her by her blood. Wound her. Pleasure is crossed with pain.

Does he feel guilty? Hardly. Like they say, the Spaniard bit went to his head. He's a vampire.

But, a last question remains:

"Where do all those objects come from, where has the preceding scene unfolded?"

Well, so intense was the pilgrimage of his nights and the impatience of his days, that G. decided to change tactics. What was needed in the Theater? What did Lotus use every day? What could she not live without?

Although his calling was great, he soon rejected the idea of a grocery store. In Lotus's kitchen, according to the laws of the Opera, almost everything was excluded. The rice with tea that she'd eat and the sesame seed oil that she'd massage herself with did not justify setting up shop. He decided on what was left. So, with his last savings, Mrs. General, the cats, and the albino jumper whom you have just seen, along with some war and hunting trophies, G. settled in Chinatown *de plein pied*. There, across the street from the theater, he opened *Divine Providence*, super store, the one the Magpies recently ravaged.

There he stands guard day and night. Sentinel in his stockade.
Today he's not going to the show.
He's waiting for them to carry a pale body out the stage door.

DOLORES RONDÓN

Since it's such a hot day, it won't do us any harm to take a walk in the cemetery: marble is cooling, almost like lemonade. There are no café tables or one-armed bandits in this garden of stone, but we'll come to that. In this part of Camagüey, in the center of Cuba, there's no end of oil portraits, of dead black men looking rosier and healthier than they ever did alive, or of two-story chapels, or reading material. Here at this crossroads, for example, you can read Dolores Rondón's poem:

> Dolores Rondón did here
> reach the end of her career,
> come, mortal, and ponder
> on where lies true grandeur.
> Pride and arrogance,
> power and prominence,
> all is bound to perish.
> And you only immortalize
> the evil you economize
> and the good you may cherish.

A Hard Profession, Dolores's. Courtesan and poet. Courtesan all her life. Poet for a day. But time dissolves it all, like the sea into the sea. Of the courtesan, and her ups and downs, which were those of the senator Mortal Pérez, nothing remains. But the poet views us, from death.

Under the poem two angels face down hold up a lighted lamp.

A lighted lamp over a ribbon inscribed in Latin.

A ribbon inscribed in Latin tied around a bunch of flowers.

And all in marble!

But let's give our two narrators the floor. Let them present the life of Dolores Rondón. They won't do it in chronological order, but in that of the poem, which, after all, is the true one.

In the provinces, the recent republican era

NARRATOR ONE (*chorus leader with a squeaky, biting voice*): Ah yes, going back to writing again, what an emetic! As if all this had some purpose, as if all this would penetrate some thick skull, occupy some driveling reader curled up in his armchair before the soporific stew of everyday living!

NARRATOR TWO (*high-sounding, solemn chorus leader, with a deep-chested voice*): That's it, decipher it or bust: all has a purpose, all is final, all returns to all, that is, to nothing, nothing is all (*his throat-rasps*) . . . with this play on words I mean that your emetic is very useful, useful because emetic, in short, with words you modify things, behaviors, the behavior of the (*he stops short, stamps his cothurnus on the floor*).

NARRATOR ONE (*very high pitched*): Behavior, future, modify: lame words. Please, it only hurts when I laugh. You have a mangy dog, I say mangy for example, well then, you take the dog, which is the word, and throw a pail of boiling water on him, which is the exact sense of the word. What does the dog do? What does the word do? And so we have: dog-word, water-sense: These are the four parts. Take them! Who pins the tail on the donkey? Here is the summary of my metaphor: lame words for lame realities that follow a lame plan drawn up by a lame monkey.

NARRATOR TWO: I'm slow I admit, but I don't get who the monkey is.

NARRATOR ONE (*in coloratura soprano*): My son, please, when will you learn! (*he looks for an easy comparison*) Now then: words are like flies, toads, as you know, eat flies, snakes eat toads, bulls eat snakes and men eat bulls, that is to say . . .

NARRATOR TWO: Men eat flies!

NARRATOR ONE: It's not that easy, but enough, we didn't meet here today for that, but to discuss, under the denomination of the Patron Saint of Small Animals, to discuss I say, the case of the mulatto Dolores Rondón.

NARRATOR TWO (*answering a riddle*): The one who reached the end of her career?

NARRATOR ONE: They're one and the same. Let's talk about her.

CLEMENCY (*red-headed and waxen youth with a high and hysterical voice*): With chapter and verse!

HELP (*red-headed and waxen youth with a high and hysterical voice*): With toad tack!

MERCY (*red-headed and waxen youth with a high and hysterical voice*): With monkey fine stone and cats fly cabala!

NARRATOR ONE (*protesting*): Oh no, out of the question! I will not stand for those three queens, horrible creatures.

NARRATOR TWO: Come on, for God's sake (a figure of speech), more simplicity, more modesty. Throw your spangles into the well and listen quietly. These are Dolores's witnesses, her attendants. Let them express themselves.

HELP (*leading a protest by the trio, real leader of the masses style, very confident*): We strive to come out!

MERCY (*sprecht-gesang*):

Like the tortoise from his shell,

like the chicken from his egg,

like the corpse from his hole, yes!

NARRATOR ONE (*frightened before the apparition of the three acolytes*): Please!

DOLORES (*Wilfredo Lam mulatto woman, voice between a guitar and an obatala drum*): You've got to get out. (*Without any gradation: a street near the station. Rundown hotels. A smell of tobacco and mangos. In the lemon-colored air the red cap of the porters, the clicking of spurs. Street cries. Jewelry vendors. Perhaps the horn of an old Ford.*) Get out of the hole. If you don't change, you get stuck. You've got to keep moving. No, it's not the mud that bothers me, nor the heavy rains, nor the puddles, nor the oxcarts, nor the electoral campaigns; it's the other people buying and selling, buying machetes, soap, knockers, scissors, earrings, rags, old cots and bottles; the others eating and sleeping.

(*The street disappears just as it had appeared.*)

NARRATOR ONE: Now do you see? She despises the essential, the place of her birth.

NARRATOR TWO: Shut up, stupid. The essential is somewhere between the *guanábana* and the *mango*.

DOLORES (*conscious of the narrators' interruption*): I'm getting out of here and I've come to sell all I've got: a wristwatch and a fine Grade A rooster. I can make it to Camagüey easy on what I get. This is it. I'm doing like Christopher Columbus, who burnt his ships behind him. I'm a high-class dancer, let the others have the box step rumba.

266

Learned, I am, well-read, no. My saints I know by heart, and I play the right numbers. Show and place.

HELP (*quickly*): Hey, what's all this about "play"?

MERCY (*erudite*): Each animal is a number of the lottery, one is the horse, nine the snake.

CLEMENCY (*in false falsetto*): Which eats toads, which eats bulls.

DOLORES: I am the legitimate daughter of Ochum, queen of the river and the sky. You got to move fast. You got to keep moving ahead, like a train. You got to get out of here.

NARRATOR ONE: That's what she thinks, that she's going, but she's staying here, here's where her career ends.

NARRATOR TWO (*grandiloquent*): She's going, she's going so that the poem may come true, so that, as I was saying, fate may exist, and the emetic be useful.

DOLORES (*who has overheard the conversation*): What? What are those two old goats over there saying? That I'm staying? That here's where my career ends? We'll see about that. Hey there, Spaniard baby! Yeah you, with the beret.

MORTAL (*blondie, piñata eyes, the man from Castille, with his pure Castillian diction*): Are you calling me?

HELP (*recitative, the voice of a hoarse soprano, glad to see the poem is following its course*): Opposites attract!

MERCY (*and he powders his nose*): Their vertices touch!

CLEMENCY (*crowned with marble garlands*): Like the snake its tail!

HELP, MERCY, CLEMENCY (*dissonant requiem*): Like the beginning its end! (*The three in* guanábana *hats, holding baskets of sugar cones, jumping over the tracks, the train is coming!*)

Reach the End of Her Career

In the provinces, after the fall of Mortal

NARRATOR TWO: Now look where we are! What did I tell you? Her attendants abandoned her, leaving her to her executioner just as they left her to her lovers before, always to the best bidder.

NARRATOR ONE: It's not their fault, they didn't mean to. They revealed the place where Dolores meets her lovers and that's all. For a few coins, for a few cartons of Chesterfields and an Elizabeth Arden lotion they've sold her, the frivolous lads. They didn't know what they were risking, they didn't know that death was watching at every step. But let's not name Lady Bones, the Lonely Anima, let us not anticipate her arrival. Trusting, they were, are, victims of the mustached fury. They should be warned: Oyá is dread and comes by everyday with her cart, mistress of the ways of the wind, of the keys to the cemetery. Dolores is going to die, perhaps is already dying so that the poem may come true. In the heat, in a bug-ridden bed she is dying, without the air conditioning she lived her better days in, always on Very Cold, without her Simmons mattresses, the best in comfort, without the rose water that once perfumed her. Lady Bones, make her . . .

HELP (*realizing the evil he has done*): All must perish!

MERCY (*and he sprays himself from head to toe with an atomizer*): We are nothing!

CLEMENCY (*and he combs his hair*): From dust to dust!

DOLORES (*With this monologue Dolores receives death. She no longer fears the grandiloquent tone, ridiculous images, folklore, verbosity itself. Dolores enters death in a major key, as she once entered life. She draws out certain words, the names of saints, in this "lyrical declamation." Tearful comicality. Here the rhetoric, and on the patios in the background, the cha-cha-cha*): The river returns to the source, the light to dawn, the wounded beast to the forest. Each one in his water. Each bird in his air. I return to the bottom of the sea, in the god Obatalá's white dressing gown, in the night, flag of the dead. I am a tree, I threw a shadow. Darkness frightens the birds, but day is coming, roosters' watch. Valley of shadow, come to me! The son of Elegua lacks neither bread, nor pasture, nor the chosen water of repose, nor her husband the fragrant fruit. Guitars, I was wood; let my death warm ye. Maracas, break, untuned goddesses. The saints had said it with their daily signals: the broken glass of water, the frisky horses, the black in the mirrors. I didn't hear. I didn't believe. I didn't open the door. Ye were calling. Let the king of the heavens open to me now with the same smile with which I now open, not to every day's lover, but to the murderer. The gods provide for the Damp House the same as they do for the earth. There will be heat, there will be wine and coffee in death. Neither bread, nor pineapple, nor open mamey, nor beheaded roosters will be wanting in my tomb. Nor the oration of the nine days, nor mourning, nor the abundant banquet with guayaba and cheese. Let there be rum at my wake. Rum and rumination. No weeping, no teeth gnashing, no torn clothing. King, receive me; I go without fear. Wind swallow me. Scatter me in the rain . . . And ye, dark servants, beasts who have betrayed me, may war decimate ye, lightning blind ye, leprosy corrode ye. Ye have promised without keeping your word, gods of whites. Dagger, be brief. Do not repeat my blood.

(*The cha-cha-cha goes off.*)

HELP: A ridiculous farewell monologue. Lacking in Camagüeyan spontaneity.

MERCY: Let the dead have fame, but the living love!

CLEMENCY: What I wouldn't do for a nice cold beer!

NARRATOR TWO: Dumb Fates. Owl faces.

NARRATOR ONE: It's late. Let's go. There's a Caridad del Cobre Fair and tonight everybody's drunk.

(*Dolores screams. The cha-cha-cha begins again.*)

(*In the brothel next door, Help, Mercy, and Clemency dance it and wave their tresses—slow whirls of flame—patting their lips, biting their fingers, pulling off their cartilage bone necklaces, breaking off their eyebrows, their faces now quartered, pale masks.*)

Come, Mortal, and Ponder

In the provinces, before the election

NARRATOR ONE (*ironical*): Remember the dog?

NARRATOR TWO (*as lost as a nun in a garage*): What dog? The one in the manger?

NARRATOR ONE: No, the other more mongrel one, that came shooting out in the first line when they threw a bucket of boiling water on him.

NARRATOR TWO: Good Heavens! Of course I remember. What's become of him?

NARRATOR ONE: You'll know soon enough. Wait. Look: they're already there, they're already arriving.

NARRATOR TWO: Who are those people?

NARRATOR ONE: The nomination people, Mortal's people.

NARRATOR TWO: The watch of the living and the dead!

(*Multitudes in the square. Cheers, applause. Pennants. Arches of triumph pop up all over the place.*)

MORTAL (*aspiring candidate to the municipal council. The voice of the first line has become authoritarian*): I . . . (*but there are defects in the microphone, in the radio. First like "static," to such a point that you can hear only one syllable, then the dial goes through all the stations. Sharp whistle.*)

(*Singing commercial*) Candado Soap leaves your clothes (*spoken, a feeble voice*) or in the Gentleman of the R (*intellectual's voice*) Wallraf-Richartz-Museum (*spoken*) and in a situation that is internal ext (*sung, Ella Fitzgerald*) in the moon.

MORTAL (*continuing the speech*): I, suh (*but the "static" returns*).

NARRATOR TWO (*afraid*): Looks like the gods are against him. He can't even begin his message.

NARRATOR ONE (*a quick giggle*): Message? For there to be a message (*repeating something he doesn't understand, and that he's just read somewhere*) there must be: number one, intentionality; two, a consciousness of the transmitter; three, a code; four.

MORTAL (*continuing his speech*): I, son of this Province, on this day have received the nomination as candidate to the municipal council of Camagüey, the loveliest land that human eyes have ever seen, to occupy a position in the government of the Republic (*applause*). Others will say that . . .

NARRATOR ONE (*erudite*): The parts of a speech are known: introduction, thesis, antithesis, refutation, and summary.

MORTAL: It's easy to promise prosperity before you're in power; for us power will not be a triumph but a sacrifice, just as the Nation is an altar, not a pedestal. We will confront those who waste and stake the national treasury in risky pacts or disturbing and reckless exchanges with planned finance and welfare programs for our peasants which includes the building of cheap housing, roads, schools and medical aid, not to forget school breakfast (*applause*), the creation of dance centers, circuses, cockfights, fairs (*applause*) as you have all requested with unanimous enthusiasm.

NARRATOR ONE (*laughing at Mortal for using the word enthusiasm without knowing its root*): Listen to that!

MORTAL (*after listening to him*): Yes, with unanimous enthusiasm, all you illustrious citizens of this glorious and twice heroic town. The voice of rebellion (*in that moment a dog crosses the square where the meeting's taking place, howling like a condemned soul out of Dante's Hell, among applause and cheers, while Help, Mercy, and Clemency scream and loose their feathers.*)

HELP, MERCY, CLEMENCY: Watch out! He has rabies!

NARRATOR ONE (*priestly*): *Canis hydrophobus, Dominus Tecum!*

HELP, MERCY, CLEMENCY: Amen!

NARRATOR TWO: Aha, those vipers again, those venomous poisons, fresh, newly bathed, bleached salmon and wearing zebra-skin boots, I knew I smelled Camels and Shoulton Old Spice. There they are, after perpetrating the most bloodcurdling crime in Camagüeyan history, the most ignoble betrayal, a fratricide that's so . . . I cannot find the adjective.

HELP, MERCY, CLEMENCY (*witches' cackles before a concoction of vinegar and salty toads*).

HELP: Poor devil, he doesn't understand a thing. He has no discrimination whatsoever. Look, it's enough to enumerate in one stroke all your errors, they are colossal, dropsical, whale-sized. Look, it's enough to point out four (*sure of himself, an academic reading his paper*): error number one, concerning the material being:

MERCY: We are neither fresh nor newly bathed, since there's not a drop of water in the whole town and we merely wiped ourselves with a rag dipped in alcohol. On the other hand, our dazzling wigs, which all are admiring as they ought, are not salmon colored as in the naïve appraisal you have uttered, but rather grated carrot color, which is not the same.

HELP: Error number two, concerning the material peripheral being:

CLEMENCY: It is neither Camels, a cigarette we loathe for its verbal allusion known to us all and which reminds us of the nickname of our childhood, nor is it Shoulton Old Spice, but rather Fleur de Racaille de Caron: *en perfumes on sait très bien à quel saint se vouer.*

HELP: Error number three, concerning the phrasing of the insult and propriety in the use of words, since each one, as we know, has its own meaning—which is what excludes all synonymy—and this can neither be changed nor transferred.

MERCY: In fact, it has nothing to do with a fratricide, since no kindred ties us to the one you believed torn to pieces, we have not perpetrated it, we shall simply be the "intellectual authors," and, on the other hand, the adjectives bloodcurdling, ignoble, belong to a past aesthetic . . . but let's not enter into details.

271

HELP (*radio announcer, angel of the apocalypse with a tenor sax, entangled in bunches of ribbons, haloed, barefoot on a sword*): And lastly, the fourth error, the least forgivable, concerning the spiral quality of the time of the being:

CLEMENCY: The famous crime, the fratricide of which you speak, in spite of having been the theme of line number two, we now being on three, has not yet taken place. It would be inane to think that the numerical order corresponds to the time sequence; that is, we have not yet revealed anything, the senator to whom Dolores's destiny will be bound has not yet appeared, since in this meeting he announces his aspiration to be councilman. Lastly, even if this had taken place after Dolores's death, we would not have celebrated by coming to a meeting, but instead would have remained close to her body.

NARRATOR TWO: Well then, what the hell are you doing here?

HELP, MERCY, CLEMENCY: The same as always—that is—taking care of Dolores—faithful and eternal as we are—moral support—lads-in-waiting—etc., etc.

NARRATOR TWO: Ah, then Dolores is coming to the meeting?

HELP: She's coming, but not exactly to complain, like us, about the lack of water, indeed not to make any complaint at all; she's coming simply because the Spaniard promised (in line one, since that one does take place before this moment, and just before)

NARRATOR TWO: And the spiral?

HELP (*without answering him, looks out of the corner of his eye, which is elongated by a golden line*): if he wins the election for councilman, which of course will happen, in order for the poem to come true step by step (which is already beginning to bore us), and without obstacles (for which I beseech you end this line right now)

NARRATOR ONE: It shall be done in a few lines.

HELP: to take her to Camagüey, and what's more, if we understand correctly (since, in parenthesis, that damn peninsular accent is a pain in the neck), he promised that once there, he was going to ask for her hand, since he can't mean cut off her hand as far as we know since it has nothing to do with the cutting off of hands as with delinquent slaves, which she isn't. So that. But let's finish.

NARRATOR TWO: Dolores, there she is!

DOLORES (*puffing, from all that running*): What a trip, holy cow! Bouncing like the dancing turkey in the circus on an electric iron! I've been bounced around in a tobacco cart drawn by two oxen over hill and dale, night and day, but I've finally arrived. And it's worth it. I'm the first, the founder of Mortal's Fan Club. I'll have six hundred pictures of him in my room, a lock of his blond hair in a locket. (*And changing her tone.*) Boy, am I hungry. Anybody have a sandwich for me?

NARRATOR ONE: Nobody, Nobody. No cheese for Jerry. Not even a scrap of ham for Tom. Tens of thousands like you have come. From the most out-of-the-way places. Haitians and Jamaicans in railway caravans. Singing and leaping from car to car, on sacks of white sugar. The trains like wakes of fire in the night, whistling, repeating Mor-tal-Pé-rez!

MORTAL (*in complete possession of the microphones and the public, under a rain of purple lampoons*): There'll be more than you've seen since the Deluge!

(*Last applause and cheers. Help, Mercy, and Clemency demand improvements, pinch each other, take off their eyebrows and prick each other. The dog passes by again.*)

HELP, MERCY, CLEMENCY: Water! Water! Water! (*And they squirm and do somersaults in the sand, they swallow red stones and slobber, the thirsty things—they think they see turrets, an oasis.*)

On Where Lies True Grandeur

At Dolores's house

NARRATOR ONE (*shaking a maraca*): He won! He won!

NARRATOR TWO (*does a somersault, falls off the hammock*): What's up?

NARRATOR ONE: Oh, I woke you up. It's just that I'm a little ahead of time. We have to shout in a few lines, at a party.

NARRATOR TWO: Are we going to a party? What about destiny? And Dolores?

NARRATOR ONE: Precisely, we've occupied all the previous lines pushing them aside with our empty talk, but since they are the essential theme of the poem we must make ourselves scarce.

NARRATOR TWO (*a bit scared*): What do you mean, make ourselves scarce? Not appear anymore?

NARRATOR ONE (*clarifying*): We will appear, yes, but as anonymous servants: hairdressers, dress designers, people who don't add up to being. As for the three Etruscan conductors of souls, who were yesterday a marvel . . . (*Without any transition: creole country dance. Guitars. The party people, the Matamoros trio arrive; rum with lemon. The sallow girls break their hips*) . . . are today Dolores's dressmaker, pastry cook and antique dealer: scissor, poison, and termite. (*The din approaches.*) Let's go! Now's when you have to shout! With feeling! Allegro vivace!

NARRATORS ONE and TWO (*allegro vivace*): He won! Mortal Pérez won!

DOLORES (*very lyrical*): Open doors and windows! The first to go are these shoes which were so tight on me, this shoulder bag, these pans. And now: bring in the water!

HELP: But honey, you know there's not a single drop in this damn town!

DOLORES: That's not the water I mean. Peroxide water: we're gonna be blonds!

MERCY: We're gonna be white!

HELP: We're gonna be pale!

CLEMENCY: Blond like corn, like light beer!

DOLORES: We got to pack. Yes, we're moving to a better house. In a fancy neighborhood. We're going to Camagüey, to Havana. In a sleeping-car suite. Call the dressmaker, say it's Dolores Rondón calling . . . Dolores Rondón . . . what a name for a councilman's wife . . . Dolores de Pérez . . . Lola Pérez Rondón . . . There's nothing you can do about it. We are the name we're born with. (*In the party, someone steps on a dog; it howls.*)

MERCY: Here's the dressmaker!

DRESSMAKER (*who is Help in disguise. In her new metamorphosis, the Fate comes with enormous scissors, her head shaved, like a mannikin, wearing a headband—a measuring tape. Lines of black stitches run across her chest.*): Light and Progress!

DOLORES: Oh, it seems to me I know you. Where have we met before? Now I know: at the wake of

DRESSMAKER (*takes a step back, to get her off the track*): Me at a wake? Never. Crysanthemums nauseate me, candles make me choke, coffee attacks my liver, sleepless nights make me sallow, etcetera.

DOLORES: I must be wrong then. But let's talk about the important things, about what they're wearing in Havana: we want bottle green silk, the kind of fur that makes you cough, necklaces, gloves, hats with flowers, and little birds and those sunglasses you can see through without being seen.

274

DRESSMAKER: Like old crossbones!

DOLORES: What?

DRESSMAKER: Like the cross-eyed, who cover their eyes, but they see, they keep seeing, they see too much.

DOLORES: Oh, right. (*shouting*) Hey what's happening, isn't there anything to drink in this house? A daiquiri for the dressmaker!

(*Cheers to victory, to Mortal.*)

Pride and Arrogance

In the capital of the province

HAIRDRESSER: There must be method to your madness. There must be method. Change lovers, Dolores. Hair color. Houses. But not gods. Your speaking high-class and not mumbling like a councilman's wife should, putting in two gold teeth for pure show and without ever having had the slightest toothache, drinking scotch on the rocks and Tom Collinses, pretending to be blind so as not to recognize your friends, going to bed with your blond servants, abandoning the poor Spaniard to the dizzying heights of the mayor's office, where, as everybody knows, he follows your advice and recruits an army of mambo dancers in your image and likeness from the farthest corners of the province . . . all this is permitted. All of it. But there must be method. You must keep up the appearance of method. There must be method within the lack of method. I'm tripping on my words. I mean that you mustn't forget the glass of water, the sunflowers, the roosters. I mean you mustn't forget the offerings to the gods.

DOLORES (*with her head in a plastic dryer. Operatic. With pride and arrogance.*): What's with the servants? First that old bag the antique dealer snickering at me, all because I asked for twisted chairs and a Simmons mattress. Then toad eyes, the housekeeper, who didn't recognize me in a two-piece suit. Then the pastry cook with her rice pudding (*and on a long high note*); I want a Banana Split! And now you, the Attila of hairdressing, after mangling my tresses, my beautiful straight hair, my skull, my whole head; after applying stinking pomades to straighten it, electric dryers to curl it, massages to straighten it again, curling irons; after leaving me scabby, scalped, bald as an egg . . . now it's method. Now it's saints. Now that

275

they're preparing another banquet, another candidacy, another party-switching, another caucus (*she's complaining, the poor thing*) . . . How much further, Catalina, will you carry the abuse of our forbearance? Madness, Method. Loaded words. Which of the two has the bigger mouth? Which swallows the other? Does madness swallow, digest, expulse method? Does method gag on madness? Do both devour, fear, flee each other? I don't know. I only know that the kitchen pots are under the bed and the chamber pots on the stove. That's the method. I only know that you've left me bald.

THE HAIRDRESSER (*almost crying*): No, Dolores. You've had too much to drink. Bloody Marys unhinge you. It's not true about your hair. We straightened it, we made it blond and purple like a piece of cloud, then we turned it into flames. You weren't satisfied. You wanted concentric ringlets, upside-down towers, ship prows. You wanted a Flavian hair style. You said: "I am Titi." Hence the aluminum dryers, the high voltage, the muriatic acids, the curling iron, the stench. That's the way of method. You wanted to be a bird, a gazelle, you loathed your slanty eyes. Hence the spinach mascara, the baby pineapple cream, the simultaneous massages, and the Helena Rubinstein beauty sunfluid. We did what we could. That's the way of method. The well-rounded, clean, classified, filed, alphabetically ordered way, in the belly of method. That's how it is.

DOLORES (*Valkyric*): No! You won't stop me, you won't tie me down like a goat. If you don't change, you get stuck. I'll keep moving ahead, always ahead, like a train. This very day I'll pack my bags. I'm going. From here to Havana. This dusty city without ships, without Chinese restaurants, I can't stand it any longer. I want chop suey, fried rice, chicken with almonds, glazed pork. I'll go wherever the wind takes me. To Peking, to Hong Kong. Bald as you've left me. Cross-eyed, lame: no matter what, I'll reach my destiny on time, like an American train. Life is a soap dish; if you don't fall, you slip. I'm going. We'll win the municipal, provincial, senatorial, national elections. I'll be the wife of a senator. I'll have more and more admirers: That's Hip Power for you!

And to you, servants who refuse to follow me, who despise victory, who want to stay buried here like the snake in its cave, to you I leave these blond pieces of straw, my last hairs, those wires you've twisted over my head; you who despise the capital, the swell life, you who in the eleventh hour abandon me, in the hour of the great election, the soya beans, and the egg roll, I free you of job and wages. Faithful, the only among a whole staff of boisterous, demanding, angry, irritated, and mad servants, my three advisors follow me: the dressmaker, pastry cook, and antique dealer. The elegance, and sweetness, of past and present. Three sacrificing souls. At least there'll be pastries, frozen meringues, and Mandarin oranges. I'm going to the ships. Bald, lame, but to Havana.

(*The drumming of typewriters. Traffic lights. Ships. Sirens fading in and out.*)

NARRATOR ONE: Do you hear it? Havana. She wanted it, she herself hastens her own destiny, jumps toward it like a fish toward the shore. She wants Havana, she wants the swell life, she wants, as she says, to imitate our illustrious Cuban classic, the adventurous Countess of Merlin. Well here is the beginning of the end: here's Havana!

DOLORES (*with the emphasis of all political apotheosis*): Faithful servants, dear shadows of myself. Let's begin the senatorial stage with a bang. I knew I'd be a senator's wife. There are the votes, there is Mortal acclaimed by the caucuses, the parties, the people themselves! The days of the province, the dust, the rooster, are way behind us. The bathtub. I want a bath. A bathtub full of rum. And then they can fan me with giant leaves. This is the life the four of us deserve. Today we'll throw gold coins to the little black boys! Bring the wig, the tightest corset, the spangle, the orchid that arrived this morning from Miami. I'm going to the Presidential Palace! (*The telephone rings.*)

THE DRESSMAKER (*answering the phone*): She's not in, Mrs. Senator is not in! (*She snickers, hangs with a bang.*)

NARRATOR TWO (*remorseful*): You got to admit it. Dolores has reached her baroque period. She's outdoing herself, beating her own record. This is all going to end like a Chinaman's spree. Her reading has done her a lot of damage. It's driven her insane. It's okay for her to learn English, which, in parenthesis, she speaks like a Haitian; it's okay for her to order perfumes and frozen flowers from Miami, but the Cuban classics have been the strongest of all. What indigestion. There she is, having herself fanned by two fat Negresses after a rum bath. Just like the "Countess of Berlin," she says. Good God!

All Is Bound to Perish

(*The telephone rings.*)

THE ANTIQUE DEALER (*who, naturally, is a mutation of Clemency. Lying on a llama skin, tightly fitted in pink and gold silk—the tail of her dress looks like a flower vase—hair in an upsweep with Cuban floral motifs. In her hand a modern style telephone; the receiver is a horn painted by an Ethiopian primitive.*): Mrs. Senator is not in, away on presidential business. (*But oh, they have terrible news for her.*) What? That's impossible! (*She jumps up—and breaks a heel. How pale she has become!*) No! (*She screams. The other two Fates draw near and scream too: wails of woe, gnashing of teeth, howls that unhinge the earth.*)

NARRATOR TWO (*at his wit's end*): What's happening?

NARRATOR ONE (*biblical, with a silvery, curling patriarchal beard, the tablets of the Law in his hands*): What had to happen. Do you remember the parable of the animals?

NARRATOR TWO: Of course I remember, but stop pestering me with your parables. What's happening at Dolores's house? What hell is breaking loose? What gods have come with the banner of death?

NARRATOR ONE (*unperturbed*): We'll get to that. Let's begin with the Cycle of Zoophagy: toads eat flies, snakes eat toads, bulls eat snakes, men eat bulls. Here's the explanation. This morning, at five. Stifling heat in the presidential suite. Eroticisms. Drinks. Etcetera. Sex changes for obvious reasons. Number one: women eat bulls. Well then, the dancer called "The Girl with the Diamond in Her Navel," (*and here the tiered mirrors, neon flowers, background curtain with gondolas, and Ravel's* Bolero, *the trademark of every striptease.*)

PRESIDENT: Enough of those Tahitian dances! That navel going around and around, making circles, opening and closing like Cyclops' eye, that navel, I tell you, is making me cockeyed, I'm getting seasick. I see it going around and around by itself, like a spinning top.

DANSEUSE: A fine homage, for someone like me who's squandered so much of her international talent here.

PRESIDENT: And I my pesos to see Camagüeyan hips.

DANSEUSE: Which I've sure suffered for. And are they stuck to your wallet? A "special performance" at the Palace. That's what they promised me. A performance with lights and color posters. I see myself stuck here and I can't believe it. No public, no bravos, no orchids in the dressing room, no telegrams. Reduced to a room and a bed. I who gave up everything to come. I, wanted at the Negresco of Paris, the Lido of Rome. I, the most sought-after, the "assoluta," the girl with the wiggly hips. Somebody's gonna pay for this!

PRESIDENT: You misread the tourist pamphlets. Business is bad. A bad beginning makes a bad ending.

DANSEUSE: You're in for a bad ending and your gang is too. I, goddess of Papeete, here with my jewels. Among crooks. I who gilded my eyelids à la Cleopatra for the palace spotlights, and bought myself a dress, a three-string necklace, a grated carrot with asparagus cream-colored wig; I who invented a "pleasing and presidential number," like Madam Rondón told me. They're all in for a bad ending. They are a bad ending.

PRESIDENT: Get out of here, zombie. Plumed serpent.

DANSEUSE: You'd do better to say Goddess of Liberty!

NARRATOR ONE (*the music stops*): And that's how the zoophagous cycle starts. Women eat bulls. Funny, isn't it? And the bull, what does he do?

NARRATOR TWO: He eats the snake.

NARRATOR ONE: Of course. The President, outraged, flies like a bat out of hell to the serpent, who is the prime minister. The reptile is sleeping, but the first magistrate awakens him with insults, since it was he who obtained, also imported, like I was saying, the liquor, drugs, and danseuse. It is, to keep track of chronologies and order, six in the morning and we are in the second stage.

NARRATOR TWO: How horrible! Each phrase of yours, which seemed banal and gratuitous, takes on great meaning, becomes part of a clockwork machinery. How great you are, author of Dolores Rondón!

NARRATOR ONE: Save your praise for the end. It is seven A.M.: the serpent is about to devour the toad. Listen:

PRIME MINISTER: You wretch, you bastard. To have sent me that revolting courtesan. That Camagüeyan tramp pretending she was an exquisite dancer from Hawaii. Look what's happened! It's all over! Don't you ever dare set foot in the Capitol building or the House again!

SECRETARY TO THE PRIME MINISTER: But my dear sir, don't get confused, don't get excited, remember the heart cannot be replaced. Our dear friend Mortal Pérez introduced me to her, she was taken from the "Army of Art" in Camagüey, her native land.

NARRATOR TWO (*cries*): Now I understand. Poor Dolores.

NARRATOR ONE: Let us keep our cold objectivity till the end. This morning at eight, while Dolores was taking her rum bath, Mortal was publicly accused of white slavery, drug smuggling, importing liquor illegally, an attempt against public morality, traitor to the party, atheist, etc. . . . and he has been declared persona non grata.

(*Holding hands, slow, weightless, the Fates revolve. Their pearly feet barely touch the floor. Their hair floating. Underwater opaqueness. Their screams reach us fragmented, broken.*)

DOLORES (*with a tragic sense of existence*): Earth swallow me! Earth swallow me! Earth swallow me!

THE DRESSMAKER: All tragedy is repetitive!

THE PASTRY COOK (*a candied metamorphosis of Mercy. Balancing on her head a tray topped with honeyed grapefruits, napoleons, fruitcakes, rum cakes*): All repetition is rhetorical!

DOLORES: Yes, earth that witnessed my birth, open now, eat me, dissolve me, turn me to stone! What fury in the saints! What a fire in my head! Servants, if you're still there, if you still haven't carried off the furniture and curtains, bring me a bag of ice and lemonade. How can I pacify the saints now? How can I go back in time, change the course of events? Ice! Fans! What a fire!

THE DRESSMAKER: Here we are, faithful servants.

THE PASTRY COOK: We are following you. We are watching your every step. We were your shadow in the full glare of day, now we will lead you into darkness.

THE DRESSMAKER: Here you are, madam. A mango milk shake. Take with ice and brown sugar the fruit you denied the gods and which they no longer accept from you. Take it.

DOLORES (*as carefree as if she were at a canasta party*): Oh, how delicious! I ow nice and sweet! Real Philippine mangos! We're lucky, all things considered, we still have the blender! (*And returning to Tragedy.*) Look at me Camagüeyans, sons of the flattest province, the mountainless, the Land of the Labyrinth of the Twelve Leagues and the Isles and Islets of the Queen; look at me, glorious lineage of cattle!

THE DRESSMAKER (*recitative*): And of the water jars filled with toads!

THE ANTIQUE DEALER (*recitative*): And of the mystical verse makers!

DOLORES: Look at the end of my career. I leave what I have. Nothing is left except what I have given away. Look at my house: the servants abandon their posts and flee, rats from a sinking ship, ants from a flooded cave; the creditors surround us. I leave it all. I part without regrets. (*In the canasta-party tone again.*) My, that was good! Is there more? (*And tragic again.*) Let the heavens break over me! Mortal is already arriving by the service stairway, hiding, as if infected with the plague, crying, his feet swollen.

MORTAL: What a pain in my feet! What grief! (*The Fates cry, snip each other's hair with scissors, cover the mirrors with black cloths.*) Quiet! I don't want any weeping, just a basin of hot water, a place to put these growing, swelling feet.

THE DRESSMAKER: Oh Mortal, what's to become of us?

THE PASTRY COOK: For whom shall we cook the pork and beans now, for whom the Spanish dishes and diction, for whom the door-to-door vote buying?

THE ANTIQUE DEALER: And God's compassionate eye, and the Valencian paella, will they return no more?

THE DRESSMAKER: Feel better now, sir?

MORTAL (*sighing*): Yes, it's easing up already. I walked too much . . .

THE PASTRY COOK: And there's still more to go!

NARRATOR ONE: So, we reach the final stage, the last judgment: Dolores steps out of her bath and sees Mortal, barefoot, with his feet on the dining-room table, one of the last pieces of furniture left. The Fates take the basin of hot water and slender, slow, graceful, they dance to the window and throw it to the street.

(*Predictable symmetry! The basin, upon falling, repeats the sound we heard when, in the euphoria of electoral success, Dolores threw her pots and pans out the window.*)

And You Only Immortalize

DOLORES (*lento, ma non troppo*): How great you are, Nothingness! How boundless! You, the unique: a god with neither feet nor head. To you my life, still river.

City without walls. I walk. The towers do not retreat. This empty square, this silence, are the same as before; this night in which I return to the point of departure and again turn into dust and poverty, this night in which I wait is again the same impatient night of my departure, my eyes as watchful as then, the offerings ready on the cabinet, a fruit before each saint. At that time I asked the four roads to open before me. I left early. Without baggage. Just as I come back. The water has not moved. The tower does not retreat.

HELP: While the others sleep, she keeps watch.

MERCY: While they sing and shout, she keeps quiet.

CLEMENCY: While they eat and drink, she fasts.

HELP: Come on Dolores! What's past is past. Power is past. The day is past. The whole city sleeps. There's not a sound in the square; we can hear the flies flying in this crummy hotel you've ended up in, across the street from the station. They're all sleeping, snoring away. Mouths agape. Sweating. Naked in their hammocks. Rocking. On the floor. Among empty bottles. Having sweet dreams.

DOLORES: I keep watch.

CLEMENCY: The flowers upon the rosemary spray Young Maid may school thy sorrow The blue-eyed flower that blooms today To honey turns tomorrow. Come sing, Dolores! And buy us a drink, like you bought us one the very night you waited for Mortal, to run away. Come down to the dance. Do not fear symmetry. The dancers, the *danzón*, the pianola, are waiting for you.

DOLORES: I keep quiet.

MERCY: To your health, Dolores. Come to the banquet. To the great stuffed pig. Stuffed with tender wild pigeons stuffed with flowers. They're all eating. They eat and vomit and eat again. Don't miss out on the young pig, the rosy suckling roasted among guayaba leaves, he looks like a baby! Dinner is ready. Hallelujah!

DOLORES: I fast.

Here I waited one night. The same dust, the same square, Mortal was coming in the morning. We were on our way to wealth and power. Nothing changed. The province stands still. But I have one joy left: the sight of your sleeping face, God, waiting for you to wake up, staying here, fixed before you, looking at you. Of myself I leave a testimony: my life written on a stone, by my tomb. No one will read it but the beggars, the gravediggers, and the windows, no one will touch it but the lizards and the red bramble, or perhaps the black couples who make love on the cool grass of the cemetery, fearless, offering life to death. I leave you these words so that you'll remember me, my life in ten lines, in marble, so that neither rain nor wind will erase it:

> Dolores Rondón did here
> reach the end of her career,
> come, mortal, and ponder

on where lies true grandeur.
Pride and arrogance,
power and prominence,
all is bound to perish.
And you only immortalize
the evil you economize
and the good you may cherish.

The Evil You Economize

The province, before Mortal's election

DOLORES: Brothers.

BABALAO ONE: Come in.

DOLORES: I come about a dream.

BABALAO TWO: Speak.

BABALAO ONE: What did you see?

DOLORES: A banquet.

BABALAO ONE: What dishes?

DOLORES: Roast suckling pig, yellow rice, and cocoanuts.

BABALAO ONE: Very good they seem.

BABALAO TWO: Elegua's favorites.

DOLORES: I saw more.

BABALAO TWO: Tell us.

DOLORES: I saw the guests, white people. And I saw parrakeets of every color around the table, talking, and in the middle of the table a large covered bowl.

BABALAO ONE: And inside?

DOLORES: All the guests sit down merrily amidst the hubbub of the parrots, I uncover the big bowl and inside I see a toad, all swollen as if it were about to burst, with red popping eyes like a rabbit's. And when I put the cover upside down on the table, inside, around its edge, a black snake.

BABALAO ONE: Holy Spirit!

BABALAO TWO: Let us see.

(They throw conch shells on a mat.)

BABALAO ONE: Let the flowers of stone, let the eyes of the sea tell us.

BABALAO TWO: They say this: you will find a white man who talks a lot and in a fine manner. The gold and the tablecloths come with him.

But stay there. Do not wish for more. Be careful. Be sure to make your daily offering, be sure not to offend the gods. Do not disown them. They are like dogs, they go away if they do not recognize the master's hand.

BABALAO ONE: And they ask for the flower that revolves like them. And honey.

DOLORES: They shall be given.

BABALAO ONE: Good days are ahead. And after, a sword.

DOLORES: God forbid.

BABALAO ONE: Stop in time. No ambitions. Make your offerings. Stop in time.

DOLORES: But where? Which time is that?

BABALAO ONE: That they do not know. Or do not want to know.

DOLORES: I don't understand.

BABALAO ONE: That's all they say.

DOLORES: After all it's just a dream. And these, a couple of shells.

BABALAO ONE: Nothing but a dream.

DOLORES: And stones.

And the Good You May Cherish

The province, shortly after the fall

NARRATOR ONE: We're already on the last line! All the themes must be caught, tied and untied, sewn, paired, mixed, slid over each other, with melodious sounds, guts full of wind.

NARRATOR TWO: May the meritorious Writers' Guild be on our side!

HELP (*orthophonic*): D. Frontal O. Liquid L. Posterior O. R. E. Sibilant S. Do-lo-res.

MERCY: Do-la-res.

CLEMENCY: There is only one letter of difference between the two. Only one. The letter on a money order from the Holy Mother's Vault in the Royal Bank of Canada. Dolores makes dolares!

NARRATOR TWO: Take advantage. Attack the main theme.

NARRATOR ONE (*is a radio announcer, as if he were advertising tooth-paste*): Yes, ladies and gentlemen, as you see, the ring master, the prime mover is still the pun, the double somersault. Thus we lose the essential: the word runs before the game as the dog before the slicing machine. He sees the sausages in him. In slices, with olives, in a sandwich . . . and he runs off. He runs off barking and, the saying says it, his bark is worse than his bite. Hence so many barking . . . but toothless, words.

DOLORES (*despondent*): Nothing is left!

HELP: Something is left. Dollars are left. We know. Your bank account is full of zeros. Come on, don't put on the poor act. Write us a check. A pretty pink one.

MERCY: We want a mamey milk shake, mamey-colored silk shirts, black and white slacks, little hats. Dark green dollars!

DOLORES: No more account. No more career. No more fat cows, they're consumptive, dehydrated, the widows of bulls, dissolved into dirt.

NARRATOR TWO: Another unhinged zoology!

NARRATOR ONE: You who said that all was useful, that all served some purpose. This is a fine situation for you. Tell me what purpose this chain devourment has, is, serving, what purpose Dolores Rondón's life serves, what purpose her death will serve. Has "behavior" been "modified"? Have the "essences" been "grasped"? Nothingness. Delicious Nothingness milk shake.

HELP (*dodecaphonic*): Where there once was fire, ashes remain!

MERCY (*baroque*): A powerful gentleman is Master Money!

CLEMENCY (*rapid requiem*): What an emetic!

DOLORES (*Dolorosa in a sacramental act*): These are the only pesos left. The last of them. For the light and water bills. Take them.

HELP (*in Duke Ellington jazz, Duke at the piano, Cootie Williams on trumpet, Ray Nance, violin, Chuck Connors, bass trombone, etc.*): We will be showing out-of-this-world originals . . .

NARRATOR ONE (*repetitive and obsessive*): As if all this would penetrate some thick skull, entertain some . . .

MERCY (*in bossa nova*): By Schiaparelli, Chanel, and Christian Dior . . .

NARRATOR TWO (*furious*): Driveling reader slumped in his chair before the soporific stew of everyday living!

CLEMENCY (*like Eartha Kitt on a gilded récamier, extremely feline*): And we will use exclusivité perfumes . . .

NARRATOR ONE: Those are the four parts that united, the essences!

NARRATOR TWO: How ontic!

HELP (*who is Ella Fitzgerald*): From the Maison Rocha!

NARRATOR ONE: All has a purpose, all is final, all returns to all.

DOLORES: That is, to nothing.

NARRATOR TWO: To nothing.

HELP, MERCY, CLEMENCY (*emblematic and signaletic*): Right!

(*Chord on a guitar.*)

THE ENTRY OF CHRIST IN HAVANA

"The serpent, the emerald clarity, I saw it by my head, splattering vinegar; but not Mortal, not even his footsteps in the dust I swallow searching for him, in the stones that cut my feet, in the red bramble. Of what did he drink? Of the pasture of what animals has he eaten? Did thirst kill him? Turn his bones to ashes? Dry his throat and eyes? Are they the ones that look at me, burnt, ashen, flanked with threads of blood? Is this the promised orchard, this absence of trees, this gnashing of teeth?"

Mercy could see herself finding him, draped in damasks, carrying her bleeding breasts on a tray. She saw herself as an infanta, flower of Aragon, open-winged plateresque bird, fixed among apples and snakes from Flemish tapestries, on her head the felt miter, the cardinal's hat of worsted tassels, the three-cornered hat, the round and octagonal gold hat; tattooed in Mudéjar borders, engraved in the heraldic purple of the Courts, written in the sky of an engraving among masts and contorted angels, pointing toward the port of Cadiz. She dreamed her face was deformed by the churrigueresque style, by provincial woodworks, by a rock garden reflected in the volute of a mimbar. She imagined herself, the poor thing, leaving the Palace of Two Waters, bent under the weight of crackling jewels, the pace of her sorrel horse punctuated by a band of Moroccan tambourines, convoyed by Indians, yes, Indians with Brazilian parrakeets, baskets of tobacco and sugar cane. She even sniffed the nearby scent of brown sugar, and of the black sweat she tasted with her fingertip, an expert sampler, and of aguardiente and rotten orchids.

That's what Mercy wanted to be, conqueror of Mortal and the world, a new Cid, bastion of Castille, inquisitor of the Mohammedans and the circumcised; she wanted to cross the Manchegan dust again, galloping over broken turrets with a drove of steeds, swaying baroque incensories over shit-stained Korans, founding monasteries, beheading Almoravide princes, then washing herself with holy water.

. . . "He would travel in the morning. The branches would sprinkle dewdrops upon his horse's mane, and would hide the sun from him as he proceeded, letting through only the necessary light. The growing clarity sowed pieces of gold in his clothing, elusive to his fingers. There were fruits so full and of such delicate skin, that they seemed like liqueurs waiting to be imbibed without the need of a glass, and there were running waters where pebbles crackled like jewels in the hands of beautiful women . . ."[1]

It didn't last long. Of little use were so many gold trinkets. Banners and rumpled rags, mitered and scabby heads: they all rot. Whose stench is it? Who tilts the scale of the vanities? On one plate of the balance, the dried, bald heads of Help and Mercy, crowning the diadems that once crowned them; on the other their bibles and viscera. Who will save them? Who's the highest bidder? Going through his Mansions, searching for Mortal dead or alive, pregnant with him, so did the Faithful fall on the Sierra of Ronda, so did the pistol shots surprise them, the cracking of Toledan swords clearing the way, the hoarse "hands up" of the bandits and hands pawing their hips, the smell of men and wine.

They defended themselves with their nails. They waved papal bulls and amulets in their faces. The blasphemers' thirst was greater. Now they're rolling on the ground, two-bit whores, courtesans for a glass of sangría, their cheeks bitten, their shoulders tattooed with enemy coats of arms. Swinging their hips they go, flamenco dancing in the farmhouses, dragging their Saint Theresa sandals, yes, with those dried and porous nougat faces, and wine-flushed eyes, bent over their nags like harassed picadors, dragging, downtrodden Easter Virgins with their false gold trinkets.

In spite of those spites they want to dance. They shout "I have the blood of kings in the palm of my hand!" and they tap their heels again and again. But they yawn. The guitars are out of tune. They fall out of step. Remain nailed to the platform. Get rings under their eyes. Cramps. They sweat. Their eyes go dry on them, and then they see by their heads a serpent, an emerald clarity.

Threadbare Virgins? Never! They retrieve their money (but their honor, oh no!—they say). Under those rags they wear silks, that preg-

---

[1] Adaptation of a poem by Mutanabbí (915–965) *wafir, nun,* number 175, translated by Emilio García Gómez.

287

nancy has been girdled by wide sashes, and they bear the signatures of Cordoban silversmiths on forged bracelets, lockets of saints' bones, charms that Mortal once wore, coffer to keep his locks in. Do you feel sorry for them, wearing the common wide hats of ruffians and muleteers? Well, underneath are turbans that are jugs of doubloons and, of the sandals, the double sole is a genealogical tree of repoussé leather. Yes, they wear their ancestry on their feet, the gaudy things; they step on the grapevines of more than one crown:

That wine made viceroyships of provinces, ennobled generations of dealers and slave drivers. They search for an impossible, it's true, but they travel equipped for anything. They peddle advertisements for gambling houses and beehives—the brothels of Malaga—; in those cells, Apocryphal beggars, fortune-tellers, procuresses bribe black princesses, houris of Magreb harems, badly castrated eunuchs who answer them with their contralto voices:

HELP and MERCY (*hands clasped, eyes turned toward the sky—and in them the cross reflected, of course*): Sad hermaphrodites, by the law of contrasts you must know of him, he slept in these beds, did you not wash his private parts in the ablutions of before and after the act, did you not kiss the rings on his feet, anoint his chest with holy oils and cinnamon, perfume the air, as he passed, with jasmine pomegranates?

And the chorus of smeared fat men answers moaning over the orange-studded crowns, rending their white cloaks.

THE CHORUS (*the languid sopranos in their cells, accompanied by cymbals*): Yes! We saw him twice, twice did he honor our beds. We tasted of his juice and today we felt his thirst more inextinguishable than the *ayma;*[2] he tempered us like guitars, filled our cups . . . he left for Córdoba, he left for Medina, he stayed, all at once, because he is everywhere!

The Wait in Medina-Az-Zahara[3]

Not capitals, but wooden caps perforated with Koranic letters; the tortoiseshell of the texts appears once and again around those heads like

---

[2] A thirst, which the ancient Arabs had, for she-camel milk.

[3] Medina-Az-Zahara, near Córdoba, palace built in 936 by Adb Er Rahman Anasir III for his favorite Azahara.

the small animals in a Zirí dynasty plate, forming praises and precepts, and from those star-shaped symmetries a jet-black foliage descends—the matted hair of the Moorish Mademoiselles—twisted around the marble columns of their bodies. At their feet, a still river, the blue dust that was once paved with ponds and fountains. In it, water within water, the Azahara had dissolved.

That murmur of cisterns now belongs to the growing bramble; that dampness, an orange glow, levitates over the ground: a garden which the sun duplicates and evaporates; those terraces, cellars, their celebrations, mournings.

Help and Mercy bend down to listen: nothing, not even the birds have remained. So do the Veiled and Vigilant spend day and night at the ruins, waiting.

"Waiting is to become nothing"—they hum from time to time, and over their quartered bodies they let serpents creep. They are salamanders, sweet vermin; they offer that stillness to Mortal.

They neither eat, nor drink, nor join their stiffened eyelids. They decipher the neighboring capitals and from that reading receive omens of The Arrival and patience. Then they smile with their floury cracks, move their pupils of white and pink radii, and think that the joyful day is near.

So passes a time that has neither direction nor measure, until a crew of excavators approaches the palace. Stucco ruins, someone points out, and they crumble. From that rubbish, dusting themselves, two lady wildcat and bible vendors step out. Again they arouse the peasants' surprise, standing there in the middle of the chorus, frozen in speech-making poses; in their baskets, felines battle among psalms.

"Not for these rough stones, oh peasants, nor for archeological treasure whatsoever did we come; but rather for signs of our lord. You look for empty palaces; we a king who deserves them. The stones are already ascending. Pray tell us if near them he has passed. His name is Mortal and "he wears the celestial robe from the looms of Almería."[4]

The Sancho Panzas want to mount their horses and run from the almond-eyed divinities.

[4] Verse from Ben Guzmán, twelfth century.

In a Dream

Questioning, the Majas jump up and down in front of the foreman. Carriers of banderillas, they wave them like double piccolos and extricate their little feet from the ground, crossing them, striking first one hip then the other with them, dancers of the Aragonese jota. Are they going to hurl a javelin? No, they run, jump, touch each other in air; the crack is that of two small mildewed plates, or of a tambourine full of water.

The foreman wants to catch them and runs below, his hands open, awkward sunflowers, following the route of the Skilled Ones.

The Dog Heads picture themselves: in levitation, disarrayed angels, made of striated cubes, heads on backward, false tresses—tiaras of stones and sticks—falling, gold in gold, in a goblet which they raise between their hands. An indigo cloth covers them and on it, concentric creases, elbows and knees are insinuated. These touch (and cross), because the Princesses are two mountebanks, and the ground the letters of the gospel.

The foreman, way below, bearded, following them with his eyes, throwing pieces of earthen jugs at them to make them trip and fall, yes, they see him with half-moon horns, lanceolated ears and a tail of black bristles wagging in the air (not to mention the other, that exposed and overflowing earthen vessel); he drools, he wants to lick their feet.

They, naked intertwined herons over a plate of grapes and laurels, nailed upon a wooden heraldry, in red on the white half, in Prussian blue on the feathered half.

Help and Mercy were sleeping on a pallet, among bull and satyr heads, knees, volutes of Corinthian capitals and pieces of Omeyan plates. So did day discover the rubble and aforementioned plate of grapes, and the foreman the other giver of fire, their bodies sweetly naked under the sheets. It is true that, as in the dream, he licked their feet. He drank of them. He left on their breasts a smell of olives. They awoke damp and startled. Help shouted: "rascals, scoundrels, satyrs." And Mercy: "heretics, fiends." They leapt from the cushions, and not to the dust but to a carpet which covered it. Where the foreman had left the trace of his calloused feet when, playing the innocent, he came to them.

"Here, oh chaste mothers, is this souvenir (*and he pointed to the carpet with a king-of-hearts gesture*), a sign of Mortal's stay here that he left before he moved on. Give it to them—he said to me—so that they will love it as they love me." (And he turned dancingly on his heel.) Let it not surprise us then that the Fat Heads, still naked, parade the carpet among the ruins. They caress it, yes, they offer it raisins, fresh cheese, and goat's milk, they stand in front of it so that the sun won't fade it, they call it "banner," or "godgiven," or "burnt water."

HELP (*yawning*): Mortal thought of our honor: a carpet to carpet us. Sold, it would make our fortune, pawned, our bed and board, traded to the looms of Almería, our heaviest jewel.

MERCY (*who perfumed it with incense*): Shut up, magpie, potbelly. Giving it to you is like throwing rare diamonds to swine. Fool, these threads of gold have meaning, Mortal's tongue is in them. A woven message; it cannot be taken for tatters.

Does Help wave hers? No. It's her laugh: little bones in a tumbler, sand dragged away by the river.

"You numbskull, you're stuffed with vulgar sayings. Nothing says nothing. Let's sell it quickly, or it will be coveted by bandits and rats. Dust comes to dust. Water rots the threads."

"Those threads of your fate are already stinking, Sancha, Pot of Meatballs. Go away! Here's your part. Finish it off in pork and beans."

The scissor grates, bites the plush along the middle, like it does the fate of the Pale Ones. It's when the carpet is already cut that they look at each other, look again and immediately embrace in a jeremiad, howling. The unhappy creatures blow out their snot, riprap their clothes, bend over as if with stomach cramps, twitched into grimaces that cannot possibly disfigure them more than they are now. They're a lament, a breast-beating, a flamenco cry that doesn't stop.

"Look what we have done" (*and they pat each other on the back*).

"It was my fault. I, the transcendental, the fool" (Mercy).

"No, mine: the sweet tooth, never full" (Help).

And they hug and kiss. But it's too late.

Note: In the carpet, FAITH, a naked young woman (she covers one breast and her sex with her hands), hurries to enter the dining room, but already in front of the door, blocking her way, is EXPERIENCE, a hook-nosed and bilious old woman. Who in turn is stopped by a lazy round-faced page covered with a hat of feathers which open like lyres before the dried face of the old woman. The women whisper and nudge each other, relishing the banquet.

The blond prince has tasted the soup and is smiling. Under the table, between his legs, a frightened boy hides and two greyhounds play. The main dish, hog or wild boar meat, has been presented in a bowl in the shape of a ship, the sail is speckled skin and the wooden mast ends in a capital shaped like a pineapple. There are three lit tapers, goblets full of nuts, and a plate of open pomegranates.

(Mercy inquired into the meaning of the cloth. She unstitched it from the lining to see if it hid a written message; she only found the unraveled back of plates and heads: islands of knots, black stitches. The scar of the stitches traced another banquet in the canvas that was like a joke on the visible one, dull and full of clods. The plate of pomegranates was a dark green patch; the dinner guests cross-eyed puppets. Next to the border a left hand pointed to a striated piece of material, separated from the rest.

Tearful Mercy resewed the carpet, pricking her fingers.)

A dark young man, HICCUPS, turns down the splendid food and gives orders to the band. Which consists of three flutists with puffed cheeks, a mandolin, harp, and drum. The harpist, almost a dwarf, seems to be conducting the group. To his right the mandolin player bends his head under the weight of an abundantly convoluted turban, and to his left, the sad drummer tightens his muscles to hold up his instrument (a barrel with two leather skins and a chain) and press a perforated piccolo in his mouth.

Next to him another character (a musician) is showing FAITH and EXPERIENCE something, but we can't see what it is, because there's a darning patch in its place.

Mercy

would redden stones with burning ash, and wait over the coals for dawn, like a thief in ambush. She would fast standing, in the dampest part of the cloister, repeat short prayers and Salve Reginas. She abandoned, for their leniency, her confessors and taking her half of the carpet (which she had unstitched again, interpreted according to numbers and stars, and made into the object of prayers), she spread it before a calvary, so that the faithful would step on it, and stain it with their scabs and tears.

She begged. She lived on bread and water. She suffered the hair shirt. She scourged herself. She drank bile and vinegar. She considered herself a strumpet and begged them to scorn her.

Her eyes sank into the back of her head from keeping watch at night, her feet were cracked from walking barefoot. She was reduced to mere bones. She lost her hair.

Note: By the right edge of the cloth, on a strip that feet had not profaned, remained an arm of the prince and the body of HICCUPS. A very pious little nun believed she saw in him our Lord. So she cut him off, framed him in a shroud, and hung him behind a door.

Help

What a smell of cinnamon! It's just that Help, along with cowbells and cowskulls, had placed fragrant timber among her tresses, certain that so much fragrance can only favor the sale. Although stiff, one would say that a hundred goats are grazing when she moves, such is the chiming of her tins. She comes wrapped in the merchandise: the purchase is the temptation to another more pleasureful one. In other words: she covers her nakedness with her half of the carpet, and apart from that, she wears only the tuneful hairdo.

So to the Palace she went. And lost both cloths: the brocade, and the one I leave to your imagination. She came out dressed, and if she was clinking, it was less from tin cans than from gold trinkets.

The marquis, who was a veteran, did not with this act do injustice to his past victories. Surprise did not unnerve him, and he consummated the conquest with the ritual chimings. When he finally sheathed his saber, they celebrated copiously with aged wines.

Note: The carpet ended up in a winter dining room. Since the scissor snippings left the prince armless, the embroiderers decided to eliminate him and with him the floral border that framed three of the sides. They hung it among horns and rifles, on a wooden closet, sewn to a blue wreath with goats and *puttis.* They made bedspreads with the fringes; the body of the prince, the victim of two restorations, ended up in the garbage.

To Help

You came out laden with gold trinkets, but you quickly went down-hill. You broke your incensory dancing the *pompompero*, your palms and heels grew calloused, you lost honor and hair. You dragged your-self, hide and bones, smeared white and carmine, down the roads of Fuengirolas like a beggarly holyman without once listening to a muezzin, or seeing the white of domes, or hearing any voice to break your fast. Your last shreds were spent on *manzanilla* and *anis del Mono;* you shuffled around, getting drunk in the holds of Magreb ships; at night you anointed yourself with perfumes and went out to wait for the harvesters. They left you their sweat, semen, and a few nickels. You returned with rings under your eyes, yellowed hair, bitten lips. You sang, you were an Arabian cantor with a great pink bow, a timbrel player; you pierced your graying pompom with an arrow of sparkles.

They called you Easy Francie, the Living-Dead. You couldn't even drag your own bones around anymore and you cursed Mortal, the carpet, and the day you were born; you were a hook-nosed and bilious old woman.

To Mercy

You deprived yourself of bracelets and of the honey crullers you so much liked; you gave up your veil for the stain and to the poor, your garments. You called yourself Ruin, Servant, you kissed the feet of the lepers and shared with them your water with noodles. You mortified your hide to the point of swooning. You enjoyed raptures, ecstasy, the gift of tears; you even got to hear voices, to see next to you a pillar of light that rose to the sky; you made light with a fistful of grass (you covered one breast and your sex with your hands); you forgot your senses and saw the emerald clarity, the serpent that appears before the chosen. The one you didn't see was Mortal, nor did you know what happened to him, nor did you remove his face from your chest, your only memory, sharper than thorns, looking at you, turning your guts inside out, buried in your heart like an amber.

So one day Mercy, who—rosary in hand—was dragging her feet over stones and bramble, thought she saw herself in the distance, advancing toward herself.

"Another miracle!"—she thanked the Giver aloud. She continued walking. Then she ran into Help.

"Let's sing!"—they exclaimed. (*And taking each other's hand*):

> There's neither scourge nor reward
> faithful the infidel
> The quick and the dead
> Dance with the Minstrel.

And they cried in their joy.

"I don't know how to say it"—sobbed One; and the Other:—"I don't know how to say it."

And so on till they calmed down, and untied their tongues. They were just turning the place into a lachrymatory with their tears when a bunch of drunken peasants came by. They sang as they walked, with canteens and sickles flung over their shoulders and a pickled stag on a pole. They laughed in a grand manner, so outrageous and insane did they find the weepers. They wanted to dance with them. They made signs with their hands touching themselves you know where, and in fun; they poked at one another. The girls seemed in such great need, with such appetites, that they threw them rolls and raisins. Although starving they tossed them back like hot coals and shouted that "the hunger they suffered was another kind; only the news of a Spaniard with skin like tasseled corn, a chaste tongue, and javelin eyes would satisfy them."

The men, laughing heartily:

"To Cadiz he goes, and on wings."

Hearing this made them so smiley and content that they asked for the same rolls and raisins they had just refused, not to mention meat, wine, and spices. Swiftly, they left.

They spent a happy day. By the next morning they were already confined in black cloth, one of them in a hairnet of starched cambric, the other with her bald disgrace still exposed. They took with them a mare, and lame at that, a missal and a jug of ginger. Had they killed a nun? Pillaged a convent? Where'd they get all those rags? I don't know.

Joy made them proliferate.

Already they play leapfrog and ring-around-the-rosy—"it is not weeping but the plucking of guitars that our Shepherd wants"—they lose the green ivy of their eyelids, they laugh, yes, just like the words say, they laugh and make haste, Mercy high on her saddle, under a fringed parasol which, opened, propels the animal when there's a good wind; Help in front, pulling the reins, parting the underbrush with her cane, crossing herself at every cliff.

MERCY: A day of merriment this is, since not of mourning. Let us not exhaust more hymnals since Mortal awaits us. He, before an absence split in two, is now a sole thirst drying us, a mute figure among stones.

HELP: Then we didn't know how to look for him. Ask for him. We felt his hunger and, crazy little feet, we ran all over the place.

MERCY: We were birds in air.

HELP: And now salamanders in fire!

Already the amazon unfolds parchments, wets her forefinger with saliva to feel the wind's direction, makes note of bird frequency, launches the filly to a gallop and hums: "east" or "northeast," with her little flute voice.

When blown from the stern their contentment is great; they think Mortal is promoting their union and pushing them toward him.

MERCY (*first voice*)

> Look at me, and you will have eyes
> and I yours, to refresh my own.

And HELP (*second voice*):

> You entered me. You anointed my tonsure
> and like burning coals left my senses.

The duo frightened birds and lizards; snakes and bucks glided behind the black bramble to spy on them. The creaking wicker of their hampers held rugs, wooden saints and carbines; in a pot, among small laurel leaves, cumin, capers, and red pepper, a deer tail and two ears clanked. A good bullfight they must have put on to deserve such distinguished trophies!

So they searched, ay, but didn't find. Wounded with love they walked, ran through the fields. They smelled only of sweet basil and rosemary; they ate only grass and flowers; painted birdies, they crossed forests and streams in one thrust, they shouted at the top of their lungs to see if he heard them; they inscribed on their rings—tin hoops that were still theirs—the word WOUNDER, and they trained homing pigeons to carry them in all directions.

They paused at every tree, to see if he had engraved his name; they distinguished the different greens in the grass, searching for the faded trace of his soles; they spent their nights in silence, watching: they heard the sap push out the buds, the gills of fish palpitate, and faraway, on the other shore, the fire in the eyes of tigers, the sleep of men, the vigil of muezzins. A warm air enfolded them as if he had breathed it; then they dreamed intensely of him, to see if he'd appear, they repeated his name till they were breathless, to conjure it: they wanted to invent him with words, count all fish, birds, and fruit, all vermin and bugs, to see if those that nourished him, that he crushed with his step, were missing.

They searched, ay, but didn't find. They wanted to give up, be someone else.

Pigeons under the moon, in great strides they crossed bridges, nights, valleys of white ruins. Finally they saw beyond the hills a light as if from many bright lamps, bounded by a strip of palms. It was the sea: between lines of sand, a line of domes; between deltas of saltpeter, the blue dot of the fortified bay.

Comforted by the view of Cadiz, garland-clustered—guardian angels of the port—they praised and exalted as they laid a tablecloth down by a stream to thus recover their health and give thanks. They were relishing sunflowers with honey and gazing at ships cutting through terraces of foam, when they heard a sound like splitting rafts, and then some cries. Striped by the shadows of willows, fleeing mountain goats were approaching the bank. They jumped over the tablecloth. They turned over the pitcher of wine. After them came two naked, soaking shepherds. They stopped at the sight of wooden bowls, the toppled pitcher of red wine, the purple-stained grass, and frightened Help and Mercy, wounded partridges, open pomegranates in hand.

The Flamenco Girls stood up, and shyly turned their faces toward the stream. With one hand they covered their eyes—Help put a little mirror in front of hers to look at the shepherds without dishonoring herself—with the other, they pointed to the pitcher, accusingly.

The shepherds stammered "a good lunch to you," and with the wet underpants rumpled in their hands, they covered what they thought most urgent: the popular gesture of Modesty. Above the damp cloths their pubic hairs showed in minute spirals; other hairs, like down, shaded their chests. They were strong and golden and had identical beards and hair. The shepherds blushed at seeing them so covered: flowered cretonne fitted them snugly like shrouds from where their hands, desiccated herons, and shaven heads emerged; a white bow on their last lock crowned them like a weather vane. Under those consumptive butterflies the Deers smiled.

And offering the shepherds the bowl of pomegranates:

"Pray do not stop, your mountain goats are escaping."

"Yes, we were running after fleeing goats, and find ourselves before wounded fawns."

And that quaint music? It's hand organs. Look: turn the crank. Don't let the roll stop. That holey roll is the music. Time as a honeycombed parchment. Look at them. The Polliwogs enter Cadiz. The boys follow them in throngs, singing ballads and clapping. The organs of Cadiz slide their sounding boxes, painted with jumping turtles, silver flowers, and Indian birds, around Help and Mercy. And they escape, they don't want that music, they want Mortal's, which is silent music.[5]

They ask around for him. The saffron-haired players follow them, big puppets rolling cranks and heads. Hoods. And the girls cover their ears, hide in the doorways—are they crying? They want to give up, be someone else.

They searched, yes, they asked, they bribed, they begged for advice from door to door. Nobody understood them. People would push them. Throw them old bread and pots of rotten soup. They caught their fingers in doors. Remained stuck there. Children threw stones at them. Cats came to sniff them.

Fragments from Help and Mercy's Log Book

One

HELP: (*Isle and Islets of
   the Queen.*[6]) Yes, I discern
   this sea's roof is of fern,
   and, its towers are lances.

[5] In this passage, and many others, may Saint John forgive me.
[6] An archipelago south of Camagüey.

Are they coral the lusters
on these insular clusters?
MERCY: No, they're holey countenances.
Don't you see that those red dots
are mushrooms and were eye slots
of turtles and drowned dancers?

Fragments from Help and Mercy's Log Book

Two

Yesterday the sea was orange-hued and calm. We saw a school of sirens come near the ship, some of them caught on to the prow and kept us company during many leagues. The sailors threw them walnuts and hazelnuts, which they like so much. It was joyous to see them frolic in the water.

Afraid of running over tritons at night, we navigated cautiously; these besieged us in bands of as many as one hundred and did not leave us till dawn, remaining tangled in gulfweed. Many birds and angels, never further than a mile away from the coast, flew by; land must be near . . . "We saw a branch of fire fall into the sea."[7]

This morning, fish, green bands in the water—islands? Help danced for the sailors, clad only in sea shell necklaces . . . I said a Salve Regina.

A wind blows from the stern and sea horses stick on to the hull. Help caught some and fried them in oil. The sailors, it seems, found them delicious. A long siesta. We're running out of drinking water.

SUBSEQUENT REPORTS identify Help and Mercy as two organists in the cathedral of Santiago, Cuba. The Bacardí Museum holds in its collection of engravings two scores that they composed and, in all probability, in their own handwriting: one is a Stabat Mater. If rather simple in instrumentation, the text is correct. The other is a vernacular song about love and Cupid's artful deceptions, followed by a quadrille for clavichord; both are undated in the original. Which is the composer of each work, and if a "Mourning Song" in two voices, for soprano and contralto, also belongs to the composer of the first, and if "To the

[7] Columbus.

pineapple and sun of Cuba," a song for mezzosoprano and piano, clearly sweetened by the Italian operetta, belongs to the composer of the second, are debatable matters, but after all, secondary.

Other news less worthy of credit—handed down by dubious oral tradition—testifies that the famous women who, following the route of the liberating invasion, entertained the island in sheds, or under white pilgrim and nomadic tents, are none other than the Moorish Girls.

Engravings of the times, anonymous or signed by local craftsmen, portray the *Ontos* Girls against a background of banners and tapers.

But if these episodes are but rough drafts, written over them have remained those that took place during the last days of Cadiz and the first of Santiago. There's a log book in which the Fixed Eyes bear witness to the exaltation which "the incandescence of the tropics" produced in them and they even indulge in a dialogued ten-line stanza, silly and metrically precise, on the Isles and Islets of the Queen, an archipelago off the southern coast of Camagüey.

It is after the landing that their common history branches off, or duplicates itself in mocking inversion, as if the facts danced dizzily around themselves.

We shall follow the version that covers the days of choral glory in the Santiago cathedral, up until the disappearance of the organists in Havana, victims of a snowstorm.

Domus Auxilii

1: "Hey, by the way, what happened to Mortal? Don't they keep searching for him, have they forgotten him?"

"Why honey!"—Help answers, and cartwheels out of her hammock. "Have some, kid, it'll cool you off"—and she gives me a guanábana milk shake.

1 (*delicious!*) tips the glass: Through the bottom I see her within a milky circle, sugar-stained and concave.

"What can I do for you, sweetie?"—she continues (*How she's changed! I say to myself.*). "Reality is a simple matter of birth and death, so why worry ourselves sick? If you don't change, you get stuck, pal, so live and let live!"

I put the glass down to hear her better. She waves her hands, shuffles around, talks with her hands on her hips.

"Look, honey, we searched for him all right, but if he turns up, great, and if not (*she yawns, ooh, it looks like she's going to swallow me*) we'll get through the day with the help of siesta. Which of the two is blonder?" (*And she raises—what sunlight!—a bamboo curtain.*)

Pale sunflowers speckle her body: reflections from a stained-glass window. Shadows of arabesques break between her hands: iron grates, city blocks of pink glass. The light scratches her, a smell of molasses surrounds her, the purple of the roofs hardly differs from that of her eyes.

ı: I've got to admit, Help, you're really at home here. The gold of these tropical fruits glows no brighter than the gold of your hair, angels of Caney county crown you with medlars, write your name on mameys.

HELP: Come on, sonny, don't be so Cuban. (*and calling*) Mercy, Mercy, listen to what this aborigine (*that's me*) is saying.

MERCY: In some mood for natives I am!—She comes in from the kitchen, half-naked, with a bunch of bananas hanging from her waist and singing:

> Mamá those singers so gay
> are they from ol' Havana bay?
> oh how I like their rhythm
> oh how I'd like to know them . . .

She flops in a wicker chair. And fans herself with a palm leaf, opening her legs in a way that to tell the truth leaves me perplexed. It's incredible how heat loosens folks up. But let's cut this short and move on to something else.

Let's climb to the lecterns of the Schola Cantorum. Before them the Passion Flowers have been decaying, extravagant vestry junk, holy water larvae. Poor things, they spend the night among these platforms, ringing the bells and oiling the organs. Their days go by in Te Deums, siestas, and bread with sardines. When they leave the cathedral, pious mustached women shout at them from behind curtains, envious of the clerical life they lead, organizing catechism and bingo parties (they nickname them The Bats). Sunday afternoons, services over, they slip away to dance at the Medlar, so they say. There they rub against mulattos and slanty-eyed natives; they go drunk to the beer halls, to wait for morning—remembering Mortal?—in the bacchanal.

That winds them up for another week of climbing the tower. But, as they say, you can't ring the bell and march in the procession, and this gig of the Little Shopping Bags is in for a bad ending.

When did the Mulatto first come before them? How did his diplomaed tenor voice, his violin, fill that vociferous old age with enthusiasm? How did he gain access, not to chapels and vestry, but to tower platforms, and to the most secret beds? He made the organs resound and, long live the virgin!, the Cranachian bellies of their organists.

HELP: "He brought those yellowing texts back to life with his sweet breath!"

MERCY: "He scared away the moths with his nigger smell!"

These devout women were already moving from the Spanish ascesis to Creole mysticism; they were the martyrs and confessors of half of Santiago (virgins they were not), but they bore one dead weight: their scales. So, seeing them pedal in vain, and finger sixteenth notes instead of thirty-seconds, and scribbles instead of eighth notes, the Bishop of the diocese, that plump good-natured fellow with clammy hands, ordered that an "expert" assist them, since "it takes more than fervor to play the organ" and "my daughters, technique is everything in divine matters." Yes, the canon was a technocrat, so the next day, come what may, he unswervingly appeared in the deambulatory arm in arm with the violinist. The latter came in a Bachian jacket, with his kinky hair slicked down; when he took up the bow, his hands fluttered like two long-tailed doves. He was merry and frolicsome, and from the minute he saw Help and Mercy he knew that high music was in store for them.

"If in the towers"—said the sepia Paganini, taking from his sleeves a lace handkerchief—"there were spiral ramps for carriages, we could set up the clavichords and, chorus raised, sing a Salve Regina that would be heard out to sea!"—And he drew in the air with his handkerchief, the form of a pineapple.

"Oh!"—breathed Help, braking with the pedal.

"Let's sing!"—ordered Bruno. And he gave the key.

Oh the sadness, my friend, of those middays! Of cockroached skies, yellow rain. Big birds would hover among the ropes of the bell tower or fall shrieking, beheaded against the lightning rod. But neither the little heads throbbing between the cracks of the boarded floor, nor the blood-clotted feathers prevented Help and Mercy from attacking the midday onion pie. They'd eat it standing, among bunches of Easter

302

ribbons, remains of ramsacked sepulchers, and moldings from the kneeling stool.

They would cry from two to four, rolled into balls among the cushions of a confessional. They would cry and sneeze, and it was neither snuff nor something similar that they smelled, but rather the fine dust of the covers, sand that would saturate the naves, suspending—golden asterisks—fleas and lice.

Figure it out: two hours daily of lachrymal secretion, with the little they'd drink and the lot they'd urinate—thus the prosperity of the east gardens: gargoyles emptied into them—and you'll see why they were drying up, like pickled lizards.

Around four, that old devil siesta would start putting the flea in their ear. To shake it out they'd ring bells and vespers a few times, drink some cane liquor (which they'd send up in a thermos bottle in the morning, along with other victuals) and they'd give their all to the rigors of the ruled staff. On the bells, fleeing the clappers, blind baby owls would bump their heads.

To judge by the concentric iridescent veins (so pretty!) which daily tears left in the felt of the cushions, the weeping season was long and full. You can see that they resisted—did the memory of Mortal still sustain them?—the sudden attacks of the honeyed heat; you can see that disorder frightened them.

Till one day: (1) They grew a little ovoid belly which waddled before them as they'd climb the spiral staircase; (2) they got bored with everything, they shat on scales and theory, they let their hairs split and dirt settle on the suspenders of their slips; (3) to everything they answered "whatever you say, pal" "no need to kill yourself." In short: siesta corroded their bones, turned them yellow, a malignant anemia; no big deal, it just gave them the Caribbean torpor (sweetly!) in its mildest form, which is the cabbage soup, and the daily *danzón*, and the mattress.

They'd remain stupified on the platforms for days on end, never descending to the maddening crowd, only opening tin cans and playing cards. So that at noon one day, the priest, accompanied by the plump theocrat, climbed the creaking steps on all fours and surprised them, at Te Deum hour, in full snore.

"Better tuned—exclaimed the servant of the servants of the lord—"are your fluty bronchial tubes, than those of this dilapidated harmonium!"

And in their drowsiness, talking through their noses, they flapped their hands in his face. "Come on pal, we're up to our necks in pedaling. We finger the keyboard all day long and not a single saint comes down. We entreat in vain. There's a great deafness up there. We've had it: our phalanx, second phalanx, and third phalanx hurt from fingering that keyboard so much!"

Now that you've heard them, darlings, you'll understand why when Bruno, jazzy violinist and steady drinker of Santiago *prú*, arrived, he found the way paved.

This will look redundant, but the classes began in perfect harmony. The virtuoso taught them Misereres, but also sarabands, so from the Salve Regina, alas, they soon went on to the chaconne. How did he introduce them to the daiquiri, the baroque crown of Oriente province drinks? How did they become so addicted to the Santiago "*chiringuito*"? Where did they learn the "*saoco*" recipe, that is: *agua-ardiente* with cocoanut milk, which they were already pronouncing like Cubans as "*agüecoco*"? Who taught them that bad habit: leaving tamales, pork pies, and deviled ham rolls among the organ strings, where they'd sometimes even rot?

Already the cover of the organ, shining more from varnish than from centenaries, was a washboard marked with whitish circles: the traces of small glasses of crushed ice, overflowing with Bacardí and maraschino cherries, which they left there, in the frantic dancing. And I say frantic dancing, because while One scribbled four or five *pasodobles* on the artefact, the Other danced off heat in the arms of the Maestro, when he wasn't in those of Rita Pla, the new pupil, an image seller and a soprano in her free time.

When they had celebrated the dancing gods, they'd go back to the lessons. How nice those trios were, with Bruno in the center of the organ and the Blond Cowlicks on either side, industriously following his hands with theirs, from C to C, from keyboard to knee, yes sir, they'd give him a finger and he'd take the rest! Do you remember Help, your hair messed by the blowing tubes, coiling your matted peroxide hair around them, golden serpents on golden pillars, musical taffy that you were, you naughty wench?

HELP (*a bit grief-stricken*): Yes, kid, of course I remember; how can I forget those times? Listen, get me a drink . . . What could have become of those waterfront bars, the Black and White, the Two Worlds, where we'd end up shipwrecked in the morning? What became of the Santiago by-the-hour hotels, those gardens open only for the few? Mercy would run naked among colonists and Haitian smugglers, dancing Lully's dances, as she would call those drum beatings . . .

(And we hear a Lully dance which becomes a vaudoux drumbeat. We go back to the times of the cathedral tower.)

At the Santiago Museum

neither detailed branches, earthly paradises, faces made of vegetables, nor patient gardens painted leaf by leaf were scarce.

Peeping out of the windows of their Noah's Arks, their manes in flames, varnished little blond giraffes passed by. Restorers had returned the eloquence of cockatoos and gold of roosters to the palms. On the same branches hummingbirds and mockingbirds perched. Among the stones, white and quartered like the giraffes, lizards slept; the one with little verticle ears, the rodent, would flit through the reeds—the raw red of its scalped hide denounced it—.

In the engravings Latin alternated with old French in humpbacked letters.

"Ara chloroptere! Boselphus Trago Canelus!"—Mercy would exclaim pointing to the little spheres of fish scales bristled with thorns: miniatures of haddock and snappers.

And the hummingbird sewn to the wood, pinned flyer.

In the Other Room

"Place of Arms on The Night of the Military Parade" and a blurred "View of Havana," by Hill, were gathering dust. Sugary Indians displayed tobacco leaves and cassava pies. Then the collection, the Punishment of the Mace, Punishment of the Mask, and Punishment of the Stocks: Negros tainted in blood, kneeling among shackles and chains.

Christ Sets Out from Santiago

Along the naves, tapers in little cups of gilded edges were blinking; in the dark those signs were bat eyes nailed against the altars or swarms of glowworms coming out of a bottle. That light of drizzled sand over Help and Mercy would change them at times into water nymphs, and other times into little candy skulls, depending on how the shadows cut them.

The murmur of crackling wax would join the sound of a rusty clock and this the steps of their bare feet. The feet of the Devout Ones scarcely touched the floor, like a hanged man's feet. Beneath the gravestones they were stepping on, among mushrooms and withered relics, lay eight mitered generations: empty eyes would look at the same archivolts, the identical days would from the lantern yellow the circles of angels in the dome, as light as mist; bundles of bones held in place the gold of the tunics that were incrusted in them, and pressed together, dried cartilage, reliquaries and chalices.

Heads bowed, Help and Mercy advanced toward the vestry. They went reading the In Memoriam engraved in the marble. They touched dark green texts with the tip of their forefingers and crossed themselves. They heard a warbling: it was Rita Pla's vocal exercises. When they pushed open the doors, they found her before Bruno who was raising a baton, her mouth open like someone who's about to spell in the first reading book Acorn Air And.

There was a lukewarm air, of wax, among the closets, and a mustard light among the holy-water pots, incensories and purple puppets with their eyelids on backward. Light filtered through a yellow awning, stretched before the baroque iron work of the window; the wind stretched it—a drum—blowing it—a sail—. Birds were crossing lines on the cloth, and the trolleycars with their long sparking trolleys, in the background of the orange square, outlined by the iron bars, were gods of codices running with burning rattles.

Mercy opened the little platinum mesh pouch that she wore at her waist and out of it came a swollen key, with a double point. She carefully sank it into the lock. The click rang like a bell.

Sprawled in a corner of the display case, elbows folded against his chest and his arm in disks, the Redeemer, foot and headless, was resting. Hooks came out of his wrists and ankles, and from his neck, cut at the Adam's apple, a great screw. He had neither sex nor knee. A tortoise-shell varnish covered him and on his stomach, pale pink. He was worm-eaten. He smelled of incense and naphthalene. On the wounded side you could see a hinge.

On a slab of white wood, stained with ink from the sign HANDLE WITH CARE, his feet and a hand of ovaled nails were exhibited. The other, which gripped a golden flagstaff, and the head, were found in the back of a drawer among broken candelabrums, little Santa Lucía eyes and scapularies.

They put him together in the twinkling of an eye. Bruno screwed on his head until the two little threads of blood which ran down from his eyes continued into those of his neck. Rita combed his beard and with a beer-drenched curler twisted his wig of blond hemp into several snail shell curls which she fastened with a barbed-wire crown. Help perfumed him with her "Attractive and Winning." She took out her string of safety pins. They dressed him in a ruffled slip, crackling with starch and on top, a blanket of rubies and stones from El Cobre Mountain, and snail shells on a string. In his bullfighter's garb he balanced on his flat feet, in the middle of the vestry.

The Christ Fans stepped back to look at him. When they came forward again, they fell on their knees.

With Green Background and Shouting

"Praised be Jesus Christ our Lord who died on the cross to redeem us!"—Help shouted praises till she was hoarse, stretching the e's of "redeem" to the point of choking, catching the impulse in soprano and, poor wretch, ending in bass.

"Have pity on us, ay!" (That was Mercy, and she struck her chest as if she were seized with Saint Vitus's Dance.)

"Long live the King of the Jews and the Cubans!" (That was Rita and she sobbed with emotion.)

And He, before Bruno, looked at himself in the mirror.

"Look how handsome, look how handsome he is!"—shouted a little black girl hanging from the bars of the window.

On the street, cars with loudspeakers passed by; the nasal twang of amplifiers came in along with the crackling of broken glass and screeching of rails.

In the tarnished space of the mirror the small doors opened and the red square of the bonnet, the lace sleeve, the black shirt frills of lively golds appeared: it was the Bishop.

"Oh, my beloved!"—and he patted his stomach.

Through the crack between the shutters you could see a brightness in the naves: the dirty silver of the altars, reddish disks dancing clumsily—copper crosses—.

In the vestry's dampness the faithful were five hanged warriors, going around and around in the same place, dervishes, spinning tops, merry-go-rounds. The grass green, bottle green floor of rhombi met the orange walls at sharp angles, forming a cuneiform space where he reigned, duplicated in the river of quicksilver.

"Hurry up, girls, we'll be leaving in a minute!"—And the Lord Bishop shook a hand bell that was heard again, faraway, returning from the dome.

And he shook a hand bell that was heard again, another time, as if it had sounded in the Kingdom of Death.

"We're leaving!"—In the naves a band of cracked drums, water-filled guitars, and muted rattles broke out.

What a hissing of prayers! What a creaking of benches! Chest beatings. Ejaculations. The weepers sounded maracas—they played maracas for this burial—and the hoodmasters their mahogany clavichords. Little devils with palm-leaf skirts and castles of yellow feathers on their heads crowded into the baptistery.

He appeared in the door of the vestry, tottering under a canopy of royal palms held up by Help and Mercy, within a white white light, as from milk curds. Canticles and cheers. Under his vault of greenery he advanced among purple strips of stained-glass windows, shadows of banners, flags.

The sepulcher awaited Him.

You could hear a flapping of wings, like droves of geese: it was the Black Oblates, they were dressed as angels.

These big Pious Babies were already lined up in the choir aisle, rosy and smelling of Eau de Cologne, in white piqué dresses and carrying large palm-leaf baskets, reciting a rosary of river pebbles and sweating into initialed hankies.

Grumpy dwarfs were stamping their feet behind the altar, wrapped in bunches of red felt ribbon.

The shrouds were replicas of his face, the standard-bearers' ensigns the color of his blood, the cornets of the Municipal Brass Band the silver of his tomb.

"Long live the King of Alto Songo!"—that was the hotheaded misses of the diocese, who had been tippling as they walked since morning. One of them rattled a maraca.

Electric tapers were lit. Crepe-paper flowers carpeted the route to the sepulcher. Make way, people, here comes the Verb of Santiago! The resurrected, sandpapered king was about to begin the voyage on his aluminum throne. The blood barely stained his nose and eyelids. Why it looked like he was going to laugh!

Now the leader shakes his baton (at his age, that's what he shakes best). And the chorus sings the first Gloria—What a triumph for Bruno! Mercy leaves the pulpy palm leaves on the pulpit staircase. She kisses him, sets him on the sepulcher.

Help shouts "Ready!" Someone breaks into tears.

The King totters, then takes off, balancing under a rainfall of jasmine. He advances toward the portico, between lamps of green glass. The flame flits over the chalk of his face, the shine of rotten fish. White and green, the rust of nails, flowers of tetanus, opens in his dried hands and pierced feet.

"Here comes the handsomest fellow of Caney county"—the children clap hands. And take out their bags of confetti.

Creole gentlemen follow him. You've got to admit, that humble vestry wine sure gives a man poise! They march in unison, foot to foot, their stomachs tucked in by In Excelsis Deo sashes.

The Minstrels march, the precious load on their shoulders: in front, Mercy sets the example in her Prussian blue rayon cloak with a cushion sewn on the left shoulder, and Rita Pla, a cushion on her right shoulder, struts in such a way that you'd think it's the lantern of The Bakers' Masked Ball that's being carried and not the Victor of Santiago on his tomb. The poor Redeemer up there, he must be eating himself up! At the rear, Help, in the best of her wigs, and Bruno hold the two back handles of the sepulcher. Look in wonder, brethren, at what four pillars carry the Blond of Blonds, at what caryatids fit for a mausoleum, in short, what four legs for a bench!

Already they're down the central nave. At his passing the faithful close their eyes, kneel; trembling, they kiss the carpet where he has passed. And make the sign of the cross. Others run. Push. Touch him. Tear white lilies from his funeral carriage.

Already they're near the portico. From the high altar you can see him from the back, outlined against the blue rectangle of night, shower of light; hands and handkerchiefs raised. The stones from El Cobre shrine, mortuary jewels, are already glittering on his cloak, stirred by the breeze in the square.

"Lower him!"—Mercy orders—"or his crown will short-circuit on the bulbs of the tympan!"

The bearers stoop. He's outside. The whole square lights up.

"Raise him again!"

And he ascends, standing erect over the sepulcher, proud as a pimp, hoisting a white flag. Behind, red stones, gold stains: the seal of his face on the Pantocrator of Italian mosaic. A silence. Rosary beads passing through fingers. Candles crackling.

The wind on the terraces, whistling through patio palm trees.

Then bells, the hymn. Gentlemen in drill suits and Panamas come out on their balconies, and little girls in straw hats empty baskets of petals. Cigar smoke sweetens the air in slow rings that will break among the fans. The square is full. The people of Santiago sing.

"Straight on, but *moderato,* gents, *per piacere!*"—orders Bruno. And the Blond descends the steps, following a gentle parabola as if on an escalator. The Bishop receives him.

No sooner did he set foot on the ground when beneath the portico appears the sorrowful, ash moon virgin. They've whitened her with rice powder, "so that she really looks pale," her mouth and cheeks, a heart. Her tears, and her seven daggers, are silver.

He crosses the square. Around him trumpets, the rim of the drums, crashing cymbals, shine. The Bishop makes way for him; covered in his hands, the chalice: over the red cloth of his sleeves, gilded lace. In front walk two acolytes swaying incensories. Sinuous ribbons of white smoke. The pale parson drops Latin mumbo jumbo as he goes, and makes crosses in the air with his right hand. Women in black mantillas and high shell combs, and stiff men with candles and branches of lilies, walk on either side.

"Come, people of Santiago, who's more stud than he, and who whiter?"— howl the Cornucopias of Craniums, beating their breasts.

HELP (*who has pinched a cloak with a black and white fiber hood.*): "You leave Santiago to enter Death!"

MERCY (*wielding a shroud in which you see Christ's face in an arrow-pierced heart with the inscription "C loves M."—Christ and Mercy*): "You enter Death to give us Life!"

The old people, bundled up, crowd together on the sidewalks, beneath the greenish halo of the street lamps. Joining hands they watch him go by in his Sunday best, and then withdraw in silence, to kneel on the cushions of the antechamber.

In cracked oil paintings the Virgin shines on her half-moon, against a blackened sky of sugar mill chimneys, and in the yellowish cardboard of screens a mulatto Christ watches over Santiago: a labyrinth of small sugar plantations and boats.

> Look at them oh crack footed King,
> because you leave they cannot sing

It's Rita, when they stop in front of City Hall where gentlemen greet him from the gates, waving hats. Little devils jingle bells, dancing on one foot before the sepulcher. Against the white façades, the hood masters play their clavichords: black stitches around the holes of their eyes.

Then the procession moves on. Empty terraces, lighted lamps, wicker rocking chairs rocking are left behind, and in the shadows of interiors: burnished clocks, mirrors, opulent pineapple goblets, the ancestral portrait.

In the night's dampness they disappear into poplar groves, into the suburbs.

Now, little by little, they are left alone. In the city the tapers' light has traced a white sign, a chalk omega, two inverted fish joined by a thread. Or perhaps a signature.

So they left the last lots behind, the whistle of the land breeze through the mangrove trees, the streaks of saltpeter on the eaves. When they started moving into the thick night, Bruno made him turn his head so that he'd see the rows of windows slowly disappear. Mercy tells that down his cheeks rolled two big tears, and also down his neck, as far as his shoulder blade.

When they straightened his head he saw before him other greens, the surprise of other birds in the calm, the Cuban peasants: little eyes behind windows, lighter than the royal palm leaves of the shutters, Chinese shadows—but in big Panama hats—in front of carbon lamps. They covered the cracks in their walls with newspapers, passed the latch, and between the planks of their whitewashed doors, they peeped out to see him go by. The huts were boxes of hemp, the cracks small yellow stained-glass windows with printed letters.

They followed the windings of a stream, the highway, they disappeared into the mist of a small forest, among the dark cones of the . . . (and here, the exhaustive enumeration of Cuban trees—horse-flesh mahogany, guamá, jequi, oak, the anona tree, and so forth—with their botanical jargon)[8] . . . until Help and Mercy, Rita and Bruno, "dead tired," left the sepulcher on the grass.

In the early morning—or was it the turning of a rattlesnake among dry leaves, the flapping of an owl?—they heard Him cough. He woke up with stiff elbows and wrists; the joints of his ankles rigid. Well you see, it's just that accustomed as he was to vestry climate, tempered by the sighs and yawns of so many fasters, the dampness had gotten into the sawdust of his bones. His fingers stiffened, one foot hard in the air as if on a step, he was petrified in a good-bye: poorly sewn puppet, raffle picture card. His meeting with the Cuban countryside, with insular space and its glowworms, had brought on arthritis.

They stretched His limbs as much as they could. They put Him through calisthenics, recited an Ex Aegypto Israel. The heat was—listen to Help—"thicker than pea soup." There was something sweetish in the air, as if near a beehive or cane juice stand.

The followers stretched—the few that were left: at the sight of the jungle the rest had resigned themselves to urban mysticism—shook the hay off their uniforms and cassocks and ran into the woods to piss.

(Tarnished cornets, and on the drums, dew.)

He felt that something was jolting Him in the knees, that his legs were giving way. A shiver ("Oh Father, have pity on me, you who have gotten me into this mess"—he thought). His whole body itched —Was it jigger fleas? He promised to scourge himself. He wasn't going to wait much longer. Listen to these morning prayers:

HELP (*who was putting the pink back into her cheeks with roucou*): Now you carry Him for a while, why it's worse than carrying a chimpanzee piggyback. He's got me crippled.

MERCY (*who was bathing in a stream*): You poke your own hellfire, you lazybones, ramrod, thick clod. Etc., etc.

Stretching and bending they finally reached a town. What a relief for their swollen feet: the square was paved in cobblestones and dark green water ran along the juncture of the stones. It overflowed from the broken basin of the fountain.

What a smell of coffee, what nice smoke spiraling out the doorways!

[8] Phonetic delights never omitted in any Cuban tract, from the *Mirror of Patience*—1608—to the present day.

Bowls of chipped china on shiny crimson tablecloths, the leaning tables, the stools, piled on top.

The women were doing the foot scratching dance, coming out in flowered slippers, the backs of them worn down: "oh boy, what a visitor." They opened their houses. Brought out lamps and hung them on the *guásima* trees in the patio, and gave away lumps of pan sugar from their cupboards. Why they combed their hair: to receive him!

The Next Day

An arcade stood facing the village, and another one almost parallel: the shadow of the first on the smooth, windowless façades. These successive arches supported unfinished walls, or ruins, a second portico, and the slope of roofs. On a stoop rested the handle of a coach, and over the shadow of its great wheels, on the adjacent wall, hung carbines, telescopes, pendulums, and perhaps pocket pistols and swords with tortoise-shell hilts. From there the early risers set forth in a throng, with great clamor and large red shawls around their necks. They brought accordions. Graters and maracas. What cute music they scratched! It would split anybody's sides! It was a thick-lipped mulatto with even, scorched kinky hair—Mercy's darling—who was shooting off like this, with his razor sharp voice:

> I have a little thing that you like
> that you like
> that you like

He wriggled like an eel, with a hand on his hip—what Dahoman rings!—pointing with the other to the object of such elliptic verse.

The aroma of honest-to-good coffee—accustomed as he was to that of incense—and that spicy odor emanating from the tables revived Him. He was delighted that they ran behind Him, that they wore down the wood of his feet with kisses, that they perfumed him with *agua-ardiente*. He wanted them to entreat Him, but with guitars and gourds; he wanted angels with royal palms. He thought himself a patriot, a Martilike orator frozen in the threads of an engraving; He pictured himself in a speech-making pose, raised to a tricolor tribune, or releasing a fighting cock with his calloused hands, its feathers crossing his dried, olive face. He would like you to see a blue sky behind him, and

313

a sun of hard fog, a waning moon, several comets. He had the calling
of a redeemer, blondie did, He liked flags.

Help immediately joined in on the fun, not to mention—which would
be knocking your head against Redundance—Rita and Bruno, who
didn't have to join it, since they had it in them since birth (according
to Mercy).

It wasn't till they were in the store, with the "hurry up, we still have
the fringes to put up," that they found out: the one they left slipping
on the cobblestones outside in the square was not the object of this
great fuss; the people were expecting a new candidate, who had
promised "to give the town running water and to build a road that
would connect them to their neighbors in nearby towns," to arrive at
noon. For him the tournament, the cockfights, the "National" band,
the tables of breadsticks and the taffy wrapped in colored papers.

Competition horses in checkered girths came from all over the
county. And on foot, pulling their reins, smiling bowlegged riders
already appeared in black and gold or blue and gold colors that reappeared on stirrups and blinders, bringing Guinea hens and Mandarin
oranges and shopping bags of limes too.

"May you be struck down with lightning!"—Mercy exploded, she
was cracking up, already wallowing in corners with some of the band
players (according to Help), knocking machetes and spats off the
walls.

"God, what am I doing here?"—and she ran toward the portico
through the steam of boiled milk, the wake of clean pitchers and the
marimbas.

She sensed that the party was leaving her. She saw Bruno call to her,
between two open-mouthed guitarists, against a background of pots
and swords.

In full force she crossed the square, fell on her knees before Christ
and cried on His navel—that's as high as her disheveled head could
reach.

"Forgive me Dear God, I didn't know what I was doing." (*and
without any sense of dramatic transition*) Help adds: "Fungus! Pustules on his feet! He's rotting, eek!"

She took one step back, and another, without turning around. She
opened her hands, drew them near her eyes, scrutinized the palms:

"And I've touched Him! I'm infected: alcohol!"

And He, to get a good look at her, squeezed his glass pupils, those opaque stones that have been dimmed by so much looking at the top of a locker. He was soaked with dew. Bagasse Christ. One foot was eczematous and green, and in the arch a milky flower, of mushrooms. His nose ran and so did the swollen edge of his eyelids.

"Alcohol, for God's sake!"—And she shot off to the store.

"And the best!"—answered Bruno who awaited her with open arms in the doorway. And he emptied on her head a glass of rum-on-the-rocks. From there he was dragged away. Help and Mercy, yoked together, pulled Him. He went on foot, tied to a beam, handcuffed. They had taken off his crown and put on a palm-leaf hat because it was drizzling, they had tossed lemon juice on his foot and cologne on his head. So that His sore couldn't be seen, they had surrounded Him with vases of wax flowers. So that the Rotten One emerged from an opaque garden whose leaves the cart's jolting could not shake off. They fell into gutters. Got stuck in bogs.

Mercy was getting eaten up by mosquitos; but stoically she sang:

> tonight it is raining
> tomorrow will be muddy,

When Help answered her the rain fell thicker:

> poor is the carter
> who pulls this cart

And the Foul One went through the drizzle, his feet among flowered urns, his legs among still flowers. Oh how it burns! Water surrounded him right up to his pustules.

"A bigamist I'll be, but not a fag"—he thought. And looked out the corner of his eye at Bruno, who was laughing, envious.

It was because the Two Women were rubbing Him with camphor balls, wrapping Him in blankets, inserting in each armpit "because you see, he had fever on only one side" a vulvous thermometer with fili-grees and Roman numerals. They even pleaded with Saint Lazarus to rid Him of galloping leprosy.

They had to cross the rising Jobabo river, and hauled the cart by looping the rope through a ring that moved along a rope tied to a palm tree on each bank. And the last just men kept the balance.

Like a rolling barrel full of stones was the noise of the waters. Red turtles leapt to the beams, held on with their little nails, disappeared into slow eddies. Trout jumped up in rapid flight, flicked their tails, spattered water, and remained gasping between planks.

"They fish themselves, God's creatures! Let's pray He doesn't decide to multiply them now!" (Help)

Below, the current dragged away torn roots, and shrubs with nests.

"And the bluish hands of drowned men, saying good-bye!" (Adds Mercy, who scarcely breathes so as not to move, "not everybody walks on water.") They left the rest of the pilgrimage in Oriente province waving handkerchiefs and sneezing. Rita wanted to catch on to the rope and swim to the other side, but they finally convinced her to stay on land. Bruno left the violin cover and three candelabrums with her, to lighten the load. What a farewell! They could still see her from the other bank, behind the strip of mud, moving the three bronzes like a traffic cop. Then she became a blur with the others. At the landing a gust of wind carried away His hat. Bruno raised Him by the head and planted Him on the grass. Then they saw those plaques of pus which whitened his leg to the waist.

They stuck their ears to his stomach, the Magdalenas auscultated Him. Something was bubbling inside.

MERCY (*her eyes popping*): "The Evil Disease!"

The sweet felp of their earlobes and the pearls of their earrings rubbing His groin certainly seemed to make Him mighty happy. What a pity there wasn't a camera at hand: he was smiling!

ILLUSTRIOUS SHORES, but a feeble welcome did He receive from those of Santa María del Puerto del Príncipe.

Listen to those welcomes the Camagüeyan ladies forced on Him, sheltered behind the shutters and rails of their windows:

a. You will leave our towers mute, but the bronze of our many bells will sink your ships. (*They had taken Him for a pirate!*)

b. Ill wind from a leprosarium, angel of rebels, leader of escaped slaves.

c. Locust of cattle, salting of the water, etc.

He, who in so many Gobelins, on so many night tables: wounded pigeon, gentleman of painted plaster, with eyes of chemical blue like a Mexican doll, He, whose signs—parallel fish, crowns, crosses and nails—embellished the glass of every paperweight and, in cement, worn down by rains, the medallions of every façade,

He, who appeared in so many family portraits.

And yet they did not recognize Him.

He scratched what he thought most symbolic of the situation (he already had Cuban habits!) and gave Bruno the "forward march" signal.

The shadows of dates clouded his face, in the black gardens of las Mercedes, the chandelier of the choir loft's arches. He wanted to lose himself in the labyrinths of the angel makers, among the goldsmith stands and old book stalls. Along the banks of the Tínima River the display cases of Spanish flea markets, beneath the yellow halo of candles, were shining in the mist: Catalan panels with beheaded saints and all the arteries of their necks; paintings of balloons rising with sacks of sand and green ribbons: in the baskets, in smoking jackets, handlebar mustaches, and spectacles, brave Matías Perezes would observe the clouds.

Bruno's Statement

It is here necessary to make note of a fact, so that written evidence shall remain which could serve the authoress in securing either total absolution or perpetual hellfire. Here it is: the Redeemer pointed to one of those balloons. It is well known that ascensions are His weak point.

I bear witness that, with the few pesos she had left, with no hope whatsoever of earning more, and much less in such chaste places, Help offered to get it for Him, perhaps because she had seen new stains on Him and knew that sooner or later she'd recover the gift. Whatever the case may be, she went out to buy it.

Every Venetian blind fell. Every salesman spat on her, threw the door in her face.

The lights went out. I hereby testify that that's how the Camagüeyan tour ended.

They saw black propellers among the palm trees: army helicopters were following them. Clean shaven young pilots descended to the villages He was going to pass through, to intimidate the people and buy Paloma de Castilla crackers. When the travelers arrived, little men in uniforms would point to them with large pencils and, terrified, take off. Through the plastic bellies of the crafts you could see them gesticulate and open maps.

317

To bother Him, the pilots powdered Him from above with bread crumbs.

Another rumble. They all stooped down—except Him, naturally, He would have hurt his pustules—but they didn't see anything. It was the subway.

There is no rule without the exception: the herbists of Ciego de Avila came out to receive him, and with a lot of noise. To entertain Him they brought out wooden serpents coiled around little mirrors, mortars, old pomander boxes with the names of leaves where letters were missing, the covers adorned with Florentine and French landscapes.

Mechanical gargoyles followed them, raising whirlwinds with their helices, five bakelite birds. Curtains of dust surrounded Him. If the three faithfuls would stop, the noise of the motors would decrease and the row of transparent machines would stand still in air, perpendicular to the highway. The whirlwinds would then spread and a spiral of straw would surround them.

If they'd flee to the grottos of reinforced concrete, or hide by the rivers, in the inns on abandoned piles, the patrol—and the dull buzzing—would escort them, forming a V whose vortex, a craft with two propellers, would plane over His head, like a Holy Spirit Dove.

HELP (*and the motors came on louder*):......(she opened and closed her mouth—was she shouting?—; gusts of wind stiffened her face. A totally bald pate.)

MERCY:......(*with calm gestures*)

Bruno touched them and pointed to the mouth of a subway. They went down the escalator, under the panel SUBWAY. With Him and the cart on their backs they passed through a lunch counter (ay, His toes were already spouting pus, falling off in pieces), the cabarets of River Side (pustules had begun on His other leg and, like a belt of rotting metals, they girded His stomach), corridors with amplifiers; on the radio the twelve o'clock noon gongs, the meowing sopranos on the Chinese programs and the Candado soap commercials.

They bathed Him in sulphur. They came up in the elevator content, out the other mouth of the subway. Motionless, like a band of scabby turkey buzzards, the helicopters were waiting for them at the exit.

The din of the choppers were breaking Help's eardrums; the corruption of the Corpus Christi, Mercy's heart.

The crafts were not following them at equal distances now, but rather, one by one, they dove down like kingfishers, almost flush with roofs and trees; then a hatch-door opened in the plexiglass shell, the copilot peered out a second "like the cuckoo of a clock" (Bruno), and took a flash photograph. The mosquito would then return to his place in the V. The next would come down.

Having reached the cherry orchards of Las Villas, He asked them to abandon him to His fate (he showed them the highway with a flabby hand, and with the other He grabbed on to a trunk), to let Him rot on the marabou.

At night they'd take off His blanket and leave Him in the open—so that the night dew would cool his sores—in the light of the V of blinking headlights. In the morning they'd find Him softened, tearful, pecked at by birds.

They hiked down the Villa Clara hills. In the distance, streaking the pink fields, you could see the black lines of the railroad disappearing under the roofs of the kirshwasser factories, branching off on the other side, crossing the pine groves and fishing villages, or else following the rivers which swept along rafts of white trunks, convoyed by signal flags and toads, until disappearing into the curve of inlets, under the red smoke cloud of the distilleries, among the tanks along the docks.

Near a curve in the road they heard call bells. When they turned the corner, they saw two yellow triangles with red edges light up and a barrier fall before them: blocking the way, an armored train had stopped at the crossing.

The bell stopped. What a silence! (They felt they were being watched.) Suddenly the cars opened, unglued boxes, and down the walls, now ramps, tanks rolled out. From their turrets came nets full of green sponges ("Giant pieces of mint!"—Help), portable radios, tape recorders whose tapes were running.

"Somehow we've got to appeal to the popular devotion!"—declared Help, and she stamped the first letter on one buttock.

Let me explain: she was dancing in front of a jukebox, and wildly, pardon me, and enthusiastically composing the Lord's texts on her naked body—which looked as if printed on brown paper—: with wooden blocks she engraved golden monograms.

No one had come to receive them in Santa Clara. She tore her clothes in anger, crossed herself, and bought a printing set: (to Him):

> I will make of my body Your book,
> they will read from me!

And Mercy (*to the frightened Villa Clara folk behind cracks—families squeezed into bunches—hidden under their mothers' skirts*):

> Come, children of God:
> Here is the flesh made word!

And Help went wild over burning tambourines and cornets from John Coltrane's band.

They came running, and *en masse*. At the beat of the drums, Help wriggled from head to toe, and from her navel, which projected an O, to the full stop of her knee letters shined all over her.

He couldn't take His eyes off the oscillating band of texts, nor hold back His feet: he wanted to dance, he knew that dance is the new birth, that after death they'll confront us with the mambo band. What a pity! He couldn't even clap hands. He stretched his arms and felt like His armpits were breaking. He was finished now: his nipples were purple, his chest in welts, his throat burning, He was choking, the ganglia of His neck hurt. If the band came on louder—the needle in the striped grooves, for Him it was like bottles breaking against each other, cornets playing under water.

"What wiggly hips!"—(said the faithful). Bruno took some steps around her, looking at her hips as if reading.

"But, what about the helicopters?"

They were there. Watching the show from the boxes. The pilots eating popcorn. Whose bags they threw away when the record was over.

Let's not even talk about Matanzas.

The Entry of Christ in Havana

What a reception in Havana! They were all waiting for Him. His picture was everywhere, endlessly repeated, to the point of ridicule or simply boredom: pasted up, ripped off, pulled apart, nailed on every door, pasted around every pole, decorated with mustaches, with pricks dripping into His mouth, even in colors—oh so blond and beautiful, just like Greta Garbo—not to mention the stained-glass reproductions in the Galiano subway. Wherever you look, He looks back.

Bruno: I'm gonna walk no more: I'm sitting right down. I'm at my wit's end: They take more pictures of him than of the Coca Cola bottle! Let somebody else carry Him. Here's where I'm staying.

And there he stayed, in a fit of hiccups.

Pictures, taken from above, but at different distances: a black spot, a winding line of the highway, tilled fields; a blond head, toes on a platform, a background of pavement, white locks, and up front His profile; close-up: His eyes. His eyes; white locks, profile; dark spot, highway.

A little black girl came running full steam ahead, with a banner waving in the breeze, white knee socks were all you could see of her tiny legs; she came running full steam ahead, her legs—pistons—were all over the place, her knees chugachugachuga—a Hittite lion—holding up high a banner that said INRI. You've finally come, she said, we were waiting for You. Her eyes became moist, she was speechless ("She swooned, in a trance, as if she had seen Paul Anka!"—said Help), she thrashed about wildly, out of joy, took a few steps toward Him, and fell.

He didn't have time to pick her up. Two others fell upon Him, more and more kept coming. Weeping and embracing Him. They came down from the hills, beating barrels and drums with sticks rolled up in rags. The women threw open their doors; dazed, they clapped their hands over their mouths; a cry; they dropped to their knees, tried to touch Him, kissed the ground where He passed. The children carried around His image in good luck charms, in little straw dolls. His name was in all the shop windows. They ate Him in mint candies. They dressed up like Him, wearing little crowns of thorns (their faces white with rice powder) and small blood flowers. It was all so pretty!

They came from every direction, climbed trees to see Him, asked for His autograph.

He coughed and suddenly felt that He was moving forward, the people pushing Him, that He was moving backward, driftwood floating in the tide, that He was moving forward again. Sweating. He had chills. They stepped on His feet. They blew their hot breath, thick fumes of Gold Label rum, into His face; the trumpets of Luyanó in His ears. (The flutists were two jaundiced and baggy-eyed dwarfs, puffy cheeks under black berets.) He felt slimy hands caressing Him, and on His thighs wet mollusk lips. The banners covered His sky, the poles fenced Him in like a palisade of red lances. He was gasping for air. He thrashed His arms in acid fumes. He really wasn't made for the proletariat: the masses stifled Him.

"I'll never make it," He said to Himself. He tightened His eyes, clinched His fists, bit His lips. He wanted to stamp and kick. Spin around with his arms outstretched (and, God willing, with knives in both hands), open a path, escape. His dangling limbs did not obey Him. (Horns, rattles, bells) His hand shook as if it were throwing dice. He tried to stop it: one foot trembled, or was it the other or His head. His hand moved on its own. His feet. He jumped. His body quivered, a goaded frog. An electric shock ran through Him. He was dancing unwillingly to a rock beat. (Balloons popped out of a balcony, doves from another.)

He listened as if someone were whispering in His ear. At the same time Help and Mercy turned toward Him. Once more (but the racket of brass bands, clapping, hurrahs): stuttering, babbling words ("African angels are speaking to Me," He thought). Without turning His head, He looked in the direction of the voices. Attentive, He heard "red," and right after: "It hurts in the back of my eyes."

He saw Help and Mercy shake their heads, stand still, raise their open hands—restored to the fervor of the catacombs—turn from white to yellow and back again to white. Now two great tears rolled down their cheeks. Now they muttered, sobbing, "A miracle, a miracle."

Then He realized He was speaking.

He heard Himself say: "I am freezing inside."

They wrapped Him in the Madonna's cloak from the main altar in the Church of Carmen. The thick cloth, embroidered with gold leaves hung straight down from His shoulders. Black cords intertwined in the shape of clover leaves and rosettes of pearls ran along its edges.

Each step of the bearers shook His blond head, his waxy eyelids, those sick eyes sank deeper. (From a distance He was the Madonna of a Siennese casket.) They threw flowers, they cheered Him. Without turning His head, with the solemnity of a princess in her Mercedes, He greeted the multitudes on the balconies. Carnations stuck to the garlands and brooches of His cloak.

"Blessed be ye, women, wise if not virgins, who have followed Me through thick and thin." He moved His forearm three times like a piggy-bank black boy who bows and doffs his cap. He suddenly unwound: His hands. They hung limp, like rags. He could not quite touch His eyelids:

"How cold they are, oh God, what a pain in the back of My eyes!" And they took off their cloaks, folded them like sashes, wrapped them around His waist. Or transported by mystical delirium ("May Your fire joyously consume me!"—said Help), they padded them, and with the same burlap filled in the gaps of His joints. They covered His hinges. They would have torn out the pupils of their eyes to give Him. They wept with only one eye, so He would not see. They turned violet, their nails black, as if the Plague were devouring them.

(Thickness of the sky: terraces of wax.

And there, over the streets, the sea: fixed foam, a strip of sand.) He glided over the mob—carried on their shoulders—swift, blinded by the flash bulbs, followed by the cameras—concave green crossed the lenses—. Majestic, He was like a redwood statue unearthed from a river bed: His eyes sockets full of crabs, His face rotted, His arms broken, His feet black sponges. Branches and leaves of holy Palm trees opened before Him, like seaweed before the hull of a ship.

Posing in place, in order of generations, the families looked down at Him from their balconies. In the foreground, right behind the railing, little boys dressed in white suits and black bow ties, were rocking back and forth on their wooden horses, chocolate cigars between their fingers. Little girls, in starched dresses, held yellow hoops next to their perfectly conical skirts, beach pails, and shovels. Behind them, austere, the fathers with mustaches and goatees, and bouquets of flowers in their hands, the mothers in their fancy curls and bonnets, wrapped in shawls. And in the background, leaning against the doors, grinning at the photographer's birdie, the grandparents, gray-haired, almost dead.

The squares: theaters with identical boxes. A parade of toy horses, hoops, bouquets, toy horses.

Such repetition made him dizzy, and the choruses too. Mercy touched His forehead with the back of her hand: It was burning. She pressed the wood and it crumbled. A white halo remaining. He had already rotted right through.

"King of the Four Roads, spare our sugar harvest!," shouted a reeling peasant with a bottle of rum in his hand, and he hung from Him, crying. Help tried to protect Him. But it was too late. The peasant had torn off a hand. A wooden stump remained, a splinter, out of which ants came scurrying.

The people came from all directions. They pushed. They squeezed together. It was a jungle of slender legs, knotty bamboo shoots supporting puffy buttocks, round like purple *caimitos*. Their trunks bent,

323

swayed back, rocked by gusts of wind. In their midst, jumping over their wide feet, frightened black boys—little frogs—zigzagged around, fanning themselves.

A grandstand had been set up—with bleachers and platforms—and a red damask canopy hung over it, supported by four gilded halberds. Banners waved. Helicopters hovered above the square. From the platforms His followers threw them black balls which opened in midair: flowers of Chinese silk. They floated: black gardens. They fell; on the petals His name was imprinted: incomplete, backward, broken.

The sky was a crumpled piece of paper. A thick tent. Slow waves rolled through it: the ebb tide of a salty marsh. Something in the air was going to break.

"Come closer"—He said to them—"look at Me."

I am He who gives the Face. The big daddy-o. Mine is the page of the Codex. Mine is the ink and the painted image. Where are you taking Me?

But an icy gust ripped open His cloak, tore down the flags.

The people trembled. They warmed each other with their breath. Their eyes were wide open. They murmured: "This is the day   terror after death   change   rot   House of the Black." They began to weep. They lowered their heads in prayer. They beat their brows. He heard Himself say: "Dear God, have pity on Me."

The families went inside: They closed the shutters. They bolted the doors. They piled up the furniture, and the children on top, against the doors so the wind would not blow them open. They covered the mirrors with sheets.

The storm raged. (The little black boys dropped their fans, clung to people's legs, buried their heads between their knees.) It grew dark. It was when they turned on the lights that they saw, in the lights' flickering cones, the white specks scrawling in the air, then orderly, with the slowness of stars, whirlwinds of sculptured water: it was snowing.

They huddled up under His cloak. They tried to warm Him "But He was already fucked up"—Help said—; and on to another prayer. The snow burned Him on the face, another kind of fever. He looked like a prisoner, a drowned man. His eyes were sunken and watery, the lids jaundiced, His lips oozing with pus, His neck bloated. Branches of black veins climbed to His throat. Knots of puffy ganglia, spongy animals, rotting between His bones and hide. When He coughed he felt something was burning inside. When He spat, bloody water stained the handkerchief. He was scarcely breathing, sounding like an asthmatic sucking in air. Hunched over. Gasping. A fish on dry land.

"Come on, You're looking great. You look just like a Virgin of Charity!" (it's Mercy, to make Him happy)

Parallel furrows in the pavement. A carpet of ceiba flowers. White moss.

And He:

"Of all the spectacles I've seen, none . . ."

A fit of coughing broke His bronchial tubes. A downpour of snowflakes pelted Him ("Tiny bird feathers!"—said Help); the whirling propellers scattered them.

"If I should die upon the road, on my grave I want no flowers" (He said)—And He tried to smile, to reassure the last of the faithful. But when they beat the drums they sprayed needles of ice.

Smooth, a tin sky covered almost the whole landscape. Bell towers and the arms of windmills jutted out over the red roofs. Open bridges, beached ships run aground: the Almendares River multiplied them. Along the snowy banks, stained at intervals by scaffolds and cranes, dying fish were jumping. Sea gulls swooped down to peck at them.

He tightened His throat. He felt that something was bursting in His neck. A taste of copper, warm salt, came up. He spat blood.

He was now a gargoyle, a snow white rag. Help, in a fit of tears, passed her hand over His head, dried the sweat from His brow, murmured in His ear, "It will soon be over, have faith, it will soon be over." And Mercy, in a fit of tears, patted Him on the back, kissed His temples, murmured in His ear: "It will soon be over, have faith, it will soon be over."

The snow slanted down. At the eaves, broken spirals, veins of white ink that He saw erased, with each gust of wind, to reappear, each time wider.

In the depths of their sockets, His eyes grew glassy. He did not move them. Help and Mercy dragged Him a few steps; they looked at each other: they turned to shout. His body shook. He was weeping. And when He calmed down:

"Why all this moaning?"—He said—. "Kicking the bucket is great fun. Life only begins after death, the life."

He was choking.

Cutting through the snow, a coach sped by.

Like zinc, from afar, the Havana lakes. Small covered bridges crossed them. On the shore there were austere towers of fortresses, palaces of cedar, tall dove cotes amidst cherry orchards, the ruins of synagogues, cut off minarets: there Infanta Street, frozen, crosses San Lázaro.

"Let's go, every man for himself!"—He heard them shout. He tried to raise His head. Then He saw the grandstand crushed by an avalanche. "Oh God"—He moaned—"Why didn't You throw in the towel?" The faithful left the square in groups, under yellow raincoats held over themselves with raised arms. The leaders carried lanterns. Helicopters spotlighted them with their floodlights: dotted lines.
"Who has stayed behind?"—(poor thing!)
And They:
"Loyal Ones, Followers, Shadows."

On the façades of colonial palaces the snow covered capitals, moldings, cement flowers. Closed gates; the blue shadow of the latches extended over the iron. Only half-moons, contorted masks, remained of the medallions with the heads of viceroys. Squirrels fled across the cornices.
Sunken gardens. Silent fountains: the tritons driveled threads of ice.

"Curtains of bread crumbs" (said Help).
"Who up there is shaking His tablecloth?" (said Mercy). One of His hands came loose. Swollen, it fell to the ground; in its palm, a sore.
It stayed there, for a moment, on the white cloth; purple knuckles. Three red drops fell upon it, from the wrist, it was buried by the snow.

The Entry of Christ into Death

He saw quick reddish stains in the snow, copper shadows. The ground moved away from him. He was losing footing. He felt he was entering another space. Burning zone, he heard water through swollen leaves, the sleep of rattlesnakes and birds, the ambush. Behind vines, the frightened flight of mockingbirds. Cascades of moss, thick dark green mats, fell from the highest fronds, clouding the day. Light tigers carried bleeding ducks in their teeth. He heard His steps in the mud, on damp leaves. With the sound of water among rocks, the strokes of a guitar reached His ear. Then the drums, yes: it was the mambo band, the one that greets us on the other side.

His body became strange to Him: a pile of rotting sticks under the snow. Help and Mercy closed His eyes. He saw himself twisted, a broken gargoyle.

Meanwhile, he crossed reverberating forests, stockades of sugar cane that ended in golden leaves. He was getting close. Already among the sputtering sparks of flowers you could see the musicians. He knew that He was going to dance. That dancing means meeting the Dead.

That if you dance well, you get in.

He saw himself crumble. He fell into pieces, with a moan. Wood falling in water. His bald, leprous head split in two. The empty holes of the eyes, the white, perforated lips, the nose in its bone, the ears plugged with two black clots. And further on, the forehead, the cold globes of the eyes, the trunk, with an arm that sank into the snow as if looking for something buried. And further up, the curve of the back. The legs in pieces; the snow buried them.

And the foot that stamped three times, the belch, the first beat. He jumped. Two more steps, two steps. He clapped hands to the rhythm. He did a turn. Holding a white handkerchief. He danced on one foot. The band players shook their little bells near his ear. "Who can beat me?"—He said to Himself. And he wiggled His hips. The musicians gathered around him. Twice they suddenly changed the batá beat of the tambourines and twice he caught up to them with a caper. He was blond and handsome. And had white feet. He whirled around. Then the other way. Superimposed on himself. He was blond. He was naked. Holding a white handkerchief. He shouted again. "Sugar!"—they shouted to Him. He laughed. He wore gold bracelets. Not as shiny as his eyes.

He didn't know that the snow had stopped. Rivulets of mud cracked the white cloth, creased it at the sewers. It was sunny. Grating rails and throwing off sparks, the trolleys, full, passed by again. The river ran. The ships cast off.

(In the parks the old men chatted.)

Then the Faithful, the Fates, crossed the square. They started picking Him up, searching in the mire. Piece by piece, they wrapped Him in a cloth with loving care. They hurried away.

They were already reaching the portals when, from the helicopters, bullets rained down.

UNDERSTANDING CHARACTERS

Note: Three cultures, at least, have been superimposed to constitute the Cuban—Spanish, African, and Chinese—; three fictions alluding to them constitute this book.

These fables share in common three characters—or themes—: Mortal, the blond Spaniard whose Castillian is spotless and who possesses the always uncertain attributes of power; Help and Mercy, also called the Flower Girls, the Ever Present, the Siamese Twins, the Divine Ones, the Thirsty Ones, the Majas . . . the Fates. (A third sister: Clemency, accidentally joins them.)

In the first narrative—*By the River of Rose Ashes*—Mortal Pérez is a lecherous old general who pursues the image of Lotus Flower, a soprano—he thinks—at the Chinatown Opera House. Here everything is looking, contemplation, evanescent reality. If Lotus Flower really is a paint-smeared fraud, Help and Mercy are gifted with (and abuse) the power of metamorphosis: chorus girls at the Opera, and two-bit whores, they will make their heads, armored arms and legs proliferate, to frighten the general—A Sivaic Band—. This will be light, the absence of light. In a *café-concert* they will coexist with their own mutations. "Grass"—hashish—and "white sugar"—cocaine—which Dragon Puss distributes, haunt this space of symmetrical arts: Painting and Torture.

In *Dolores Rondón*, Mortal is only a politician of emphatic oratory in his stages of councilman, candidate to the Senate, senator and ex-senator. But these ups and downs mark the life of Dolores Rondón, a Camagüeyan mulatto. This story—sound, action: theater—spells out a ten-line poem engraved on a tombstone in a Camagüey cemetery. Her only work, Dolores Rondón wrote it as an epitaph. The one-act farce, in ten "moments," respects the order of the lines (not the chronological) and the demands of its genre.

In *The Entry of Christ in Havana* Mortal is an absent young lover who is going to become a metaphor of Christ. Help and Mercy search for him; the desire for Mortal that ails them will turn into a thirst for eternal life. Here the two women will illustrate two main currents of Hispanic culture—Faith and Experience in the tapestry—opposites which polarize the continuous turns of the text: if the beginning evokes a certain pompousness, Zurbarán, soon the *vanities*, Valdes Leal, will appear; if Mercy quixotizes, Help is a Sancho Panza collection of proverbs. With a wooden Christ and Bruno—the Prince and his guest, Hiccups, in the tapestry—both will go on a pilgrimage through Cuba. The corruption of that wood corresponds to the corruption of time, and context: growing anachronisms, other landscapes superimposed on the Cuban, the reiteration and unreality of snow.

Curriculum Cubense introduces the characters. Help behaves awkwardly in the Self-Service; the delirious description of her photographs, which she hands out to all present, is not enough to impose another image of her. As for Mercy, she comes back frustrated from her visit to the House of God. In the Domus Dei, "the absence" of the one she searches "is almost present." Both want to disappear, to be someone else: therefore the constant transformation, the wealth of cosmetics, artifices.

The general desires Lotus Flower; Dolores desires power; Help and Mercy, the body of a man, the soul's salvation. This man is the same, those worlds attract, will unite, reflect each other: in the midst of the Sivaic Band a Yoruba altar appears, in Christ's reception in Havana, Chinese decorations. Dolores's monologues emphasize this mirror quality. Among its constant figures throughout the centuries, Rhetoric has catalogued the *excusatio propter infirmitatem*, that confession of modesty, of incapacity before the theme to be developed, that must precede all discourse. I don't use it here (although denial is one of its forms): the impertinence of the preceding pages declares it for me, more than enough.

Carlos Fuentes was born in Mexico in 1928. His published works include *Where the Air Is Clear* (1958), *The Good Conscience* (1959), *Aura* (1962), *The Death of Artemio Cruz* (1962), and *A Change of Skin* (1967). His works have been translated into many languages. He lives in Mexico.

José Donoso was born in 1924 in Santiago, Chile. He received his A.B. from Princeton in 1951. He has taught English literature at the University of Chile and has been a writer-in-residence at the University of Iowa. His books include *This Sunday* and *Coronation*, which won the William Faulkner Foundation Prize for Chile in 1962. He lives in Spain.

Severo Sarduy was born in Camagüey, Cuba, in 1937. His works in French translation have established him as a leading avant-garde writer. *From Cuba with a Song* is his first book publication in English. He lives in Paris.